Urban Australia and Post-Punk

David Nichols · Sophie Perillo
Editors

Urban Australia and Post-Punk

Exploring Dogs in Space

Editors
David Nichols
University of Melbourne
Parkville, VIC, Australia

Sophie Perillo
University of Melbourne
Parkville, VIC, Australia

ISBN 978-981-32-9701-2   ISBN 978-981-32-9702-9 (eBook)
https://doi.org/10.1007/978-981-32-9702-9

© The Editor(s) (if applicable) and The Author(s) 2020
This work is subject to copyright. All rights are solely and exclusively licensed by the Publisher, whether the whole or part of the material is concerned, specifically the rights of translation, reprinting, reuse of illustrations, recitation, broadcasting, reproduction on microfilms or in any other physical way, and transmission or information storage and retrieval, electronic adaptation, computer software, or by similar or dissimilar methodology now known or hereafter developed.
The use of general descriptive names, registered names, trademarks, service marks, etc. in this publication does not imply, even in the absence of a specific statement, that such names are exempt from the relevant protective laws and regulations and therefore free for general use.
The publisher, the authors and the editors are safe to assume that the advice and information in this book are believed to be true and accurate at the date of publication. Neither the publisher nor the authors or the editors give a warranty, expressed or implied, with respect to the material contained herein or for any errors or omissions that may have been made. The publisher remains neutral with regard to jurisdictional claims in published maps and institutional affiliations.

Cover image: Sophie Perillo

This Palgrave Macmillan imprint is published by the registered company Springer Nature Singapore Pte Ltd.
The registered company address is: 152 Beach Road, #21-01/04 Gateway East, Singapore 189721, Singapore

Acknowledgements

The editors would like to thank all contributors and the efficient, engaged and hardworking staff at Palgrave Macmillan, particularly Joshua Pitt who commissioned this book.

Richard Lowenstein declined to be officially involved in this collection, a decision we respect and which has of course shaped it—whether positively or negatively can never be known. We would however like to thank Richard and all at Ghost pictures for initial encouragement—without which we are unlikely to have proceeded—and other acts of generosity.

For advice, ideas, information and encouragement, we are also grateful to: Jim Betts, Andrew Bonnici, Josh and Ollie Brook, Sarah Charing and the excellent librarians at the Architecture, Building and Planning Library at the University of Melbourne; Steve Connell, Kathryn Davidson, Marie Hoy, Sooryadeepth Jayakrishnan, Victoria Kolankiewicz, Martie Lowenstein, Chuck Meo, Tim Millikan, Bruce Milne, Tony Moore, Greg Perano, Lauren Pikó, Dean Richards, Eddy Sarafian, Dave Sloggett, Elizabeth Taylor, Felicity Watson, Melynda von Wayward, Henry Vynhil and Brendan Young.

Contents

Introduction 1
Sophie Perillo

If You Were a Freak, You Were Equally Excluded 9
Sam Sejavka

It Was Filmic 23
Peter Farnan

I Was In-Between Two Worlds 27
John Clifforth

The B-Side of a Single? An Autobiohistoriography 35
Stuart Grant

In My Mind the World Was Safer 51
Karen Ansel

Let's Go and Get in Some Trub 61
Edward Clayton-Jones

Everyone Was Interchangeable 67
Jules Taylor

We're the Most Fabulous People Australia Has Ever Known 73
Cornelius Delaney

It Was Never Pistols at Dawn 81
Cathy McQuade

Bowie Queues 87
Bruce Butler

Excerpt from Comic Book 101
Jerome Gaynor

Rock Star in Space 105
Zora Simic

The Intimacy of Distance: Re/Reading *Dogs in Space* 123
Laura Carroll

'Someone's Been Fucking Using This for Meat Again':
18 Berry Street and Melbourne Sharehousing
in the 1970s and 1980s 141
Molly McKew and Katherine Ellinghaus

Richmond and 18 Berry Street Revisited 157
James Lesh and David Nichols

'Making It': The Ears, INXS, and Music Scene
Restructuring as Seen Through *Dogs in Space* 175
Sarah Taylor

The Strange Life of 'Shivers' and Its Place in *Dogs in Space* 209
Lisa MacKinney

'The Fucked Room': Situating the *Dogs in Space*
Soundtrack and 'Rooms for the Memory' in the Diffusion
of the *Dogs in Space* Story   227
David Nichols

Say Clitoris: Queers in Space   247
Simona Castricum

Fun House: DIY House Venues and the Melbourne
Underground   261
Carolyn Hawkins

Finding 'Places to Be Bad' in Social Media: The Case
of TikTok   285
Sorcha Avalon Mackenzie and David Nichols

Coda: 'What It Feels Like When a Subculture
Appears'—Richard Lowenstein Interview, 2009   299
Trevor Block

Bibliography   307

Index   323

Notes on Contributors

Karen Ansel is an internationally renowned visual effects specialist. Previously a musician, she began performing in the Melbourne art/punk scene of the late 1970s before becoming an influential member of the Australian band The Reels. She lives in the United States.

Trevor Block is a 'man of words'.

Bruce Butler has worked in various roles within the Australian music industry over four decades promoting new local talent. He currently teaches Music Business at RMIT and Collarts passing on his experience to a new generation.

Dr. Laura Carroll is a Melbourne writer. She is a Research Associate in the College of Arts, Social Sciences and Commerce at La Trobe University.

Simona Castricum is an architecture academic at the University of Melbourne. As a musician, she performs as both a solo artist and one half the duo SaD, as well as a DJ and community radio broadcaster on PBS FM.

Notes on Contributors

Edward Clayton-Jones is a well-known musician originally from Melbourne and presently living in Sydney. He was a member of Plays with Marionettes, The Wreckery and Nick Cave and the Bad Seeds. He continues to write, record and perform.

Dr. John Clifforth is a GP and singer/songwriter currently playing in various Melbourne bands.

Dr. Cornelius Delaney was born in Melbourne Australia. At 17 he changed his name to Nique Needles and started to play in post-punk band Microfilm before going on to form his own band The Curse. The Curse played around Melbourne for a couple of years until Delaney left town and went to Sydney. He found work acting in the theatre at first, then over the next 5 years appeared in several feature films. In 1985 he won an Australian Film Institute award for Best Supporting Actor for his work on *The Boy Who Had Everything*. In 1986 Delaney played the character Tim in *Dogs in Space*. In 1988 he won Best Actor in A Science Fiction Film at Fantascienza: The Rome Science Fiction and Fantasy Film Awards for his performance in *As Time Goes By*—a kooky Australian Sci-Fi film about a surfer who travels in time to find his long lost father. Throughout the '90s he exhibited his paintings regularly and in 2000 enrolled in university where he completed a Ph.D. in Visual Art.

Delaney now lives in the south of France where he continues to paint, exhibit and play music as Darky Valetta.

Katherine Ellinghaus is an Associate Professor of History at La Trobe University. She writes about settler colonialism, transnational and comparative history, and the social and cultural history of the United States and Australia.

Peter Farnan is a song writer, composer, producer, performer and teacher. He is a founding member of Australian rock bands Boom Crash Opera and Serious Young Insects.

Jerome Gaynor is an artist from St. Louis, Missouri.

Dr. Stuart Grant is a low rent academic at a shitbox provincial university in the arse end of nowhere. He is guitarist and singer in the primitive calculators.

Carolyn Hawkins is an artist, illustrator and musician living in Melbourne. She plays in local bands Parsnip and School Damage.

Dr. James Lesh is a heritage researcher, writer and consultant is interested in the enduring potential of heritage to enhance cities and urban life. James is currently based at the University of Sydney School of Architecture, Design and Planning.

Sorcha Avalon Mackenzie is a Melbourne-based artist specialising in intaglio etchings and drawing.

Lisa MacKinney is a historian and musician (guitar and organ) based in Melbourne, Australia. Past and current musical projects include Taipan Tiger Girls, Hospital Pass, Super Luminum and Mystic Eyes. MacKinney's Ph.D. thesis is the first ever book-length study of New York pop group the Shangri-Las. She writes regularly for Australian classical music magazine *Limelight* and occasionally for UK music magazine *Uncut*.

Molly McKew is a Ph.D. candidate at the University of Melbourne. Her current research focuses on the countercultures of the 1960s and 1970s in inner-urban Melbourne.

Cathy McQuade was bass player in the 'classic' line-up of The Ears after which she played in popular Sydney group Deckchairs Overboard. She released her first solo album *Perfect Storm* in 2018. She was twice awarded 'Best Original Score' for her soundtrack to the 2018 film *The Widow* at both the Los Angeles Crime and Horror Festival and the Independent Short Awards.

David Nichols lectures in Urban Planning at the University of Melbourne, with a focus on history, culture, community and place. His previous books include *Community: Building Modern Australia* (co-edited with Hannah Lewi), *Trendyville: The Battle for Australia's Inner Cities* (with Renate Howe and Graeme Davison) and *Dig: Australian Rock and Pop Music 1960–1985*.

Sophie Perillo is an interdisciplinary performance artist, musician and writer. She has devised independent and collaborative performance works for Artist Run Initiatives, major galleries and festivals. She has performed in Melbourne bands The Ancients, PSA and Hi God People. Her research and writing is centred in gender theory, performativity and theatricality.

Sam Sejavka is a writer, outlier, hep C treatment advocate, musician and father to Polly. He was and is the singer in The Ears through their many incarnations as well as leading a host of other Melbourne bands since the late 1970s. He has had a long and successful relationship with the theatre both as a playright and an actor.

Dr. Zora Simic is a Senior Lecturer in History and Gender Studies in the School of Humanities and Languages at the University of New South Wales. She is a historian of twentieth century Australia and her research interests include past and present feminisms, postwar migration and popular culture. In her spare time, she writes book reviews and makes music playlists.

Jules Taylor worked in the music industry while playing in various 'little bands' in Melbourne, most famously Thrush and the Cunts. She was also volunteers co-ordinator for 3RRR-fm, after which she spent time in the film industry. She is a psychotherapist.

Dr. Sarah Taylor is a postdoctoral research fellow at RMIT University. Her Ph.D. research examined the history of live music in Sydney and Melbourne, using a combination of Geographic Information Systems (GIS) and interviews with musicians. She has over ten years' experience working with maps, databases, and software development. She has performed with music group the Taylor Project since 2006.

List of Figures

The Intimacy of Distance: Re/Reading *Dogs in Space*

Fig. 1   Laura, Melissa and Katrina, Berry Street, 1989
(Photo by Ruby Richardson)   129

Richmond and 18 Berry Street Revisited

Fig. 1   18 Berry St, Register No. F3256, September 1972.
By permission National Trust of Victoria   168

'Making It': The Ears, INXS, and Music Scene Restructuring as Seen Through *Dogs in Space*

Fig. 1   Map of publicly listed live music performances by The Ears in Greater Melbourne, 1979–1981, grouped by venue. Details in Table 1   180

Fig. 2   Map of publicly listed live music performances by INXS in Greater Melbourne, 1979–1981, grouped by venue. Details in Table 2   184

List of Tables

'Making It': The Ears, INXS, and Music Scene Restructuring as Seen Through *Dogs in Space*

Table 1	Publicly listed live music performances by The Ears in Greater Melbourne, 1979–1981, grouped by venue	181
Table 2	Publicly listed live music performances by INXS in Greater Melbourne, 1979–1981, grouped by venue	185
Table 3	Publicly listed live music performances, same week of different years, Melbourne	195

Introduction

Sophie Perillo

This book collects impressions and analysis not only of the 1986 film *Dogs in Space*, but also—as per its title—the geographical and cultural world in which it was created.

It also looks at the film's own changing fortunes. In a 2016 article published by *The Conversation* to commemorate the 30th anniversary of the release of Richard Lowenstein's *Dogs in Space*, David Nichols and I wrote about initial responses to *Dogs in Space* by those with a stake in the value and virtue of 'punk rock':

> The inclusion of some 'terrible' music, and the depiction of the bands' performances as a backdrop for violence, drinking, drug taking, ribaldry and so on, lent the film an air of decadence. To many in the mid-1980s, this seemed to indicate that Lowenstein was misrepresenting a serious, artistic, politically charged era.

S. Perillo (✉)
University of Melbourne, Parkville, VIC, Australia
e-mail: perillos@unimelb.edu.au

The critic Vikki Riley – who played in a band, Slub, with musician and actor John Murphy, who actually appeared in *Dogs in Space* – disliked Lowenstein's approach. Writing in *Cinema Papers* in 1987, she argued Lowenstein had lost an opportunity to capture a 'magic atmosphere' that had 'given way to clichés and tokenisms'. He had, she wrote, refused 'to acknowledge any effort at subversion that the punks in the film make'.

However, we wrote, 'as *Dogs in Space* celebrates its 30th anniversary, it feels like the world has caught up with the film. Many who dismissed it— including some of its cast—have revised their opinion of the production. They now see it as capturing an era more truthfully than they were able to appreciate in 1986. At the same time, a new audience has emerged who respond to the film on very different terms'.[1]

Few expected, upon its release in 1986, that *Dogs in Space* would have a longer life than a limited cinematic and video release. Yet in these testimonies from individuals involved in the 1970s share houses, in inner-city music and in the making of the film itself we see a new understanding of the value of that period and milieu. There are also numerous significant ideas and meanings within *Dogs in Space* and the diversity of contributors, and approaches to analysing the film, its cultural impact and the world it documents, reveals the film's remarkably wide-reaching appeal.

In a country like Australia, where a tendency to devalue culture has historically undermined the value of much of the film, music and art produced within it, it is unusual that such a film as *Dogs in Space* even had a chance of being made. It is also possible that the various names associated with Melbourne's post-punk music scene of the late 1970s, such as Nick Cave, Rowland S. Howard, and others from the art and film scene, as well as appearances from figures like fashion designer Alanna Hill, who became famous following the film's release, have assisted in its longevity. But it is also possible that it is something core to the film's depiction of alternative culture(s) and society that make it far more universal than a mere depiction of a time and place. I do not consider this film primarily historical: it continues to influence subsequent generations who are able to relate to the lifestyle it depicts.

The idea for this book first emerged when I was curating a season of films, *Carlton to the Yabba: Australian Film from the 70s to Now* at the small but important Dane Certificate's Magic Theatre, in 2015. I invited Stuart Grant—a participant in late 1970s Melbourne music and in *Dogs in Space*—to introduce the film to a (largely) new audience. Seeing the film again, Stuart's opinion of it changed; he began to question the truth of its historiography. He continues his reflection on the film within these pages.

Something that has surprised me in the creation of this book is the personal accounts that it has encouraged from those contributors, both directly involved in the film and whose experiences help contextualise it culturally. During the commissioning, writing and dialogue surrounding this book, it has veered from its initial intention—of focusing on the film from the perspective of the director and others involved in its making—to one that encompasses perspectives from a vast pool of academics, musicians and cultural figures. The collection ultimately resembles an ethnographic account, with an interwoven balance of personal memoir and academic analysis which works together to illuminate the film and its position in culture, society and history.

I was a baby when *Dogs in Space* was released. My first encounter with the film, at the turn of the twenty-first century, came from at least three teenage obsessions: with films about music; the films of Noah Taylor; and with the world of inner-city share houses. The music films (for instance, *Empire Records* or *High Fidelity*) were intriguing, but never very satisfying. Taylor was the anti-heart throb at time when everyone around me had their celebrity crush. His persona across films such as *The Year My Voice Broke*, *Flirting* and *The Nostradamus Kid* was self-deprecating, funny and knowing; he made it clear that everything was bullshit but that it was necessary to negotiate the bullshit to find oneself. The Noah Taylor persona would always come through even if it was inconvenient in the film's narrative; it was simultaneously awkward yet self-assured. Not satisfied with heteronormative macho big-chinned poster boys—even the 'alternative' ones were highly masculine and hard to connect with—I identified with the kind of person he represented. He wasn't a rock star in his movies, but simply weird, a social misfit. Taylor does appear in *Dogs in Space*, but his (unnamed) role is negligible; he appears in one early scene and a party scene, a larger part for his character apparently left on the proverbial cutting room floor. But it was fitting that he was there.

Films like *Dogs in Space* showed me a world I could compare to what I'd researched on the bohemian lifestyles of figures like David Bowie, Lou Reed, Patti Smith and Iggy Pop. But this, like me, was *Australian*. Similarly, the film's music clip aesthetic appealed; it was not dramatic or overwrought, just people hanging out; its non-linear narrative made the whole film rebellious and punk in its refusal to adhere to a mainstream Hollywood-style arcs. Anything I could identify as embracing mainstream appeal, I liked less.

Though the suburb of Richmond lay between the suburb where I grew up and central Melbourne, it meant very little to me. By the time I was old enough to explore the city by myself, Richmond meant Bridge Road—commercial, cheap, boring shops selling generic clothes—a place I didn't want to go to—and Victoria St, which was known mainly for restaurants; I felt no connection to the area and nor did I connect *Dogs in Space* with Richmond.

However, when I was 14 or 15 I had a close friend who lived in Westgarth St., Fitzroy. She had an older brother and sister, both of who were in their early 20s and lived in typical share houses in the same area. We'd often stay there and sleep in her sister's bed while she went to some party. She was in some ways not unlike the Anna character in *Dogs in Space;* she was professional and successful, but also liked cool music and smoked weed. I remember once observing her while she slept on the couch, and thinking, 'this is what it's like to be an adult'. I was engaged with punk and grunge aesthetics and it was great to see people who *did things*, who were vibrant, part of a creative atmosphere. I wanted to be a part of Melbourne's creative culture; I was drawn to performance artists like the 'Delapidated Diva', Emma Bathgate, and her celebration of the feminine grotesque and subversive cabaret. I was aware, too, of cultural figures like Vali Myers, who were a part of that world and a continuity from a distant past both local and international.

So I was interested in Fitzroy and St Kilda. I spent a lot of time wandering around Fitzroy and I knew different places like the café-bar Rumbarella's, which featured in the film *Love and Other Catastrophes*. I knew there was something important about it and I wanted to be cool.

More importantly, I liked anything subverting bourgeois ideas moralistic ideas of how to live a life. I wanted to be nomadic, didn't want to own a home, have children or be a lawyer like everyone else at my school. My goal was to be an artist—not even necessarily a successful artist—but to be like the characters in *Dogs in Space*, whose lives were like their artwork, disillusioned and nihilistic, with no solid hopes for future. I connected with that because it reaffirmed the way I failed to fit into the mainstream culture.

The chapters in this book approach many of these ideas—and some others—in a range of different ways and styles. The first section is, in large part, concerned with reminiscences from people directly involved with the world we would now typify as belonging to *Dogs in Space* (of course, without the film, interest in this time and place would certainly be far less notable). Many of the contributors who discuss their experience of either cultural creation in Melbourne in the 1970s, or involvement in the making of *Dogs in Space*, or both, are at an ideal place to contemplate both their own creative enterprise in the light of the film's sustained popularity and its ongoing relevance. Sam Sejavka, around whose life *Dogs in Space* was arguably based around, discusses some early, formative elements in his upbringing and nascent creativity which illustrate a much more rounded and accomplished man than the self-obsessed and selfish 'Sam' of *Dogs in Space*.

Sejavka's chapter is followed by short reminiscences from two men who were peripheral to the *Dogs in Space* world but whose memories of that time are invaluable for that reason. Peter Farnan, a school friend of Sejavka's, engineered some early recordings by The Ears and was in many regards a fellow traveller to that band; John Clifforth moved in slightly different circles during The Ears' existence but would later form a band, Deckchairs Overboard, with The Ears' bass player Cathy McQuade and, still later, would work with Troy Davies, a legendary figure in the lives of both Sam Sejavka and Richard Lowenstein.

Stuart Grant's piece is a rumination on the impact of *Dogs in Space* on his own life and presents some counterpoints to the conventional understanding of punk culture. Karen Ansel is an example of someone for whom punk opened doors into a range of creative worlds, and whose remarkable early career saw her—as a member of The Reels—appear on *Countdown* numerous times, a world that bands of the *Dogs in Space* milieu could only dream about.

Edward Clayton-Jones, Jules Taylor and Cornelius Delaney were all participants in the 'original' scene of the late 1970s, and all involved in the film's production. Clayton-Jones and Delaney (known either as Nique Delaney or Nique Needles, the name under which he had an extraordinarily successful acting career in the 1980s) were labelmates in the 1970s, with the groups Microfilm and the Fabulous Marquises respectively. Though neither was a 'little band', both groups were regulars at the Champion Hotel. Jules Taylor, on the other hand, was a little band aficionado, with Thrush and the Cunts her best-known vehicle. All three discuss the dichotomy, and pleasures, of being asked to re-enact one's earlier life in a big-budget cinema production.

Like Karen Ansel, Cathy McQuade leveraged pop success early in her career from unpromising 'punk' beginnings as bass player for The Ears; she was a member of Deckchairs Overboard and also, as mentioned by Sarah Taylor in her chapter, provided vocals for the hit single 'Sweet and Sour' by The Takeaways.

The first section of the book is concluded with images from Bruce Butler's exceptional archive of materials from the 1978 Bowie queue, a legendary moment in Australian alternative culture which affected the lives of many who participated.

It would be a mistake to imagine that the second part of the book is not about 'experience'. Although most of the authors within this section were in no sense participants in the late 1970s counterculture, their responses and understandings of *Dogs in Space* and many of its tropes are no less engaging. An extract from a comic book by Jerome Gaynor, detailing his own reactions to and understanding of the film as a teenager in the American suburbs, begins this section. Zora Simic then examines her own (and the world's) responses to INXS, Michael Hutchence and *Dogs in Space*. Laura Carroll gives a forensic reading of some of the film's conceptual threads and its relevance to all those who, for good or ill, romanticised the inner-city share house life it depicts.

Katherine Ellinghaus and Molly McKew contextualise that same share house life in a chapter on the rising phenomenon of countercultural domesticity, utilising interviews with individuals far more ideologically driven and pure than the *Dogs in Space* household. James Lesh and David Nichols examine the geographical place of the Berry Street, Richmond house in which the film was set, bringing forward the role of public housing, protest, and gentrification in the preservation and use of the house.

Sarah Taylor's chapter on the Ears' and INXS' engagement with the music industry, comparing the two bands' experience and interaction, as well as comparing the industry in the late 1970s with the present day, reveals not only assumptions about the two groups and their relationship to the music business, but also provides a reminder of the way that the film's original audience would have perceived its depiction of performance and ambition very differently from contemporary viewers.

Lisa MacKinney's chapter, an analysis of the song 'Shivers', explores some of the background and value of a song which plays a central role to the film, running deeper than many casual consumers may have grasped. David Nichols discusses the legacy of the film's soundtrack album in the subsequent chapter.

Simona Castricum's chapter could, in some respects, have nestled appropriately in the first section of the book; it is a memoir, but it is also of course an analysis. Her overview of the impact the film has had on her life is a counter to anyone who would dismiss it as arcane.

The final two analytical chapters explore elements of the *Dogs in Space* world that do not directly connect to anything germane to the film itself, or the events it depicts. Yet both respond, in different ways, to aspects of the film which are among the many which perpetuate far beyond 'Melbourne, 1978'. Carolyn Hawkins' chapter on unofficial music venues is a piece of social research which provides not only a contemporary marker of the desire for music or art consumers to socialise outside the realm of sanctioned space, but also serves to show how much has changed in understandings of the commercial value of a music scene to the classic 'creative city'. Sorcha Mackenzie and David Nichols investigate a world which, while largely geographically removed from Melbourne, resonates with many of the ideas explored by the counterculture in the late twentieth century. They ask whether it is still possible to be rebellious in the conventional platforms of twenty-first-century social media.

The collection ends with a brief interview with Richard Lowenstein, conducted by Trevor Block close to a quarter of a century after *Dogs in Space* was originally released. Lowenstein has directed many fine fiction films—*Say a Little Prayer* is a somewhat forgotten masterpiece, and *He*

Died with a Felafel in His Hand is rightly celebrated—but he has also directed four documentaries that tease out elements of the *Dogs in Space* legend: *We're Living on Dog Food*, *Autoluminescent*, *Ecco Homo* and, most recently, *Mystify*. It might be imagined that, as much as the contributors to this book, and its editors, are fascinated by the *Dogs in Space* world and its dichotomies, Lowenstein, its creator, is at least as intrigued.

We would not presume to suggest this book is complementary to those films, or even that it is a counter to Lowenstein's published *Dogs in Space* diary which, at time of writing, had not been issued. We are aware, however, of the phenomenon of *Dogs in Space* as one which has a considerable distance yet to run.

In 2016, we contributed to a seminar at Monash University run by Dr. Tony Moore, author of *Dancing with Empty Pockets*. One attendee was a man in his twenties who came to the seminar entirely because of his enthusiasm for *Dogs in Space* which, he said, had been a part of his teenage years in the Riverina. Every weekend, he said, his friends would party to the video of the film, revelling in its debauchery and hedonism. What surprised him, following our presentation, was the discovery that the film was based on real events; a fact that had never occurred to him. It is realities like this which surely show that the *Dogs in Space* world is both rooted in a time and place and yet entirely free of any geographic or temporal anchor, and that its quality as a film and an evocation will continue to propel it much further beyond 'Melbourne, 1978'; its release date in 1986; or, for that matter, the present day.

Note

1. D. Nichols and S. Perillo, 'Dogs in Space, 30 Years On—A Once Maligned Film Comes of Age', *The Conversation*, https://theconversation.com/friday-essay-dogs-in-space-30-years-on-a-once-maligned-film-comes-of-age-56288, accessed 4 January 2019.

If You Were a Freak, You Were Equally Excluded

Sam Sejavka

I'm Sam Sejavka. I'm a writer and a singer. I'm twenty years old, but in one week's time I'll be twenty-one. Allow me to briefly describe my life up to this point. Half way through my HSC year at St Kevin's College, I left home and school and took a flat in St Kilda. I was seventeen. Shortly after that, suffering from nervous tension, I spent some weeks in a private psychiatric hospital. Though I never returned to school, I did sit my exams and managed to do pretty well, particularly in English. I lived a reckless life in St Kilda, spending time with the basest of the creatures who abide there. I wrote all this time, though the results were dubious. I was young and over-stimulated by my new found freedom. I was seeing a girl called Irene, but broke up with her around the turn of the year.

Before long, I was evicted for general rowdiness and spent a week or so wandering in St Kilda, staying at hotels and such. I was undergoing another personality crisis, but this time it was not quite as severe. I took up a new flat in Armadale and attended university, which I loathed. After two or three months I left, again undergoing a kind of crisis. I had done not a skerrick of work in

S. Sejavka (✉)
Melbourne, VIC, Australia

this time. I found myself completely uninspired. I moved to Sydney, found a flat in Kings Cross and wrote. I viewed myself as something like the protagonist from Orwell's Down and Out in Paris and London—but under a shadow of inexperience and pretension the work I did was pretty well unreadable. [Woe the day I first read William Burroughs] I made no friends there. I never went out. I became a lonely bum, trying to live his twisted idea of a dream. I must say though that I was brave. I've never had quite the same attitude to food since I found myself starving up in Sydney. At times I would go to a nearby homeless shelter to partake of a dreadful brown gruel I will never forget.

In time, I found I no longer had the stomach for that kind of life and returned to Melbourne. I rented a house with George in Richmond and lived there six months, leading a wasteful sort of life. We had trouble with hoodlums in that place and were forced to leave suddenly with the house in a wreck. Though I pined for female company, but in its absence George and I enjoyed ourselves concocting and realising all manner of eccentric schemes. I left for a new flat in Armadale, determined to write as diligently as I could—and I did for while, but again it was forced, meaningless stuff. Inspired by William Burroughs, and much to alarm of my parents, I joined The Church of Scientology. Though my involvement was pretty marginal, [probably because I had no money,] it remains one of the stupidest things I've ever done.

In September, for several weeks, I camped out for David Bowie tickets. This was to be a turning point. I was introduced to heroin and LSD, though I'd had my fair share of other drugs previously. I made many friends and by the time of the next queue—this time for actual seating—I could almost have been described as gregarious. I spent those three weeks stoned in as many ways as it is possible to be. This is where the idea of the band was born. The night of the concert, my basement flat flooded and I could no longer live there [I'd forgotten to turn on the pump]. I moved home and around the turn of the year, The Ears began to practise.

In January 1979, I went to a science-fiction writer's workshop in Sydney where, among others, I encountered George Turner and a young Lucy Sussex. My next accommodation was a share house with school friends Mick Lewis (guitar) and Tim McLaughlan [keyboards] and here The Ears developed. We played for the first time in February. I returned to Melbourne Uni and could stand it this time only because I had found a girlfriend, Elise Valmorbida, with whom I fell madly in love. But I was far too immature to make something like *that work and the relationship had decayed to nothing by the end of the year. The group was playing regularly by now. I rented a new flat in Armadale, where I decided to once more quit university. Soon after that, I moved to a house in* Berry Street, *Richmond with Mick, Tim and Richard Lowenstein. I was a night bird, socialising as widely and wildly as I was able, living a life of utter debauchery. They were the days of the Champion Hotel, The Ballroom and The Exford. The end of the year came and I had frittered it agreeably away. It was 1980, I was nineteen. I was in a group and things were fine in a twisted sort of way.*

I stayed in Richmond till March, then moved to Elwood, to the flat where I began this diary. I turned twenty. Our first single was released. I pursued women. We hired a manager, then a different manager. I went to parties. And in August, I met Christine. There followed the most rewarding period of my life thus far. I was not prolific, I was not together, I was just unreasonably happy. We slept together almost every night. I was totally, without qualification, in love. And love was what was most important. Soon after I met Christine, my father died. But the grief eased with time. Then on the twentieth of March, Christine overdosed and died. Now it's the twenty fifth of March; I'm sitting out the front of Milton St, watching some placid old people mulling over the detritus of their lives. Mine is a pain equalled only by the pleasure that it echoes.

25 March 1981 thurs 2.30 p.m.[1]

My mother met my father at Greswell, a tuberculosis sanatorium in North-Eastern Melbourne which in later times became a drug rehab.

She was a country girl from Tasmania who had worked hard to become a nurse. She was always very quiet about where she got her degree (in Georgetown, I think, or Burnie) because those poor Tasmanian towns tended to have shoddy reputations.

My dad was an emigre from Latvia, who contracted TB about four years after his arrival in Australia. He had been conscripted to fight for the Germans in a unit called the Latvian Legions. This was a part of the Waffen SS, whose role was military in nature.

I think they were given a blood group tattoo or some other tattoo by which they could be identified as SS. He had this massive gouge in his flesh. I never knew what it was, I still don't know for sure, but I think it was where he must have dug out the tattoo. I imagine that involvement with the SS in any form would have affected his eligibility to emigrate to Australia.

He was always paranoid about this. And about Soviet spies. Most of the other children of Latvian parents went to Latvian school on the weekends, but he wouldn't let me near other Latvians.

He arrived here in 1952, through a post-war immigration programme. He was required to work on a forestry project for two years, which further degraded his already poor health. During the war, he'd had his kidneys frozen. This was towards the end, the winter of '44–'45, when the Germans were retreating from the East. He was in a platoon of Latvians commanded by a German lieutenant from which he deserted twice. The first time he was caught but, for whatever reason, was not shot. The second time, he'd noticed the German lieutenant slinking off towards the back and sensed that he was going to do a runner. He figured that, as long as he stuck with his officer, he couldn't be accused of desertion. So that's what he did, despite the lieutenant wanting nothing to do with him. For a while he followed, twenty metres behind, but eventually they wound up walking together, through the forest, in the snow. Later, they rounded the top of a hillside to see a road at the bottom and a Russian motorised column. The Russians spotted them and opened fire. The lieutenant was shot dead. My dad fell too, pretending to have been hit. He would only have been eighteen at the time. It's hard to imagine that kind of fear. The Russians assumed they were dead and did not bother climbing the hill to finish them off. For a long time, my father was too frightened to move. He just lay in the snow pretending to be dead for so long he actually froze his kidneys. I learned this from my mother. There must have been so many stories I never heard because I never spoke of such things with my dad. I've no idea how he got from that hillside to an internment camp in Germany and thence to Australia. I've got some photos of Berchtesgaden, Hitler's retreat, so he must have passed through there at some point. It remains a mystery. I didn't get on with my dad so well and we never really talked. I was somewhat weird from the word go, and he couldn't get his head around it. I got on much better with my mum because she was sort of weird as well.

The film-maker Paul Goldman's mother became friends with my dad in the internment camp. They had some kind of thing going. The story is that he climbed over a barbed wire fence to get an apple for her from an orchard, but he tore his trousers, and she sewed them up for him—all very romantic. At the same time, in Melbourne, my mum was being avidly pursued by Dr. Goldman, Paul's dad, who was working at the same hospital as her. It's the most amazing coincidence. Paul put up the money for the first Ears recording, so he was very much a part of the Ears story. The tale of our parents' shared friendships emerged the day we brought a test pressing back to my parents' place from the Astor factory. When my mum was told Paul's surname, her questioning rapidly revealed the fact he was *that* Dr. Goldman's son.

So, my mum was a shy, country girl, my dad was a paranoid ex-German soldier. I think they may have wanted more than one child, but they only managed to get me. They were straight as a die. My mum was very religious and my dad happily went along with it.

He was an engineer by trade but couldn't use his qualifications in Australia. He worked as a design draughtsman instead, designing machines, making blueprints—I've still got some of those at home. At one point, he was designing ovens for Tip Top bread. I remember his blueprints for this giant cone with all these little loaf-sized holes in it. He always had a good job, but his health was really bad. He almost died of a heart attack when I was five, and he was one of the first people to have an artificial heart valve implanted. He lived a lot longer than they expected him to, but he was always really sick; kidneys, heart, blood pressure. Eventually he died of a stroke.

My parents were dedicated to being good Australian citizens. My father identified strongly with the term 'New Australian'. He was *proud* to be a New Australian. He had a noticeable Latvian accent and claimed to know five languages: Russian, Latvian, German, Polish and English.

Around grade four, I started getting bullied by one of my teachers. It was serious stuff for me. I used to sit in the shower crying. There were nightmares. I remember threatening my parents that I would run away from home if they sent me back to that horrible Mt Waverley Catholic primary school. Eventually, they got the message and somehow, with both of them working, they raised enough money to send me to St Kevin's College in Toorak.

I was super-competitive at school and always very good academically. I was about twelve, I think, when I decided I wanted to be a writer. I got a typewriter for Christmas that year, an Olivetti Lettera 32, and started writing poetry. Between Years 10 and 11, I found a job in a plastics factory and raised the money to attend a science fiction writers' workshop run by some international SF bigwigs who were here for a world convention. Christopher Priest, who's still writing, and Vonda McIntyre, who's since passed on.

I met a number of well-known science fiction writers around that time: Robert Silverberg, Ursula Le Guin. I got to know George Turner quite well. He was a very well-regarded Australian science fiction writer.

I remember how excited I was at getting an honourable mention in the *Herald* poetry competition. A writer was what I was going to be. I was determined.

The first time I heard David Bowie, I was pretty young, sitting in the back of the car, with my parents upfront. The song was 'Space Oddity'. There was something in that music which absolutely captivated me. From that point on, I was a David Bowie freak. I still am, I guess. He provided the soundtrack for my later years of school, along with Lou Reed, Leonard Cohen, even Tangerine Dream.

I was also obsessed by the Beat Poets, Burroughs, Kerouac, Ballard, anything that was intellectually edgy. I had some supportive teachers too. Once I was allowed to write an English essay about Arthur C. Clarke's *2001*. But then year 12 came along. 1977. And that meant the Sex Pistols. I started acting out during that year. I only attended the first two terms. I began to dye my hair, which at the time was extreme. When my mother first saw me blond, she told me I'd never be allowed back in the house. I don't know if she really meant it, but I took her at her word. I got myself on the dole and found a flat in St Kilda.

I cracked up a bit around that time. I spent about three weeks in a rest home with some very disturbed people. I don't how mentally ill I was, but I rather liked the *idea* of being mentally ill. I remember my mother bringing me three packs of Camel 20s a day. It was her way of caring. In a way I was still acting out, but there was definitely something wrong at the core. There was an element of—I don't want to call it narcissism—it was almost like I was searching for material to write about. I've got seventy pages stacked away somewhere that I wrote in that place. I'd be surprised if they contain one ounce of sense.

It was while I was there that I spoke on the phone with my literature teacher Brother McCarthy. He explained to me in precise detail the concept of anal retention. And I really have to give a nod in his direction for that, it really pulled me up, helped me—to that point I had been inclined to think that anything which came out of me was inherently fascinating.

Those were times when all I wanted was to be like William Burroughs or David Bowie or whoever. I was thinking in terms of writing still, but I would sing Bowie songs in front of the mirror. I remember that first flat I had, that mirror, I remember singing in front of it, endlessly.

We weren't really seeing bands at that time. But we were hanging around a lot on Fitzroy St. which was extremely sleazy then, me and my friend George. He was also portrayed in *Dogs in Space*. He played himself, the guy on the motorbike with a camera, who had the vigorous sex upstairs. Ring a bell? Apparently, he went quite wild when they filmed that scene, and, according to Lowenstein, they had to cut most of it. Crazy George, that's what he was called.

He was a good friend, but we were really bad for each other. We did a lot of stupid things. We lived together for a while in a house in Stephenson St, Richmond, a few doors down from Kath Pettingill's brothel. At one point, we decided to have a party, so we photocopied hundreds of invitations and posted them everywhere. Then we sourced about thirty chairs, mainly kitchen chairs, probably from hard rubbish piles, really rotten, covered in filth and mould, and arranged them around a sort of small arena that we'd made. Then we bought a pig from Victoria Market. It was maybe half-grown and we released it into the arena. We were seventeen. The idea was that people could sit and watch the pig snuffling around... we had grand ideas for this party.

Bikies showed up, inevitably, and started breaking down the walls and cupboards. The last we saw of the pig, a huge Coffin Cheater or whatever was walking down the street with it under his arm.

The house was a complete wreck but we still had all those awful kitchen chairs. The property backed onto the railway just down from South Yarra station, so we spent an entire night walking down to South Yarra station and back, porting these disgusting chairs and kind of lining them up in neat rows on the platforms, back to back, as if they were official seating, so the next day the people coming to work would encounter them—like, really quite a lot of them—neatly set up for them. We never saw what happened, but we still laugh about it.

We used to climb electricity pylons too. I'm surprised we survived that. You know Glenferrie Road near Kooyong Station—those pylons there? Once we climbed to the top of one, took off all our clothes and climbed down naked.

I'll tell you another amusing anecdote. I was at George's place one evening, shortly after my dad died. He had a car, so I asked him if he could drive me to my dad's grave, to pay respects. When we arrived at the cemetery, it was getting dark and the gates were closed, but there was a hole in the fence. It took us ages to find his grave in the dark but, shortly after we succeeded, we began to see lights in the distance, people on the hunt, people with barking dogs on leads. They came steadily closer, and we got really scared. Of course, it was the cops, with a dog squad, and they found us lying flat, perfectly still on the ground, pathetically trying to avoid their notice. There were a lot of them. There seemed to be a lot of dogs too. I was terrified. This one cop seemed to be panicking, saying stuff like, 'Sergeant! I'm losing control of Brutus!' or whatever. Ultimately, they marched us off the premises, and drove us to the station in separate divvy vans.

They charged me with something quite serious. Criminal trespass with intent—something like that. When it got to court, they accused me of 'lying flat on a grave' as if I was some kind of occultist. They called witnesses, cited precedent but, at some point, the magistrate actually asked *me* what I was doing there. I told him 'I was visiting my father's grave'. He asked the prosecutor, 'is his father buried there?' And the answer—'well, there is a man with the same name as his father buried in the cemetery'. Then the magistrate asked me 'why do it at night?' I said, 'it was getting late, and I really wanted to visit him', then 'why the urgency?' and I said, 'It was Father's Day!' and he like, rolled his eyes, banged the gavel and said 'case dismissed'.

I used to get in trouble with the police a lot in my youth, I'd be picked up on the street, put in the back of the van just because I was a punk. Or billposting, you know? I was billposting for the mafia at one stage, glue buckets, rolls of posters and no car. I actually got a conviction for that.

Looking back, the Bowie queue at the MCG was quite significant. We were out of school by that stage—was it '78? As soon as we heard he was coming, we vowed we would be first in line, no matter how long we had to camp out. And we succeeded, ultimately, spent two or three weeks in sleeping bags, but that was just to get the tickets. Later, we had to queue for seating allocation. We met a lot of people. Bruce Butler. Harry Howard. Marie Hoy… The Crauford-Wall sisters, they were dangerous girls. It was pretty extreme, at least for me. I injected heroin for the first time during this period. Anaesthetised by Mandrax, Erica and I pierced each other's ears with safety pins…

It was here that we met and became friends with the meat and potatoes of the scene. We found the place for which we'd been searching. Melbourne was a lot less cosmopolitan then, it was grey, grim and conservative.

It was as if all the colourful people—and I don't mean hippies—found each other during those weeks. Everyone who was lost out there in the suburbs, looking—not knowing there were other people like them—found each other during those weeks. For good or for ill. Bowie and punk rock. Though, on the face of it, they may seem antithetical, somehow, in the Melbourne of that time, they merged to create a subculture.

The first real gig I went to was at the Matthew Flinders. My mum dropped me off there by myself to see The Ferrets and picked me up after. Before long, it became a thing; I'd go out to pubs with male friends from school. Radio Birdman at the Tiger Lounge. That was memorable. A girl took me back to a very cushy joint in South Yarra and practically raped me. Then we were trooping off to see the Boys Next Door at the Ballroom, or The Models at Bananas on the Esplanade. And before long we were in the era portrayed by Dogs in Space. I was 19 or 20.

During those years, I moved through heaps of apartments. It was a deliberate thing. I wanted to always keep moving, from place to place. I moved to Sydney for a while, to a bug-infested hovel behind the main strip in King's Cross, where Deans Cafe is (or was). Moved back. Moved on. Always.

I didn't attend the last term of year 12, but I did really well in my exams, even in French, which is bizarre. I started a BA at Melbourne Uni then deferred, then the next year I went back but my heart wasn't in it. I'd already gotten together loosely with a few school friends and formed a band. We were inspired by the whole punk rock paradigm—who says we had to know how to play a musical instrument to get on stage and make a racket? So we formed… I think it was The Spastics. It was during my second and last deferment from university that we became The Ears. I was living in a house in Malvern with Mick Lewis, the guitar player and Tim McLaughlan (keyboards). Chuck Meo, who played himself in *Dogs in Space*—he was the drummer.

It might've been interesting if The Ears had stayed together a bit longer. We were getting ever more popular, but we broke up for some typically stupid reason. We never had that arty suave thing that the Boys Next Door managed to project, and we certainly had little in common with the north-of-the-Yarra bands like Whirlywirld or the Primitive Calculators—though we often played on the same bill. It never really mattered, at that stage, whether you were working class or middle class or whatever class: in Melbourne, if you were a freak, you were equally excluded. Stuart Grant had a political edge and Ollie Olsen *seemed* political. They had a 'what we're doing is more important than what you're doing' vibe about them. The Ears were just crazy fucks. Apolitical nutjobs.

A year or so in, Paul Goldman put up $500 and we went to York Street to record a couple of songs, 'Leap for Lunch' and 'The Crater', with a guy called Daffy behind the desk. Stuart was the producer. With $500 we were able to pay for the studio, for the pressing, for posters, and a two-colour sleeve. It seemed like a huge amount of money. We were so grateful to Paul. It was an independent release, obviously, and you'd be hard-pressed to find a copy now. The cover showed a guy gouging out his own eyeball with a spoon. I think it actually did quite well on the 3RRR charts.

We were completely incompetent, but that wasn't unusual for the time—it was practically a dictum of punk rock. But prior to punk, it was unthinkable. It was a liberating thing, I never thought I could be in a band. I remember Mick had this little flat in Hawthorn, a reel-to-reel tape player, his Top Tone guitar and a shitty microphone. That's where the 'magic' happened. The very fact that we thought we could do music was so heretical, but punk let us do it.

The band shown in *Dogs in Space* felt a bit insulting in comparison with the reality of The Ears. Not that we were the best band or anything, but we did generate a vibe. We cared about the monster we'd created. Tim McLaughlan, who's dead now, he made his own synthesisers, he was a tinkerer, he had this old electric organ and discovered that if you put a resistor in there, a capacitor here, and soldered them just so, it made a crazy sound. It was great. Unstable but great. Our lighting guy was much the same—he went on to do lights for U2. Our sound engineer wound up doing the biggest acts in the world. He's a multimillionaire.

We released our second single through Keith Glass and Missing Link records. 'Scarecrow' was the A-side and it was pretty good. There was some fantastic cover art by a guy called Tony Harding, the brother of Christine Harding (on whom the Anna character in DIS was based and who, like myself, was from Mt Waverley). But we chose a different cover, for stupid pseudo-commercial reasons. By not staying true to ourselves, we were already hammering nails into our own coffin.

I first saw *Dogs in Space* at Richard's production offices in South Melbourne. I'd called to find out whether they had a first edit. They did. 'Come in and we'll play it for you'. I watched it alone in a room containing nothing but a TV and a VCR. I'll never forget that day. It was only three or four years since my girlfriend had died, tragically, of an overdose. You know how deeply you love when you're young? I was that deeply in love with Christine. Her death was unbelievably traumatic for me.

I sat there, in that room, bawling my eyes out through practically the whole thing. I finished, dropped the cassette on a desk and left. I walked the block in a daze, in emotional shock. The film had such huge emotional resonance for me, despite any number of factual errors or what not. It felt very very close. And I felt very angry that it seemed to suggest that I had introduced Christine to heroin. I hadn't. I was not only hurt but confused over this.

After hearing the story, this black American actor I'd been working with at the time had said: 'oh, man, you really have to get a lawyer. They won't charge unless they get a result'. This was true in the USA at the time but not here. With little to no rigmarole, the lawyer I found saw me out the door. I sent a letter to the censors and got a similarly dismissive response.

Christine was someone I loved profoundly. The truth that we shared a taste for heroin does not diminish that.

Craig Ellrick and his girlfriend Janet had returned from Thailand the day before. They were more Christine's friends than mine, but we were reasonably close. Earlier that night, The Ears had played at the Jump Club and, afterwards, they'd suggested going back to mine for a taste of the nice gear they'd brought home from abroad.

Both Christine and I... we both OD'd.

My last memory was of holding Christine upright on the bonnet of a car, a VW beetle I think, slapping her face, in a tumult of loud frightened voices.

This memory is a flash. Did it happen? Did it not? But later, then I really woke up. Dawn was approaching. I was walking around a flat, my neighbour's flat, with an awful feeling, like an oppressive weight. Something really bad had happened, I knew. But I wasn't sure what. I'd OD'd, obviously...

I looked out into the back yard. There was an area of very long grass, and somebody was standing in it. Peter Walsh (he played Anthony in *Dogs in Space*). He didn't look right. I saw him walk, very slowly, past the door, along the driveway. Then I must have fallen back to sleep.

I woke up some hours later in my neighbour's bed. In Troy's bed. I remember looking around, but I was unable to focus. Craig McGee was in the doorway. I saw his face and I knew. The world was heavy, grey, choking.

'Where's Christine?'

'She's dead'.

Dogs in Space did not attempt to reproduce this moment. But for me, subjectively, even its omission was hard to sit through.

Note

1. https://sailsofoblivion.blogspot.com/search/label/THE%20EARS?updated-max=2008-08-30T10:19:00%2B10:00&max-results=20&start=40&by-date=false.

It Was Filmic

Peter Farnan

On a Friday afternoon in 1979, I went to visit The Ears at their house in Wattletree Road, Malvern. I got off the tram and there, graffitied on a lamp post, was the inscription: 'Dogs in Space'. Tracking across the road (this is a one-shot so stay with me), it was scrawled elsewhere: on a fence, a wall, another lamp post, a surreptitious secret code. When I got to the front gate of the house, it was written on the footpath in much larger letters. Coming up to the porch, it was scrawled on the front door too. The door was ajar so I pushed it open. There was the band set-up in front of me in the living room. 'Hi Petey. Do you want to hear our new song, "Dogs in Space"?' They counted it off and smashed it out, fully formed; 30 seconds of guitar noise over a two-note bass pattern, a verse, an intoned chorus, a momentary sparse tom tom interregnum and then all of that again, and again one more time; a perfectly formed tri-partite avant-garde pop song. The experience was like a purposefully shaped episode, a subjective tracking shot culminating in a song. I did not think this in hindsight. It was clearly apparent at the time.

P. Farnan (✉)
Melbourne, VIC, Australia

© The Author(s) 2020
D. Nichols and S. Perillo (eds.), *Urban Australia and Post-Punk*,
https://doi.org/10.1007/978-981-32-9702-9_3

Throughout that period, my experience of The Ears was filmic. I would find Michael Lewis and Sam Sejavka in the backyard throwing bricks at each other. Sam would go 'you cunt' and he'd hurl a brick that would glance off his Mick's calf. Mick would go 'you bastard' and throw it back. It was played out in a kind of slothful, rock-monsterish slo-mo. Each missile would bounce off the paving, kiss a foot, scuff an arm, whistle past an ear. They would almost kill each other, but not quite. It was a performance, a scene. And at the time, I quite decidedly registered it as filmic.

There was a retinue of straight people who didn't factor into the darkly glamorous side of the story. One rung below the stars (and a rung above the parents), we had cars and amplifiers, knowledge and access to synthesisers and tape decks. We were the support crew. And, we never made the cut of the film.

I recorded 'Dogs in Space' at the same Wattletree Road House (not as portrayed in the film—Berry Street came later). I had the band distributed around the house. We recorded extended beds of squalling noise which I would, dub-style, drop in and out of the mix. Cathy McQuade was in one room playing a saw. I forgot to tell her she could stop. I remember, some time later, after the take, pushing the door open and there was Cathy, still diligently making strange noises in an empty room; a chair on ugly lino, light streaming through the window; a perfect image.

I went to school with Sam Sejavka, Mick Lewis and Tim McLaughlan. I'd known Sam and Mick since grade 5. We were part of a cohort at school in the 1970s, the much-maligned, spurned arty types. We coalesced around drama and theatre where we put on plays and pretentiously created spontaneous art happenings (instead of rehearsing said plays) for our own amusement. We staged The Tempest. Sam was a natural fit for Caliban, where his tortured writhing prefigured his stage persona in The Ears.

We were all aware of Roxy, Eno, Bowie, as well as prog, Kraut and 'cosmic music' (care of the record store, Pipe Music, in Melbourne—an epicentre for marginalised geeks in pre-punk days). Sam was an early adopter of Tangerine Dream. Another school mate inducted me into Springsteen and Patti Smith. Nothing funky—Joni and Patti were just about the only women. I was stuck on prog, but others were attracted to Lou Reed's dark and ominous persona, not so much for his taut language, but because of his 'drug-fuck-you' attitude. It was a remarkable furnace of creativity and ideas, partially because we were in opposition to the prevailing culture of sport and anti-intellectualism.

Post-school Mick Lewis and Tim McLaughlan moved into a flat in Hawthorn. They had a tape recorder and they started making fantastic, whimsical pieces of music; the 'tape recorder as an instrument' ethos but with none of the Art School pseudo-intellectual baggage. Tim was tinkering with electronics. He was gradually assembling the burbling, snorting, buzzing device that became his home-made synth in The Ears. I would drop around and piss myself at their creations. I distinctly remember one called 'Cut My Toad'.

Meanwhile, I was being taught composition by Ron Nagorcka at Melbourne State College. He started chastising students who handed in piano manuscripts for being too orthodox. I was exploring putting contact bugs on balloons and attaching them to parts of my body and amplifying them. I was filling my bags with Art School pseudo-intellectualism. When I listened to what Tim and Mick were doing it all made sense to me. But I was also a bit of a musical snob because I could play and they couldn't. They talked about forming a band and everybody laughed because nobody could play an instrument. But they did it. And off they went.

The Ears began in the early 1979. I 'mixed' them at their first gig at a loft party somewhere near Hardware Lane. It was appropriately chaotic. Eggs were smashed on peoples' heads and I started kissing a girl and didn't mix anything. We recorded their first demo, partly at Melbourne State College where we had access to Moogs and a VCS 3 synth. I remember the songs 'Brick Woman' and 'Sagging Insects'. I understand the songs made it to a compilation that Bruce Butler has curated.

They progressed lightning fast. Cathy McQuade, a real musician, joined and they became a slightly slicker proposition (but with attendant cyclonic, cinematic organisational chaos). Within months, we made a second set of recordings at that house in Wattletree Road: 'Golf Course', 'The Crater', 'Dogs in Space' and something else I can't remember. We were on a four track, but we were running tape loops (all that contact mic stuff I was doing at college) on another two track.

Soon Tim McLaughlan, their synth secret weapon, was out 'cause he could only make noises; he couldn't play notes. I played keys with them live at the Champion one night because they went 'maybe we should get a keyboard player'. They wanted to be like the Models, who were cool with the Ballroom crowd but also played tight little pop songs with nifty synth lines. I loved the Models, but I thought The Ears were more interesting when they were like The Residents. There's footage that Richard Lowenstein shot that night at the Champion. I'm somewhere in the bottom of the frame looking out of place; I wore brown, wilfully refusing to accede to the prevailing aesthetic for black.

Sam and Mick (and Tim I think) moved to the Berry Street house—the location mythologised in the film *Dogs in Space*. I went there many times—usually to watch *Countdown* on a Sunday night—but I don't remember Richard Lowenstein at all. They just said 'there's some guy upstairs who does film at Swinburne'. There was also 'some longhaired guy' who they were dismissive of. Many were written off as nonentities. I was still living with my parents (a very nonentity thing to do). Sam would sometimes visit. My parents remember him fondly but with: 'he was troubled, wasn't he?'

That first year of The Ears was indeed a perfectly framed cinematic piece. Gradually, I drifted away from that scene (which I was never really a part of). The Ears sailed on and became more and more orthodox, losing their chaotic art-anarchy in a fumbly quest for *fame*, that ghastly word that shaped so much of the 1980s. They became serious. So did I. I started Serious Young Insects and begun my own negotiation of that dreaded decade. Richard Lowenstein went on to make pop clips and some very good films. I still haven't met him.

I Was In-Between Two Worlds

John Clifforth

The House with the Eyebrows

I grew up in West Heidelberg and so as a teenager I used to go to places like the Q Club and the Berg, which was Heidelberg Town Hall. There'd always be fights and there'd be sharpies and punch ups. I saw Coloured Balls there, for example, that was tits out, everybody fighting, it was ridiculous.

My first band was The Cuckoos, the singer was Shane Lowe, and his sister was a girlfriend of Nick Smith's from The Millionaires, so I knew him when I was 14. My first experience of the Carlton scene was going to Nick's house, it was mad, it was this other world, growing up in West Heidelberg and going to Carlton. He was the first person to introduce me to the Carlton scene and he played me *Ziggy Stardust and the Spiders from Mars*. He mimed Mick Ronson doing the solo in 'Moonage Daydream'—we'd smoked some Zombie Grass and I'm like, this is incredible, I've never experienced anything like it.

J. Clifforth (✉)
Melbourne, VIC, Australia
e-mail: drjohn@apmed.com.au

When I moved to Carlton, Tim Brosnan who was living next door used to borrow my amp to play with The Millionaires. I knew the whole band and I went to their first shows. Nick was a very charismatic, funny guy, he gave different names to the band members—Tim was Boyd Compact, Nick was Nicky Lafayette, Steve Leeson was Buzz Deluxe, Henry Vynhil—actually I think that was his real name. They were a little bit influenced by Todd Rundgren, a little bit of Roxy Music. Tim was way into Hendrix and played like him. He soloed like crazy, but he couldn't play rhythm very well. I guess they were almost referencing the same things Skyhooks were, but with a bit more glamour. Nick ended up writing a lot of songs with Joe Camilleri.

I was living at 919 Rathdowne St. Carlton. Thanks to me it's called the house with the eyebrows, because I painted them above the windows one night for fun. I shared the house with another medical student, Stephen Johnson, Greg Perano knew him. I used to think Greg was a bit like—have you ever seen the movie *The Birthday Party?* Greg and his friend Peter would come round and harass Stephen in the way two mysterious men harassed Robert Shaw in that film.

919 was in a group of shops and 917 next door had these hippies living there, Tim Brosnan lived there, after his stint with the Millionaires he was in the Dots, and other bands. He lived there with this other guy Craig and a bunch of girls; it was basically a hippie share house. They were obsessed with music; they'd jam all the time. Along with Steve, I lived with Ken who ended up joining one of my bands. Ken wasn't studying, he worked with Tony Antoniades in a polythene pipe factory in Fitzroy. There was a bunch of other medical students on the other side at 921. I would sometimes go over there to do wine bottlings or whatever these middle-class kids from the western district were doing. That would be one hat, then on the other side would be the bonged-off-your-brain jamming community. I was between two worlds.

But there was this sense of growth, coming out of the kind of anarchy that was going on at University of Melbourne at the time. There was a transition from the hippie dinosaur bands culture of that period to younger kids looking for something completely new.

I played guitar and wrote songs. I played Greg some tunes I'd written and he said 'let's form a band' and we formed True Wheels. We classed ourselves as New Wave—via *Talking Heads 77,* Jonathan Richman and that sort of style. We covered Eno's 'Baby's on Fire', songs like that as well as our own material. There was a bit of scene in Carlton at that time. We used to play clubs, put on our own gigs. We played Martini's a lot, the Kingston, the Tiger Lounge, The Mitre Tavern. We did one gig with Jab at the Toorak Anglers Hall, which we promoted ourselves. Bananas was a crappy room above St Moritz on the Esplanade, St Kilda where you'd go after hours, after you'd been somewhere else, it was open till two or three am. It had the shittiest watered-down alcohol you could get, it was a complete dive. A lot of the time if you were in a working band it wouldn't be too exceptional to do two or three gigs in a night, so you'd do one gig, pack up, go and play Bananas. It had bleachers almost. It was tiny and rough. One night two groups of guys decided it was a good place to meet for a brawl, baseball bats and golf clubs flying. We just kept playing.

We used to play gigs with the Boys Next Door, play at Universities, union nights, little clubs, a corner in a pub, places like that. We'd do gigs with impromptu bands, often they were university students, architecture students probably. They'd get together for the night and wear some funny outfit and get a drum machine and just muck around. Then there were bands that were trying to do something a bit more serious, I suppose. It was up for grabs. It was all new, breaking new ground. Babeez was the first punk band—'what's that!'—it was all brand new, unchartered waters. Trying to find something that was a little fresher, a little bit more edgy maybe, a bit more existential than the blissed-out hippiedom that we'd come through from the late 1960s, early 1970s.

I had to be pretty disciplined actually. There was a point at which—my head was in two places—in final year I played in two bands, and I had to stop smoking pot for two months prior to the exams. I was a terrible student, but I did go to lectures every day, coping with a heavy lecture schedule, seven or eight hours a day. Sometimes if I went to see a band in North Court, there'd be joints going around the whole time and you'd end up getting pretty out of it, I'd go to lectures and miss tons of it—when the exams came I'd have to get notes from other people—I'd learn enough to pass by rote and then immediately forget it because summer came round and I'd be playing music. There'd be times I'd bow out of it, 'I can't be in that milieu for a while, while I get this out of the way'—that was the way I dealt with it.

I had friends who were junkies and I'd try to get them off, it was horrible, it was really hard to do. I think there was a period where people felt it was pretty glamorous and important to be junkies so they'd force themselves to get over the initial nausea and then—there were people who did feel normal when they took it, they had low endorphins or whatever. Heroin suited those people.

In the 1970s people were opening up to all sorts of new things to do with medicine, it was the beginning of acupuncture, holistic medicine, naturopathy, herbal medicine. I didn't have any moral judgement at all, I felt that chemistry and chemicals were up for grabs in terms of what suited you, what worked and what didn't. A lot of my friends were doing absolutely nothing except playing music and I couldn't do that all the time.

Troy Davies

I think Troy was every bit as capable of being a performer as Iggy Pop. The way he sings, it's so stylized and his capacity to write clearly and evocatively that was something Troy had as well, it just had to be guided. I have every belief that Troy could have gone further but he was all over the shop. He had this incredible stamina and it got him into trouble as well.

Troy was such a Puck like guy, he was extremely talented and very very funny. He could make you laugh hysterically, bring out the devil in you, he would really seriously make you do things you wouldn't normally do with anyone else. A very conservative friend of mine went and got a tattoo with him—it's a tiny little snail, I think, on his arse.

We made the Eccohomo single 'Motorcycle Baby'. He'd say 'I can *do stuff*, but nobody knows'. I said why not? You've got Michael, he could be in the clip, I had some backing grooves that I'd written, and he started doing this semi-rap stuff, it wasn't really singing, it was more like telling stories over it. He started doing this character of a butch guy with a motorcycle and a girlfriend, and it ended up becoming developed in the studio with Sherine Abeyratne singing, 'venus in leather, venus in furs', words he'd come up with. Those demos, I've got about four of them, there's one that's like a bizarre Suicide song, but it's called 'New Dress', and there's another one that's called 'My Hair', which is about a guy and a woman—and the woman goes out and does some sexual favours in order to get her hair done, and the boyfriend finds out about it and gets angry, Troy doing the voices of the characters seamlessly and totally off the cuff.

I'd just be rolling around. He'd be saying 'play it, don't tape it, play it don't tape it' you can hear him saying it over and over again he didn't want anything to be the definitive thing. But I would tape everything and edit it later. 'Motorcycle Baby' was really the only one. He did another thing with Ollie Olsen I think.

Deckchairs Overboard

The Cheks were this kind of power pop band I formed with Paul Hester. We made a demo tape which is on Spotify now, there were two record companies around we were interested in—in Sydney, Regular Records because they had Mentals, Icehouse, and they were kind of emerging as an independent. Men at Work had signed to CBS, and there were international labels but the main independents were Mushroom and Regular, we'd worked a lot with Mushroom; they had a company called Premier artists who were an agency, our manager was somehow connected to Premier. Michael Gudinski really wanted to sign us but Paul and I were really interested in moving to Sydney and signing to Regular, and I think we even signed as The Cheks. Steve Carter, the bass player, had a child and lived in Sunshine, he didn't want to move to Sydney. He was a very competent bass player but every time we wanted to do something funky, he didn't have a clue. We did a great demo tape at AAV with Jim Barton who's a fucking amazing producer, and I guess we could have had quite a bit of success. But my life probably would have been a lot less enjoyable if we'd stayed in Melbourne. Because we'd decided to move to Sydney we were like 'why don't we just change everything'. I liked Cathy [McQuade], her style, what she'd done in The Ears, I just liked her as a person, and so we thought, 'let's get her, we'll be like Talking Heads, it'll be a cool look, and she's into funky stuff', which we were becoming more interested in at the time. We did a bunch of rehearsing, we swapped instruments. I played bass on a few songs, Ken played drums.

We called ourselves 'I Can't Remember'. We played with Split Enz under that name. When we got to Sydney Martin Fabinyi said 'you can't have that stupid fucking name', we were in the boardroom and they had these director's chairs, we spent about five minutes thinking and we said 'deckchairs ... board ... deckchairs overboard ... Martin we've got a new name!' We called ourselves that, dicked around in the studio for a while writing an EP, played around for a while.

In Sydney with Deckchairs, we were trying to find a balance between Talking Heads-type songs about alienation, to playing dance music but with serious themes. We got to the point where we had to come up with some stuff that was radio friendly, I wrote 'Walking in the Dark'. Then along came Prince and he was doing funk but making it a lot more accessible in the pop vernacular, with a rock edge as well. It was very appealing and it turned us onto a more upbeat approach, a sense of elation in our music. I think that had an effect on INXS too—Andrew and Michael were always good songwriters but I think they moved to that kind of thing on *Kick* in particular.

I was good friends with Michael, around that time we'd see each other a lot, we even wrote songs together, nothing much came of those. I think it was probably just sitting around, singing, yelling out, playing guitars or whatever. It was more of a sharing of ideas, at parties, we'd just be singing. In Sydney, I hung around with people like Michael, Deborah Conway, a friend I shared a house with called Nick Conroy, had a band called Ditty Dimwits, the actor Andrew Gilbert and his brother. We lived in Potts Point and there were a lot of little clubs around there, The Manzil Room, there was a place called Exit which I loved. Dance clubs like Critter Canyon.

In Sydney venues opened later, you could play a show at a leagues club and come back and play a late show. Newcastle was very strong for us; we used to go up there a lot. Melbourne was different—we actually drove to Portland and back to play, you'd get back at four in the morning, just horrible. The gigs were kind of spread out and not particularly—there weren't as many as in Sydney because Sydney had the leagues clubs. The scene in Melbourne—weirdly, it seemed like the weather had a bit of an influence on us too at the time—the weather was better in Sydney, people would go out more, there was the surf scene, and I think there were fairly strong agencies in Sydney as well, Dirty Pool had Icehouse, Cold Chisel, Angels. There wasn't really much in the way of management in Melbourne, Melbourne was a bit less commercial I suppose.

After a while, Paul Hester left the band and Cathy and I became Deckchairs Overboard. We signed a deal with WEA after *Walking in the Dark* and virtually rewrote our repertoire for the Deckchairs Overboard album. The milieu at the time, the mid-1980s, was a strange one—there were places like Stranded which Gun Club played, basically those indie bands from England played there, a mix between a dance club and a venue, it didn't have a big stage. I guess it was a tiny version of The Hacienda in Manchester. Our favourite gig though was probably the Trade Union Club, which we played pretty frequently.

I was good friends with Colin Hay and I'd seen how Men at Work had gone. I think *Countdown* had a big influence, putting Australia on the international scene. There were groups that stood up with international acts. We always thought there would be a possibility of getting recognition overseas if you got good enough product. We mixed our album in New York with John Morales and Sergio Munzibai—they were DJs, they'd done mixes for a whole lot of international acts—we were like 'great, we're on equal footing with those people'. I loved that time and ended up living in New York. I was writing songs with Shepherd Solomon there and after playing little clubs for a while we started shopping our songs to publishers, live in their boardrooms. We ended up getting a huge publishing deal out of it, signing a deal with EMI and moving to LA.

The beauty of being able to come up with something that's interesting and captures the zeitgeist, it can take you anywhere—that was our feeling at the time. There was no cultural cringe from me. Just blind audacity!

The B-Side of a Single? An Autobiohistoriography

Stuart Grant

A barely sustainable tissue of lies.

* * *

This essay is a historiography of a set of competing histories. There is too much history here, too many histories, too many things that happened and didn't happen and are still happening; and the historiography only justifies a clearly stated intention to inflict further abuse. The past continually rewrites itself. And as Nietzsche wrote: "For by excess of history life becomes maimed and degenerate, and is followed by the degeneration of history as well."[1]

In 1973, I was fifteen years old. I had close-cropped hair with short rats' tails at the back. I wore tight striped ribbed cardigans, three-buttoned high-waisted checked pants with wide flares, and platform shoes with large bubble toes. Every boy I knew of my age in Melbourne dressed similarly. We didn't call ourselves sharpies or skins. It was just how we dressed. In

S. Grant (✉)
Melbourne, VIC, Australia
e-mail: stuart.grant@monash.edu

North Springvale where I lived, there were a few small stretches of local shops, usually a milk bar, a fish and chip shop, a small supermarket, a post office, maybe a laundromat or a doctor or a florist or a pet shop. The first of the big malls, Chadstone, Southland, and Northland, had been built in the previous decade, but they weren't yet the all-encompassing hubs of social and commercial activity they are now in 2019. Most shopping was still local and we only went to Chadstone to go bowling. Our parents shopped at the small supermarkets and milk bars. Each stretch of shops belonged to a gang that hung out at it. My gang hung out at the Sandown Park shops up the road from where I lived. We played football for Sandown Park and Mulgrave. The local shops nearest to my house were the turf of a local Catholic gang who had gone to St John Vianney's Primary School and now went to Clayton Tech. Members of my gang went to Clayton Tech, Lyndale High and Springvale High. We had gone to Springvale North State School, diagonally opposite St John's. In primary school, we were at constant war with the Catholic kids. In the songs, we used to sing about them we called them Catholic dogs. There were no Italians or Greeks in our gang. They were greasy wogs and spags, stinking garlic-eating spaghetti munchers.

These allegiances were crucial to our social belonging and survival: school, gang, religion, country of origin, football club. They were markers of position and identity in a pecking order of violence. The main marker of social position, within the gang, and between the gangs, was how good a fighter you were. My gang was not a gang of good fighters. We were lowly placed among the local gangs. The Catholic gang nearer where I lived were much better fighters. When I went to the shop to buy bread and milk for my mother, I had to run the gauntlet. I would look down, take the insults, say nothing. Sometimes I would get pushed around but never took a real beating off those guys. I took my beatings elsewhere, in Dandenong, at the Saturday night dance, Freedom, where every week hundreds of teenage boys from all the surrounding suburbs would gather to kick the shit out of each other.

This was a masculinist, working-class culture of violence. Women's liberation was a weird left-wing thing that happened in America and to rich people. The word feminist was not yet in circulation. My mother worked the same hours as my father, but when she came home, she cooked and cleaned until she went to bed and waited on my father while he watched TV. His jobs, out in the garden, the painting, and maintenance, remained undone. As kids, we played in the wild long grass his laziness grew in the backyard. Domestic violence was the norm. Pack rape at parties was commonplace and considered a joke. We were beaten at school and at home. Teachers would have their favourite strap, a long piece of leather, often polished, trimmed, and preserved to give maximum pain effect, and in our eyes, the length, shape, and painfulness of the individual teacher's strap were integral to their identity. We were strapped indiscriminately, for small transgressions, and just to generate an atmosphere of fear to prevent possible further transgressions. It was considered good for us, to make us men. Girls didn't get the strap so much. The violence perpetrated on them was more hidden; ingrained and insidious in the classroom, to supplement the tacitly accepted rape and beatings at home and in the streets.

Outer suburban Melbourne, rows of small, not quite identical brick veneer and weatherboard houses, was a working-class culture where we were being trained to be soldiers, factory workers, and domestic servants. We knew that the smartest among us would be office workers, with a small number getting to go to Monash University to train as schoolteachers. Other smart ones would do apprenticeships and become plumbers, cabinet makers, carpenters, bricklayers, toolmakers, sheetmetal workers, and boilermakers. The rest of us would be labourers and process workers in the factories. We were guaranteed work. This was a coherent social system, creating masculinised and feminised bodies and persons to function in an integrated society and economy. It was sustained by the traditional working-class virtue of knowing your place. But then, the 70s happened, the end of the Vietnam War, the Whitlam government, and the factories started closing down. We started to hear about this thing called the economy, which was in crisis. Unemployment soared, the dole was raised, the streets of Melbourne flooded with drugs: ounce bags of grass from Queensland for 30 bucks, hash from Nepal, India, and Pakistan for 120 bucks an ounce, acid tabs in the form of clearlights and microdots, cheap speed for 10 bucks a gram, and as the seventies went on, Thai white powder, Chinese rocks from Penang, Palfium, pethidine, Ritalin, Valium, barbiturates, and other fruits of easy chemist busts. Some of the tough guys with the striped cardigans and platform shoes were becoming hippies and disappearing into the rainforests of northern New South Wales and far North Queensland; some were marrying the girls they got pregnant and sitting at home on the dole shooting up pharmaceuticals into veins clogged with chalk deposits from the sulphates and other chemicals. This was a historic rupture in Melbourne's cultural and social fabric. By 1975, working-class suburban thugs were starting to die of smack overdoses. Literally dying out.

In 1972, I was playing in a boogie band. Melbourne boogie had been the sound of my childhood. Carson, Chain, Ida May Mack, Sunbury, Thorpie, the Coloured Balls. High ceilinged outer suburban halls reverberating with the sound of Gibson SGs played loud through Vase amps with deep-voiced, soul-influenced shouting singers. Blues-based, one-chord, minor key grooves that went on forever, danced to by circles of platformed-booted short-haired sharpies, elbows bent, fists clenched in a robotic punching motion. This had been a tradition since the early 60s with bands like the Purple Hearts, the Throb, and other raw Australian responses to the British invasion bands and their imitators in the USA. The sound had evolved in these outer suburban halls and a few inner-city clubs, and at its acme, before the glossed-up sanitised cabaret version in the form of AC/DC, when the sound of the Aztecs thundered out of the wall of amps into the audience at Sunbury, it was received by two overlapping main strands of Melbourne youth culture: the remainder of the suburban thug sharpies, and the burgeoning hippie culture. The rolling dotted crotchets of the blues boogie sound were heard as the soundtrack of a good kicking by the sharpies, and were the site of interminable drug-induced meandering jams of the hippies. In the mud of Sunbury, sharpies and hippies mingled, in a haze of booze and acid and chillums. But by 1975, the youth culture of Melbourne had reached a turning point. The hippy and sharpie cultures had reached their peak and had nowhere to go. Both were unsustainable. The working class was dying. The hippies were burning out. A new reality was taking hold. The opening scene of *Dogs in Space*, in which a bunch of sharpies confront some punks, captures this moment of cultural rupture.

* * *

Richard Lowenstein's film is a detailed and nuanced socio-cultural time capsule; a history written less than a decade after the events it depicts. The opening scene reveals and foregrounds this historiographic motive from the beginning. The movie is a personal historical reflection on a period of change. The title of the film refers to a song which refers to a certain historical event of the time. The wandering eye and ear of the camera moves through rooms of people, representative of different subcultures of the time, embodying certain different phases of the cultural shifts which were occurring, and listens to them discussing significant and insignificant events of the day. This technique is a key moment of the film's overt historiographic intent. It is not just a story about the competing interests of love and heroin, but the deployment of a conscious and articulate historiographic methodology. This essay picks up and carries forward Lowenstein's method. At the most objective sense, I was there as a historical cultural artefact undergoing the change depicted. At a subjective level, I knew the people on whom the characters of the film were based, some of whom were playing themselves or other characters in the movie, and I had participated in some of the events depicted. At a historiographic level, I played a role in the stories the film tells and have influenced and been influenced by their reception and telling. I was in the film briefly, playing myself. I took a very specific prejudiced stance at the time on what I perceived to be the historical inauthenticity of the film, and it has substantially influenced the course of my life since. This is part of Lowenstein's genius. He created a complex historiographic knot through the layering and intertwining of two close periods of time, through the events and the people, and overlapped them in a dense multiplying mesh of connections that, in my case, gave me my experience in a way in which I had never had it. I take this forward in this essay by first, as I have already done, reflecting on my experience of the social and cultural prehistory of the film in ways I never would have thought without it having been made; second, by describing my experience of some of the events of both the period depicted in the film and the period in which the film was made; and third, noting my own contemporaneous judgments of the film; and explaining my current completely different understanding of it, and the role the film has played in shaping the last ten years of my life, thirty years after it was made. I can say conclusively that I would not be who I am today without *Dogs in Space*, I would not be doing the things I do. I would not know many of the people I know. My past, even the past before the film, would be different. This film has affected me profoundly. It took me nearly 30 years to get *Dogs in Space*, or more accurately, to drop my identity guard long enough to let it get me, and to realise what an important document it is, and what a sophisticated and artful example it is of the power of the central temporal substance and mission of film.

* * *

The opening scene of the film captures the aforementioned historical moment of cultural rupture. The old Melbourne working-class youth culture confronts a whole new animal. As someone who had previously been the sharpie kid you had to be in Melbourne's violent suburbs of the early 1970s, the years 1974–1976 were lost. Too young to be a hippy, and too socially dislocated to get a real job. In those two years, my peers and I listened to jazz, country, blues, and other historical forms, mined the history of psychedelic 60s music, kept an ear to the pop of the time, and were seduced in the pot haze of the new glossy sound of west coast soft rock. And there was disco everywhere. We loved disco. We were too cool for disco to be uncool, like it was for many. Even though it culturally belonged to young mature office workers, we heard it as the site of new sounds, a new kind of soul music, and the most exhilarating technological and musical innovations in production and structure. The 12″ disco single was a revolution in pop music. But it didn't belong to us. We had no music of our own, no scene, no distinct recognisable youth culture, no belonging as we had had to our gangs as kids, and as our older brothers and sisters the hippies had had to their acid-induced delusions of a new world.

By early 1976, I was 18 years old, somehow ended up living in Adelaide, working in a shit office job, not knowing what I was doing. As a musician, I was still playing blues and folk songs without much interest, going through the motions. One day I walked into a record shop off Rundle St and heard the first Ramones album, and Suicide's "Rocket USA", off *Max's Kansas City 1976*. My life changed immediately and irrevocably. I had never heard anything like it, but I knew I needed it. It struck something in me, rang a cultural chord, the magnitude of which fills with me awe when I look back on it. I can see now that no event before or since has changed and shaped the subsequent direction of my life more than that moment. I started to write punk songs. I knew of the MC5, the New York Dolls, the Stooges, and was a big Velvet Underground fan. I hated the laboured, self-conscious attempt to appear intelligent of David Bowie and Roxy Music, and all English art school rock, and had little interest in Krautrock, but none of this post-gathered prehistory of punk and the electronic punk I ended up playing had made much of an effect on me up until that moment. History is written after the fact. These threads weren't drawn together and didn't make sense until after the Ramones. The supposed tradition of the roots of punk was a story gathered in retrospect. The Ramones made it imaginable as a tradition. Plus they sounded like the Beach Boys. This was their genius. And the nihilism of their lyrics combined with this gathering of sonic elements sounded necessary and apt to the frustration and lostness of my generation. Similarly, and in my case more efficaciously, Suicide imagined a future for a past that only became visible and audible in the combination of sonic and cultural elements they brought together. Like the inside of a demented Elvis head working on a factory production line. But this music was not a progression. It was a rupture. It broke time. It made a new past visible. History goes backwards. And the following December 1976, shortly after "Anarchy in the UK" was released in the morning and banned in the afternoon, I came back to Melbourne to make a punk band.

In early 1977, I got together with a bunch of high school friends, moved into a house in St Kilda and wrote a bunch of songs about nihilism, death, and drugs. We called ourselves The Moths. We were children of the Whitlam era. We believed it was our birthright to be paid just for being there, that work was an anachronism that would soon die out and that humans would be delivered to a higher destiny. We lived on the dole, which was generous. Rents were low and drugs were cheap. The Moths played once and went through a series of different line-ups, but by the end of 1977, punk was dead. It had lost its exhilaration, couldn't get fast enough or loud enough. The punk edge was blunt. You couldn't get the abandonment of that initial thrash and rush that it gave for that first year. We needed something to keep the ugliness and brutality alive.

And we hated playing with drummers. They slowed down and expressed themselves too much. We hadn't yet learnt to make the Suicide component of our sound. In 1978, we moved to Fitzroy, bought some state of the art equipment, a Roland CR78 drum machine, a Roland System 100 synthesiser, and a Wasp synthesiser, and started making a more savage, brutal, primitive, noisy kind of music. We called ourselves the Primitive Calculators because I thought it was an apt description of the human mind. There were no personal computers yet. The pocket calculator was the most advanced personal electronic equipment at the time. The AI of the day. Humans appeared primitive in comparison. We started to play a few gigs. Nobody, or at least only very few people, liked or understood us. We were angry, contemptuous, incompetent, unlistenable, and hated everybody and everything, especially the Melbourne punk scene, which was always more influenced by English art school rock, and in our opinion, with only a couple of exceptions, it had never been anything more than a bunch of private school haircuts. Still, slowly, through late 1978 and early 1979, a scene built around us. We had met John Murphy, Ollie Olsen, and Arne Hanna of Whirlywirld, and although we hated their pompous new romantic English sound, we also hated the same people as them, and our little scene, based on this shared hatred, became a lot more substantial. We moved to North Fitzroy to two adjoining shops. Whirlywirld lived in one, the Primitive Calculators in the other.

One day in early 1979, Dave Light from the Primitive Calculators was rehearsing a song with Lee Smith, one of our friends who hung around our shop. They said they were a new band called the Leapfrogs. I said we should invite our friends and the people in the small scene that was building around us and Whirlywirld to all make little bands and play together at our own nights so we didn't have to play at the Crystal Ballroom, Tiger Lounge, Hearts, and the other conventional punk and music industry venues which the now mainstream punk bands were playing at. We started to stage nights playing with the little bands we were making as our supports at new venues like the Champion Hotel in Brunswick St. and the Exford in Chinatown. Other bands started to contact us about playing with us and started to hang around the scene.

That year, one of the bands which were popping up around us, a band called The Ears, asked me to produce their first single. I found myself in York St studios with an engineer called Daffy, who had also recorded the Primitive Calculators single and the Little Bands EP, producing a meandering jagged song called "Leap for Lunch". All I can remember of it was the line "dressed like a salad and arguably real", that the singer had an annoying yelp of a voice like XTC, The Cure, and Talking Heads, all of whom I hated, that the drummer slowed down and sped up, the homemade synthesiser kept breaking down, and they were more art school than I liked. Although I haven't listened to it since the day it was recorded, I remember the B-side was a strange thing featuring this home-made synth. Me and Daffy decided to use the studio to make what we took at the time to be a howling psychedelic wall of noise. The song was called "Dogs in Space".

* * *

When I submitted this article to the editors, they pointed out to me that the song "Dogs in Space" was not the B-side of the "Leap for Lunch" single. They were mildly apologetic in tone, suggesting that maybe I had produced the song but it wasn't the track that eventually made it to the vinyl, and perhaps it was replaced by the song that did, "The Crater". I, however, was enthused. As I said above, I had not and still have not listened to it from the day we recorded it until now 40 years later. As soon as I went and listened to the song a few days ago, I knew it was the one we had recorded and that my memory of the song which gave its name to the band in the film and the film itself was an amalgam of memories of seeing the Ears live when they supported the Calculators, and from recordings of the movie soundtrack. But my false self-serving memory, that the title came from a song that I produced, which I have repeated so many times to so many people, is the ultimate proof of my argument concerning the interestedness and fallibility of history and historiography.

This is further emphasised by my memory of Richard Lowenstein. In the first draft of this essay, submitted two weeks before this writing, I wrote that I wasn't sure but I thought I remembered that Richard Lowenstein had been involved in the financing or some other way of supporting the single, or he might just have been a fan of The Ears who was hanging around the studio at the time. I wrote that I had a memory of a quiet, keen, respectable looking kid. I postulated that I thought it might have been him, it might have been someone else, it might have been a composite that I'd made up out of a few different people. I also noted that at the time, in 1979, I had been crippled with self-obsession and drugs, so in 2019, two weeks ago, I wasn't sure. On doing a little research after the editors pointed out my mistake on the song, I looked at the sleeve of the record online and saw that Paul Goldman was Executive Producer. At that point, it all came together for me. My memory of young Richard Lowenstein was actually a composite of him and Paul Goldman. As I noted two weeks ago, that's history. And this is historiography. I had a Richard Lowenstein in my memory who I though may or may not have existed, but who I now know was only partially him.

* * *

In 1980, the Primitive Calculators broke up. I spent a couple of years out of the country, and came back in late 1982, formed the Bum Steers, Mr. Bum and Ruby, and joined Use No Hooks, a project of Mick Earls and Arne Hanna. In 1983, I moved to Sydney. Mr. Bum was a cabaret singer doing Tom Waits-style versions of jazz standards and was my main act at the time. We were doing better business In Sydney than in Melbourne, so it made sense to move there, and me and Ruby and the absurdly handsome Phil Nichols, the pianist, hated Melbourne and wanted to get out of the place. I swore I would never come back to Melbourne unless they paid me. I have stuck to that commitment to this day. I have never spent one unpaid day in Melbourne since 1983.

In 1985, I was a working cabaret singer in Sydney, singing funk, soul and jazz, doing weddings, RSL clubs, and functions. I received word from some of the other former Primitive Calculators that someone was making a movie about the Ears and we were going to be in it. I was bemused. As far as I was concerned, the Primitive Calculators and the associated scene was in the past. Punk had failed and turned into new romanticism. The world had not changed. It had gotten worse. The musicians of the Melbourne punk scene had become part of the Mushroom/Premier Oz Rock industry. The supposed forefront of popular music in the 1980s was in the main a vacuous English fashion parade. The haircuts had won. The stupidity and gullibility of the listening audience had prevailed. I was too busy making a living out of being a workaday singer to be bothered with a dead thing from the past. I was living the ongoing stream of my life. I proclaimed to anyone who would listen that I would never write another song because I had nothing to say to this corrupt world. My past was disposed of. I had no interest in it. And I was too addicted to heroin and martinis to care.

I came to Melbourne for the making of the film and the recording of our track "Pumping Ugly Muscle", which I'd written in 1978, eight years earlier. We recorded it at Richmond Recorders with Tony Cohen and Ollie Olsen. It was a very different thing from how we had originally sounded. Much more rock and less electronic noise. On the final version Ollie Olsen ruined it by putting stupid screams all over it, I think by Marie Hoy, but maybe not. It was done after the fact. I had no say in it and I didn't give a fuck. The whole thing seemed like a sad joke of people dwelling in imagined past glories of a period that was just a shitpit of incompetence, anxiety and hate, as far as I could remember. I still can't listen to it to this day. Piece of stupid shit.

* * *

However, the making of this film was the inception of a strange historiographic fold which substantially changed my life. They were making a film in 1985 about 1979. As I look back on it today from 2019, that six years, at the time, felt like a longer temporal gulf than the 33 years has since the film was made. I was going to say it still does, but that would be a lie, confected for exaggerated effect, maybe, but not entirely. I'm not sure. Time obscures time. But it is in this little knot, of the six-year duration and what it felt like then, compared to the 33 years since and what it has felt like going through that, compared to the feeling today of looking back on both periods, compared to the raw data of the turning of the earth and the numbers of days and nights, that the weight of time develops. The experience and significance of time is tied to cultural, social, and personal meanings. My response to the making of the film at the time was, like my general attitude, cynical, self-obsessed, and drugfucked. I thought it was entirely inauthentic, even though I hadn't actually thought through what that term meant. I found myself in a room at the Crystal Ballroom which was already being remembered as the site of some sort of golden creative flowering, five years after I had last played there, but which I had always seen as the graveyard of the spirit of punk, and of any true creativity in the new music of the late 1970s. The Crystal Ballroom was the site where the Primitive Calculators cleared the room of punk luminaries by playing the first-ever live drone music Melbourne had heard. Now, in 1985, the room was full of young people I had never met and people that I had known for years, who were all playing pastiche characters based loosely on types of people we had known six years earlier. But the haircuts and clothes were contemporary 80s styles, nothing like, to my view at the time, those we had actually worn in the 70s. More worryingly for me, although I didn't realise I was responding to it at the time, the film was participating in a story that was being created around the Little Bands which had very little to do with what actually happened. The Primitive Calculators appeared in the band night scene of the film, which was clearly based on a Little Bands night, and original Little Bands posters were used in the film. But the Calculators were starting to be remembered as a Little Band. Worse still, other people were being credited with founding the scene. In this movie, I was watching history being rewritten, but, as I said, I didn't realise it at the time. But still, it was a history which would not have been written at all without the intervention of this film, which was understandably rewriting the history in a way which would serve its own commercial imperative and the interests of those actively engaged in the film's making. As Nietzsche taught us, history has uses. It always serves a power agenda. But in pertinence to my own life story, it is clear that without the making of *Dogs in Space*, it is likely that the Primitive Calculators would have been consigned to the trashcan of history. So if the film had never been made, had never told its lies, I would not be here telling these lies right now, writing this article.

The production company making the film offered us a shit deal for our songs, asking us to sign all our rights away forever for a pittance. As a working musician, this was not acceptable to me. I got a lawyer and kept the rights to my song and made a dance version, which Phil Nichols and I did on a Fairlight in Sydney, with Andrew Bell, who, over a decade earlier, had auditioned for, but never made it into Skyhooks, an event which shaped his life irrevocably, which also ties into another interesting connection. When me and my friends from high school first moved to St Kilda in 1977 and formed The Moths, we met Steve Hill, the original singer in Skyhooks, who was a totally fucked up junkie who became our first regular heroin supplier. Steve was a beautiful man, who died relatively young of his addiction. But that's another story. Anyway, in 1987, me and Phil and Andrew released our completely different dance music version 12″ single on Chase records (Primitive Calculators 1987), and it is still the best version of the song, like a fucked up Prince record, far better than the stupid *Dogs in Space* version with the screams on it or the older version from the 70s, which has also been released in some form or other, I think on Chapter records. I still, in 2019, play another completely different version of the song in the Calculators, and it now sounds more like a Kanyesque hip hop than any of these other versions. This song, as a historical artefact, keeps changing to reflect its contemporary sonic environment.

After my few days on the film set, I left Melbourne, went back to my career as a cabaret singer, and didn't think much about it until the Sydney premiere of the film, which I attended with disgust, and I then forgot about it for 25 years. In the meantime, I lived a life, sang in soul and funk bands, worked as a jazz singer, and in cheesy Latin bands.

In 2008, I got a job at a university in Melbourne and returned to live in that city for the first time since 1983. In the ensuing 25 years, I had lived mostly in Sydney and in a few cities across Asia. Shortly after my arrival, we were asked by one of the more well-known haircuts of the 70s Melbourne punk scene to put the Primitive Calculators back together for a festival. Our music had been reissued by Chapter and other labels across the previous decade and had apparently and incomprehensibly influenced new generations of Melbourne musicians. This was amusing but also kind of gratifying, because we had always been so convinced of our own cultural import and ethical rectitude. It may have been this sense of the importance of what we were doing that gave such temporal weight to that six-year period between 1979 and 1986, and the subsequent judgment of the inauthenticity of the movie. But when I was looking back at all this from 2008, my judgment of the movie changed completely. It became clear to me that *Dogs in Space* had been integral to this discovery and influence of the Primitive Calculators. The film had provided a marker to the band's existence and given an artefact in a few snatches of performance and a couple of recordings, even though the band in the film was not the band in the 70s, the music wasn't anything like it had been originally, and the context was an inauthentic 80s recreation. So again we had been remembered all those years later in a form and occasion that was itself an inexact remembering of another time. The film had kept the name of the band alive which had led to Chapter records releasing our original 70s recordings in the early 2000s. This layering created a historiographic richness and depth, which, although in my mind was inauthentic, again, in an unthought, unexamined, hackneyed idea of the term that I was still carrying around, it gave the band the appearance of more substance than it actually had originally had.

* * *

At the time I returned to Melbourne in 2008, the film, this inauthentic recreation, was being again recreated in its own right, in what I now understand as its own authentic inauthenticity, and was about to authentically change my life again. In 2009, shortly afterwards, Richard Lowenstein made the documentary *We're Livin on Dog Food*, about his own film and the scene it sprang from. This was another historiographic move to perpetuate his living interpretation of the events. I saw this as an opportunity to do two things. First to start re-rewriting the history of the Primitive Calculators and the Little Bands, to reestablish the "truth" as I saw it of the origin of the scene, and second to manufacture a new history which bloated the importance of the band and the little scene that sprung up around it. I did the interview for the film as a blueprint that set the future reputation and reception of the band as uncompromising, not fitting in, always self-destroying, annoying little dickheads. I also used it as the platform to continue the band, in which I am now, in 2019, the only original remaining member, and which has now been recording and performing for a further ten years, while the original band didn't exist for even two.

* * *

This is an extraordinarily dense, complex layering and crystallising of histories, historiographies, authenticities, inauthenticities, and the interests they serve, which are built not only into the method, structure, and content of the film *Dogs in Space*, but which Lowenstein continues and complexifies with his later historiographic strategy in the documentary. Lowenstein uses the time gap of the ensuing 25 years to position *Dogs in Space* as temporally congruent with the time it documents, despite its later reinterpretative role of that time. In the interviews, he blends reminisces of the original events with memories of the making of the film, blurring the original temporal rupture it initiated. This temporal muddying utilises and perpetuates the cult status of *Dogs in Space*, accentuating it as a living, changing, evolving cultural artefact. The ageing participants in the documentary have lost the nuance of the more detailed temporal perspective in the length of time since, in their emotional engagement with their own personal histories and narratives, and in the fog of memory. As I have elaborated above in the description of my own case, *Dogs in Space* has shaped the lives of all of these people in some ways and to some extent, as a touchstone of their own histories and identities. And, as attested by the interest of the editors of and some of the contributors to this volume, it continues to affect the lives of people who weren't even there as they use it to decipher their own cultural prehistories.

* * *

I could go on, but I can't end. It does not seem appropriate to come to a conclusion here. This essay is an autobiohistoriography. This history is still writing and revising itself. I am still alive. Many of the participants in the movie are dead, and some of those are gruellingly memorialised and recreated on facebook pages by other participants and some much younger people. *Dogs in Space*, as a historiographic cipher, remains a living, changing, evolving, cultural artefact that continues to pile up the lies, stories, memories, and interpretations of which history and life are made. This is the genius of the film and its maker.

* * *

Oh. And let's not forget. In the movie, Heroin, the main character, defeated Love, its antagonist.

Note

1. Nietzsche, Friedrich Wilhelm (1957) *The Use and Abuse of History.* 2nd rev. ed. (New York: Liberal Arts Press), p. 12.

In My Mind the World Was Safer

Karen Ansel

I had to find a way to pay rent and I had been making my own clothes since I was a kid. I'd left home at 17 and travelled around Australia for a year and came back to Melbourne. I found work at the Australian Ballet Company doing costumes. Ballet costumes are based on eighteenth-century corsetry and the craftsmanship of haute couture. Layers of silks over calico and hand-beaded. The pattern cutter there was brilliant so I got my skills and professional finish working there. I had this craft of design and sewing that was portable and could help me pay the rent wherever. I was living in a Victorian terrace share house on Edinburgh Gardens, North Fitzroy, commuting into the Australian Ballet costume department in Spring Street and going to see bands all the time.

Music had helped me since I was a kid. If I got near a piano I could play by ear. Early teens I would haunt Discurio (record store) to educate myself—folk, swing, blues, finding links from one thing to another. When I was a kid, there was a commercial radio DJ who would play 40s swing and then blues and then pop then Dylan. I'd go and try and find the link.

K. Ansel (✉)
Melbourne, VIC, Australia

Melbourne musicians seem to look deep into the bones. I didn't know about jump blues but you could hear this flavour in like Daddy Cool, hear it on the radio and then go find out about the core. Then in the late 70s, the Sex Pistols, Clash, Buzzcocks, X-Ray Spex happened. It was the attitude. Undeniable. And energy. Also that you didn't have to be a musical virtuoso to get on stage. It seemed out of reach before then, dominated by the Eagles and accomplished musicians, then here's this total energy coming out of nowhere.

At the same time, I was seeing English magazines showing what London fashion design stores 'Sex' and then 'Seditionaries' were doing—Vivienne Westwood. It was inspiring. I wanted to contribute here and I thought I could open a store. I found a storefront in Caledonian Lane beside Myers and started a punk shop I called 'Trash'. I'd been introduced to Uschi Flett who had also been doing costumes for bands and theatres like me and I partnered with her. 'Trash' was kind of a meeting place more than a business. I employed Ollie Olsen to attend the shop, his first job. Debbie Harry, doing her first promotional tour for Blondie, came in and was photographed there and said some kind words so it had a profile. Office girls would buy things. Mary Madigan, an exotic dancer who performed as Doody and choreographed amazing, subversive routines bought my leopard-print catsuit with a tail. Jane Clifton, singer for Stiletto then, bought from us.

Rowland (Howard) and Ollie hung out. I had a workshop up Little Bourke Street in a warehouse space where I was living then so I would leave the shop to make stock in the day. I'd be screen-printing T-shirts that was a newsprint with photo in bright pink, 'Krupa Kills Cats at Atlantic City Opening' because I adored Gene Krupa. Black lace one pieces, vinyl minis, zips. I'd buy shower curtain fabric and make full circle skirts which I got sunray-pleated over in a factory in Northcote. The city was full of resources like that—old local family-run factory businesses where you could get anything done. 'Trash' made no money. I kept being told by people that they had come to the shop but it was closed. I was too naive in business and too busy to look into it further. Years later one of the shop assistants came clean and told me that he got bored and used to close the store and go to the pub. He wouldn't have got the importance of trying to get a return from a creative business that I'd worked for to get started. I had a bit of attitude back then that most of the punk bands were boys who had attended public school or alternative schools or had supportive parents and I didn't see how they thought they had it so rough, from well-heeled families. I didn't appreciate the lyricism then that I do now. The lost boys and lost girls from all walks.

There was alienation. I was born in Mount Beauty, post-war parents on the Snowy Mountain project, then we transplanted to this wasteland suburban development when I was four, so there was that dislocation. I was a latch key kid, looking after the house and the meals. My parents did not have a happy marriage. My Dad developed MS (Multiple Sclerosis), diagnosed early, developed slow, inexorable. My mother was undiagnosed but in retrospect had the traits of borderline personality disorder, spreading fabrications all around and rage behind a facade of normalcy. I was a caretaker. Things at home were unpredictable and could be cruel and I was a kid who wanted to make it easy for everyone. Family life was shredded. It was confusing. Being invisible was the best way to survive. Then as a teenager I started to look ahead. The path in those suburbs, you're expected to get married—that's it, that's your path. I was creative, there's got to be another way. Music helped. Books, art. I discovered Buddhism doing a geography project at 14. There were signs pointing a different direction. When I finished high school, I felt that for my survival I had to get out. At 17, I left and worked and travelled around Australia, went through the outback. I've occasionally heard through the years that 'you must have been so brave', but it didn't feel like that. Somehow in my mind the world was safer. I got out of a deadened nowhere. That isolation. I had anger about where I'd come from, wanted to express it.

I got back to Melbourne, started running 'Trash' and then the small bands had started so there was a lot of places to play. Art students out of Caulfield Tech like Boys Next Door were playing, all of Ollie's bands, lots of gigs. No women. The door was open with three chord thrash and in '77 no girls were walking through. Uschi's boyfriend Nick Rieschbeth had a house in Richmond with a studio and PA and one day we were bemoaning that no women were in punk bands so he sort of dared us to shut up and start writing. We took a leap. I picked up the synths that were laying around the place. I had a mini-Korg, an MXR digital delay feeding through a Lesley speaker and a patch Korg and started writing songs and getting further into synths. I had a affinity with electronics. (My first job at fourteen was inputting the betting tickets as data to the computer before the races at the Clayton TAB.) Half the band was influenced by Captain Beefheart and the other half by The Buzzcocks, X-Ray Spex and Giorgio Moroder. We wrote a bunch of songs and rehearsed a few covers for a couple of weeks and jumped on stage. First gig at The Tiger Lounge I played a saxophone for the first time and apparently hit a high C. I didn't know. Made the bass player a meat vest which he took off when it turned rancid under the lights and flung it into the audience, which flattened Tracy Pew on the dance floor. That sort of gig. The Crystal Ballroom, Bananas, Martinis, The Jump Club, and so many small bands forming, falling apart, re-forming. You could play a few gigs a week. Bands played one after the other on one stage. We'd run around the city checking out what everyone was doing. For *Dogs* Richard (Lowenstein) hung about The Ears, around The Ballroom. Thankfully he and Ollie put Marie Hoy into that Ballroom scene in '*Dogs*'. For all the punk ethos then, the girls were still being the muse, looking cute and looking on. I would run into Ollie or there'd be bands I'd go to or gigs where we were supporting. Boys Next Door, Eric Gradman's Man & Machine, Whirlywirld and people backstage. I wasn't doing drugs. I was still working, had keep myself together. Later when heroin came in and started to dissolve everyone, it seemed to take hold of the boys from privilege quickest, the dissolute glamour with the safety net. I stayed away. Survival instincts kept me away. I had only myself to pay my rent. I did drink a lot.

'Trash' had folded in on itself. Synthesisers captured me. There was Felix Werder's studio in the city. He was a master. He ran this course where he wrote the Pythagorean theory of music on the board, pointed to the synths in his studio and said have at it. Influenced all of us in Melbourne into electronics—Ollie, Andrew Duffield, everyone. The band played the small bands' circuit, had a floating group of musicians (Nick Seymour, Bob Starkie, Stephan Fidock). We supported The Reels a few times, played at The Tiger Lounge in Richmond one night. The Reels were ska pop at this stage. I was getting into Giorgio Moroder and funk and I'd written this song called 'Dream Kitchen'. I think Dave Mason was looking for the next direction for the band and something in it struck him. Dave and

I and Craig (Hooper) hung out and we just got on. Dave and I had a strong aesthetic affinity from the start. He was subversive and looking for a change of direction musically. Plus he liked the idea of a girl in the band and asked me to audition. After the audition, Dave and the band gave the tick, so I moved up to Sydney.

The lineage from that Melbourne art/punk scene spread wide. The Reels were trained musicians. I played by ear. It was a challenge. Even though I couldn't read music, I had a good ear. I could 'hear' my parts and programmed, knew when I had the sound I 'heard' and stopped messing around with the sound and then played the parts I heard. Polly could score for marching bands. For *Quasimodo's Dream*, we went to a warehouse on the ports in Glebe to work on this new direction. Polly, Craig and I on synths started doing all this machine stuff. Remember I had come from that Melbourne art/punk scene and there were no limits. It was a process of deconstruction in rehearsals, a steel forge factory meets primal scream therapy and Todd Rundgren. We would tape the jams in rehearsal, listen, extract the workable sections and work them over. It looked as if it might not work, then it started to gel. Craig and I worked over and over on an arrangement for 'After The News'. Polly would piece together other arrangements that made sense to him musically. Dave was confident, fearless about letting it happen. It was still pretty loose when we went into record at Alberts. We decided to do some covers, a kind of sampler for *Five Great Gift Ideas*. I suggested 'Band of Gold'. Dave of course came up with 'According To My Heart'. Then followed recording, designing, touring. Dave and I worked on the concepts for the tours.

I met Michael (Hutchence) around that time in Sydney. Michael was a searcher. He found us all. He'd seek out like minds. He had apparently come and seen the Reels a few times when we were out on *Five Great Gift Ideas*, (before *Quasimodo's Dream*). He reached out when INXS were recording *Underneath the Colours*, asking Dave and me to sing backing vocals. So I first met Michael in the studio. Backing vocals on 'Stay Young'. By the way, this says something about Michael, that he reached out then. The Reels were not in the same realm of INXS, Cold Chisel, Midnight Oil, and pub rock Marshall-stack bands. We had tiny Bose speakers and headsets mics. We'd been on Countdown, accepted as quirky in the beer barns. That Michael recognised enough there to support and that he reached out to us speaks to who he was. He would actively seek people no matter what contrary perception, search out some kind of creative community for himself. I saw him do this over and over through the years. So we met in the studio. This would have been around 1979. After that session, we just walked around Darlinghurst all night, the Cross, neons and nightlife, talking. It's who Michael was. He and Michele (his girlfriend) became my friends. To me, he was like that great male friend in high school if you were lucky enough to find who would say don't worry, look over there's Kurt Vonnegut, here's Lou Reed, what about the Velvets, that kind of friend. He was sensitive, intuitive. I know he was a chameleon, and to me, for all his high-voltage sensuality, he had just as high a percentage of artist nerd. He had magnetism and a wicked sense of humour.

It was in London, '84 that I met Richard. I'd met him through Michael. Richard had been around The (Crystal) Ballroom and punk in Melbourne, so we must have crossed paths like all of us did then, but by then I'd left for Sydney and was touring with The Reels so I didn't get to know him, although he shot 'Talking to a Stranger' in and around my brother's place at the beach. Then Richard started doing INXS clips after Michael reached out him. By '82, I was burned out from touring and recording and working in The Reels and still broke and starving, living in squats in Sydney while management had their swimming pools, same old, lots of work, no money. I'd been wanting The Reels to leave for London but they wouldn't. Around this time on tour I had an vision about computer animation, it was only just starting, and so I left The Reels, went back to Melbourne for a bit, then set off for London, the only place in the world then that had a CG course I could do. It was for BBC employees at Middlesex Poly, Fortran language, very early. INXS were in London around this time and that's how I met Richard and Lynn-Maree (Milburn), in London through Michael. We all went to see the Bad Seeds there, Michael admired Nick (Cave). They both met backstage then for the first time. They looked like two big cats circling each other without moving. Nick snarled, Michael lapped it up. Michael, like he always did, persevered and they became fast friends through the years. Like I said, he found us all. I'd finished my course and I was heading to Italy I thought. Richard was going to Cannes for *Strikebound* and INXS were playing in Nice, they were huge in France at that time, and Michael said visit, come and hang out.

In Cannes, Richard and Michael went off on a notorious long night's adventure of parties up somewhere in the hills South of France and Richard had a meeting the morning after with a producer and Michael still there for the hell of it. Richard's original pitch about corruption in the banking sector apparently had the producer's eyes glaze over, and Richard looked at Michael and started another pitch on the fly, 'Oh and Michael's going to be in this idea I'm working on about punk…' and Michael apparently picked up on it and hooked the producer. He'd probably started writing it, but can you imagine, Richard hungover in the hotbed of Cannes, improvising the inception of *Dogs in Space*.

I made it back to London, still making the rent sewing clothes for various clients, Paula Yates one of them. I would go to their house in Chelsea and sometimes wait hours for Paula to turn up for fittings, she was notoriously late. Bob would be on the floor on the phone saying 'This thing is global'. Turned out to be organising Live Aid. He'd get up and stir the stew on the stove for his girls, caring for them. I was relieved when I heard Tiger had gone to live with her sisters and Geldof later because I felt she would have stability and freedom from what I had seen in the house back then. After doing the course at Middlesex Poly, I couldn't find work in London in computer animation. The software and hardware were astronomically expensive so you had to find large companies to work at to get experience. At that time, my focus was to come back to Melbourne and try to start work in CG there. When Richard came back to London and heard I wanted to come back to Melbourne, he offered me work doing costumes on *Dogs*. Mindful I think about Michael's comfort with who was around him on set.

Richard had written *Dogs* based on his experiences of his time in a share house. The characters were composites of friends and events that he and his girlfriend, Lynn-Maree had had. The film budget was low. Clothes we wore back then were from op-shops but at the time of the shoot, only a few years later, the op-shops had been bought out. Classic 40s overcoats, 60s mini skirts, laddered hand-knit jumpers that would be slashed, classic shirts that were painted over and slashed. We would go to the warehouses that baled up clothes for overseas and riffle through it for pieces which would reflect the op-shop buys in the 70s. It was a small team working on the costumes, with me and Lynn-Maree and Jacqui. Richard had photographic reference for the characters. For original costume, I dramatised a little and tried to design with an eye to the character and story arc so it might age a little better for film. I took from the script and there was guidance in reference photos and character through Richard and Lynn-Maree. If there was some fabric I found that would fit a character, I could consult to assess that even if it's not something the character wore at the time, if he/she could've have, they would have. There were some signature pieces that needed to be made again, like the jockey shirt for Sam's character which I took off the photo reference, made new and we then aged with bleach and sandpaper. Some pieces would be interpreted. If fabrics could be found, like at Job Warehouse in the city where there were walls and walls of period fabrics, I would discuss the design and be able to get an opinion if it would be something the character would have worn then, even if it was not a replica. For *Dogs*, it was film, not documentary, so there had to be a bit of creative licence to express character, and have it read better on the screen. Richard had known the characters. For all the humour in the script, the events were tragic and shaped people's lives. It deserved respect and I was hoping to get the spirit.

The producer had found an empty warehouse space on Bridge Road which connected down the alleyway from the Berry Street house where the shoot was taking place and we set up the wardrobe department there so we were right on site every day. Lots of stories from on set. One I can say was day the second AD and I saw this actor. We were looking at him. She and I had heard Stephen Spielberg had bought the rights to Tintin and we looked at each other and went, 'We've got to write we've found him!'. We obsessed. 'Who is this guy? He's perfect'. When he turned up, he had the whole look down for his character, took one look at him said you're good to go. It was Noah Taylor. He had it from the beginning.

Michael getting onto the project was controversial with his cohorts. I don't think his management wanted him to do it, because they had no control, but he wanted it. That was an expression of him, his respect for that cultural community. His willingness to sacrifice time to get involved. His respect for the relationships he forged during that period, like with Ollie which led into Max Q. It took some guts for Michael to stand up to management and say no I'm going to do this. He was in his element on set, he expanded into it. He'd been on set in LA with his mother when he was a kid. He was a great mimic in real life too. Years later I met up with him in LA. He'd had Tiger by then. She was just a baby and he wanted me to meet her. We spent some time with her. I'd been working in the States in visual effects for film then for many years. Michael was looking for a change and I think he was thinking of pursuing acting seriously. He wanted to get a sense of how it was after I'd left the music industry and went into film.

After *Dogs*, I was focused on computer animation. I did some more work on costumes, like for 'Listen Like Thieves' the music video Richard did for INXS. Then I worked in Melbourne and Sydney companies getting experience in CG before leaving for the United States in the early 90s to work in visual effects for film. There is a bridge there in visual effects linking back from *Dogs*. Ollie and Michael bonded during *Dogs* and when they did Max Q, together, I had started to work professionally in computer animation. For Max Q's 'Monday Night By Satellite' directed by Jeff Jaffers, I did the Mandelbrot Set fractals for the backgrounds. I believe it was the first time the Mandelbrot Set had ever been used in a music video. I started to work in the United States doing visual effects at Industrial, Light & Magic. It was a small team then, the digital department, a kind of 'skunkworks' to figure out how to get this (digital imagery) on to film. Scanning, recording, rendering, it all had to be invented, hardware and software, working out how to move it all forward was inspiring, and another story. In a way, the road's never left me. Stagnation was the thing to drive away from, following instinct and going towards something new.

Let's Go and Get in Some Trub

Edward Clayton-Jones

The first band I was in that actually recorded was Piano Piano with Ron Rude who was a bit of a weird guy who was up in Belgrave. My first professional gigs were with Ron when I was 17. It soon became apparent that life on the road with Ron would be hell. I'd made friends with Pierre Sutcliffe and he made an offer I couldn't refuse: 'Do you want to get out of Ron's band?' 'Yes please'.

I am pretty grateful to Ron because he did give me my first break, and Belgrave wasn't very far to go, and despite his idiosyncrasies, I did learn a lot from Ron about recording and just the business in general, though it was a fairly short tenure. But I learnt a lot more from being in the Marquises and subsequent bands, Plays With Marionettes, The Wreckery, Nick Cave and whatever.

Playing with Ron, the first stop was the Champion Hotel, Fitzroy, and that was really the blooding ground for a whole lot of people—obviously

E. Clayton-Jones (✉)
Sydney, NSW, Australia

Lisa (Gerrard), and Sam, x amount of gigs and these guys were playing—though it seems we all managed to keep busy, though there were some godawful gigs in great places and some great gigs in some godawful places, to paraphrase Ian Hunter.

It was 1979 the first time I think that I was there, or 78—it was a great place, you know, because there was a very young group of people, and the guy promoting the place, a guy called Laurie Richards, he was brilliant, you know—on the back of the whole punk thing, he was just letting anything go, Little Bands, all that sort of stuff. Really cool, or not-so-cool experimental outfits, Primitive Calculators and all that sort of crew, Stuart Grant, Ollie, all of that. People from the other side of the river.

I made my move, shortly before joining the Marquises, away from Rowville to St Kilda where the band all lived at the time. My parents were in complete turmoil, so I don't think they even noticed. That's a bit unfair on my parents but it was a pretty ugly time at home and it really lent itself to me buying into punk and the whole nihilist ideal and getting out there and me pursuing my passion which was electric guitar and music in general.

I lived with Chris Walsh, who also played in the Marquises. Those guys were a little bit older than me and I was involved in this local Waverley Youth Group thing to run a night of bands at the local civic hall, with a little group of local kids, despite me not being from Waverley, I still managed to stick in there. We did a show, the Reals played which was Chris' band, and we had the Boys Next Door, it was the first time that I met those guys, and that was really kind of great. I don't even know if they were the Boys Next Door yet, it's going back a long way, but they looked the part. I hadn't quite made the transition to being a punk rocker, I was pretty green, still going to school, so… we ran this night and that's how I first got to meet Chris and Garry Gray and those cats.

My first gigs with Ron I was playing bass, because I was just hungry to do whatever, and then I played keyboards with the Marquises and guitar and sang a couple of songs and before joining the Marionettes where I actually got to play more guitar and I did a bit of keyboard and synth.

So I was in this share house in Clyde St, with Chris with a couple of girls and the band used to rehearse there and it was like a classic *Dogs in Space* type house, if you know what I mean. Everyone was just kind of hanging out doing whatever, and on the weekends we were all drinking like fish and other things as well. I was known as 'the guy behind the bar' because there was a fixed bar in the lounge room, and I broke up with my girlfriend and I had nowhere else to go, so I just thought fuck this I'll sleep behind the bar. So I did. I wasn't really very fussy. It was just a space to crawl into, it was alright.

I was a bit of an apprentice, so you know it was an eye-opener, we're all still good friends today so it speaks volumes about the level of camaraderie, and all the people from that time are all very close and protective of each other and supportive of each other, which I think is pretty cool.

I probably met Sam at the Champion. Sam was really kind of weird. There's a certain affectation to Sam, or there certainly was, always seems to be a bit affected. But Sam was very funny but not very approachable or easy to have conversations with, certainly when he was playing or getting ready to play, doing all that sort of jazz. Sam went out with my girlfriend's sister, Christine Harding, *Dogs in Space* is based on her—so that sort of all happened.

We loved Christine, she was complicated, funny and crass, she was nothing like Saskia's character in DIS, no bad reflection on Saskia, she did what Richard directed her to do. I'm pretty certain Richard never met Christine. We used to go to Sam's house and stuff, and I moved into a house with Christine's sister Anne. We were all old friends and became entwined a bit later on, and so there was Christine and Sam and there was me and Anne, and we were hanging out a bit, and Christine was older and Sam was a bit older, and they were going down a different path in some ways—they had a car and we didn't. I wasn't very close to Sam. In those days, I was close to Mick Lewis, who was the guitarist in The Ears. And we loved each other. We used to go to the Southern Cross on dole cheque day and drink fluffy ducks.

Sadly, Mick and I never played music together. I think we would have been good, because he was a really unique guy, very funny and a great, he really was quite an interesting guitar player, for the time, he was using heaps of effects which other people weren't tending to do so much. I just loved Mick, he was cool. And it was ironic again that I should play him in *Dogs in Space*. I think it was kind of Mick's set up, I know that he said to Richard if you don't get Ed to play me I'm going to sue you.

So, I already knew Richard, I lived with Richard briefly—like, you know, everyone knew everyone. And Richard's girlfriend at the time Lynn-Maree Milburn was one of Anne's old pals and one of our little circle of friends.

So anyway Mick Lewis, and Gus Till, Gus and I are friends still, Gus was a real musician, like he could read music and everything, he was a bit more serious and capable I think in a lot of ways, Gus is pretty impressive, I was playing keyboards—I was a long way short of being able to play anything like Gus, but I wasn't a dedicated keyboard player, in my defence.

I did a couple of years of classical guitar while I was in school and found that wasn't really taking me where I wanted to go. But I was really very dedicated to the instrument, so all I did was play, living where I lived it was easy to do that because there was not much else to do. And it was easy to make a lot of noise and get away with it. And then I met a guy whose name was Robert Davies, a Scottish guy, big guy, who was doing lessons and he was in a band called Palais, this was in the 1970s, and so he'd get write-ups in *Juke*, his nickname was Bomba, they'd say 'oh, Bomba's picture's in *Juke*, he's so cool', but he was a fantastic guitar player, I probably learnt more from him than the rest of them combined, he was the real deal, he was a blues player, that's what I wanted to learn, and that's what he taught me, and a lot of other difficult things that I never really mastered, and he pointed me in the right direction, and he drank a lot of scotch and coke, he probably should have had a better mixer but it was fine at the time. Bomba was a fantastic mentor really and he was really helpful in getting me up the next step.

The biggest change that happened in my playing happened when I joined Plays With Marionettes, that was a real sink or swim thing. I have to give Robin Casinader a lot of credit for my third musical—not 'instruction', but he challenged everyone to do his arrangements, he and Hugo were very prog rock when they were at school, at Melbourne Grammar together. The cotton fields of Melbourne Grammar! So I think the early things like Dum Dum Fix were straight from things like Genesis and Yes and King Crimson and all of those kind of bands who were all about being fancy and quite the antithesis of what I was about. And just as I was changed by the Marionettes so too, they were changed by me. I brought a pop sensibility to the band that they weren't that interested in prior to that. I was actually mixing, doing front of house for them before I joined the band.

I'd heard a lot about them, I went and had a look at them, they were fantastic, but I thought they sounded terrible. And I said look, if you want me—I'd be happy to do front of house for you because I'm sure I could do a better job. This is after the Marquises but they knew who I was, and sometime after that I got a call, can you come down and mix us because our mixer's not shown up. So down I went. So I was in the gang pretty much. Then one day Hugo and Frank and David and Mariella del Conti came to my flat and said 'we want you to join the band' and I was very surprised actually, and thrilled. I knew it was going to be pretty fun, and it was, it was very primitive and really we grew a lot in the brief time I was in the band, we went from cardboard boxes to real drums and we had a Hammond B3 organ, like a real one in a road case. Someone stole it and they left the road case behind… it was unreal. But anyway, time in the Marionettes was time well spent, it was a good time and it's something I reflect on.

Hugo had an affiliation with St Martin's Theatre, as an actor and as a writer, he had a play, *Sweaty Weather*, Hugo was a bit of a renaissance man. He didn't paint, though, thank god. So he was a bit of an actor, a playwright, so… everyone was in *Dogs in Space*, to greater or lesser degrees. Casting him as Pierre was really funny. He's just like nothing like Pierre, nothing.

The Pierre I know wouldn't have any trouble saying clitoris, but maybe he was saying clit-awris. You know, he's from Avondale Heights, who knows what he says. But the Frankie Teardrop on the front of the car thing, that's true. In fact, he did far worse than that. He was standing on the *top* of the car. Tracy Pew was driving it, it was going down outside Hearts, Polaris Inn. For fun! For fun, for fun. It was all about 'trub'. 'Let's go and get in some trub', that was Pierre's thing, trouble.

I was this kid from the outer suburbs, I'd go 'oh no I don't want to go to the police station Pierre,' he'd be 'come on, you fuckin' idiot', off we'd go, get in these shopping trolleys in Acland Street… just amazing. Amazing.

Dogs in Space was kind of offered to me more or less. I did go and read for it but it was a foregone conclusion. Richard's main problem was that he knew I was using a fair bit in those days, and he was worried I wouldn't be able to make it on set so I assured him it would be worth far more to me, and again this was another turning point, because I got out of this relationship I was in which was very negative and *Dogs in Space* enabled me to move away from that which was timely and really cool. I think Richard had me in his sights to do the Mick part and it wasn't any great effort on my part, and I was just uncommonly lucky to be able to be in that production because it was just an awesome experience. It certainly changed my life. And I think at that particular time it… potentially saved my life.

Everyone Was Interchangeable

Jules Taylor

For a band that barely played one-and-a-half times, we're still so famous. People say to me, 'were you around in the blah blah blah days' and I go 'yeah'.

'Oh, did you ever play in a band'
'Yeah.'
'What band did you play in?'
'Ah – I don't really need to tell you.'
'Yeah, yeah go on'
'OK… Thrush and the Cunts.'
'Oh, no way! We love Thrush and the…'
'You don't love it! You don't know it'
'Yeah but we love the *name.*'

I mean really, please no! We didn't have any musical qualities, sorry but we didn't. It embodied the spirit of the time and the little bands.

I grew up in Queensland then went to New Zealand when I was nine, I'd been working in the record industry in New Zealand as my first job, straight out of school. I was into quite free form jazz and abstract heavy metal. When I came to Australia I ended up in Melbourne and somehow I found out about a job going at Climax Records, in Universal Studios. By then punk had happened but I went for the interview in a flowery skirt, I was a little bit of a hippy. When I got the job I went to the op shop and bought a whole set of black clothes! 'Ok, yeah, got this'.

Music had changed in my year of travelling around Australia—it was so exciting, so vibrant and wild, so raw but it still had that freeformness to it that I loved, so that just tapped straight into my love of music. I love that freeform style. From there I met Stuart Grant, and Ollie Olsen, you just had to stand for a day in Climax Records and you met everybody.

It was a punk and reggae record store. I don't even know how Max got involved but he was there when I arrived, and Little Mark used to work there, he had this encyclopaedic knowledge of punk music, he was amazing and knew so much about music. I'm not even sure he was paid! And Max. Max loved reggae music but he also loved punk. When he'd order music, boxes and boxes of records would appear, and the whole shop would be just filled, and when people knew that the shipments were arriving, you'd see these hordes of black-coated op-shop dressed people arriving. You had a lot of early ska bands and people like that wanting to pick up the latest reggae and ska music as well. It was a really exciting time.

At some stage Climax Records had to move, Universal Studios were renovating, so we took a shop in Gertrude Street, and it had sort of rooms out the back, and they became rehearsal rooms, and I became friends with a lot of the little bands. Everyone needed members and I became involved in Ronnie and the Rhythm Boys with Stuart and Denise and Frank (Lovece)—I was one of the vocalists in Ronnie and the Rhythm Boys, and then I was in Thrush and the Cunts, which was an all-girl band with Denise.

What I loved about it was everyone was interchangeable, there was nothing solid about it, that appealed to me. I wasn't a serious musician, but I loved the fact that I was able to create some expression myself. I think that at the core of the little bands, particularly with some of the stronger personalities there was a political philosophical framework that they were speaking out of that didn't appeal to me, but that was fine. I think for me it was much more of a social, experimental, creative expression.

I remember once thinking—I was at a little bands gig and standing around and I remember thinking, in a righteous drunken mood, 'I'm probably the only working class one here'. Knowing my roots—going, 'fuck I'm the only working class one here, in this little band troupe tonight!' Not being proud of it, but noticing it: *here we all are.*

I'm not sure where the serious politics came from, it didn't have such a strong meaning to me. But I did like the idea of everybody being able to have expression, I liked that they had stupid names like Too Fat to Fit Through the Door. Some of that black humour came from the political climate in Europe. I was introduced to a lot of interesting literature and art, and my mind and my eyes were opened quite dramatically during that time. Who wouldn't want that?

Thrush and the Cunts only played a few times. I remember the one time, only because I was so petrified, we played once at the back of Climax Records and I remember being so shy, I had terrible stage fright, that I remember people yelling at me, 'look up! Look up!' I'm just not a natural front person. I wanted to play the drums, really I wanted to be a drummer! I do remember being yelled at, I was in the toilet vomiting, because I was so nervous, someone yelling at me from the stage, 'Jules! Will you get out here!'—once I was actually up on stage I somewhat overcame it. I do remember screaming at people—I remember absolutely strutting my stuff along the stage and yelling at people about sexually transmitted diseases. So I did let loose.

I left Climax with that Little Bands 4-track EP, and went to England, we all decamped from here—Nick and the Boys Next Door had already gone and so Ollie Olsen went, and Stuart and Denise and there was a whole lot of us and we all went to England. Nick Cave and Anita, and some of the band, were staying in a squat in North London.

I was the one who was going to try and sell the little 4-track EP. I got a couple of interviews, an appointment with Rough Trade. I took this little 4-track EP, everyone else was too scared to go to this appointment with me, I remember this guy saying, 'oh no it's too weird for Rough Trade'.

'What? *Too weird!?* I don't know how to take that!'

There were a lot of Australians from the Melbourne punk scene living in England, out of all of them I ended up getting a job. It was with Beggar's Banquet and 4AD because I had the music store experience. That was fantastic, I was really lucky to work with them especially, it was great to work with the Cocteau Twins/Bauhaus early in their career. I raved to Ivo Watts-Russell about the Birthday Party. I dragged him along to their gigs, I said 'you've got to come and see them!' I worked there for nearly two years.

Then I came back to Melbourne and I was unemployed, Climax records had folded, Max was trying to sell all the records at Camberwell Market, I was sitting in Baker's, the coffee shop around from the Universal Theatre that is now Mario's, two weeks back from London, and Peter Cole (Artist) who was on the board at 3RRR was there, he used to come and buy reggae/punk records from Climax. He came up to me and said 'you are just the person we need!' and I went 'what?' and he goes 'I've just been at RRR. What have you been doing?'

'Working in London, working at Beggar's Banquet'
He literally said, 'What are you doing *right now*?'
'I'm having a coffee with a friend!'

'No you're not, you're coming to RRR' and he dragged me to RRR and arranged an interview for the next day, Brenda Kelly, the previous music and volunteers co-ordinator, was leaving and I got the job. No radio experience whatsoever, oh my god, I was petrified! That was extraordinary and amazing, I feel so blessed to have been a part of that.

I was there for two years. Then I worked with the Rich Kids, I worked on film clips for bands—a Dragon film clip at the Corner Hotel, upstairs on the roof. I think I worked on a Beargarden film clip. So I just ended up picking up work. I worked with John Hillcoat and Evan English and Paul Goldman—I worked little bits and pieces within their growing early careers, and I'm not quite sure how I ended up as the runner on *Dogs in Space*, but I was also a little bit involved in pre-production with Glenys Rowe and Lynda House. So just a little bit, but I became friends with them. That was my job, I ended up getting a job as a runner.

The runner is the person who runs between the production office and on set. If the set needs something, you are the person that needs to go out and get it. The production office needs to communicate with the set, call sheets, you're a gopher for everybody, you drive people around who need to be driven around.

Part of my job was to pick Michael up and drive him to set. He was staying in South Melbourne, in a serviced apartment just off Kings Way. It was very low-key. He was very focused, really professional, he was good, I remember once something happened and we didn't come back through the Botanical Gardens way, something to do with the traffic, and we got stuck in a bit of a traffic jam in the city. I didn't know him that well, only in a very casual way. I wasn't anybody of significance. But I remember we were having this conversation and he was a deep thinker. He was an amazing deep person, who had huge spiritual questions. I was really surprised. I said 'I don't know how you balance such a deep, inquiring mind with this other facile world.' I remember him saying, 'you have to have a great sense of humour, you have to take it really lightly'. I'll always remember that conversation, thinking 'it's nice to see another side of him'.

It was a pretty wild film set. There were lots of drugs, I'm pretty sure, there was lots of cocaine—no not *lots* of cocaine, but there *was* cocaine. There was a feeling that it was a bit like a film clip for a band, yet there was a very serious nature to it, but there was that quality to it as well. I don't know how that came about, whether that was Michael's presence, or Richard and Michael, they were thick as thieves.

Michael seemed to be really interested in Ollie, and I think he had a good connection with him. I don't think he was interested in Thrush and the Cunts—I think he was interested in some of the music—I remember being in the recording studio and feeling he had a common language with Ollie and that they spoke a common language musically. Definitely.

When Thrush and the Cunts did 'Diseases' for the film it was a bit subdued. It was not necessarily a song we were terribly familiar with, it didn't really have lyrics, it was very spontaneous, it was a bit odd to then go into a recording studio. I would imagine Ollie and Richard chose that track, they would have thought about all the little bands in those days, and then maybe they chose Thrush and the Cunts more for the name than the music.

I knew something was happening here that would stand the test of time. I remember when I first saw *Dogs in Space* I didn't enjoy it. I thought it was making fun of some serious subject matter, some of that was quite close to my own heart, in my own life, I didn't really enjoy it very much at all. I didn't find it very believable, but even then I knew it captured something. It had gotten something but it was too soon and too close. Now I enjoy it, I just go 'woah' and I can laugh, and I've got beautiful memories, I've got that great distance, and I was involved. I think it was the accumulation of talent that was there as really potent, there was some extraordinary talent working on that film, you could just feel that potency, you knew that something was happening, something was being captured.

I made another record, 'Rock Rock Daddy', when I was still at RRR. Richard Lowenstein made that clip—and Andrew shot it—and Lynn did the make up! Same team from *Dogs in Space*. I don't disown it, when I was trying to be Madonna for a moment.

When I was at RRR I opened up the Hardware Club, then I did the single, that's all that time, then *Dogs in Space* then after that more film clips working with the Rich Kids, and then I opened up my second nightclub which was Razor then went to Sydney to live. I had my breakthrough, whatever you call it, 'I've got to change my life'—I trained as a film producer and never produced another film again! Film school nearly killed me. I started working in counselling… I thought 'oh my god as a film producer all you do is psychotherapy'. I thought I'd rather do it for people who really need help. That's exactly what happened.

We're the Most Fabulous People Australia Has Ever Known

Cornelius Delaney

I started life down on the Mornington Peninsula at Carrum by the beach. We did a stint in Sydney in 1969 and 1970, then came back to Melbourne and lived in East Doncaster—which was then way out in the suburbs. My dad took over a hotel in the city when I was about 12. He'd been a cop, so for him, the next best thing was running a pub where all his mates came and drank. It was on the corner of Russell Street and Latrobe Street, across the road from Russell Street Police station, the City Court and the museum. It was demolished in the 1980s.

I met the taxidermists from the museum, they used to drink in the bar. Once they showed me the skin of a greyhound pickled in a garbage-bin full of formaldehyde, or something. That was one of the few redeeming things about living there though. Living in the city on my own at that age was kind of weird. Because my mates from school lived in the suburbs, I guess that prompted me to become part of that inner-city St Kilda scene. I used to put on my regalia of safety pins and badges on the tram and go to the Seaview Ballroom to see La Femme when I was like 16.

C. Delaney (✉)
Melbourne, VIC, Australia

When I was 17, I started playing bass in Microfilm. It was the first band I was in. Gordon Pitts was the driving force behind Microfilm, it was his project. Marshall Butters was the guitarist and Lisa Gerrard was the singer. We used to play at the Champion in the early months of 1980. I was just a little kid.

Because my old man had been a cop back in the early 1960s, he knew all these old hotels. When he found out I was going to the Champion he was horrified, because he remembered it as the pub that murderers would go to in the 1950s. It was a crims' pub and a filthy, unfriendly place. The punk nights were run by this guy called Terry Rogers, a kind of emaciated Keith Richards type who'd become a punk. He seemed like an old guy back then, but I guess he was only in his early 30s. He was going to be the manager of Microfilm, who probably seemed like a good package—mostly because of Lisa with her Botticelli blonde hair, her old wino's coat and fishnet stockings. It was the beginning of 1980 in summer, so it's daylight-savings and still light at 9 p.m. We'd gather in an upstairs room looking out the window at the fellahs in the park across the road having a meeting with their flagons of 'goon'. It felt kind of dangerous. Someone was always getting stabbed in that street. To keep their licence, the Champion had to serve sliced Strasbourg sausage and pieces of white bread, which was awful, but I wasn't 18 yet and with the dole being only $70 a fortnight, you were grateful for a top-up from the murderers' pub.

I remember driving in the 1959 Morris Minor van out to Ron Rude's recording studio in Belgrave to record a single. It was all very backyard and under-equipped, but it was my first studio recording experience—I thought we were already popstars! At the time, I considered myself a serious artist anarchist who rejected pretty much anything and everything, and screaming about how fucked the system was seemed like a career path. I imagined we would be on *Countdown* in a few weeks. I'd made up the name Nique Needles while I was still at school. Gordon was 22 then, so he was like the grouchy older guy and he says: "You're not putting 'Nique Needles' on our record, ya fuckin' idiot!" My nasty 17-year-old persona wanted to put as much space between me and my family as I possibly could.

I moved into this big old terrace house on Spencer Street in North Melbourne with Gordon and Marshall. It had been a brothel decades earlier and had about 15 rooms with an enormous bedroom upstairs big enough to rehearse in. You lived with ten people, so the rent was only about 8 bucks each. Lisa, our singer, lived round the corner with the singer from The Marching Girls.

The Marching Girls were John Cook, Des Hefner and Ronnie Recent (Brendan Perry) and they'd just arrived from NZ where they'd apparently been huge popstars as The Scavengers. They played regularly at the Champion and I used to talk to them. Lisa sometimes sang with the Little Bands at the Champion too. The Little Bands were the Fitzroy crew, whereas the more punk-rock type of rock and roll bands came from St Kilda. The junk bands—the Little Bands—was kind of revolutionary as a scene, but it was hard to sit through some of the acts. I say 'hard to sit through' because you couldn't dance to it. I think Lisa and Ronnie developed the ideas that began Dead Can Dance out of the Little Bands… and that was the end of Microfilm.

From the same era, there was the Boys Next Door—totally mezmerizing. And The Ears, they were kind of mysterious and strange, and funny. They weren't ever gonna be Skyhooks or Sherbet, but I think they liked the idea of following Nick Cave and the boys over to the UK. They eventually became Beargarden (and did get on Countdown), but that was never as interesting as The Ears had been. Who else? There was Dave Graney's band The Moodists, they were sophisticated and kinda funny. And The Curse of course, we were supremely awesome. We had a backdrop with wildebeests painted on it and used to decorate the stage with pigs' heads we got at the market.

Melbourne was also intensely boring. The nights when you didn't go to the Seaview Ballroom or The Champion you had to find something to do and usually it was with the 15 people you lived with… thinking stuff up. We used to *make stuff.* If we weren't actually doing a film course, we helped the students in the house who were, to build props and shoot scenes. We drew images from obscure films on the walls and went to see stuff like *Alphaville*, *La Grande Bouffe* and Buñuel's *Simon of the Desert…* films that nobody had heard of. We played with state-of-the-art recording technology, like reel-to-reel and 4-track tape recorders! Maybe the actual residents of the *Dogs in Space* house thought it was cool to be stupid, we on the other side of town however, thought it was cooler to be well read and smart. Camus, Satre, Hesse, Dostoyevsky... Bourgeois brats we were!

I think something *Dogs in Space* missed was how politically and intellectually engaged the young Melbourne crew were. We read Camus, we attempted to read Jean-Paul Sartre. Sartre died in 1980, but we were aware of who he was, what he said and that he had died. We thought visual arts was dead and making a painting to hang in a gallery while you're off somewhere else was not confronting enough. For us, being in a punk band was a kind of in-your-face art form. Our attitude towards the clothes we wore, how we cut our hair and the way we all lived on top of each other for years and years—there was thought behind that and of course, a lot of amphetamine-fuelled intense nights talking. I think that's lost in the film, as though it was all just mad, youthful hedonism—it wasn't always.

I started The Curse with my best friend John Rowell at the beginning of 1981. John played synthesizer, Adrian Chynoweth played guitar and Graeme Scott played drums. I played bass and sang at first. My main interest was writing lyrics, but after six months or so I realized I couldn't get it together to actually sing and play bass at the same time. I just wanted to sing anyway, so we got Nick Barker to play the bass. He was a great bass player long before he was famous.

The Curse was a lot heavier and more psychotic than other stuff I'd done. Microfilm had been like a cool, French noir kind of thing—Gordon and Lisa's aesthetic. The Curse started out around the time that *Junkyard* was released, and we were inspired by that thundering bass, scratchy guitar and lunatic singing. The faux American hillbillies and hotrods aesthetic worked well in a Melbourne context. Remember that summer when the clouds of smoke and dust blotted out the sun? The Ash Wednesday bushfires—it was kind of a *Mad Max*, *Razorback* aesthetic. I'm talking about aesthetics because the look of everything and the way it all felt was as important for us as the music.

John and I were almost joined at the hip for a couple of years there. He used to call himself 'Sid Blood'. I remember him being so drunk one New Year's Eve, eating a giant piece of raw meat and swigging bourbon from a bottle out the back of the Ballroom, in the gutter in the laneway. I suppose that's kind of horrific and primitive, but it was also an important aspect of our aesthetic. We'd write stuff inspired by that moment—by our own horrendous behaviour.

We tried to make the music as demented and as creepy as we could. Someone called it 'lollipop voodoo' or 'dancin' on your grave music'— which I liked. We started to get pretty good after a couple of years, we played regularly and had a bit of a following. We supported Psychedelic Furs at the Seaview Ballroom and even Iggy Pop, and we did a RRR live-to-air thing. Now, of course, no trace of us remains. I even lost the cassette recording I had for years in a suitcase.

In 1983, I got fed up with it all and left town. I went to Sydney with Jo Kennedy, my girlfriend at the time. She'd just finished the gig doing *Starstruck* and that was utterly bizarre.

Melbourne back then was dark and sophisticated, moribund, dank and mysterious—French clowns and 1950s sci-fi, poetry and tragic unrequited love. Sydney was skinheads and ska-bands, Doc Martens and fights. Melbourne was Joy Division; Sydney was The Ramones.

Anyway, after *Starstruck*, Jo got a gig in the theatre. She brought the script home to learn her lines and there was this other character in it. I auditioned for that other character—a boy with brain damage—and got the part. It was my first acting job and it radically changed my life. That was *The Kid*, by Michael Gow and it played from May until October 1983 at the Nimrod Theatre, now Belvoir Street Theatre.

After that, for the next few years, I was apparently the most employed actor in the country. So by 1986, I'd been working quite regularly in Sydney. I'd just worked on *Bliss*—based on the Peter Carey story—and I heard Richard Lowenstein was casting this thing. I wanted to play the character Davis, based on The Ears' guitarist Mick Lewis. I didn't want to play the daggy character! Compared to Tim, Davis was a kind of dark, gothic fiend. But there was more laugh value in Tim—though I didn't see it at the time. I think from the bunch of Sydney actors that Richard had to choose from, I stuck out as a possibility because I'd been involved in that Melbourne crew earlier.

In retrospect, *Dogs in Space* was the best film project I did. I'm not very proud of any of the other work I did as an actor. *Dogs in Space* was a hoot to make too. Suddenly getting a few grand a week to play a funny character in a story that I had actually been part of only five years earlier… that was astounding. What else? That science fiction thing I did called *As Time Goes By*, was a cartoony, comic book thing. I was the blond-haired lead character, which was interesting to do, but not really my gig. Apparently, there is no print of the film in existence anymore. It made it to video but I don't think it was digitized. I won 'Best Actor in A Science Fiction Film' for it at the Science-Fiction-Fantasy Film Awards in Rome in 1988. I suppose if I reflect on that period now, as a serious old geezer, I think: Well, I was actually a broken, egomaniac child-man, with emotional issues and a drug and alcohol problem, going from one expensive bout of madness to the next for a few years. From the outset it was doomed to fail, but it was personally cathartic.

Dogs in Space covered a bizarre moment in Australian history, and in the context of *Strikebound*, it also becomes an historical document. It was extraordinary that we were all involved in it, and it was Sam's life and Richard's life and Tim's life, and we were all hanging around at a party in 1980 in February, and then six years later we're getting paid to recreate the same party. When we did a big crowd scene or the scenes we shot at the Ballroom, people like Ollie Olsen were there, Little Band people were there, and there were people from the Ballroom gigs. Suddenly you had a vast mob of this crew, and you could go: 'Oh yeah, we were really at this gig six years ago!' But with that mob of people, it was like: 'Yeah, of course that was going to happen to us... We're the most fabulous people Australia has ever known'. And for us it felt kind of true.

At the beginning, when I was told Michael Hutchence would be involved, I thought: 'Ah fuck, that's a terrible idea. Him? He's just a popstar, he's not even an actor'. But to meet the guy, he was great. He was very sweet, very funny, very self-effacing about what he was doing—which was coming back from a fucking world tour! He was delighted to meet all of us street punks, and we all had a great time with him. I think he had a great time with us too. I remember being with a little group of people out somewhere, raving at him: 'What are you fucking doing being part of this horrible system?', and 'What are these fucking songs you're writing?' and all this shit. His manager comes up and grabs him by the elbow to drag him away from us: 'Michael, we're out of here'.

When he'd come to Sydney he'd look me up. It might have been the following year, they came back from another world tour—so I go and see INXS play. Someone gave me some particularly strong psychotropic substance at the concert, which was illuminating at first, but after the concert I'd kind of had enough. There was lots of sushi and champagne and fabulous rockstar stuff, but I was seeing insects everywhere and starting to sweat like Hunter S. Thompson. I thought I'd better duck out the back. So I go outside and suddenly I'm in this cyclone fence cage type of thing, with thousands of screaming teenage girls crawling all over it like bugs. It was one of the most horrific things I've ever experienced.

I found my way back inside and tried to calm down and drink some orange juice. Later that evening I must have looked like I was having a hectic experience and Michael says: 'Don't worry, I'll give you a ride home'. So we get into the stretched limo and he goes to his place in North Sydney. Then he leaves me alone in this enormous limousine at 2 o'clock in the morning and I'm trying to ring up my friends (A phone in the limo in 1987!) to say: 'Hey! Are you awake? You won't believe what I'm doing... I'm driving across the Harbour Bridge in a stretched limo tripping outta my skull'. But of course, no one was awake. So I went back to my lonely house in Rozelle and sat in the kitchen listening to John Lennon singing 'Across the Universe' on the radio. It was a poignant moment. So yeah, I went out drinking with Michael a few times. That was 1987 or 1988. Then he moved overseas and I didn't see him again. He was a beautiful guy.

I knew Sam Sejavka quite well from going to see The Ears play every week for a couple of years at the Exford and just about everywhere else in Melbourne. Whenever they'd do a microtour of Sydney as Beargarden I'd go and see them, usually at some fuckin' horrible place like the Rooty Hill RSL. In a Rooty Hill RSL context Beargarden were like a 'gay hairdresser band from Melbourne'.

I met Tim McLaughlan the first time The Curse played in 1981. It was with Tim's band, which I think was called Din—a kind of bizarre noise band. When I got the *Dogs* gig, I bought a slab of beer and went around to his place in Northcote to talk to him about it and pick his brain. I can't remember much of what he said because I got so drunk, which was kind of normal for me back then in my Bukowski years. Maybe I exaggerated his little speech impediment a bit.

Being one of only a few Sydney actors on the film, I thought Saskia Post moved into that challenging clique of people quite gracefully and charmingly. I remember her as a beautiful, funny girl who was also a talented and dedicated actor. I'm surprised she didn't become a household name. Again, it's the way Australia often treats talented people, it crushes them or disregards them, doesn't really value what they have, what they do, what they are.

Tony Helou was the other Sydney actor. Tony, who I'm sure went through all the acting-school stuff to get into the business, was very determined to establish himself as a serious actor and not some party punk off the street. I remember having some serious conversations with him about acting. And here's me, just a blow-in! I was able to get work because I was young and beautiful, but really I didn't have much skill or much idea of what I was doing at all—but Tony was very serious. When I heard he was ill recently, I sent him a note and said: 'Don't worry man, doctors don't always get it right'. Sadly, he died not long after. He was a good guy. I didn't see him again after *Dogs in Space*.

In fact, he and John Murphy died within a week of each other. I remember John Murphy from gigs back in 1978. I used to sneak out of my parents' pub and go down to gigs at RMIT Storey Hall and see NEWS. Remember NEWS? He played drums in NEWS, and he was the punkest looking punk I'd ever met. By 1986 though he was kinda fat and fucked up—he was on crutches because he'd fallen over at Richmond Recorders while we were making the film. Yeah, so, we're all dying off. In a couple of years, we'll all be gone.

Hedonism perhaps consumed a lot of us, but the horrific events unfolding *now* kind of retrospectively validate our position that society is fucked, consumer capitalism is fucked, politics is fucked and everything's fucked. We were saying that thirty-five years ago when we were just kids, we actually had a pretty good instinct for what was coming.

It Was Never Pistols at Dawn

Cathy McQuade

I first saw The Ears at Melbourne University. I was doing Law/Arts. When I saw them play, I thought they were the worst band I'd ever heard. But they were so bad, that it kind of tipped over into something really special. Tim McLaughlan had this synthesizer which he'd constructed himself. It was really a random noise generator. It didn't correspond to anything he or the band was playing, and the randomness of it—it sounded like a machine that had cranked itself up. They were the most bizarre act I had ever seen. I was 17 and had only ever played in a high school band doing Status Quo covers up to that point ….so of course I was determined to join them.

I wasn't the orchestrator of anything in The Ears. Sam, the lead singer, had this pretence of being hopeless. He looked like he could barely hold himself upright, and it's actually not true at all. He's really clear what he wants to do. So the line-ups would change, plans would roll out, like 'we're going to do a single'. Because I was at Uni, I wasn't seeing it as my big career, so I just rolled along with it, at least at first.

C. McQuade (✉)
Melbourne, VIC, Australia

One of my favourite memories, perversely, was The Ears playing with La Femme headlining. They were a sharpie band really. In that time when the lines were blurred, it was moving from the mid-1970s into the late 1970s, and punk was not clearly defined. These skinheady bands were neither fish nor fowl. La Femme were basically this westie band full of tough people. They had bleached hair, so their look crossed over into punk territory. The line, actually, if you had to be brutal, was around education. They were a band for the bogans, the guys who'd see the Angels as well, the tough guys. It was one of our only trips out to the suburbs with The Ears. We played first, and the reaction was… muted hostility. It was like entering a strange, scary universe. The audience looked at us like we were aliens and we thought the same looking back at them.

I became really good friends with The Ears' guitarist Mick Lewis. We actually shared a place together—in fact we used to sleep in the same bed, although we were never sexual. It was quite a sweet relationship. It was in Camberwell of all places, in a place which would be unthinkable as a student house now. Cookson St., just opposite Camberwell station. I'm not sure what the period was but those flats were gorgeous. Each of them had a garage and the garage had an upstairs loft, Mick lived in our loft.

Mick used to watch telly all night and smoke White Ox, the most hideous—it's disgusting roll your own tobacco. (there were two, White Ox and Champion Ruby) I would get into bed with him, we'd watch television and I'd fall asleep. He'd keep watching all night, smoking away. I'd deferred Uni to earn money to go overseas, so I'd taken this hideous job in the tax office (working alongside Mark Seymour) but that's another story. I'd wake up, crawl out of bed to go to work in the morning, and Mick would still be awake. Then he would go to sleep after I got up. So we had this ridiculous lifestyle.

When Sam would bring new songs they were always really rudimentary. The thing that always astonished me was how little musical skills were contained within the band. That's probably where a bit of tension happened. I was always thinking 'shit, they know so little'. In the early days, with that kind of music, it didn't matter, but I was getting frustrated.

I was removed from The Ears. Why? That question was never answered for me. If I had to speculate, I think that it was a territorial battle. Although initially I was a passenger, this was not a natural role for me, and I probably stopped being an Indian and started wanting to be a chief. Once I started to settle into the band, I started writing songs. Sam wouldn't let me write lyrics, but he would accept the music for two or three songs; they still do one that I wrote, when they do their gigs. I think that wasn't something that sat comfortably for him. There is also that thing that, although people always pay attention to the guy who's the lead singer—you naturally get attention for being a girl.

There was also a conflict about the lifestyle thing—I never took heroin, so in a way I wasn't part of that inner sanctum. I'd have a few drinks, but I never hit up anything. Sam would float around, just live that life. I was always more ambitious in a way. Later, when Gus was in the band, and Berry St had disbanded, I'd turn up for rehearsals on time. They'd just turn up three hours later. They'd drift in, sit down and want to drink coffee, beer and Big Ms and smoke cigarettes and just hang out, and I'd be like, 'aren't we here to make music?' To me, it seemed like they weren't very serious about their music, but I guess we just had different rhythms and how we wanted to go about it.

When Gus came, along adding the synth, the sound transitioned from punk to new romantic, new wave. The bass parts were still those melodic riffs running up and down the fretboard—they hadn't moved into the white boy funk sound yet—so it was still more of a new wave sound. So yeah, it was a gradual transition. I was surprised when the new songs came up; how *candy* they sounded to my ears, very poppy. I didn't have any sense of what the overall vision of the band was.

With 'Scarecrow', the mood was moving towards Beargarden's sound—that's what was happening. Carl was besties with Ross Farnell; they were huge fans of the band Japan. I think that probably contributed to 'hey we can do this thing, and we'll have Gus, and we'll have Ross and it'll be this lovely white boy funk thing, and it'll create a nice vehicle'.

INXS were a great example of a band who understood the roles everyone played. They really—until Michael met with personal misadventure, definitely understood that the structure worked as a whole, and that kind of discipline worked so well.

Any slight that I'd felt from being thrown out of The Ears disappeared when I was asked to join Deckchairs Overboard. They had a record contract with Regular Records, which felt like the big time and it meant leaving the Melbourne scene for Sydney.

The whole auditioning process for Deckchairs was pretty weird. I wasn't even told I was being auditioned. John Clifforth and Ken Campbell were best friends. But it was like *1900*, the Bertolucci movie, best friends but worst enemies, tied together through life, the polar opposite journeys. The first rehearsal I went to wasn't really a rehearsal: 'come and have a jam, a jam, yeah?' but they were checking me out for the job. Paul Hester and I started jamming and clicked straight away. Then it started building into an idea. Our songs were built up from the feels. I'm pretty sure that is how 'That's the Way' happened. Very different from The Ears. It went well for a while, but later on in the afternoon two of them started getting into a fight…. a serious fight. They were strangling each other, and the other guy hurried me out, he took me out of the room because he was worried I might not want to join the band. I mean, god, common sense should have told me, *don't* join them. There was so much anger in that band. But I still did.

Berry Street was where Sam was living, and that's where we were rehearsing. Richard lived there too, and so did Peter Walsh and Aldo Pace, who became 'Luchio'. Richard was all part of the same world. Richard was never a participant; in a sense he was already the film-maker, almost the anthropologist observing. It was a contained two-storey house, but so many people were moving in and out. Perfect for a film-maker.

It didn't surprise me Richard went on to make *Dogs in Space* and I heard rumours that the project was going on. I was never asked if I wanted to be a part of it, but even I was living in Sydney I never understood why they got some angular stranger to play me? Everybody else was in there. I can only hypothesise. I was in New York, recording an album with John Morales, so maybe I seemed out of reach—though Michael Hutchence did it! I don't know, I don't understand why people make some decisions.

I like the sense of movement in *Dogs in Space*, it's Altmanesque, and I like that the camera's not landing on anybody, it's just taking in the textures. I think it does have that sense of one of those shared households with people coming and going and moving through the environment.

Some of the re-creations of the band world, when you see them on stage, the roughness of it and people bumping into each other, I thought that were pretty good.

My main issue is more about the internal world of the band. Richard never really got the humour. I think he went for a clichéd idea of the self-immolating nihilistic ill-fated on-a-train-on-the-way-to-hell musician. Actually that was not how it seemed to me. It was much more like *Withnail and I*. They were middle-class boys, they were extremely educated, and you don't get that from the film. They were really literate and really smart with it. The things that they'd do—they were almost like exercises in absurdity. Why do you do this? Because it's the most stupid thing you could do.

Sam had a girlfriend for a while called Erika—he wrote the song 'Brick Woman' about her. The reason was because a brick was the thing she was least like. It was all about turning stuff on its head—Mick and Sam also had a game named after a friend of theirs called Purbrick, Simon Purbrick, because the word 'brick' was in it. It involved hurling yourself at a brick wall because that was the stupidest thing you could do. So therefore we'll make a game out of that. It was almost a worship of stupidity. The thing where they went and got a sheep—that was just one of those random things, 'I'm bored, what shall we do?' 'I don't know, let's go to the country and get a sheep'.

So I guess I was disappointed; Richard could have dug deeper, though maybe that's not what he saw. I saw it. And because a lot of the humour, and the sense of perversity was held by Mick Lewis, I was really aware of it, having had such a close friendship with him. The flavour of the band, what the band was about, was really heightened by that stuff. Richard didn't show any of that. They all looked a bit po-faced and serious. That's my main criticism of the film.

Michael nailed Sam's body mannerisms in the film; it was an amazing performance. But any of us who know Sam know that it's a mask, underneath there's a guy who's scheming and manoeuvring. It sort of undersells him in a way. Everyone's going to have a different take on what any situation, any scene was. You talk to a bunch of different people they'll all have different takes on it, maybe all a little disappointed that the way they saw it is not the way that it was portrayed. Clearly, that was how Richard saw the scene.

If you think what we'd come through musically, a period of heightened emotion, the seventies, bombastic music like *Journey to the Centre of the Earth*…and scorching guitar solos, our world, and the stripped back music we were making was a kind of reaction against that. In a way, the film is consistent with that ethos. It's just that later on, looking back, I'd like to feel who these people are, instead of just looking at them as a kind of wallpaper. But I guess it's accurate in a way, the sentiment of the time; that's what was going on. People were avoiding being real.

I went to the *Dogs in Space* wrap party. I was down in Melbourne, I don't know if I was playing gigs or just visiting my family, but somehow I got word that the wrap party for the film was going on, so I went. So many people asked me why I wasn't in the movie—I didn't have an answer. But there were no bad feelings. And just as I was leaving, at the end of the night, someone called my name out. Adam Briscomb, a boy I had grown up with, one of my dearest friends, who I had lost touch with, had acted in *Dogs in Space*, we reconnected that night. So it ended up being really special. That's the whole thing—all of this stuff went on under the surface. It was always civilized; it was never pistols at dawn.

Bowie Queues

Bruce Butler

The following pages feature photographs taken by Bruce Butler during the two 'Bowie Queues' (one for tickets and another for the event itself) as well as the actual show, in 1978.

A 'Bowie Queue' was recreated for the opening scene of *Dogs in Space*. Butler, who would go on to play key roles in Australian music—including operating the Australian arm of Virgin Records, which was to sign the post-Ears group Beargarden—met and befriended members of The Ears at this event. Sam Sejavka discusses some aspects of this period in his chapter in this book.

These images show:

B. Butler (✉)
RMIT University, Melbourne, VIC, Australia

© The Author(s) 2020
D. Nichols and S. Perillo (eds.), *Urban Australia and Post-Punk*,
https://doi.org/10.1007/978-981-32-9702-9_11

1. The MCG sign advertising the show.

2. Bruce Butler

3 and 4. Two scenes in the ticket queue.

5. Group shot on site, including Butler, Mick Lewis (later to be guitarist for The Ears) and 'Little Mark' Ryan.

6. Erica Waters—who Sam Sejavka was to write about in the song 'Brick Woman'—Bruce Butler, Mark Gason and Paul Storm.

7. Group shot from the queue

8. The frame of the main tent with rubbish bins which were used for fires.

9. Tim McLaughlan (later to be synthesizer player for The Ears)

10. Lewis

11. Lewis, McLaughlan and Sejavka

12. Sejavka and Lewis

13 and 14. Sejavka

15 and 16. The front row of the show, 18 November 1978.

Excerpt from Comic Book

Jerome Gaynor

The following pages are part of an unfinished comic book by St. Louis artist Jerome Gaynor, who describes it as 'pretentious early-20's gibberish' and says: 'I never published it at all, no one's really seen it… the pages… comprise the least silly part of a REALLY, very pretentious and self-consciously obscene (because I was so punk) anarchist/Marxist rant that I did back then'.

J. Gaynor (✉)
St. Louis, MO, USA
e-mail: jerome@oldstlouis.com

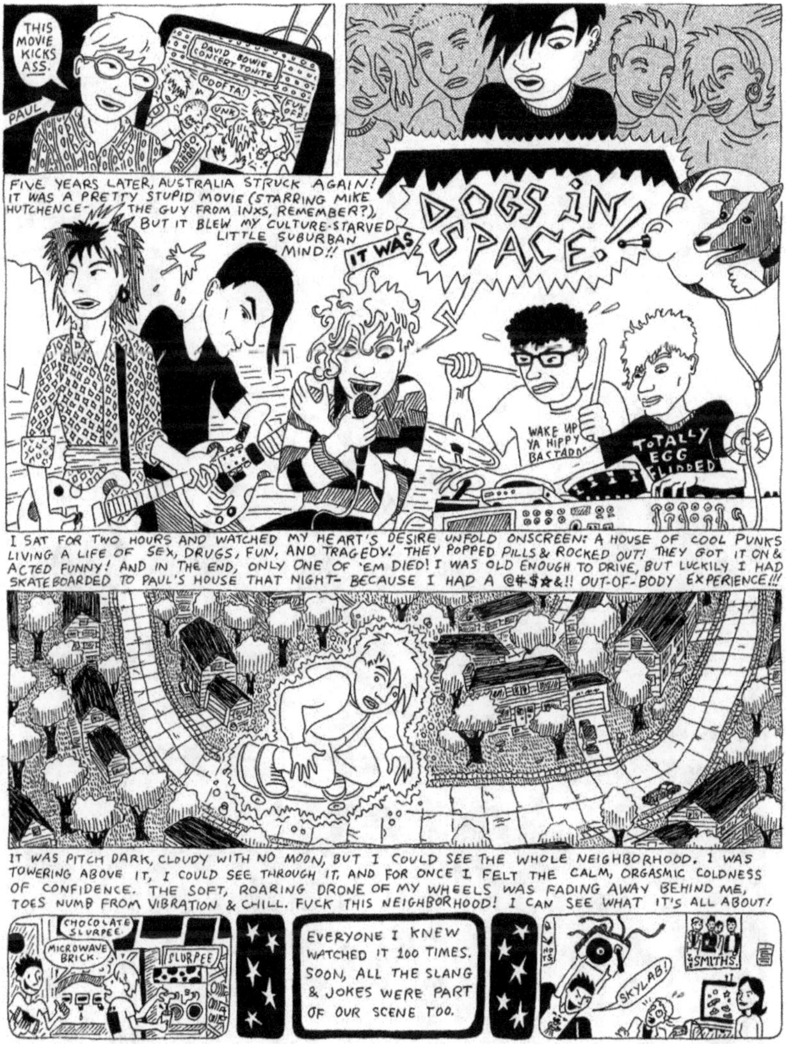

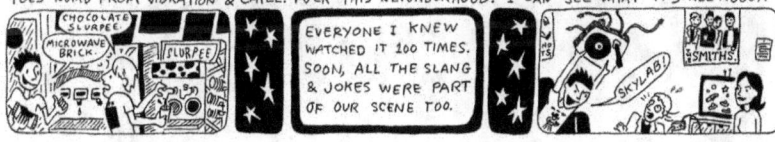

J. Gaynor

BUT NO ONE TOOK IT AS MUCH TO HEART AS ME. I DREW PSYCHIC, ELECTROMAGNETIC CONNECTIONS, AND FELT DIRECT COMMUNICATION OCCURING - THROUGH THE EARTH'S CORE - BETWEEN MELBOURNE, AUSTRALIA AND MELVILLE, MISSOURI. I KNEW EVERYONE IN THE MOVIE... EVEN THE RECURRENT EXTRAS IN THE BACKGROUND HAD PERSONALITIES, HISTORIES. THEY WERE MY BEST FRIENDS.

EVENTUALLY, EVEN MY FEELINGS STARTED BLENDING WITH THE FEELINGS EXPRESSED BY THE CHARACTERS IN THE MOVIE. LIKE, IF I WAS MAD, I'D FEEL LIKE SOME GIRL FROM THE MOVIE WHEN SHE'S MAD. MY SLANG & FACIAL EXPRESSIONS WERE ALL IMPORTED.

-IT SOUNDS PATHETIC-

I KNOW, I KNOW...

BUT I DON'T CARE.

I MEAN, SHIT...

WHAT DID YOU SPEND YOUR HIGH SCHOOL YEARS DOING?!

ONE DAY, WHILE PAINTING THE FENDER OF MY SCOOTER, I SAID TO MYSELF:

THE FUNNY THING IS, THE SAME TIME I WAS DREAMING OF AUSTRALIA, THERE WERE PROBABLY A MILLION AUSTRALIAN KIDS WATCHING "90210" AND DREAMING OF LIVING IN AMERICA!

THE MODERN WORLD IS JUST SO UNCOMFORTABLE FOR EVERYONE... WE'RE ALL CHASING SOME SORT OF FANTASY.

SPORTS, SOAP OPERAS, COMIC STRIPS, SIT-COMS, MOVIES - WE FILL OUR MINDS WITH SIMPLE STORIES SO WE WON'T HAVE TO THINK ABOUT OUR HOPELESS REAL STORIES. GLOBAL WARMING, WORLD WAR, ECONOMIC RECESSION: HOW CAN WE FACE THEM?!

WHEN YOU LOSE THE ABILITY TO BE DISTRACTED BY FANTASY MEDIA, IT CAN BE PRETTY HARD TO LIVE DAY-TO-DAY WITHOUT SINKING INTO ANXIETY and DEPRESSION.

EVEN MICHAEL HUTCHENCE, THE STAR OF MY BELOVED "DOGS IN SPACE" - A WORLD-FAMOUS ROCKSTAR- KILLED HIMSELF JUST LAST WEEK!!

Rock Star in Space

Zora Simic

The hackneyed lyrics from INXS's 1984 hit 'Dancing on the Jetty' about the world arguing with itself once struck me as so profound as to warrant epigraph status in my 1986 diary. In that momentous year, I turned thirteen and as a measure of my new-found maturity, switched my pop allegiances from the Uncanny X-Men to INXS. It seems laughable now that the cartoonish X-Men with their comically posturing front-man Brian Mannix and throwaway lyrics ('Everybody wants to work - nah nah not me!') were genuine rivals to INXS—a proper grown-up band with songs about war and film clips shot by a bona fide film director. But they were at the 1985 *Countdown* Rock Awards. During that soon-to-be-infamous ceremony, held in April 1986 at the Melbourne Sports and Entertainment Centre, INXS and X-Men fans hurled abuse at each other and some even 'scuffled'. At home, I watched transfixed, in my usual *Countdown* viewing pose—sprawled on my belly on the carpet, hands under my chin. The

---

Z. Simic (✉)
University of New South Wales, Sydney, NSW, Australia
e-mail: z.simic@unsw.edu.au

X-Men fans and the X-Men themselves seemed to be enjoying it all rather too much, it was embarrassing and I didn't like it. The INXS fans were just as loud, but the band themselves were cool. They had credibility. The X-Men would never get bigger than this, but INXS—they were already massive and were just going to become more so. Plus, their music sounded *mature*. I switched bands.

At first, my defection involved little more than re-arranging the posters on my bedroom wall, begging my mum to buy me *The Swing* on vinyl and scrawling 'INXS RULES' in texta on my duffel bag. By the time I was fifteen, however, being an INXS fan was who I was. My best friend Leanne and I camped overnight in the Liverpool Westfields car park to get tickets for their *Kick* tour, chased various INXS members around Sydney and got part-time jobs to pay for the merchandise. We met other obsessives who sometimes shared their secret information, but we also kept a wary distance because those girls took fandom to the next level and it pained me to think about how some of them were old enough and cashed up enough to follow the band around the country. Some of them also seemed rather more sexually experienced than me (which was not hard). I dimly recall a mother and daughter fan duo who showed us photos of themselves wedged between Kirk Pengilly and Tim Farris on a backstage couch. They were holding stuffed devils with fresh autographs on them, and they were both wearing very low-cut tops. Then there was the intense young woman who presented drummer Jon Farriss with an entire toilet roll with the words 'I love Jon' written over and over. He was my favourite too, or equal favourite with Michael, and I cursed myself for not having thought of such a distinctive show of devotion. Instead, I wrote fan fiction that I kept to myself. A recurring scenario was a grown-up cosmopolitan me having to decide whether to marry Jon or Michael. These dilemmas were usually enacted either in Hong Kong, where I know the two of them sometimes lived, or in Prague, where the band filmed all the *Kick* music videos. These sophisticated cities were far from my western Sydney fibro home, but I was convinced a peripatetic, love-triangle existence was right up ahead. I just had to get my year ten certificate first.

Meanwhile, the *Countdown* Awards that marked my coming-of-age soon disappeared from Australian pop culture. Eager to distance themselves from screaming teenage girls possessed by footy-style tribalism, the Australian Recording Industry Association (ARIA) cut their ties with *Countdown* and launched their own awards ceremony the following year. The often shambolic but always entertaining *Countdown* Awards were held and screened just one more time, right after the last episode of *Countdown* went to air in July 1987. Word has it Michael Hutchence met his future girlfriend Kylie Minogue, then a soap star and not yet more famous than her sister Danielle (later Dannii) that very night. When Michael and Kylie's love affair hit the news in 1989 I had already started to move on from INXS—to The Smiths (who had already broken up) and buying *NME*, four months late—but this sensational coupling was unacceptable to me. I was done.

Or rather, I was finished with INXS, but not with Michael Hutchence. Right up to his tragic death, he intrigued me in the way people you once worshipped sometimes do when you begin to see them as human. And for all of his sexy swagger and genuine celebrity, there was something endearingly sincere or even a bit sad about Michael Hutchence. He is now remembered as Australia's first proper rock star—as well as possibly its last, to draw on the title of a 2017 television documentary about Hutchence—but for me he was the first mainstream idol I encountered who also wanted to be 'alternative', or what we once called 'indie'. In doing so, he was my gateway to more interesting things. One of those was *Dogs in Space*, a film I now genuinely enjoy, but pretended to, back when I was a teenager. Indeed, for a time, I even lied about having seen it when I hadn't because the movie was slapped with an R-rating and only had a limited cinema release. I dimly recall scouring the Saturday paper for session times and despairing because it was only showing at the Valhalla in Glebe, an inner-city Sydney suburb that may as well have been Paris from my outer suburban vantage point.

This chapter is a tribute of sorts to a rock star who tried to transcend his anointed role, but never quite escaped it. I approach *Dogs in Space* from the perspective of the once-besotted teenage fan who did not quite get it, in the context of his wider career, and as the paradigmatic example of Hutchence going 'experimental'. I consider his friendship with director Richard Lowenstein, whose own tribute to his close friend, the documentary *Mystify: Michael Hutchence* (2019) presents a vivid portrait of a sensitive artist tragically undone by a brain injury, the ugly side of fame, and in distant third, 'has-been' status. Their friendship is a crucial part of the *Dogs in Space* story. Lowenstein was in the unique position of aiding both INXS's success through his music video direction, and Hutchence's forays into more alternative scenes, beginning with the film. Yet Hutchence, as Lowenstein recognised in his consistent championing of the singer's role and performance in the film, was not simply invited to bring his celebrity to *Dogs in Space*—he contributed substantially to its genesis and its distinctive energy. As a former obsessive fan, it's been especially fascinating, for instance, to consider how the women involved with the film, including his lead co-star Saskia Post, reacted to the presence of an international rock star on their set.

Firstly though: Michael Hutchence, the rock star celebrity, and his place in Australian music history and popular culture more broadly. This may seem an unnecessary task for readers of a certain age, but given Hutchence has been dead since 1997, and that his old band went on without him in tepid tribute, a refresher and reappraisal is in order. One early review of *Mystify* exalts Hutchence as a 'genuine rock god' who belongs in 'the same company as Mick Jagger, Jim Morrison, and Robert Plant'[1]—three other rock gods, I would add, who also tried to expand the possibilities of that category, to varying degrees of success. This review was also hardly the first time Hutchence had been likened to Morrison and Jagger in particular. So unprecedented was he on the Australian rock scene, there was no one local to compare him to. His own bandmates reached for the same tired comparisons in their 2005 'official autobiography', albeit with additional flourishes:

> Michael was the last rock star of our times: he was as slinky as Mick Jagger, as commanding as Jim Morrison, and as fractured as Kurt Cobain. Michael truly was a postmodern rock icon, his lyrics were Romantic poetry and Utopian idealism delivered by a Shamanistic Valentino.[2]

For the film reviewer in *The New Yorker*, however, it was some of these same qualities which made Hutchence, or at least his character, such a turn-off: 'his role seems to have been conceived as a combination of Jim Morrison and Renoir's vagrant Boudu, and he's awful'.[3] Later, in the wake of *Dogs in Space*, Richard Lowenstein was offered the job of directing the Jim Morrison biopic with Michael Hutchence in the lead role. Both declined, though interestingly Hutchence's next film role was as Romantic poet Percy Shelley in the 1990 sci-fi flop *Frankenstein Unbound*. He was only in one scene, and the movie was deservedly panned.

So, What Were You Doing in 1979?

On the set of *Dogs in Space*, Sam Sejavka asked Hutchence, who played Sejavka in the lead role, this question. In the exchange, captured by Lowenstein and later featured in the documentary *We're All Livin' on Dog Food* (2009), Hutchence answers rather awkwardly: 'I was 19 and had just joined up with INXS in a serious way. Just before that, this was my surrounds, more or less'.[4] The last sentence does not sound especially convincing. Perhaps because Hutchence knows that in 1979 Sejavka *was* doing 'this'—being part of the inner-Melbourne punk scene—while he wasn't, not really. He was in INXS, a band which by 1986, the year *Dogs in Space* was filmed, was such a successful and professional unit that Hutchence had to fight with band management to get eight weeks off to make the movie.

Dogs in Space captures the 'little bands' scene which briefly bloomed in inner-city Melbourne in the late 1970s—so-called because bands would form, play a few gigs, sometimes consisting of just a few songs, then disappear or reconfigure. INXS (or the Farriss Brothers as they were first known) formed in the northern suburbs of Sydney around the same time the film is set, but they were from another universe, the pub rock circuit where bands toured the country non-stop for years on end, sometimes playing several gigs in one night. This period of rock history, spanning the 1970s and 1980s and spawning 'Oz Rock', has been nostalgically mythologised as the golden age of Australian live music, including (not surprisingly) by its participants. According to INXS's Kirk Pengilly, for instance, 'the Australian pub scene in the first half of the eighties was a unique culture that will never be equalled – it was a phenomenal, organic meeting of talent, timing and community.' He goes on:

There were no regulations, so the music went loud and late every night in smoky, sweaty, beer-soaked rooms that got so packed and hot, the condensation dripped from the ceiling like rain. ...Naturally, those conditions bred many a fight, even though there was very little room to move, let alone throw a punch. It was rough and tough and crazy and fun.[5]

Oz Rock was a homosocial world, where the wives and girlfriends mostly stayed home, and the Oz Rockers confronted 'real' Australia and 'real' Australians in country pubs and suburban beer barns. Even when lamenting the grind of the road, the tough-nut audiences and the brutal venues, the men of Oz Rock (and most Oz Rockers *were* men, give or take a Chrissy Amphlett or a female backing singer) presented a fresh iteration of the masculinist Australian Legend in their reminiscences. For Jimmy Barnes, lead singer of the quintessential Oz Rock band, Cold Chisel, life on the road was 'as far from reality as you can get',[6] but also, for him, life-saving and redemptive—even if his band, once the biggest in the country, barely made any proper money at all, and his alcoholism raged out of control.

In Australia, unlike England, the punk scene was a mostly middle-class phenomenon (which *Dogs in Space* captures well), but most of the Oz Rock audience was working class with a sense of 'personal alienation' that was an 'expression of the oppression embodied in that class position'.[7] INXS all came from comfortable middle-class backgrounds—or in the case of Hutchence, a transnational and exotic one (as a teenager, he lived in Hong Kong and Los Angeles)—but it was to these audiences that they first played.

During their ascent, INXS were a support act for Cold Chisel on a New Zealand tour; an experience remembered fondly by both bands as debaucherous fun (Barnes introduced them to cocaine, and an irate father stormed the hotel looking for his teenage daughter, who was having sex with Hutchence in the bathroom at the time).[8] Still, despite a mutual commitment to hedonism and a shared ability to hold an audience, honed 'from playing beer barns every night', INXS were clearly for Barnes (as well as teen fans like myself) a very different kind of band: more pop, than rock, with a lead singer quite unlike other Oz Rock front-man. Barnes recalls:

Michael had this whole animal presence on stage. And you know, the guys in the audience either loved it or the band, or they wanted to fucking kill him and hated them because of it.[9]

From early on then, INXS stood apart from the Oz rock bands they shared line-ups and good times with. As a musical genre, Oz Rock has what Jon Stratton has described as the 'Australian sound', defined by whiteness (of influence, as well as constituency) and steeped in the Australian big ballad tradition.[10] INXS, however, were 'one of the first white bands to sound so much like a black funk band but without losing their edgy white rock roots'.[11] Nile Rodgers, the black music producer who in the 1980s was arguably the most influential in pop music, produced their 1983 hit single 'Original Sin'. But even before then, their music was distinctly more rhythmic than power-chord driven Oz Rock; as their former promoter Harry Della recalls 'INXS was the first band to create a dancing scene at their gigs - and that was new'.[12] By the band's own estimation (and that of some programmers at US college radio stations) their peers were edgy new wave pioneers like Talking Heads, Blondie and Elvis Costello. As such, unlike Cold Chisel, INXS did not 'sound' Australian[13]; indeed, their manager Chris Murphy surmised that not many US journalists realised INXS were Australian until their third or fourth tour.[14] Eventually, being Australian became part of INXS's international appeal, or rather, INXS's increasing fame in the USA and elsewhere helped make Australian popular culture internationally appealing in the 1980s.

What also set INXS apart, of course, was Michael Hutchence. From their earliest gigs, he transformed from the soft-spoken, sensitive and short-sighted thin young man with a skin problem he was off-stage, to what his sister Tina described as a 'stage character', with 'full on, in your face presence'.[15] He prowled the stage, teased the crowd, seductively tossed his brown curls and projected a raw carnality that attracted the women to the front. To be sure, the rest of INXS also radiated 'an earthy, unmistakable heterosexuality',[16] which bassist Gary Garry Beers later surmised was part of their appeal, particularly in the USA where the band offered an alluring Antipodean antidote to the Sensitive New Age Guy model of masculinity then in vogue.[17] In Australia, meanwhile, their overt sex appeal was a novelty in itself, first on the pub scene and then in music videos, a format

Australian bands and performers were comparatively slow to take advantage of. Oz Rock was profoundly masculine, including its audience, but INXS, and especially Hutchence, exuded a more sexually confident form of modern masculinity which attracted and welcomed a female audience.

Various scholars have given Hutchence, and to a lesser extent INXS, credit as Australia's first properly sexy rock stars. Historian Frank Bongiorno observes in his history *The Eighties: The Decade That Transformed Australia* that Hutchence, as a 'somewhat androgynous figure' who was noted for his 'legendary sexual confidence', as well as his shyness, 'was far removed from ocker masculinity'.[18] For Greg Young, the major reason Hutchence has been referred to as Australia's first and only international rock star is because he unapologetically and brazenly brought sex and sexuality to the stage and screen. Historically, Young argues, normative, hegemonic Australian masculinity has assumed homosexuality as a given for male performers, with one consequence being that men in pop and rock bands defaulted to caricatured male (Skyhooks), sex-less or anti-pop (Cold Chisel).[19] While it's certainly possible to quibble with some of the finer points of Young's thesis (where does AC/DC's Bon Scott fit?), his commentary on INXS (and especially Hutchence) stands up. They were not afraid to sex-up, and even queer, their look and sound. As Young notes, if at first, INXS chose to market themselves with the 'well-worked mythology of the hard-working Australian pub band compromising a team of talented affable larrikin mates rather than talented sexually available / desirable young men',[20] their global success emerged from taking the latter approach, or at least having it both ways. Live performance remained integral to the band's success, including as a measure of their increasing local and global fame. In 1985, INXS were the only Australian band to be part of the international Live Aid telecast and in the same year they headlined the Rocking the Royals gig, where they performed in front of Prince Charles and Princess Diana in Melbourne. But INXS were also one of the first major Australian bands to take music videos (or film clips, as we called them then) seriously. They approached Richard Lowenstein to direct the video for their single 'Burn for You' from their 1984 album *The Swing* after admiring his work on the Hunters and Collectors' video

'Talking to a Stranger'. It would be the first of sixteen film clips Lowenstein would direct for the band and he became so strongly associated with INXS that they affectionately referred to him as a seventh member.

INXS's film clip artistry, and Hutchence's on-screen desirability, peaked with the suite of videos Lowenstein shot for the band for the *Kick* album, but was already on display in a pre-Lowenstein-era clip, 'The One Thing' from their breakthrough album *Shabooh Shoobah* (1983). In the soft-focus clip, INXS sit gorging on fruit and other delights at a banquet table, in the company of beautiful women, including Karen Pini from the TV soap opera *The Young Doctors* and model Michele Bennett, soon-to-be Hutchence's long-term girlfriend and later, the last person to speak to him while he was still alive. In the thick of it, but also somewhat separate, Hutchence sings directly, and sultrily, to the camera. Once my INXS obsession set in, it was this clip I recorded off the television and watched over and again (Jon Farriss also looked rather breath-taking). And it was also the clip that first caught the attention of Ollie Olsen, music director of *Dogs in Space* and later Hutchence's music collaborator in Max Q, when it came on one Saturday morning on *Sounds* in 1982: 'I thought, *ooh-err*. They look like an international band. That singer looks like an international pop star. This was before they were'.[21]

By the mid-1980s, INXS were a *zeitgeist* band in Australia and the USA, though not in England where they were somewhat mocked by the music press and compared unfavourably to more critically respected Aussie exports like The Birthday Party, then later Nick Cave and the Bad Seeds, and The Go-Betweens. In Australia, the height of their fame came arguably in the years 1984–1988, spanning the albums *The Swing*, *Listen Like Thieves* and *Kick*—and the film *Dogs in Space*, which Richard Lowenstein hoped would be a box-office smash on the back of all of those teenage fans. As we shall see, the R-rating smacked on the film by the censorship board ensured this was not to be. As it happened, *Dogs in Space* was released to limited screens the same summer INXS were touring the country on the 'Australian Made' Tour, with Lowenstein in tow as documentarian. 'Australian Made' was an ambitious series of massive open air-shows, with a line-up which also included Mental as Anything, the Triffids, the Saints, the Divinyls and the Models. Most of these accompanying bands were not Oz Rock in the narrower musical sense, and the inclusion of the arty Triffids and the Saints—Australia's, if not the world's, first punk band—was at the alleged behest of Hutchence. Assorted band managers, and especially INXS's Chris Murphy, were keen to capitalise on cultural nationalism locally, and the 'Australia' brand internationally, but the plan to rival the scale of the recent tour by Dire Straits was not to be. Depending on who you read, the tour was either a noble failure, a mixed success or a misfired feat of hubris on the part of INXS and Murphy. It marked the first signs of local backlash against INXS, but it would still be a few years—after *Dogs in Space*, after *Kick* and after Kylie—before the carefully cultivated INXS 'brand' properly lost its shine.

Dogs in Space: A Mid-Eighties Fantasy

Michael Hutchence (born 1960) was twenty-six when he made *Dogs in Space*, and Richard Lowenstein (born 1959) was around the same age—an ideal age for a rock star on the rise, but rather precocious for a film director. Indeed, Lowenstein was described as Australia's youngest feature film director when his debut feature-length film *Strikebound* was released in 1983.[22] He was about to travel to the Cannes Film Festival with the film when he got a call from INXS's management beckoning him and his collaborators Troy Davies and Lynn-Maree Milburn to northern Queensland to make 'Burn for You'. Not long after the singer's death, Lowenstein would recall this first encounter as at once a culture clash and a life-changing moment:

> I first met Michael reclining on a banana lounge in a cheap motel in MacKay, Queensland… the three of us Troy, Lynn and myself, had been persuaded to leave our black-clad, rain-soaked Melbourne to make a video in the absurdly sunny and tropical clime of North Queensland… when they finally dragged us out of the dark confines of our motel room, we walked our black clad gothic bodies over to the pool to see five bronzed males wearing Raybans, Hawaiian shirts and board shorts… One of these (the most effusive) was Michael with his eager puppy-dog gleam and a smile to die for.[23]

The director and singer started talking about the song and video and according to Lowenstein 'I found out right away that he and I did see things alike. And that was it - I was sold. It was the start of a long friendship that changed my life'.[24]

In the official INXS autobiography, the 'Burn for You' clip is nostalgically described as 'a priceless portrait of INXS in their youth, in their prime and on the verge of becoming the biggest band in the world'. Lowenstein, then a stranger, 'had just met them and had no idea what he was walking into, but he got what they were on about and captured them openly and honestly'.[25] The director was swiftly initiated into INXS's world and Hutchence into his. Somehow Hutchence ended up in Cannes too, where Lowenstein apparently pitched *Dogs in Space* to an Australian film producer over breakfast with Hutchence at the table, 'more or less asleep in his croissant' after an all-nighter. Hutchence, improvised Lowenstein, would star in the film. Writing, funding and INXS management approval all came later.[26]

The anecdote of *Dogs in Space* taking shape while Lowenstein and Hutchence were on a bender in the South of France obscures the director's already existing interest in documenting the Melbourne punk and share house scene he was part of in the late 1970s, as well as the contributions of other key people associated with the creation of *Dogs in Space*. But it's nevertheless a wonderfully illustrative story about their friendship and creative partnership, as well as the film itself. They had a lot of fun together, but also took each other's creativity and ambitions seriously. INXS presented themselves as a band of brothers, and of course three of them were actual siblings, but Hutchence and Lowenstein seemed like the true kindred spirits. Each man has been described as naturally shy and they even looked alike, though some press coverage (like Lowenstein himself sometimes did) emphasised their physical differences as a quick way to mark them out as opposites, an improbable pair—Hutchence, the sun-kissed, hedonistic rock star from Sydney, Lowenstein, the pale, black-clad auteur from Melbourne.

Lowenstein and Hutchence, as well as those close to them, contributed to the mythology of their friendship as opposites attracting, but another version—also proffered by Lowenstein—of alter egos seems more fitting. In memorialising Hutchence, Lowenstein described him as 'the part of me that I didn't follow... the kid that played air guitar in front of the mirror... the sex machine rock star all the girls loved... he was the yin to my yan [sic]'.[27] Yet in becoming so closely involved with Hutchence and INXS, Lowenstein did get to at least vicariously experience rock stardom, to an extent that his work with them derailed or sidelined his feature film career for some years after the release of *Dogs in Space*. For Hutchence, meanwhile, his friendship with Lowenstein—and via him, with Ollie Olsen, Nick Cave and Peter 'Troy' Davies, among others—opened up creative and social vistas outside of the band, from early on in INXS's rise to international stardom. While never as drearily dismissive of his teenage or mainstream fan-base as some pop stars have been known to be, Hutchence nevertheless clearly wanted to extend himself beyond what was required of him in INXS. Variously described as charming, adaptable, attention-seeking, people-pleasing and edgy, Hutchence had been drawn to subcultures and new experiences since his youth—including acting, an industry he first encountered through his mother Patricia Glassop's work as a make-up artist for film and television. She recalls her son 'had huge respect for Richard's work and longed to associate himself with his style of creative-cool'.[28]

Making *Dogs in Space* together was clearly mutually beneficial for both director and star, though there was a certain amount of naiveté on both sides. Hutchence fought hard for the role of Sam, or rather with his management team for the time to do it. He apparently tried heroin for the first time to prepare for his part as a heroin-addicted punk,[29] and Lowenstein and others involved (including Sejavka himself) praised Hutchence for his work ethic and fidelity to the 'real' Sam. Hutchence was keen to take on a part that was not expected of him or his kind. As he told film critic Jim Schembri:

> It's certainly not a role that is sort of helping one's ego or glorifying yourself. I wasn't in a Porsche going 'Hi girls! Let's play tennis!' In a way I had to do a movie like this because otherwise I wouldn't be taken seriously.[30]

However, once the movie was released, both in Australia and in the USA, critics and viewers were somewhat mixed in their opinions as to whether Hutchence could act, or whether playing a punk from the late 1970s was that much of a stretch from being a rock star in the 1980s. (As the 'real' Michael Hutchence was by all accounts well-spoken and engaging and that he played what was evocatively described in one review as possibly the 'screen's first post-literate anti-hero'[31] I do applaud his performance.) Subsequent reappraisals have been more uniform in praising both the singer and *Dogs in Space* (and especially the film), even if some new or recent fans of Hutchence have mistakenly confused it for a biopic and found it wanting.[32]

As for Lowenstein, Hutchence's involvement got his film funded and until the censors decided otherwise, the writer/director had high hopes of attracting a teenage audience. *Dogs in Space* was not yet finished when he was already promoting it as the 'youth market *Crocodile Dundee* of the summer of '86'.[33] Hoyts Cinemas were on board too, when the Board of Classification issued an R-certificate. In retrospect, the R-rating slapped on the film because it purportedly glamorised drug use does not seem so surprising given the Federal Government's high-profile anti-drugs stance and policies. And while Hutchence in a starring role would definitely have lured teenaged me to the cinema, I'm fairly sure I would have still had to pretend to have liked it anyway if I had actually been able to see it at the peak of my INXS obsession. I was into John Hughes movies, not arty films without much plot. I suspect I would have wanted Anna to somehow tame Sam, albeit in a cool sassy way, not die of an overdose in his bed. Still, I was also very into music videos and *Countdown* (like the characters in the film) and as Craig McGregor noted at the time, *Dogs in Space* is 'almost an extended play rock clip: from the opening *Mad Max* street car sequence to the closing funeral tableau, with Michael Hutchence in nifty double-breasted suit singing "Rooms for the Memory"'[34] (In contrast, rock critic Stuart Coupe found the closing sequence the most jarring: just when he'd begun to forget the actor playing Sam was a 'semi-famous rock'n'roll star', the last three minutes rolled out as a 'promotional video clip for Hutchence'[35]). So perhaps it could have gone either way for the teenage audience that never eventuated.

As it happened, Lowenstein tried to no avail to edit the film to satisfy the censors and together with Hutchence, criticised the R-rating on the press circuit as a missed opportunity to educate a young audience about the realities of drug use. Hutchence raged to Schembri: 'They've given [*Dogs in Space*] as hard a time as possible, and I think it's an absolute crime!'.³⁶ What is most striking about these interviews now is not so much their justifiable anger at the Censorship Board, as their shared commitment to the film and to each other's contribution to it. Lowenstein was unwavering in his praise for Hutchence's performance, and Hutchence doggedly prepared for, performed in and promoted the film at a time when INXS was otherwise all-consuming. On the eve of the film's release, Lowenstein told critic Ed St. John:

> For about two months he became Sam, to me. It was quite amazing, actually. I was very impressed because we had to shoot the film between all these touring commitments to INXS, at a time when they had a huge American hit, but Michael was incredibly professional and together.³⁷

The 'huge American hit' was the single 'What You Need' (1985) from the INXS album *Listen Like Thieves*. Lowenstein directed the groundbreaking live-animation video, a true feat of art direction, and the one that made them big on MTV.

Hutchence's fame did not merely facilitate the financing of the film; his presence and Lowenstein's work with INXS informed the look and the feel of *Dogs of Space*. Lowenstein has described *Dogs in Space* as 'pretty much a mid-eighties fantasy', while Ollie Olsen later shared he was more nostalgic about the making of the film than he was about the period it depicted.³⁸ Lesley Speed noted that the 'film's ostensible setting in the late 1970s is implicitly imbued with a 1980s perspective'. Eighties Goths and performers out of time mingle with musicians who were there the first time around. For Speed, this compression of 'a broad range of memories into a limited diegetic space and time' is one of the film's key strengths, rather than a sign of inauthenticity, illuminating as it does the theme of transition.³⁹ Hutchence's role in this 'fantasy' is less commented on, perhaps because it's so obvious as to not require comment. Yet the documentary *We're All Livin' on Dog Food* (2009), as well as fashion designer Allanah Hill's memoir *Butterfly on a Pin* (2018), gloriously brought Hutchence's impact to the fore, especially to the women on set.

The collected recollections in *We're Livin' on Dog Food*, of Hill, an extra on the film, his co-star Saskia Post, and artist Emma De Clario, also an extra and only fourteen at the time, make a marvellous and frankly lustful tribute to Australia's first rock star, as he transitioned from local to international stardom. Looking back, over twenty years later, Post wistfully regrets not having sex with him. She recalls 'I remember being quite struck by him. He's very charismatic, you know, he's a spunk. He's incredibly attractive'. Hill—who shared Hutchence's insecurity about not having been part of the punk scene depicted in *Dogs in Space*—found him 'totally vulnerable', but also magnetic: 'Any girl that spends ten minutes with Michael Hutchence in a room, you're gone, you're completely gone. He was that fucking charismatic.' For De Clario, the whole experience was life-changing—she lost her virginity on set, tried smack for the first time, and got to pash Michael Hutchence. She remembers being keenly aware of his presence and dressing and performing accordingly: 'it was all for Michael'. Like others on set, she sensed his shyness and also the liberation he experienced being away from the 'whole mainstream thing'. Yet his fame and his sex appeal were inescapable: 'He had that very unusual charisma of fame, that real physicality of fame, he was famous, and it…was amazing. He was so international'.[40]

Watching them, I am freshly reminded that during their relationship, Kylie Minogue—Australia's sweetheart—said Michael Hutchence helped her discover sex. He told an interviewer his favourite hobby was 'corrupting Kylie'. Now some thirty years later (how can it be?) Kylie has shared previously unseen footage with Lowenstein and is helping him promote his documentary on Hutchence, mostly by elaborating on the 'corrupting Kylie' theme. The footage is both sexy and sweet: Michael and Kylie cavort on boats, on the Orient Express and in hotel rooms. They send each other faxes, a distinctly 1990s style of courtship. Michael loved women and women loved Michael—this is the narrative arc Lowenstein has chosen to emphasise in *Mystify*, and he knew him well. When asked during the Q and A of the screening I attended, why there was barely mention of *Dogs in Space* (only fleeting, unreferenced scenes from the film and outtakes), Lowenstein shared that he'd wanted to examine Hutchence's acting aspirations, but the British producers were not enthused. The audience were assured there will be more on the future DVD release.

Conclusion

After *Dogs in Space*, Michael Hutchence's next break from INXS was to make the Max Q album with Ollie Olsen in 1989. The album, a critical success, was a happy compromise between Olsen wanting to make a pop album and Hutchence wanting to make an 'underground' record.[41] He cut off his trademark locks and stepped out with Kylie, two moves I disapproved of at the time but that have now been narrated by various biographers and insiders as bold emancipatory steps forward in keeping with his experimental way of living. Yet the flipside to this story is that Hutchence could never bring himself to leave INXS, no matter how frustrated he became with management, their relentless touring schedule or their increasingly dated sound. He also, by all appearances, became a cliched rock star—living in the South of France, dating a supermodel, dodging tax and the paparazzi, hanging with Bono—just as grunge came along and declared his kind obsolete. To some, including his last serious girlfriend Paula Yates, the tragic circumstances of his death in a Double Bay hotel room in November 1997 were interpreted through the sexy rock star lens: Hutchence, the story went, had died of autoerotic asphyxiation, a kinky act gone wrong. The coroner declared suicide by hanging.

Hutchence's death, and later an INXS miniseries and television documentary, prompted reappraisals of both INXS and their charismatic lead singer. Lowenstein has been a central figure in this revisionist turn, but he never stopped being interested in Hutchence in the first place. The eventual DVD release of *Dogs in Space*, the documentary *We're All Livin' on Dog Food* (2009), special meet-the-director cinema screenings and now the *Mystify* documentary have continued to showcase the friendship and creative partnership between Lowenstein and Hutchence, as well as Lowenstein's unabashed fascination with, and close proximity, to Hutchence. Lowenstein won praise for his work before INXS came along, but filming Michael Hutchence, with and apart from INXS, has arguably been his greatest work and most sustained project. At one point, Lowenstein was even contemplating a biopic. Both Hutchence (through death) and Lowenstein (by making music videos, films about share-houses and documentaries about his interesting friends) have had 'what ifs?' hang over their careers and legacies. Yet what they did do together—*Dogs in Space*, all those INXS videos and we can include *Mystify*—were more than enough, mid-eighties fantasies that continue to find new audiences.

Notes

1. G. Fuller (2019) 'Mystify: Michael Hutchence', *Screen Daily*, 27 April, https://www.screendaily.com/reviews/mystify-michael-hutchence-tribeca-review/5138837.article, accessed 9 June 2019.
2. INXS and A. Bozza (2005) *INXS: Story to Story: The Official Autobiography* (New York: Atria), p. 300.
3. Anon (1987) 'Dogs in Space', *The New Yorker*, 26 October, 22.
4. R. Lowenstein (2009) We're Livin' on Dog Food [film].
5. INXS and Bozza, *INXS: Story to Story*, p. xi.
6. J. Barnes (2017) *Working Class Man* (Sydney: HarperCollins), p. 154.
7. J. Stratton (2007) *Australian Rock: Essays on Popular Music* (Perth: Curtin University Press), p. 59.
8. INXS and Bozza, *INXS: Story to Story*, pp. 70–71.
9. INXS and Bozza, *INXS: Story to Story*, pp. 69–70.
10. Stratton, pp. 57–59.
11. INXS and Bozza, *INXS: Story to Story*, p. 101.
12. INXS and Bozza, *INXS: Story to Story*, p. 69.
13. Jon Stratton has persuasively suggested that Cold Chisel never made it big internationally because their Australian sound did not translate to international audiences (Stratton, Australian Rock, p. 59).
14. INXS and Bozza, *INXS: Story to Story*, p. 81.
15. T. Hutchence and P. Glassop (2000) *Just a Man: The Real Michael Hutchence* (London: Sidgwick and Jackson), p. 59.
16. INXS and Bozza, *INXS: Story to Story*, p. 101.
17. Gary Garry Beers: 'I think that American guys tried too hard to be sensitive - which wasn't what women wanted either. That's why they loved us. It was simple, we were just like, "Hello! We're Australian, we're men, we're confident, and we love to fuck. How are you tonight?"'. INXS and Bozza, *INXS: Story to Story*, p. 138.
18. F. Bongiorno (2015) *The Eighties: The Decade That Transformed Australia* (Melbourne: Black Inc.), p. 220.
19. G. Young (2004) '"So Slide Over Here": The Aesthetics of Masculinity in Late Twentieth-Century Australian Pop Music', *Popular Music*, 23(2), May, 173–193.

20. Young, '"So Slide…"', p. 182.
21. J. J. Brown (2014) 'Ghost of the Year: Was Michael Hutchence Happy?' in C. Ryan (ed.) *The Best Music Writing Under the Australian Sun* (Melbourne: Hardie Grant), pp. 279–296, 281.
22. Glenys Rowe (1984) 'Richard Lowenstein: On the Rock Clip Road to Feature Films', *Metro Magazine: Media & Education Magazine*, 64, 20–23.
23. https://michaelhutchence.org/richard-lowenstein/, accessed 9 June 2019. https://michaelhutchence.org/memories/family-and-friends/, accessed 9 June 2019.
24. INXS and Bozza, *INXS: Story to Story*, p. 112.
25. INXS and Bozza, *INXS: Story to Story*, p. 112.
26. Hutchence with Glassop, *Just a Man*, pp. 100–101.
27. https://michaelhutchence.org/memories/family-and-friends/, accessed 9 June 2019.
28. Hutchence with Glassop, *Just a Man*, p. 101.
29. Hutchence with Glassop, *Just a Man*, p. 100.
30. J. Schembri (1986) 'Hutchence Sends a Message', Melbourne *Age*, 26 December, 30–31.
31. C. Rickey (1988) 'Dogs in Space Takes a Look at Punk Rockers in Australia', *The Philadelphia Inquirer*, 19 January, 5.
32. See discussion in comments at Amazon listing for *Dogs in Space*, https://www.amazon.com/Dogs-Space-Michael-Hutchence/dp/B007RP4CQO.
33. E. St. John (1986) 'Dogs in Space and Other True Stories', *Stiletto*, 36, December, 33.
34. C. McGregor (1986) 'Now on Film: A Generation Lost in Space', *Sydney Morning Herald*, 6 December, 52.
35. S. Coupe (1986) 'Generation of Sex, Drugs, Rock n'roll', *Sydney Sun Herald*, 14 December, 115.
36. Schembri, 'Hutchence Sends a Message', p. 30.
37. St. John, 'Dogs in Space', p. 34.
38. S. Hussey (2009) 'Punk Moments: A Conversation with Richard Lowenstein', *Metro Magazine: Media & Education*, pp. 162, 169–171.
39. L. Speed (2009) 'Win and Lose: Subculture and Social Difference in *Dogs in Space*', *Metro Magazine: Media & Education Magazine*, pp. 162, 160–165.
40. Lowenstein (2009) *We're All Livin' on Dog Food*.
41. Brown, 'Ghost of the Year', p. 285.

The Intimacy of Distance: Re/Reading *Dogs in Space*

Laura Carroll

Falling to Earth

In 1962, Stanislav Lec wrote 'Myth is gossip grown old'.[1] For a film so rooted in microlocal observations and ideas about time and place, *Dogs in Space* is also interestingly, fruitfully loose about whether it belongs to the space of its setting or to the space of its making. To a sector of its first audience which was embedded at a small but significant distance from the milieu, setting, and period of the film, and therefore intimately familiar with some of its materials but not with others, this looseness had a generative effect. It meant that markers the film apparently intends as pointers back to the flowering and disintegration of unique and distinctive cultural moment—something that happened once and is now over— could be understood instead as points of entry into a story cycle which is endlessly renewed and therefore can be joined at any point. Not elegiac but prophetic: maybe even utopian.

L. Carroll (✉)
La Trobe University, Melbourne, VIC, Australia

Dogs in Space opens with a sacrifice that is both mythic and real: 'a dog named Laika' is blasted into Cold War space, to run out of dog food and die more alone than anyone else ever in the history of Earth, and to become an endlessly reproduced image of life rendered surreal by superpower aggression and domestic 'technofear', to borrow a concept from Neil of *The Young Ones*. The blue light of the cathode ray television's screen belongs to the childhood memories of the people *Dogs in Space* is about, but also to the visual experience of later generations who inherited shitty old televisions and other discarded technology, and built homes, lives and worlds out of this scavenged material. *Dogs in Space* will periodically return to rebroadcasted Cold War space footage, using it to paste together the joins between episodes in the narrative but also to offer an Olympian, ironic perspective on the intense but quotidian situations the narrative unfolds.

The film then arrives at street level with a collage of materials which consolidate its layered relationship to time, place and genre. Iggy Pop is quoted, like a sage; a passenger in a hot rod shouts recreational abuse at someone unseen and the car hoons away through the night, Iggy singing now, between the pylons of a bridge to a disorderly street rabble of people with phenomenally good hair, yelling, drinking, embracing, fighting, sprawling on the ground, encamped in clouds of smoke and rubbish under a sign that reads DAVID BOWIE CONCERT NOV 18. The first of the opening credits is MICHAEL HUTCHENCE. There's a confrontation between the occupants of the car and knots of people on the street; the car revs off and some of the street people give chase while others worm further beneath their blankets.

The sequence is captioned MELBOURNE AUSTRALIA 1978, but, gentle reader, do yourself a favour and grant me the claim that this marker, naming a specific (but not too specific) place and time in the past, is easy to miss and is also contradicted by other perspectives mobilised in the film, not all of which are compatible with the others. The place is not just the abstraction 'Melbourne Australia': it is (sorry) concrete: the street is Punt Road, the bridge is the one that holds up Richmond Station, and the rabble is camped on the footpath outside the Melbourne Cricket Ground (MCG). Seeing the film, you either know this or you don't; like a Wittgensteinian duck/rabbit, you can be aware of the doubleness but it's not possible to actually see both aspects at once. Likewise, the year 1978 is in the past for the moment of the film's production and release and for every moment since, yet the post-apocalyptic atmosphere of rage unleashed on the street belongs to a vision of the near future which was particularly strong in the mid-1980s—the Star Wars programme, Chernobyl, Mad Max—but also has never not felt like the future assuredly awaiting us once western liberal democracy finally coughs out its last, rancid, stinking breath. Put together, this slicing both ways, this subsonic dissonance emphasises the spaces and gaps between the fields of the film's narrative, and it is within these interstices that its audiences have found spaces to imagine, and generate, meanings far beyond the local yet always nourished by it.

> [The primal scene] often has the attractiveness of giving a sort of tragic pattern to one's life. It is all the repetition of the same pattern which was settled long ago.[2]

You either know this or you don't: David Bowie really did perform at the MCG on 18 November 1978, and there really was an epic, multiphase ticket and then door queue outside for weeks beforehand, and in it there really was a young artist called Sam, and also many other far-out types who got to know each other there for the first time, and this event really was documented and immediately mythologised, by the participants and others, as the birthplace of something—a primal scene, if you like.[3]

> Melbourne had this atmosphere that someone had done something and gone away, and all these people there who were part of this larger story. It was attractive, full of enigmatic late teenage, early-twenties people who lived out these bohemian dramas.[4]

But *Dogs in Space* is not a documentary about that scene. What it is, in some sense, is a re-enactment of it. As Inke Arns has argued, re-enactment is a distinctive artistic strategy peculiarly fitted to thinking about our relationship to historical situations and events when the 'permanent availability of media representations [of history] renders all forms of authenticity increasingly remote':

In this situation artistic re-enactments do not ask the naive question about what really happened outside of the history represented in the media - the "authenticity" beyond the images - instead, they ask what the images we see might mean concretely to us, if we were to experience those situations personally. In this way artistic re-enactment confronts the general feeling of insecurity about the meaning of images by using a paradoxical approach: through erasing distance to the images and at the same time distancing itself from the images.[5]

'I was with my parents in the Toyota Crown, near the corner of Stephensons and Waverley Roads, urging my mother, repeatedly, to turn up the radio - because whatever was playing was blowing my mind', Sam Sejavka asserts, implausibly, in a 2015 reflection on the place of David Bowie in his own pantheon of heroes. 'It was *Space Oddity*. Probably the early-70s re-release. And, though I was yet to know it, I was snared'. Writings about Bowie's entrance into the lives of provincial children often have this cringey, selfconsciously eschatological flavour: Morrissey, for instance, writes of seeing Bowie perform in 1972 as 'touch[ing] the hand of this inexplicably liberating reformer; he, a Wildean visionary about to re-mold England, and I, a spectacle of suffering in a blue school uniform'.[6] *Dogs in Space*, however, opens its dialogue with the past, present and future not in a doomed attempt to reconstruct the unrecoverable moment of Bowie's descent to the turf of the MCG, but with a carefully delineated Bowie-shaped hole, an aperture, conceived of from the beginning as a space for personal engagement with images without demanding that they be 'authentic'—much like 1970s Bowie himself. 'He left spaces for his followers: not just the hierarchy of stardom and fandom but a strange, astute, uncanny folding of one into the other…He taught us to be critics of our own enthusiasms'.[7]

By the mid-1980s, David Bowie was a permed and peroxided caricature of himself and I found him faintly embarrassing. I didn't warm to Michael Hutchence either: I knew the record companies and music magazines assumed and required me, a teenage girl, to like him but 'the figure of carefully tended ambiguity' he cut seemed an insult to my intelligence.[8] The people who did interest me greatly were Rowland S. Howard and Nick Cave, and I knew of them in the manner Dave Graney remembers in the passage quoted above, as people who had 'done something and gone away'. This knowledge did not produce in me a desire to go to the distant Europe an cities where they'd decamped. Instead all my aspirations centred upon getting to Melbourne. From where I stood there was no reason to want to go anywhere else.

A Projected World

> Provincials from the bush or small towns arrive in the great cit[ies] of Australia with a projected world in their heads: a world they believe stretches in wait for them outside their rented rooms; an impossible cityscape of ethereal encounters, which fades eventually, to be replaced by the real one. The real one is no less strange; but who's to say that the other city doesn't exist somewhere - that city glimpsed in the mind?
> —C. J. Koch[9]

> There will always be somewhere hipper than wherever you are.
> —David McComb[10]

I don't know how the people who made *Dogs in Space* spent New Year's Eve, 1989; nor do I know what the people who the movie is 'about' were doing. I sure don't know where *you* were or what it was that *you* got up to. But here's what *I* was doing. At midnight, I was standing in the disco of the Lady Bay Hotel in Warrnambool. I wore thick black stockings and school shoes, and a lace minidress which twenty years before had been worn by my aunt to the wedding of her eldest sister. Three hours earlier I'd desecrated that beautiful garment by cutting a hole in the side and stitching a rough pocket there to hold money, lipstick and my fake ID. Dancing around a handbag featured in none of my plans for the immediate future. In my mouth lay the tongue of a tall and uninteresting man who was dressed as if for going to work in an office. Even while I was kissing him, I knew he was a philistine. I knew also that I wasn't going to go on bothering with all this Warrnambool shit for very much longer.

Warrnambool is a large coastal town three hours' drive to the west of Melbourne. The town presented me and my friends with Sportsgirl and Katies, commercial top 40 radio, Tom Cruise at the pictures, boyfriends who played footy and drank beer or surfed and smoked dope, and the prospect of a wedding in the Catholic church in Lava Street followed by work in a shop or factory. From its beaches, the metropolis is remote enough to seem exotic and alluring, but also close enough to seem, and be, real and accessible—if not immediately, then as soon as transport can be organised. For Australians situated within reach of a major city, the obstacles to be navigated are composed of timeliness not distance. Can I get there soon enough, not will I ever get there at all?

We waited, surviving on refractions and shadows of a forgotten and more interesting world gleaned from the ruins via op shops, and on videotapes and bits of paper and music which slightly older people carried home from the city on weekends. My friend Ruby turned eighteen first. Her dad and brother got a derelict car off their farm and fixed it up for her. It was a white F. J. Holden and it had a cassette player. This cassette player had only one function and that was to play the soundtrack of *Dogs in Space*. "'I'm living on dog food!" It was a lot of time and energy expelled repelling yuppie materialism', said my friend Melissa, thirty years later (or four months ago, take your pick). We didn't know about any of that Bowie-concert-Sam-Sejavka stuff I mentioned earlier, and I suspect we wouldn't have cared. We didn't recognise Marie Hoy (who seems to me now the glowing, smouldering reactor at the heart of the entire movie) or Ollie Olsen. But we knew the *Dogs in Space* house was real. Because of the neon PELACO in the sky, we knew that *Dogs in Space* was in Richmond, and because of the street sign saying Berry Street, we could and did use a Melways to pinpoint the location of the house (Fig. 1).

The 'arbitrary act of reading'[11] I performed on the film was to take it as a love letter to the inner city share house as an aesthetic experience, and inseparable from this, as an argument for the Wildean politics of privileging aesthetic values in the making of decisions about how to live one's life. I also understood it as a formal demonstration of the independent worth of the practice of making, and making something of, sharp observations, as the movie does, of characters and situations and actions that might

Fig. 1 Laura, Melissa and Katrina, Berry Street, 1989 (Photo by Ruby Richardson)

otherwise be deemed beneath notice. I appreciated the high comedy of these pleasures coming bundled up in share house living rooms, in all their enervation and shit filthiness, and to me, this—the bundling—was the most beautiful thing in the world, and I was ready to immerse myself in it.

Going In

> Hacking out the perfect alternative lifestyle in the city, fostered by cool, free people who would gather and let me become one of them. Chasing this simple dream and that would heal everything.
> —Neill Overton[12]

> If we are to live here, it won't be as an isolated colony of freaks
> —Walter Tevis[13]

The largest flat plane in *Dogs in Space* is the front elevation of the Berry Street house: a porous membrane with openings that never close. Even so it wasn't obvious to me how you actually get across the threshold of a house like that. When the door is always open, it's hard to learn the password. I'd never lived in a two storey house; I didn't even know anyone who did. At my first share house interview, I was ushered in to stand before a queenly presence who reclined across her throne, looked me up and down and murmured 'Cool boots' before a lackey escorted me out again. I then went to an address in Fitzroy: a more experienced person would instantly have recognised this as an irretrievably fucked-up household. The door stood open. I called out and someone appeared in the dark hallway. The trainee architect who drunkenly showed me the vacant room just wanted someone to pay rent. He accepted me. I was thrilled.

People come into the Berry Street house via a range of gestures at once mythic and real. Some people already live or somehow belong there. Others insert themselves, slowly and smoothly or hard and fast. Leanne is the only person who makes a determined first entrance into the house and she is also, I think, the only person who is altered by her residence there—at least, she eventually begins to dress like a new waver. Does this mean she begins to see some value in the project of making friends with people not like herself? I choose to believe it does.

Early in the film, there is an evening of arrivals. Anna's Beetle coasts to a halt and she clambers out, in her nurse's uniform, and with her two girlfriends rushes inside, bringing conversation, energy and money, brushing past 'the girl', a waif in a school tunic sitting on the front steps with her hands clasped around her knees. In the kitchen Jen, who is straight out of Helen Garner, is trying to fry something but 'someone's been fucking using this for meat again'. Chuck, always best at coming into the house, comes storming tensely in and slams the door, kicks something, yells a greeting and throws his keys at the wall. Grant ambles in, saying things about politics in a very 'Said Hanrahan' voice. Barry and a white woman walk postcoitally down the stairs, discussing politics in a mode that is the opposite of Grant in that the tendency of it is not moaning about the decline of everything that's lost but eagerness for the revolution to come.

The night the band plays, Grant tells Jen that Leanne, who's just arrived in the house, escorted by relations who actually look like they're from the 1970s as opposed to everyone else in the movie, was Luchio's first one night stand. 'Luchio got her in Wangaratta', Grant says. To me, 'Wangaratta' sounded like another name for 'Warrnambool' and much as I hoped I was the type of wafty junior siren represented by 'the girl', I feared that in actuality I was Leanne: the opposite of cool; false, crass, obnoxious, all body, weaponised sexuality, and worst of all, nasal. Later, I would enjoy her careless disdain for conventional femininity and her lack of selfconsciousness. Later still, I would think that she walks a very important line, evaded by everyone else in the film, the line between waiting annoyingly to be deemed cool enough to be brought inside and pushing in uninvited.

A few weeks ago, I was driving on a rural highway with Kate, who was with me the night I moved into the house in Fitzroy. She said: 'I met Gary Foley about fifteen years ago. The first time we talked I couldn't place how I knew him. I actually didn't realise Gary was in *Dogs in Space* until I watched it again recently. I think the film had given me a sense of personal connection to him'. I glanced at her profile; her eyes were fixed on the road ahead. I said 'Do you remember, on the dashboard of Ruby's car, we had a set of hands stolen off op shop dummies, and when a car came, on a bit of road like this, we used to use them to wave at the driver?'

Mapping the House

We should learn to live more on staircases. But how?
—Georges Perec[14]

Is it something to do with this house? You found it. You got the upstairs room.
  She could have had the upstairs room if she'd wanted it.
—Helen Garner, *Honour and Other People's Children*[15]

That house in Fitzroy was beyond awful and my room was awfullest of all. The trainee architect's mum brought him food! She really did do that! I soon learned that in two-storey share houses, with their stark but always shifting division of communal and individual spaces, upstairs bedrooms are the ones with status. The house proles always dwell in the dark downstairs lean-to additions and the house Establishment, which is always hereditary in the sense that the longest-standing occupants rise to the top, lives in the quieter, privater, higher-ceilinged upstairs rooms with long windows opening to the balcony and the sky over the street. *Dogs in Space* registers efforts to undo the inherited strata—intentional efforts, and also the work of something like entropy or nihilism. It pays attention to the ways attempts to share urban space differently are inherently volatile. It shows it how easily the jumble of the experiment reverts to the forms of rentier capitalism, to deterioration and decay.

  The social topography of the Berry Street house explores this thoroughly, without sentimentality or romance. The two upstairs front rooms are occupied by Grant and by Tony and Jen—hippies, relics from an already fading moment of progressive personal and social politics, once pathbreakers, now immobilised by sex and dope, stuck in a rut. Luchio, literally the house's sexual underclass, occupies a room furnished with frustration, a desk, an Elvis poster, a polyester leopard skin blanket and a jar of instant coffee, directly below Grant's and repeatedly subject to the sonic invasions of Grant's upstairs activities and the visual intrusions of Grant pashing a series of hot women in the street outside the window. Tim, the house ironist and purveyor of corn, lives upstairs in a bowerlike room festooned ransom note style with clippings, bits of tinfoil and toys, and 'the sex maniacs' Sam and Anna share a den across the hall from Luchio's room, and diametrically opposite to it.

Nobody ever does learn to live on the staircase of the *Dogs in Space* house but all its other communal spaces—the dysfunctional kitchen, the entropic black hole of the living room, and the bathroom that is nightmarish beyond the power of language to convey—are so heavily lived in that they are losing their original forms under the blurring brushes of present and past efforts to remake and remodel the spaces. Several people appear to 'live', after a fashion, in the living room where the TV is always on, and beside it stands a decaying chrome and vinyl kitchen chair upon which nobody can sit because it is permanently occupied by a yellow Johnson Bros plate of food and cigarette butts. The bathroom, where Sam unconvincingly plays at being a monstrous child, is cluttered with painted tin cans suspended in an arrangement poised maddeningly between Art Brut and something you can put into the bin once it has scared away the flies of another summer. Nothing is ever cooked or eaten in the kitchen, unless you count cereal, dope and magic mushrooms.

Dogs in Space does not offer a cheering portrait of share house life but it does render that life intelligible, finding meaning in disorder and demonstrating the utility of the process Fredric Jameson, adapting Kevin Lynch, described as 'cognitive mapping' of a hitherto alienated urban space. 'Disalienation in the traditional city', Jameson writes, 'involves the practical reconquest of a sense of place and the construction or reconstruction of an articulated ensemble which can be retained in memory and which the individual subject can map and remap along the moments of mobile, alternative trajectories'.[16]

From Clutter to Collage

In Annandale people didn't feel pressured to be other than what they were. And since they were all sorts of different things, they created between them a collage full of engagingly "innocent" intricacies. In a way Annandale was simply an undigested cultural stew; yet its very lack of formal or visual cohesion or readily apparent charm, grace or drama allowed a more satisfying aesthetic to emerge, if one looked at it long and hard enough.[17]

Dogs in Space looks long and hard at share house life, and as early reviews of the film disgustedly noted, it does so without artificially imposing anything you could call 'readily apparent charm, grace or drama'. Nevertheless it's not a documentary, as I have been arguing, but something closer to re-enactment, and what emerges is subtler and more interesting. The share house is depicted as collage, sculptural and graphic, with exposed joins and rough edges where different types of materials push against each other. As in *The Young Ones*, that other great comic meditation on share housing, energy derives from revelling in friction between a set of supremely mismatched stock figures, with each one's tics amplified and eternally repeated in a manner that belongs to the tropes of comedy but also to the real purgatorial horror of enforced domestic intimacy between untidy people who don't love each other. *Dogs in Space*, however, employs tics and repetition as organising principles at the level of narrative, and in this way, it simultaneously marks the rhythm of share house life and its always fragile equilibrium. Cries of 'Ballaraaat!' echo through the movie. Crane shots rise and fall and rise over the house, street and sky. Volkswagens hurtle across intersections, past blurs of traffic lights. Egg Flip Big Ms are everything. Sam never greets Anna without pulling her to the floor and kissing and embracing her. An angry woman punctuates the film by breaking things, throwing food, screaming abuse; it's never quite clear what's prompted her transcendental rage (but it earns her the right to the greatest sentence any girl ever shouted off a balcony in the entire history of cinema: 'Suck my motherfucking dick!'). The strains of the Eno sex record—never getting past the album's first track, 'Skysaw', 3 minutes and 26 seconds—penetrate the air over and over and the irritation of house residents forced to listen to it never diminishes. In the central sequence beginning with the band arriving at the pub and ending with Anna and Sam injecting heroin and having sex, 'Shivers' is heard in a series of different versions, exploiting this oddly magical song's uncanny capacity for endless return without resorting to the dubious invention of a primal moment when it was somehow 'authentic'.

The shortness of lenses used to film the house flattens out its rooms and creates a persistent feeling that there are more people and things in its spaces than they can logically contain. The visual field of the house is a radically open structure, layered and pocketed, filled with shifting middens of debris, bodies, food, ashes, printed matter, pieces of furniture, and other unstable, ephemeral, ambiguous materials like the stuff members of the 1980s Melbourne artists' collective known as Roar remembered using to make work: 'Some of us lived on unemployment benefits but after food and rent there was little left for art materials... Among the more inventive solutions were pizza boxes, Venetian blinds and Real Estate Agents' signs that were taken in the middle of the night'.[18] Or like this, from a description of the Australian artist Mike Brown's prizewinning 1966 work 'Times Aren't Whot': 'A heap of household debris of electric plugs, torn sheets, and clock springs, together with the wreckage of torn paintings, all tied together with string and wooden stakes'.[19] Sam and Anna's room is a three-dimensional collage, with an almost unreadable visual field sliced into layers by planes of coloured light and indecipherable assemblages of objects. The room is full of metal grids, a shopping trolley, a TV, tangled hunks of cables, tape reels, model aircraft, pram wheels, cut-outs, bundles of cloth. The film depicts only three types of legible action in this intimate space: fucking, taking drugs and sheets being changed by Sam's mother. Narrative modalities—romance, tragedy, satire—are collaged by the film in exactly the same way as characters and settings. The bigger questions asked by the film concern what kind of order might manifest itself out of this process.

I moved to Melbourne to study art, or perhaps it was the other way around? The first year of my course, taught by people who spoke of themselves as the maligned artworld keepers of the flame of realism, consisted only of drawing charcoal still lifes. Drawing in colour was not allowed. Mike Brown lived in a house a few doors down from mine. He'd painted murals like jigsaws or ants' nests all over the inside and outside walls. He looked, with amusement and enough kindness, at the pages of my compulsorily monochromatic journal and said, 'who are you trying to please?'

Dropping the Bundle

> Somebody has to cope! And once you start, they expect you to cope for them as well, and you're never allowed to drop your bundle ever again - and then the buggers hate you and tell you you're authoritarian!
> —Helen Garner, *Honour and Other People's Children*[20]

> Eventually everything within the building would merge, would be faceless and identical, mere pudding-like kipple piled to the ceiling of each apartment. And, after that, the uncared-for building itself would settle into shapelessness, buried under the ubiquity of the dust.
> —Philip K. Dick[21]

> She said, "I'll never forgive you for the way you were at the end of Rowe Street. You were so cold and efficient - you didn't seem to care. And for me it was the end of the world."
> —Helen Garner, *Honour and Other People's Children*[22]

The saddest moment in *Dogs in Space* is when Tim drops his exquisitely fragile bundle of a homemade synthesiser on the hallway floor and it seems like he thinks he can't fix it. This is heaps more tragic than Anna's death, which is handled by the film in a way that ought to set your teeth violently on edge. Obviously, there is some sort of commentary intended on the general concept of selling out in the way that Sam parlays his 'grief' into career success, if that is what is depicted in the film's closing scenes, which capture a late 1980s sense that, as Frank Bongiorno writes in a different context, 'capitalism was not quite over yet, and the market soon demonstrated that there was money to be made from being "poor" and "marginal", yet "hip" and "stylish"'.[23] But the movie implicates itself in the same dubious cultural politics it critiques, simply by deploying the death of a beautiful young woman as a means of inserting a full stop, and thus forcing a narrative arc, onto material it otherwise mostly represents as cyclical series of episodes.

As Alice Bolin recently identified, the instrumentalising of 'dead girls' as plot devices, epitomised by Laura Palmer of *Twin Peaks*, is an omnipresent obsession of postmodern popular culture, often in work of the highest artistic order, and for women engaged with this culture the dead girl is a trope that can take some surviving.[24] I think I survived *Dogs in Space*'s destruction of Anna in two ways. First, I allowed myself enough distance to view the whole getting-into-a-neon-limousine business as the unfeasibly large ball of cheese that it is, to thus take a momentary step back from intimate engagement with the film's images and laugh at them instead, a tactic which I continue to like and recommend. Second, I took advantage of the quality I've been arguing this film possesses of being ambiguously elegiac or prophetic, readable as about a past or about a future.

The 'bundling' going on in *Dogs in Space* does not happen of its own accord. The household is held together by someone, and at visible cost to herself. From the Bowie concert line onward, where it's Anna who stands up and says 'Fuck off' to the sharpies in the car while Sam hides, it's plain that it's Anna who earns money, buys crumpets, drives the car, answers the phone, pays for beers, does hair, lends underpants, provides sex and relationships counselling, appreciates the band's output, and bends over backwards to maintain her volatile relationship with Sam. In return for all this giving she receives, not to put too fine a point on it, what appears to be extremely hot sex—but not much else. That this is a grossly unequal exchange is registered in the way that every person Anna passes as she takes final leave of the house offers her something. Barry and his friend walk in, offer her a drink, she shakes her head. The living room kids offer her TV, cough mixture, pills; in the kitchen, Tim offers her a fried egg, Tony and Jen offer her a joint. Chuck waves keys at her and walks by; Grant invites her upstairs and she shakes her head, no. Luchio in his doorway holds up his jar of instant coffee—Anna smiles, no. 'The girl' outside offers her nothing but an affectionate look as Anna tucks back a strand of her hair, and then she's gone.

For a sector of *Dogs in Space*'s first audience embedded at a small but significant remove from its setting, period and milieu—that is, for me and my friends and kids like us—the film's textured surface was readable as a map. But a map for what? For what our lives were about to become? For what we needed to be wary of? For what we should simply laugh at?

At some point in my first years in the city, I had a brief relationship with a man who was a bit like Sam. What he sort of made up for with Byronic good looks he utterly lacked in any sense of humour. He called me (cringe) his little goth girl. That relationship ended abruptly. One night I bled onto his mattress, and when he woke me up to show me the extensive mess I did not feel the tiniest bit bad about it, because why had he thought it was okay to bring me into his bed without even putting a sheet on there? I went out to the living room and sat down on the couch next to Chris, who had come to Melbourne from Newcastle and lived in the room across the hall, and I described to him what had happened, and he laughed till tears ran down his cheeks. I last saw Chris a couple of months ago. We had lunch at the chintzy cafe across the road from where I work. As we walked back, I told him about this essay. 'Oh, *Dogs in Space*', he said. 'That's on point for us. That was the street where the cool people lived'.

Notes

1. S. Lec (1962) *Unkempt Thoughts* (New York: St. Martin's Press), p. 71.
2. L. Wittgenstein (1966) *Lectures and Conversations on Aesthetics, Psychology and Religious Belief* (Oxford: Blackwell), p. 51.
3. B. Butler and A. R. Jones-Dean (2019) 'Dogs in Space: The Melbourne Ticket Queue', Bowiedownunder.com., http://www.bowiedownunder.com/lowheroes/14.html, accessed 21 February 2019; S. Sejavka (2015) 'David Bowie and Me: Sam Sejavka on the Moment His Melbourne Changed Forever', *Melbourne Age*, 3 July, https://www.smh.com.au/entertainment/david-bowie-and-me-sam-sejavka-on-the-moment-his-melbourne-changed-forever-20150627-ghz1hc.html, accessed 24 January 2019.
4. D. Graney quoted in D. Nichols (2016) *Dig: Australian Rock and Pop Music, 1960–1985* (Portland: Verse Chorus), p. 404.
5. I. Arns and G. Horn (eds.) (2007) *History Will Repeat Itself: Strategies of Re-enactment in Contemporary (Media) Art And Performance* (Frankfurt am Main: Revolver Books), p. 43.

6. Morrissey (2013) *Autobiography* (London: Penguin), p. 64.
7. I. Penman (2017) 'Wham Bang, Teatime', *London Review of Books*, 39(1), 5 January, 10, 21–26.
8. F. Bongiorno (2015) *The Eighties: The Decade That Transformed Australia* (Collingwood: Black Inc.), p. 220.
9. C. J. Koch (1986) *The Doubleman* (London: Triad Grafton), p. 155.
10. D. McComb quoted in Nichols 2016, p. 395.
11. H. Bloom (1975) *A Map of Misreading* (Oxford: Oxford University Press), p. 68.
12. N. Overton (1986) *The Neon Eclipse* (Ringwood: Penguin), p. 23.
13. W. Tevis (1976) *The Man Who Fell to Earth* (London: Pan Books), p. 134.
14. G. Perec (1997) *Species of Spaces and Other Pieces* (London: Penguin), p. 38.
15. H. Garner (1980) *Honour and Other People's Children* (Melbourne: McPhee Gribble), p. 79.
16. F. Jameson (1991) *Postmodernism, or the Cultural Logic of Late Capitalism* (Durham: Duke University Press), p. 51.
17. R. Haese (2011) *Permanent Revolution: Mike Brown and the Australian Avant-Garde 1953–1997* (Carlton: Miegunyah), p. 138.
18. T. Allen (1995) *Roar, and Quieter Moments from a Group of Melbourne Artists 1980–1993* (Roseville: Craftsman House), p. 40.
19. R. Haese, M. Brown, and C. Nodrum (1995) *Power to the People: The Art of Mike Brown* (Melbourne: National Gallery of Victoria), p. 54.
20. Garner, p. 103.
21. P. K. Dick (1979) *Do Androids Dream of Electric Sheep?* (New York: Ballantine), p. 15.
22. Garner, p. 80.
23. Bongiorno, p. 224.
24. A. Bolin (2018) *Dead Girls: Essays on Surviving an American Obsession* (New York: HarperCollins).

'Someone's Been Fucking Using This for Meat Again': 18 Berry Street and Melbourne Sharehousing in the 1970s and 1980s

Molly McKew and Katherine Ellinghaus

The sharehouse depicted in *Dogs in Space* was inspired by director Richard Lowenstein's own experiences of sharehousing in inner in the 1970s, but it was also a real house.[1] 18 Berry Street, located in the inner eastern suburb of Richmond, reportedly sold for more than one million dollars in 2012, its price tag indicative of just how gentrified the suburb has become since the 1970s.[2] Lowenstein lived in the house during the 1970s with Sam Sejavka, lead singer of the band The Ears, on whom the band in the film is modelled. The house, like other aspects of the film (such as the death of the character Anna), has both a real and fictional status, which has only increased as the film has gained a "cult" following, and continues to be viewed and discussed. Using newly conducted interviews with sharehouse residents in 1970s and 1980s Melbourne, as well as memoir and secondary analysis, this chapter seeks to find precedents and contexts for the kind of housing

---

M. McKew
University of Melbourne, Parkville, VIC, Australia

K. Ellinghaus (✉)
La Trobe University, Melbourne, VIC, Australia
e-mail: k.ellinghaus@latrobe.edu.au

arrangement depicted in *Dogs in Space*. The history of the sharehouse as a pragmatic arrangement arising from rising student numbers, as well as a means to political ends, is also discussed. We show that while the *Dogs in Space* house is, in large part, an imaginary construct—indeed, for much of the film a kind of utopian fantasy—it is rooted in a post-war history of counterculture and inner-urban change, and a rite-of-passage familiar to many Australians since the 1960s.

The house in Dogs in Space is occupied by a group of punk musicians forming the band after which the film is named and a couple of other housemates: Luchio, an engineering student, and Jen, a feminist and vegetarian. Throughout the film, we see the main characters, Sam and his bandmates, and Sam's kind-of-girlfriend, Anna, attending gigs and parties, drinking, taking drugs, going on reckless drives, and in between these activities, lying around in the squirm-inducing grub of the sharehouse. Sam and his bandmates are childish and impulsive, and Sam is often depicted crawling on the floor or rolling on the ground with Anna, giggling. The penultimate scene of the film is that of Anna's death from a heroin overdose and sees Anna walking through the house to say goodbye to each housemate, finally leaving (to heaven?) in a glowing limo with an unusually well-coiffed Sam. In this house, the inconsistency of income streams, meals and basic hygiene are contrasted with the rigidity and stability of the outer suburban lifestyle. It seems as if only one of the inhabitants is studying or has any sort of routine, and Sam does not seem to eat unless Anna or his mother brings food to him. This wild contrast with the suburban home is illustrated in a scene where Anna, upset with Sam, drives to her family in the suburbs: a 1950s double-fronted brick home, conspicuously quiet aside from the soft flicker of the television and the chewing of scheduled lap meals.

The bumping together of different lifestyles within the intimate space of the shared home can be discerned throughout the film. Luchio is desperately studying for his engineering exams and attempting to resist the partying and casual sex culture surrounding him. Various people frequent the house, or perhaps live there, including a second-wave feminist who speaks often and earnestly about the patriarchy and male domination; an Aboriginal rights activist; a buff hippy who is always wearing yoga pants;

and a schoolgirl who never seems to leave, every now and again throwing coy looks at Sam. The different ways in which the characters live are apparent in several interactions: an early scene shows Sam skulking into the kitchen with a blanket around his shoulders, peering into his clean and healthy-looking housemate's cereal bowl, to which his housemate says "its food, it's been a long time since you've seen anything like this"; Luchio, the student, slams the door on a too-loud rehearsal muttering "fucking arseholes"; Jen, the vegetarian "hippy" throws a saucepan on the floor shouting "someone's been fucking using this for meat again"; and a business suit-clad Anna gets pulled into a bathtub by Sam on her way to a job interview. In this sharehouse, the film seems to say, you could meet diverse types of people and experiment with different types of lifestyles—and you could live your politics through your way of life—eschewing careerism, structure and expectations of marriage and family. *Dogs in Space* is about much more than hedonism and excess, but is a film that sheds light on the countercultures of the 1970s and the intimate political space of the sharehouse. In the house, a range of political sensibilities, lifestyles and kinds of young people coexist.

A viewer in 2020 can easily forget the political context in which this subculture arose and the way in which the lifestyles therein were challenging to the political status quo. The counterculture was significant because it both responded to and created huge cultural and social shifts through the politics of lifestyle. The ways in which the people in the *Dogs in Space* sharehouse lived were expressions of the politics of lifestyle—they are eschewing the 9-5 lifestyle, the moral puritanism of the post-war period, and their politics are present in their day-to-day interactions and living patterns. For the most part, *Dogs in Space* has been regarded by scholars as an unconventional cult film that attracted attention because of its encapsulation of the excesses of the punk subculture, its candid depiction of drug use and its famous lead actor. Most discussions of the film centre on punk music and drug use and very few focus on how this scene was part of the countercultures of the 1970s in general and the sociopolitical context of Melbourne's inner suburbs at that time.[3] Lesley Speed has examined the context of inner-urban gentrification and the rise of the creative communities of sharehouses that underpin the film. Speed highlights aspects of the Whitlam era as factors which underlie the viability of such a house and such a subculture, for example, free university education, liveable doles, affordable inner-urban rents and high unemployment rates. She draws attention to the inner-urban gentrification that happened in the 1970s and the emergence of the inner-urban, middle-class cosmopolitanite—the new creative, urban-dwelling middle class, of which the *Dogs in Space* sharehouse was a precursor.[4] Rebecca Harkins-Cross has also discussed the film's depiction of sharehousing. Harkins-Cross argues that "musical cred aside, it's the portrait of slummy sharehouses that bestowed *Dogs in Space* its cult status. This is a house that all Melburnians have lived in at some point, or at least gotten boozed at".[5]

This chapter aims to move beyond the depictions of sharehouse culture which only emphasise alcohol, drugs and grunge. By placing the film against the broader historical, political and cultural context of Melbourne's inner-urban countercultures in the 1970s, which precipitated the *Dogs in Space* sharehouse, we explore the extent to which the counterculture depicted in the film was a common political reaction to the conservatism of Australia during this period.

Sharehousing in Melbourne: 1960s–1980s

From the 1960s, due to rising university attendance, young people began to sharehouses in the suburbs surrounding Melbourne's universities. The hubs of activity at the time were initially Carlton and later Fitzroy, both close to the University of Melbourne, and Prahran in Melbourne's south, attracting young students from Monash University or Prahran Technical College. These sharehouses posed a moral challenge to 1950s conservatism, and inner-city areas gathered a reputation as the home of "trendies" or "hippies" who were experimenting with lifestyle. University student counsellor Ray Priestley articulated this when he said in 1964 that sharehouse lifestyles threatened students' health and academic progress:

> The outcome is a group of fringe dwellers who because of such things as under- nourishment, minor ailments, weariness, boredom, and homesickness lose their capacity to cope with their work or to respond in any active way to the challenges of undergraduate life. They become particularly

vulnerable to the temptations of the bottle, the pep pill, and in extreme cases to the dope pedlar.[6]

Throughout the 1960s and into the 1970s, an alternative lifestyle emerged in these inner-urban suburbs revolving around the arts, activism, partying and sharehousing. Self-exploration and independence from family was key, and for many young people, the sharehouse became a space to connect with those with similar values, and their primary support network. It is impossible to ascertain exactly how many sharehouses emerged in Australia in the 1960s and 1970s and where they were located, as group houses were only identified as a distinct category by the Australian Bureau of Statistics in 1986.[7] This period also saw an increase in the proportion of youth as part of the population and an emerging youth culture: between 1966 and 1971, the age group 20–24 had increased by 25%, and youth cultures were strengthened through an increasingly sophisticated and available media.[8] Sharehouses were the natural home of this youth culture and a place in which young people could create a life separate from the authority of parents. A 1986 study based on 1981 ABS census data on housing in Australia identified changing social expectations around marriage and home ownership as a factor leading to increasing shared housing. It found the incidence of shared accommodation rose from 13% in 1966 to around one-third of housing in 1981—though this includes homes shared with extended family, not merely unrelated adults. The study pinpointed five types of people who share with other adults, one of which was "people who desire to be in a communal setting for ideological reasons". Its authors conclude that "either for ideological or economic reasons, the Australian dream may not have the same allure as it did in the past or its realisation may have become more remote".[9] Many young people shared homes for purely financial or practical reasons, requiring a cheap place to live while at university or at work. Many others, though, shared homes because they were attracted to a particular subculture or ideological milieu. In these sharehouses, young people could discover pastimes and people they otherwise would not have encountered.

More often than not, sharehouses are depicted in pop culture as chaotic and transient, as places where sheltered young people encounter strange and magical characters, houses filled with drugs and alcohol and laced with dirt—as in *Dogs in Space*. These homes have been the subject of other well-known representations of Australia in this period. Helen Garner's 1977 novel *Monkey Grip* and its 1982 film adaption depict a young single mother, Nora, in love with the drug-addicted Javo, who drifts in and out of her communal homes in the inner north borrowing money for drugs, providing inconsistent love and eating her food. Nora's life consists of her writing in her diary, reading, swimming and going to gigs and parties. Similarly to *Dogs in Space, Monkey Grip* is remembered for its portrayal of sharehousing, drugs and partying more so than other aspects of the film (such as the fact that Nora was a resourceful single mother, feminist and was raising her child alone). Sharehousing was also infamously represented in Lowenstein's 2001 film *He Died with a Felafel in His Hand*, described by Luke Buckmaster in 2015 as a "beer-splattered kaleidoscope of communal living".[10] But these representations of the sharehouse lifestyle can obscure the context in which sharehousing arose and the political implications of this way of life. Many counterculturalists who lived in sharehouses had a genuine desire to put politics into practice to experiment with newer ways of living, in a sense taking responsibility for the changes they want in the world. While many sharehouses were occupied by people living chaotic, hedonistic lives, this does not mean these houses were devoid of genuine political sentiment and a conviction that this generation could challenge the strictures of the past.[11] For many young people, such houses were a way of exploring and living their progressive values. Advertisements in countercultural magazines like the *Living Daylights* often specified desired traits—people would advertise for gay housemates ("camp guy requires semi screaming queen"), vegetarian housemates ("peaceful type freaks") or those with "emotional openness". As Alex Griffin describes in his ode to the sharehouse in a 2014 essay: "The real freedom is the space to express yourself, to explore your own identity, outside of the surveillance of family. A room of one's own not just to write, but a house in which to create yourself".

Interviews with counterculturalists who lived in Melbourne's inner-urban suburbs in the 1960s and 1970s reflect this: "Bruce", for instance, remembers sharehousing as the beginning of his growth as an individual and as a political person—"[It] started my life. That would have been '74 I think, late '74. And then my whole world expanded ... oh so fast!"[12]

Other interviewees spoke about how pursuing a countercultural lifestyle touched the most minute and intimate parts of day-to-day life; down to what they wore' their relationship with their family; what and where they ate; and the language they used. One, Suzanna, said that as soon as she moved to Carlton, she knew she had to start wearing black, and would not have dreamed of eating supermarket-bought breakfast foods like cornflakes. Instead her and her friends ate muesli thinking that they were, as she said, "changing the world one bloody cup of rolled oats at a time!"[13] It is in sharehouses that an intimate politics was performed, where lifestyle choices became symbolic of a critique of the status quo, or of the kind of world people wanted to inhabit.

Interviewees described shared homes with various degrees of structure. Some were transient, loosely organised homes where housemates drifted in and out, and some were structured collectives motivated by politics or particular ideologies, and where there were regular meetings, rosters and shared resources such as bulk foods and even childcare. Many houses were somewhere in between—where housemates shared some sort of political or ideological connection, and communal dinners and a kitty for groceries was the norm. Interviewees described a variety of households: gay, lesbian separatist, actor, anarchist, musician and communist houses.

In structured collective homes, the politics of lifestyle was made explicit, and often the minutiae of everyday life were placed under political scrutiny. One interviewee, Sofia, was part of an economic union, made up of a network of sharehouses in Fitzroy who pooled their incomes and redistributed the money between the members each week. Each Thursday, one of these houses would host a shared vegetarian dinner, the treasurer would ask each household what they needed for the coming week, and the money would be distributed accordingly. Most people in this union were artists and actors, and Sofia recalled that there was no resentment at sharing income because they all believed in each others' hard work and artistic ambition: "it was a sort of a communitarian community where you do art, it was saying that art wasn't for the elite and it was for everyone". However, Sofia does recall heavy and intricate discussions of things like whether somebody really needed new dining chairs—each member had to request how much money they needed for the week and justify it. Further, this collective was motivated in part by environmentalism and distributed bulk food goods, meaning any wasteful behaviour was frowned upon.[14]

Laila lived in structured communal shared homes in Carlton and Fitzroy in the early 1970s. In 1974, she published an article in *Farrago*, the University of Melbourne student newspaper, in which she wrote: "to me, the way people live is political. What most people see as a 'natural' way to live, in a family, with private property and privatised lives, is in fact, a value judgement imposed by a dominant middle-class culture and ideology".[15] Forty-three years later, Laila reflected on her years living in communal houses in Melbourne and Sydney. The houses she lived in were conscious collectives that were created with the intention of sharing resources and providing an alternative to the nuclear family. For Laila, these sharehouses were a way of creating a way of life that answered to her values, somewhere where women and men could mutually support each other in their personal (e.g. childrearing) and political pursuits. There were many house meetings:

> We had rosters, we had rosters for everything, we had rosters for the kids, there were often men, husbands or fathers were still around, they might be living in another alternative house, there were new relationships, and all of that was up for discussion. And the most conscious, there were two households like that for two years and it was run a bit like a military machine I have to say.[16]

Actress and singer Jane Clifton also lived in collective houses in this period. She was involved in an actor's collective, the Australian Performing Group, and lived in an associated collective house, a towering structure next door to the Pram Factory theatre. She emphasises the structured and communal elements of her home; her memoir, *The Address Book*, discusses the ways in which the politics of these spaces put communalism and sharing above individual privacy and ownership. As she says, "you were never alone in the tower, even when you wanted to be". She describes the politics behind the lack of privacy: "privacy was of course, a bourgeois concept and people barged in and out, willy-nilly, to use the toilet while you were in the shower or bath, and vice versa. You learned not to give a shit".[17]

These experiments with collective living were seen as politically important, and tense meetings in which very personal material was discussed were a feature of many shared homes in this era. Because many structured communal homes were run by consensus, housemates had to discuss elements of their personal lives honestly and in great detail. Of these homes, Laila says "there was some heated discussion. But in the end there wasn't any bad feeling … we might ask someone to leave, if they didn't fit in or something like that".[18] The personal challenges required to live collectively were seen as symptomatic of the individualistic ways in which most people had been brought up and thus challenging personal behaviour was acceptable because it had a broader political purpose.

Some sharehouses, on the other hand, were on the other end of the spectrum and were more unstructured and haphazard shared spaces, where political goals were not necessarily shared and nor were resources. Gina, who shared a home in Fitzroy in the 1970s, articulated her preference for this model of sharehousing:

> I am not attracted, and still not attracted to anything structured. What I did was kind of organic. People were individuals within a house and their individuality was respected. If people have particular peccadilloes you just respect it. So no, the idea of a commune intellectually I agree with, but it wouldn't be for me… The way the house was, people could live their own lives, they could be who they wanted to be, they weren't forced into a particular set of rules.[19]

Despite the fact that they were not explicit political collectives, politics and ideas often permeated the space of these houses. Interviewees revealed that shared values and intellectual connection—whether this was intentionally sought out—were in fact important to the atmosphere of the house. When pressed, Gina said that all the people who lived in that house were left-wing, artistic people—theatre performances were put on in the space for nights on end, and often meals were shared. I also asked Sarah, who lived above a fruit shop in Lygon Street in the 1960s whether her home was communal—and although she says it wasn't, it is clear that intellectual connection was important to the atmosphere of the space:

Nah, we just sort of... I think we weren't really, we just shared the house, we didn't share much apart from arguing over the kitchen table, arguing about something, about how we were going to organise people to be taught better, how they should be taught from the age of two, should the state take over or not.... We had these wonderful arguments... one of the young women there was an early education specialist... we had all the answers in the world then.

For most people, intellectual connection, sharing ideas and food, and hosting visitors and conversations were central to the enjoyment of sharehousing. The joys of discussing politics and being expressive, open and opinionated were articulated in some interviews. Many spoke about being attracted to a lifestyle and a space where the conversations were "real" and there was intellectual liveliness, and contrasted this with their family homes where conversations were superficial and concerns were individualistic. Bruce, who moved 25 km north from Parkdale to Carlton in 1973, said he was attracted to Carlton because he liked that there was a culture of "displaying what you believe".[20] Many counterculturalists also spoke positively about living in a milieu where no one was "told" what to do and there was no pressure to follow the conservative life trajectory of earning a good wage, marriage, children and home ownership.

Thus, in shared homes, lifestyle choices and day-to-day habits (including living in a sharehouse in the first place) were indicative of one's broader politics and were a way of resisting conservatism. Hence Sarah's insistence on eating muesli, Clifton's reminder that you couldn't just close your bedroom door, and the countercultural preference for market shopping, European foods, and Italian wine and coffee were political as well as personal choices. Eating the food of migrants was not only convenient because the counterculture shared space with migrants in these innerurban suburbs—but it signified a progressive mindset and a cosmopolitan and communitarian outlook. Radical activist Michael Hyde describes well his fascination with the cultured ways in which his new housemates in a communist household near Monash University in the late 1960s ate:

> These people cooked beef casseroles with red wine and small black things called olives, ate European rye bread with caraway seeds, and bought six different kinds of cheese from the Prahran market (where was the Kraft

cheddar?) .... My new tribe did not eat spaghetti, especially not out of a tin. They bought something called pasta, sometimes dried and sometimes flat strips of freshly made egg pasta, which also came in squat tubes and long sticks. And they could cook.[21]

Sharehouses within these countercultural spaces were diverse and varied—but what bound them was that they were resisting conservative pressures through a lived politics. They were creating a new way of life through a series of lifestyle choices that revolved around shared space and shared food, intellectual stimulation, self-expression, an aversion to mass-produced products and an eschewal of careerism and material gain. Clearly, the *Dogs in Space* sharehouse was unstructured, chaotic and hedonistic. The lifestyles of those who lived there varied—but each lived in a way that was true to their own values—there was no overarching authority dictating to anyone how they should live in the space.

Dogs in Space depicts a particular type of sharehouse in the countercultural milieu. Drugs are a large feature of the house, as is dirt, parties and general chaos, contrasting with other modes of countercultural sharehouse living that were more structured, organised, political collectives. However, perhaps Lowenstein was showcasing something that was more than hedonistic, glamourous and childish, but is depicting an era where lifestyle choices were political, as the ubiquitous 1970s slogan, "the personal is political" proclaimed. Sharehouses in this era were spaces in which you could experiment with a progressive lifestyle and eschew conservative pressures—in the *Dogs in Space* sharehouse the partying, music and drugs meant much more than pure hedonism.

Both Lowenstein, the director, and Sejavka, on whom the film is based, have suggested that the depiction of drugs and hedonism in the film have overshadowed acknowledgement of the political context of the 1970s. In a blog post, Sejavka recalls doing interviews with Lowenstein for the documentary film *We're Living on Dog Food* which was included in the 2009 DVD release of Dogs in Space. He admits to being sceptical about whether the subculture surrounding the house was truly unique, noting that all youth movements carry a similar energy and excitement. But after the interview with Lowenstein, he "began to suspect that there might really have been a special something about the scene back then". He explains:

> Twenty-five years ago, it was a smaller, greyer, far more conservative city. There were no street cafes. Restaurants rarely had bars and you could count on two hands the number of 24-hour establishments. You'd be hassled for wearing hats in pubs and chastised by war veterans for wearing second hand medals on the tram. You could get beaten up as a poofter for wearing anything even remotely peculiar. The only alternative scenes were the sluggish festering hippies in Carlton and Fitzroy, a gaggle of Maori drag-queens in Fitzroy St, and the tribes of skinheads and sharpies in Holmesglen and Bayswater. Musical offerings included pub rock, more pub rock and maybe a bit of flaccid folk rock … Because the city was smaller, because it was so disobliging of strangeness, there was a tendency for the weirdos to find each other and congregate for safety.

Sejavka reminds us that the "weirdness" of the group of people and the way in which their embrace of eccentricity, diversity and creativity represented a real, and political, challenge to conservatism. These inner-urban countercultural communities were spaces of comfort and respite for those who felt alienated by conservatism. He uses this example:

> An example I like to use involves the freakish hair colours most of us sported to varying degrees. In the Melbourne of 1980, if you caught sight of someone across the street with dyed purple hair, the odds were you'd know them. The scene was that small. Today, well, you wouldn't bother looking twice.[22]

In an interview with Sally Hussey, Lowenstein echoes these sentiments:

> A lot of people forget how conservative the seventies actually were. You see it now in hindsight: "the hippies happened; there was the sexual revolution, society was pretty liberal". It wasn't. The mainstream society in 1979, especially in Australia, was incredibly conservative.[23]

By reading Lowenstein's film in the context of the social changes of the 1970s—a rising student population, a bourgeoning counterculture, the emergence of shared housing and resulting changes to the inner-urban space—we can discern more than simply a depiction of drugs and excess. By exploring the social and political context in which the *Dogs in Space* sharehouse arose, it is clear that houses such as these represented challenges to the mainstream. These houses were independent spaces in which young people could explore various interests, create art, connect with those with similar creative or intellectual interests and, at least for a time, eschew the twin conservative pressures of career and family. The depiction of the Berry Street sharehouse was borne out of a countercultural movement that both responded to and created cultural and social change through everyday lifestyle. Lowenstein's film is thus much more than a film about drugs and hedonism, but demonstrates the ways in which the day-to-day lives of subcultures or activists during this period, and the houses in which they found each other, worked to challenge the conservatism of post-war Australia.

Notes

1. G. Stanton (2017) 'Dog Days: The Making of Dogs in Space', *FilmInk*, 22 November.
2. S. Fitzsimons (2012) 'Dogs in Space Share House Up for Sale for $1 Million', *The Music*, 2 October, http://themusic.com.au/news/all/2012/10/02/dogs-in-space-house-up-for-sale/.
3. Literature from cultural publications such as *Film Ink* have discussed the intentions behind Lowenstein's film, issues with representing drug use, and distinguishing fact from fiction, e.g. S. Hussey (2009) 'Punk Moments: A Conversation with Richard Lowenstein', *Metro Magazine: Media and Education Magazine*, 162, 157–159, and Stanton (2017) mentioned above. Other articles discuss the initial reaction to the film when it was released in 1986, and particularly its R rating (M. Kitson [2004] 'Saskia and Hutch: Doggy Style', 1 June). Other literature focuses on the punk scene of Melbourne in the late 1970s, and the drugs and alcohol therein, reflecting on the hedonism of this particular subculture and the extent to which *Dogs in Space* is a romanticised, uncritical representation of this (K. Bail [1987] 'Putting the Bite into Dogs in Space', *Cinema Papers*, 61, January, 7). Some argue, like David Nichols and Sophie Perillo in *The Conversation*, that these criticisms are not warranted, and that the film is a useful and

meaningful picture of a unique era (D. Nichols and S. Perillo [2016] 'Friday Essay: Dogs in Space, 30 Years on—A Once Maligned Film Comes of Age', *The Conversation*, 15 April).
4. L. Speed (2009) 'Win or Lose: Subculture and Social Difference in Dogs in Space', *Metro*, 162, September, 160–165.
5. R. Harkins-Cross (2013) 'Punks in Share Houses, Dogs in Space', *Lifted Brow*, 17, April.
6. G. Davison (2009) 'Carlton and the Campus: The University and the Gentrification of Inner Melbourne 1958–75', *Urban Policy and Research*, 27(3), 255.
7. Sophie McNamara and John Connell (2007) 'Homeward Bound? Searching for Home in Inner Sydney's Share Houses', *Australian Geographer*, 38(1), 71–91.
8. S. Blackburn (ed.) (2015) *Breaking Out: Memories of Melbourne in the 1970s* (Willoughby: Hale and Iremonger), p. 10.
9. Edwards et al.'s 1986 research on the emergence of shared housing in Australia from the *Journal of Population Research* sampled 4560 households from the 1981 ABS census data, finding that one-third of all households were sharehouses, an increase from 13% in 1966. The ABS definition, however, included financially independent adults living with parents or other family members and elderly parents living with their adult children. They also found that non-family adults sharing residences were 73% under 30, and men and women were equally represented in these houses. The study identifies five factors that have resulted in increasing numbers of shared homes, one of them "people who desire to live in a communal setting for ideological reasons". P. Edwards, J. Jones, and J. Edwards (1986) 'The Social Demography of Shared Housing', *Journal of Population Research*, 3, 130. Craig Maher's "Building Activity and Socio-Economic Change in Inner Melbourne 1961–1981" shows that there was a rise in smaller and non-family households in the inner suburbs in the 20 years between 1961 and 1981, and that marriage rates in inner-urban suburbs declined from 42 to 34%. This illustrates the changing demographic of the inner-urban space and the increasing numbers of non-married young people in the inner-urban space. C. Maher (1985) 'Building Activity and Socio-Economic Change in Inner Melbourne 1961–1981', *Urban Policy and Research*, 3(1), 3–12.
10. L. Buckmaster (2015) 'He Died with a Felafel in His Hand Rewatched—A Tour of Sharehouse Excess', *Guardian*, 1 May, https://www.theguardian.

com/film/2015/may/01/he-died-with-a-felafel-in-his-hand-rewatched-a-tour-of-sharehouse-excess.
11. There has been some work on shared housing in memoir and reflective essay. Lyndal Walker has examined her own experiences sharehousing in her 20s (L. Walker [2012] 'Share Houses', *Meanjin*, 71(4), 60–67), Alex Griffin reflects on the legacy of sharehousing in *Voiceworks* (A. Griffin [2016] 'A Brief History and a Short Future of the Imaginary Sharehouse', *Voiceworks*, 104, 19–25) and Fiona Wright does the same in an essay published in the *Sydney Review of Books* (F. Wright [2017] "Perhaps This One Will Be My Last Share House", *Sydney Review of Books*, https://sydneyreviewofbooks.com/perhaps-this-one-will-be-my-last-sharehouse/). These pieces reflect on the legacy of the sharehouse lifestyle and also touch on gentrification, reflecting on the economic tide that pushed working class and migrant populations out of the suburbs that they now enjoy, and the coming tides of young professionals or "yuppies" that now push their creative middle class further from the city. There has also been some work on the importance of shared housing in histories and sociologies of subcultures and countercultures—though much of this is not in an Australian context. Stephen Vider's research published in the *Journal of Gender and History* looks at the emergence of gay communal living in the US context in the late 1960s and 1970s, arguing that "although largely neglected in most accounts of 1970s gay politics and culture, communal living – sharing a house, an apartment or land – was widely discussed and practiced as a central strategy of gay male liberation" (S. Vider [2015] 'The Ultimate Extension of Gay Community: Communal Living and Gay Liberation in the 1970s', *Gender & History*, 27(3), 865). There is some work on the importance of communal and shared homes for gay and lesbian people in this period; however, this research has not extended into a more general discussion of the importance of communal and shared homes for countercultures in general.
12. Bruce interviewed by Molly McKew, Melbourne, 4 June 2018.
13. Sarah interviewed by Molly McKew, Clifton Hill, 4 July 2018.
14. Sofia interviewed by Molly McKew, Fitzroy, 20 June 2018.
15. L. Fanebust (1974) 'Beginnings', *Farrago*, 52, 20.
16. L. Fanebust interviewed by Molly McKew, Footscray, 17 February 2017.
17. J. Clifton (2011) *The Address Book: A Memoir About My Homes* (Camberwell: Penguin), p. 296.
18. L. Fanebust interviewed by McKew.
19. Gina interviewed by Molly McKew, North Fitzroy, Victoria, 15 June 2017.

20. Bruce interviewed by McKew.
21. M. Hyde (2010) *All Along the Watchtower* (Carlton North: The Vulgar Press), p. 23.
22. S. Sejavka (2009) "The Resurrection of Dogs in Space," *Sails of Oblivion*, 6 May, http://sailsofoblivion.blogspot.com/2009/05/resurrection-of-dogs-in-space.html, accessed 9 June 2019.
23. S. Hussey (2009) 'Punk Moments: A Conversation with Richard Lowenstein', *Metro Magazine: Media and Education Magazine*, 162, 157–159.

Richmond and 18 Berry Street Revisited

James Lesh and David Nichols

In 1969, when Frank and Annemarie Mutton moved house, they were unconventional amongst middle-aged Melbourne couples. Annemarie (née Annmarie Böhn) had been born in Munich in 1919 and came to Australia in 1938. Her second husband was Frank, a unionist, educator and a fitter and turner.[1] Their mixed backgrounds (he was Anglo-Australian, she ethnically Jewish), their communist sympathies, activism and dedication to community and anti-war movements[2] were not, however, the most unusual thing about them. To the perturbation of their friends, the Muttons had committed a bizarre act: they had moved to Bowen Street, Richmond from elegant East Melbourne (just one suburb away).

J. Lesh (✉)
School of Architecture, Design and Planning, University
of Sydney, Camperdown, NSW, Australia
e-mail: james.lesh@sydney.edu.au

D. Nichols
University of Melbourne, Parkville, VIC, Australia
e-mail: nicholsd@unimelb.edu.au

This chapter is an exploration of two interrelated facets of Richmond's changing face in the 1970s, as it metamorphosed from an extensive period as a suburb of apparent slums and endemic poverty to exhibiting the initial signs of gentrification and wealth for which it is better-known today. About two kilometres east of the city centre, Richmond was one of Melbourne's first settled suburbs (since the 1830s) and was still generally known as a working-class neighbourhood in the late twentieth century. Set and filmed between 1978 and 1986, *Dogs in Space* provides an opening to discuss twin directives of Richmond's gentrification related to that of consumption, specifically the embrace of historic environments by upwardly mobile social groups and the imposition of conservation controls to retain those historic environments.[3] During the 1970s–1980s, Richmond transitioned from condemning to embracing its nineteenth-century streetscapes and structures. People in Richmond, in turn, sought to retain those aesthetics and forms through the imposition of heritage protections, including for the Berry Street area and specifically Number 18. This chapter examines the presentation of Richmond's heritage in *Dogs in Space*, and the real-world measures taken to retain that heritage by residents and conservationists either decade of the film's release in 1986.

Identifying Urban Heritage in *Dogs in Space*

Notoriously, the legend of the production of *Dogs in Space* is bound to the rise of property values and the related social changes in Richmond in the years prior to 1986. The Berry Street area itself was saved and conserved in the early 1970s for its Victoria-era heritage, as will be discussed below. The desire was to make the film in the heritage-listed Number 18 Berry Street, which had served as a share house in the early 1980s for some of the people who inspired the film's characters: Sam Sejavka described it in 2009 as 'that ratty, shambolic, dangerous, vigorous household of ancient Richmond'.[4] It was also, in itself, a particularly striking building, and its position on a T-junction allowed cinematographer Andrew de Groot to plan effective and striking camera angles from the exterior.

The film does not explore Richmond as a terrain in the way that (for instance) *Spotswood* (1992) does for Melbourne's inner west or *Head On*

(1997) for the city at large. Only a few of the locations outside the house, and the T-junction of Berry and Eucalyptus Streets, are identifiable as Richmond. That said, Richmond as a locale is important, in part for what it was not. Carlton, Fitzroy and St Kilda were the famous inner-city cultural hubs of late 1970s Melbourne. Despite the presence of, firstly, Highett Street's Kingston Hotel (where the Pelaco Brothers operated a pub rock venue in the mid-1970s) and, secondly, the Tiger Lounge in Bridge Road, Richmond was nevertheless another place.

Richmond was (and is) a liminal space in Melbourne's geographies. It was neutral territory between those that lived north and south of the Yarra River, avoiding the north–south dichotomy discussed in *We're Living on Dog Food* (2009). Despite bordering East Melbourne and being the entranceway to the leafy eastern suburbs, it belonged to eastern Melbourne in name only. Notably Mick Lewis, Cathy McQuade, Tim McLaughlan and Sam Sejavka, key members of the Ears, all came from Melbourne's eastern suburbs and many of the most important developments in the evolution of The Ears took place in what might be considered the deeply middle-class environs of Wattletree Road, Malvern. In short, Richmond is appropriately atypical for the *Dogs in Space* story. It should also be noted that Sam Sejavka had moved from the Berry Street house to a flat in Milton Street, Elwood, by February 1981. The following month Christine Harding (on whom Saskia Post's character, Anna, is based on in the film) died in the Milton Street flat.[5]

Pioneers and Politics in 1970s Richmond

When the Muttons moved to Richmond they were, of course, pioneers.[6] Their peers were families such as that of Philip Andrews, a British-born Anglican minister. Andrews, his wife and four children were following a grand and for many humbling traditions. The Andrews family chose to live in public housing in the area, a sacrifice which, of course, meant one less home for those who could not afford one. These educated and/or middle-class arrivals in Richmond were treading in a world still in many ways marked by the desperate poverty Janet McCalman records so eloquently in her oral history portrait of Richmond, *Struggletown* (1984).[7] They endured what Andrews called, in a talk he gave for ABC Radio in 1973, 'the wacky, warped and smugly benevolent comments all of us who live here have to endure from people who somehow think they are better off'.[8]

As Annemarie writes, mainstream leftist politics in 1960s Melbourne was commandeered from Richmond: Jim Cairns, one of Labour's most prominent and promising federal politicians, lived in nearby Hawthorn 'but the Richmond Town Hall was his base'.[9] Clyde Holding, the leader of the state's Labour party, and opposition leader from 1967 to 1976, lived seven minutes' walk from Bowen St in Waltham Street (itself 100 metres from 18 Berry Street).[10] This political sphere, crucial to state and national party functioning for the left, was described in official City of Richmond history as 'colourful and parochial'[11] but it might more accurately be described as corrupt. The corruption also spread to local government and the 'Richmond municipal "bumbles"' as one letter-writer, C. A. Loughnan, described them in 1924 were often regarded as moribund, self-interested and unwilling to act in the interests of its residents except in the most broad-brushed and reactive of ways.[12] Fifty years after Loughnan's disparaging comment, the best that could be said about Richmond's council, perhaps, was said by Andrews—himself an A.L.P. supporter—in 1973: 'They are just a group of old people who don't know what the issues are'.[13]

Richmond was slower to gentrify than many other inner-city suburbs of Melbourne. In 1974, University of Melbourne architectural historian George Tibbits set students the task of assessing statistical data on Richmond against stereotypical assumptions about the stigmatised area:

> That it is inhabited by a high proportion of low income earners, recipients of social service benefits, single men etc., that in the last twenty years its population has declined (except where Housing Commission flats have been built) and the proportion of owner occupied dwellings has increased, the turnover of tenants has been rapid, and the poorer occupants are being displaced by higher income groups.[14]

One student, G. Gilmour, chose to survey an area within Hoddle, Lennox, Bridge and Victoria Streets—that is, directly north of Berry Street. Some of the author's findings can no doubt be applied to the late 1970s situation depicted in *Dogs in Space*. Examples include the revelation that only half the dwellings in the target area contained residents who owned cars, marking the Berry Street household—with its embarrassment of VW beetle riches—as an anomaly.[15] Others, such as that the area had a high proportion of single people[16]—specifically, single *men*, an ill-defined category probably meant to indicate divorced, separated or unlikely to marry. In this, they are difficult to distinguish from those who were yet to be exposed to any such choices. Another student surmised that Richmond had not only a high proportion of separated and divorced men, but *also* a high proportion of single men over 21.[17]

Gilmour found minor, circumstantial evidence of professionals living in 'trendy' housing stock in the area.[18] We see very little evidence of such people in *Dogs in Space*, but Annemarie and Frank exemplified this rising and, in many respects, new social strand. Shortly after moving to Richmond, Annemarie was delighted to make a likeminded friend who had moved from down-at-heel North Melbourne to straitened Richmond: Anthea Eyres. An English-born nurse, Eyres and her architect husband David were living in Erin Street, parallel to Bowen. They had struck the template for Melbourne's inner-urban activism in the mid-1960s when, in tandem with the local church and some self-categorised middle-class residents in that suburb, they helped found the North Melbourne Association. Anthea and Annemarie quickly became core members of another inner-urban activist group, the Richmond Association.

As Annemarie writes in one of two short memoirs penned late in life:

> As soon as we arrived... we were invited to attend a meeting at Anthea and David Eyres' in Erin Street... Their front room was filled with people all there to discuss the proposed building of a second Housing Commission block of flats. Several cottages had to be demolished, people to be displaced. High rise buildings were to house families newly arrived from all corners of the world and Australian-born, endemically disadvantaged families as well.
>
> Amongst the people who gathered in that front room were those who opposed these developments for purely economic reasons. They had bought houses in an inner suburb for convenience, renovated and embellished existing old housing stock. Commission buildings threatened their investment.[19]

Mutton and Eyres were untiring; the Richmond Association's first and most important duty (in its members' eyes) was the defence of older housing from the redevelopment programmes of the state Housing Commission. ('If you want to pick a fight in Richmond, just walk down any street and say you are from the Housing Commission', Clyde Holding told the *Melbourne Age* in 1970).[20] Perhaps befitting Richmond's reputed 'roughness' (though not reflecting the relatively genteel Association, which for Mutton was 'motivated by a mixture of idealism, humanism and realism')[21] the resistance to the Housing Commission in north Richmond was zealous. Mutton writes of the Association's assistance to 32-year-old Antonia Georgiopoulos, a Richmond homeowner who sought to prevent the compulsory purchase and demolition of her home by the Housing Commission:

> The going became tough. Police protected the removalists, we took the furniture back. In this midst of this was the Greek woman and her three boarders. She owned her house, the compensation from the Housing Ministry was insufficient to rehouse herself, certainly not in the area.
>
> When we knew we had lost, we marched to the Commission offices and stormed in. We all said our piece, we were incensed, inflamed by an overriding power in our own humanity.[22]

If Lowenstein addresses any aspect of 'people power' in *Dogs in Space* it is to parody it, not least in the group speak of the unimaginative political activists who visit the Berry Street house. These individuals are railing against society, rather than local issues, but for Lowenstein the realities of both disadvantage and resistance in Melbourne's inner city across the twentieth century were well-known and understood. His activist, historian mother Wendy, was the author of one of Australia's best-known and loved oral histories, *Weevils in the Flour*. When that book was published, in 1978, she was, it was reported:

> Working at the Richmond Community Education Centre under a grant from the Schools Commission to assemble resource material to stimulate an interest int eh district by the community and local schools.[23]

Lowenstein's previous two notable films, *Evictions* and *Strikebound*, derived from his mother's works, dealt with staunch activism in the face of institutionally derived force. But while he chose, arguably with good cause, to ignore local politics, and deride political rhetoric (The Ears had 'zero political conscience', he says in the first of the director's commentary tracks on the 2009 DVD release) in favour of a series of universal stories set in an atmosphere of inchoate rebellion and (small 'a') anarchy. Nevertheless, the Richmond of *Dogs in Space* contrasts effectively with the suburb of forty years earlier, a connection made comprehensively by Wendy Lowenstein in 1978:

> It's similar today with the unemployed... People who tell the kids today that they 'battled and got through' and that the kids aren't really trying, forget that they were employed in the Depression because they were young and cheap... Today I hear young academics talking about how everyone helped each other. Nonsense. Family relationships were strained or fell apart... There was an erosion of human rights and dignity...[24]

The claim, therefore, that Lowenstein located his film in Berry Street Richmond because it was the place where he lived with Sam Sejavka in the early 1980s is, of course, correct. However, it does a disservice to Lowenstein to imply that his imagination was limited to this historical reality or that *Dogs in Space* is some kind of documentary-romance hybrid. Lowenstein had extensive understanding of the Richmond's history as a down-at-heel slum, and his comment on one of the *Dogs in Space* commentary tracks, where he suggests one actor represents an oral historian documenting the Little Bands scene, is a doffing of his cap to both his mother's profession and work, and shows that his film portrays 'what it feels like when a subculture appears', as he remarks elsewhere in this book.

Paying a Visit to 18 Berry Street

The fortunes and functions of the Berry Street area, including Number 18, mirrored that of the suburb more generally. Sections of the area were some of the suburb's more-distinguished pockets due to its associations with notable colonial individuals, though less than a two minute walk away was found industrial and manufacturing niches. On the northern side of Richmond Hill, Berry Street cuts between Waltham and Church Streets, and frames northern side of Hodgson Terrace (named after the colonial-era politician James Hodgson). To the north Bridge Road—a long and popular shopping strip—runs parallel (the proximity of Berry Street to this street is apparent in the scene of Little Mark (Martii Coles) buying ephedrine at the chemist at no. 224). The basic street layout of this part of Richmond had been established by 1853, within a couple of decades of Melbourne's establishment in 1835 and at the beginning of the gold rush (1851–1960s).[25] Few permanent structures had been constructed along these streets in the 1860s[26] but by the 1880s, the Marvellous Melbourne economic boom period, however, this part of Richmond had been built up with a mixture of factories, shops and housing for wealthy and working-class people.[27]

As with Richmond, the Berry Street area was a mixed industrial and residential area. Its mansions were built by and for gold diggers and merchants and its terraces by property speculators for the blue-collar working classes. Within close proximity of the residences were small scale industry, allowing both white- and blue-collar workers a short commute by foot between home and work. By the 1970s, this pattern of development and way of life had been consistent for almost a century. A notable change might be noted in the publication of Brian Carroll and Arno Roger-Genersh's *Richmond and East Melbourne Sketchbook* in 1976: there were already 115 'sketchbooks' of historical sites throughout Australasia and the publishers, Rigby, had covered Fiji before it was deemed appropriate to set foot in Richmond. What is notable, of course, is that this Sketchbook covered both Richmond and its far more bourgeois cousin to Melbourne's east: the times for Richmond were changing.[28] In 1980, urban historian Graeme Davison—who had only the previous year published his trailblazing study of 1880s Victorian-era Melbourne, *The rise and fall of Marvellous Melbourne*—prepared a historically themed walking tour of Richmond within an edited collection called *Melbourne on Foot*. Davison concluded his Richmond walk around the Berry Street area and described how the surrounding blocks were 'cut into smaller allotments with narrow street access and covered with rows of cheap wooden cottages'.[29] He even identified 18 Berry Street: 'The two-storey wooden house facing Eucalyptus Street (1889) shows the efforts of one speculative builder to make the most of his small plot of land'.[30]

Sites from the Berry Street area appear across the film. The most obvious of these is the house itself. It was built in 1886 for Henry Frencham (1816–97), whose wealth was a result of gold prospecting.[31] He claimed to have discovered the Bendigo goldfield in 1851.[32] Frencham chose to commission a two-storey timber terrace, unusual because the 1880s Melbourne boom-era houses were typically constructed from brick. Perhaps Frencham had less means available to him than it would at first appear—after all, he was seeking reparations for his apparent Bendigo find in the 1880s—or, may have simply preferred the timber style. Unlike Number 28, a relatively large and unique structure for the Berry Street area, many of the nearby properties are single-storey timber homes. Some of the larger and smaller buildings were of the 1850s, some were speculative 1880s working-class terraces as on Waltham Place, and others were twentieth-century infill constructions.

The Berry Street area also contained industry. The Pelaco Factory and its neon sign in Goodwood Street on the northern side of Waltham Street make many appearances in the movie, for instance; in his 2009 commentary with Ollie Olsen, Lowenstein refers to it briefly as 'famous'. The Pelaco Factory replaced the 1850s mansion 'Richmond Hill' (built for merchant James Henry) in 1928.[33] Neon signs were a notable feature of modern twentieth-century manufacturing industry across Richmond, and Melbourne more generally. One of the most famous of these, today, is the Skipping Girl Vinegar sign on Victoria Street in Richmond, which is still lit at night, unlike the Pelaco sign. Due to its location on Richmond Hill, the Pelaco factory and its sign were visible across the suburb, a landmark and a way-finder for Berry Street-area residents. For the music scene, the Pelaco sign had an even stronger resonance. The Pelaco Brothers, a mid-1970s Melbourne music phenomenon, took its name directly from the brand, its distinct 'Australianness' and perhaps, the local ubiquity of the sign. It is unclear whether, when Lowenstein cast Joe Camilleri as the angry Berry Street neighbour in *Dogs in Space* he was aware that Camilleri had been a member of the group. Although the factory building is now an apartment block, the sign—its neon tubes functioning once again after extended neglect—is on the Victorian Heritage Register, for its putative 'historical and social significance to the State of Victoria'.[34]

In the 1970s, the Berry Street area was considered ripe for urban renewal. Areas that integrated residential and industrial functions, and indeed Victorian-era areas generally, were out of favour with authorities. The City of Richmond appointed UDPA Planners to consider redeveloping the Berry Street area and so the firm began making inquiries in 1972.[35] The desire to knock down and rebuild nineteenth-century neighbourhoods was common across Melbourne in the 1960s and 1970s. Historic environments such as Berry Street were assumed to be slums in need of comprehensive redevelopment. The most comprehensive instances of urban renewal—that which the Richmond Association were seeking to foil in the early 1970s—were undertaken by the Housing Commission of Victoria, whereby entire suburban blocks were levelled for high-rise modernist-style, pre-fabricated, concrete social housing.[36] Richmond was no exception, and four high-rise social housing project towers were brought to fruition within the municipality. These brand-new buildings transformed Richmond's skyline, joining older landmarks such as the Pelaco sign. The new buildings also increased Richmond's population for the first time in decades; it had been in decline as residents died or aspired to new standalone homes further out in the suburbs.

Five years before the action begins in *Dogs in Space* 18 Berry Street was, in any case, decreed safe from the threat of Housing Commission redevelopment. This may in part have been because Clyde Holding lived nearby, although noted activist, architect, minister and, later, Labour Minister Andrew McCutcheon claimed in 1981 to have successfully campaigned, in the previous decade, against a 'demolition bid' by the Commission against Berry St specifically.[37] The progressive federal Whitlam Government was not six months old when Holding approached Tom Uren, the Minister for Urban and Regional Development, to suggest that the block within Darlington Parade, Bridge Road and Church and Waltham Streets be a guinea pig for the government's first foray into 'community planning'. Residents—many of whom had resisted repairing or restoring their nineteenth-century homes lest the Housing Commission compulsorily purchase them for renewal projects—would now be given the opportunity to renovate.

Indeed, the specific attempt to renew Berry Street went nowhere. It was 1972 and the passion for comprehensive renewal and high-rise housing was waning. Finance would soon dry up in the face of the 1973 energy crisis and subsequent economic downturn. Moreover, an inquiry by UDPA Planners motivated the Victorian National Trust to undertake a study of the Berry Street area. The National Trust swiftly designated the Berry Street urban conservation area. While such a designation had no force in law—heritage planning did not get full legal backing in Melbourne until the 1980s—it was a sufficient deterrent against development for sympathetic municipal authorities and property owners. Further, the mid-1970s witnessed a popular heritage social movement, incorporating the National Trust and local resident groups such as the Richmond Association, which together brought about a broadening popular appreciation of nineteenth-century inner-suburban heritage.[38]

18 Berry Street took on particular resonance for the National Trust. A field survey was conducted by a local informant, who believed the house to be historically important. So, in addition to the conservation area, Number 18 was listed in the National Trust classification register on 28 September 1972. 18 Berry Street's owner since 1960, Giovanni Loriso, was quoted in the *Melbourne Age* newspaper in 1973 expressing relief that 'something was being done at last'. He added that he had only recently 'found out that my house had received a C classification from the National Trust and I was a bit worried'.[39]

Drafted by architectural historian Miles Lewis, the citation for 18 Berry Street read: 'One of few surviving two-storeyed timber terrace type houses, defaced by recent alternations to the verandah' [Fig. 1].[40] Perhaps in the minds of conservationists, the ceremonial exploding of the verandah in *Dogs in Space*'s notorious party scenes ('suck my motherfucking dick') served a restorative function! In addition to uncovering the history of Number 18, the informant had also identified Loriso as the owner and occupier of the house. It was Loriso who had removed the iron balustrade and lace and rebuilt the verandah. In a letter to Loriso, the National Trust wrote: 'May I compliment you on the well-kept appearance of the house?'

After Loriso moved to Melbourne's northern suburbs, 18 Berry Street would become the sharehouse for which it is known due its portrayal in *Dogs in Space*. However, the sharehouse had to be recreated to be fictionally

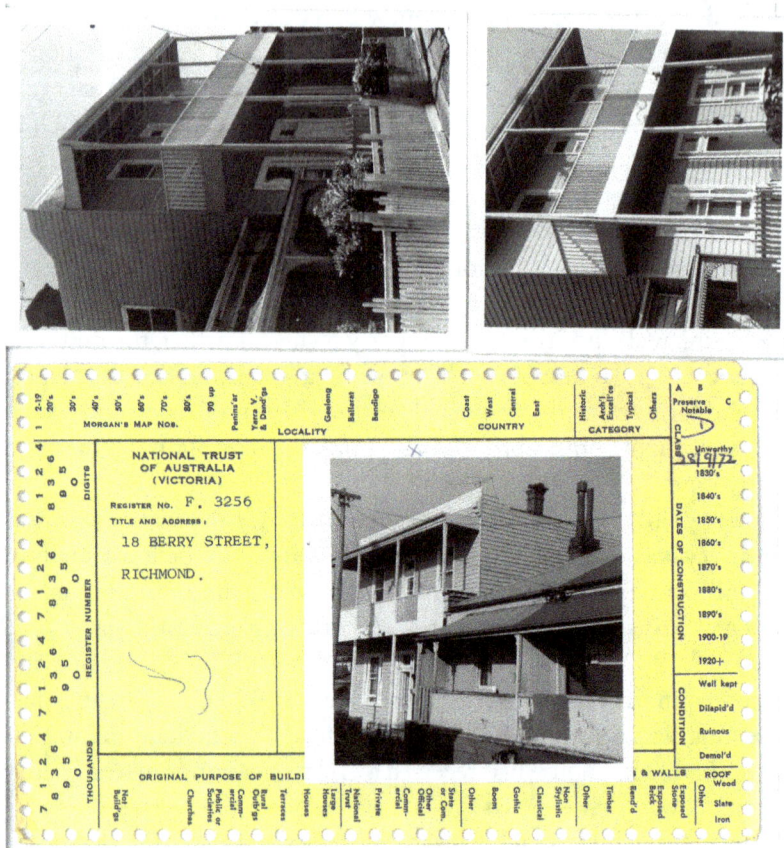

Fig. 1　18 Berry St, Register No. F3256, September 1972. By permission National Trust of Victoria

portrayed in the film. In 1983, it was sold, and its new owners for much of this decade were D. and V. Pownall, who now lived in increasingly attractive and gradually gentrifying Richmond.[41] The 1980s witnessed a continued boom in the restoration of heritage homes—an amplification of a trend which had begun with inner-suburban terrace houses in the 1960s—and many do-it-yourself guides for the inspired homeowner were published in this era.[42] In the short time between its sharehouse status and the day in October 1985 when director Richard Lowenstein and producer Glenys Rowe knocked on its door to inquire about its use in the film, the interior of 18 Berry Street had been upgraded and improved. It would require 'de-renovation' to replicate its earlier ad hoc and bedraggled nature. After filming, 18 Berry Street was restored to its renovated status. Nonetheless, old habits die hard when it comes to stereotyping urban environments: it was still possible, in 1991, to describe Berry Street as 'a streetscape... that epitomises the Struggletown of old'.[43]

Conserving *Dogs in Space*?

It was predominantly on historical and architectural grounds that 18 Berry Street was protected in the 1970s by the National Trust. This approach to the house was repeated in 1985 as part of its inclusion within the municipal City of Richmond conservation study and again in 1988 when it was added to the Victorian State Heritage Register.[44] As a result, 18 Berry Street was symbolically recognised by the National Trust and legally protected from demolition at a local and state level. Certainly, this meant the façade, and likely the two front rooms, of 18 Berry Street would be protected into perpetuity. In 1984, the entire street was depicted in the *Age* as one of four examples across Melbourne of 'urban conservation areas'.[45]

Of course, 18 Berry Street had become famous for another reason in 1986 beyond its nineteenth-century origins. *Dogs in Space* had become an Australian cult classic. And so, in the late 1990s the citation was updated to conserve Number 18 for social reasons due to its association with the film:

> The Residence at 18 Berry Street Richmond is of social significance as the primary location for the filming of the Australian film *Dogs in Space*. *Dogs in Space* portrayed the sex, drugs and rock 'n' roll subculture of the late 1970s, one of the first Australian films to do so with a degree of mainstream success. It starred, among others, singer Michael Hutchence, and was an important cultural reference point for young people in the 1980s. The house is still readily recognised by many who have seen the film.[46]

It would be reasonable to say that in Melbourne's cultural imaginary 18 Berry Street is today more famous for its portrayal in *Dogs in Space* than for its associations with colonial prospector Frencham. Yet, the ways that the house is protected respond more appropriately to its nineteenth- than its twentieth-century heritage. Nineteenth-century historic fabric is conserved, but there are hardly additional conservation cues or measures at the site that this was the place where *Dogs in Space* happened. Further opportunities exist to embrace the urban heritage of *Dogs in Space* in Melbourne, in Richmond, on Berry Street, and online.

Civic actions are also serving to interpret Richmond as '*Dogs in Space*' territory and, perhaps, to provide new attractions for pilgrims who gravitate to Richmond to explore the film's built legacy. In late 2018, the City of Yarra's mayor, Danae Bosler, announced a plan to erect a statue of Michael Hutchence in Richmond, the result of lobbying from members of Hutchence's family who recognised his strong connection to Melbourne ('most of his best friends still live there', said his sister Tina) although he had never lived in Melbourne, much less the suburb of Richmond.[47] Although the news articles proclaiming the statue plan mentioned *Dogs in Space* as the Hutchence-Richmond connection, it was also mooted that the statue would be placed close to another celebrating a genuine (and still living) Richmond icon, Ian 'Molly' Meldrum, talent co-ordinator for *Countdown*. This signifies an ambivalent place for Hutchence between 'pop star' and 'actor in *Dogs in Space*' although he was, of course, undeniably both.

The history of Richmond, as a renowned Melbourne 'slum' suburb for much of the twentieth century, was one of desperation and disadvantage. It is, we posit, important to note Richmond's unreconstructed 'slum' status in the minds of many in the 1970s, and perhaps even 1980s, when some of the events depicted in *Dogs in Space* took place, and when it was made. It is also important to note that, as a filmmaker, Richard Lowenstein was well aware of the suburb's history.

Between the mid-1970s and mid-1980s, Richmond and 18 Berry Street were in transition. In its engagement with the relatively recent-past, *Dogs in Space* portrays the political, social and cultural shifts of the era. In that short period of time, 18 Berry Street transitioned from migrant home to communal sharehouse and to middle-class stronghold. Richmond itself became newly valued for its nineteenth-century heritage amidst the area's gradual gentrification. Various forms of urban nostalgia for the not-so-recent-past fuse in the film: from the wide-angle shots of the Pelaco sign to the use of the de-(re)stored heritage-protected house. The 1986 film vividly illustrates changing 1970s Richmond and 18 Berry Street. *Dogs in Space* momentarily restores a counter-cultural version of the 'Struggletown' of old, a final and enduring affront ('fuck you') to the people who were once again transforming Richmond. There goes the neighourbood.

Notes

1. A. Mutton *Then and Now,* memoir in possession of D. Nichols, p. 1; M. Schaller (2017) From the Danube to the River Yarra, https://www.sbs.com.au/yourlanguage/german/en/explainer/danube-yarra-river, accessed 1 May 2019.
2. Anon (1970) 'National Service', *Melbourne Age,* 21 March, 11.
3. L. Lees, T. Slater, and E. K. Wyly (eds.) (2007) *The Gentrification Reader* (London: Routledge), p. 113.
4. S. Sejavka (2009) 'The Resurrection of Dogs in Space', *Sails of Oblivion,* 6 May, http://sailsofoblivion.blogspot.com/2009/05/resurrection-of-dogs-in-space.html, accessed 9 June 2019.
5. S. Sejavka (1981) '25 March 1981', *Sails of Oblivion,* https://sailsofoblivion.blogspot.com/2008/01/25-march-1981-thurs-230pm.html.
6. Cf. N. Smith (1996) *The New Urban Frontier: Gentrification and the Revanchist City* (London: Routledge).
7. J. McCalman (1984) *Struggletown: Public and Private Life in Richmond 1900–1965* (Carlton: Melbourne University Press).
8. P. Andrews (1973) 'Blessed are the Poor—Part 1' transcript of *By The Way,* ABC Radio Broadcast 12 November in possession of D. Nichols.
9. A. Mutton, *Then and Now,* p. 46.
10. C. Holding (1964) 'Labor's Policy on Education', *Melbourne Age,* 16 June, 2.
11. City of Richmond (1988) *Copping It Sweet: Shared Memories of Richmond* (Richmond: City of Richmond), p. 237.
12. C. A. Loughnan (1924) 'Richmond Slum Areas', *Melbourne Age,* 12 August, 12.

13. Anon (1967) '14-Hour Day "Underwork"', *Melbourne Age*, 12 April, 1; R. Warneke (1973) 'Children with Their Own Police Dossiers', *Melbourne Age*, 28 December, 2.
14. D. King (1974) 'Richmond Survey', University of Melbourne Thesis, p. 2.
15. G. Gilmour (1974) 'Richmond Stereotype—A Demographic Analysis', University of Melbourne Thesis, p. 5.
16. Gilmour, 'Richmond Stereotype', p. 7.
17. W. Hogan (1974) 'Population Characteristics, Richmond', University of Melbourne Thesis, 72.
18. G. Gilmour, 'Richmond', p. 12.
19. A. Mutton, *Then and Now*, p. 44.
20. Anon (1970) 'Labor Would Stop House Wrecker', *Melbourne Age*, 16 May, 3.
21. A. Mutton, *Then and Now*, p. 46.
22. A. Mutton, *Then and Now*, p. 47. See also V. Basile (1970) 'The Force Triumphs: Stronghold Falls in Siege of Mahony Street', *Melbourne Age*, 15 May, 3.
23. N. Dexter (1978) 'A Depression Relived', *Melbourne Age*, 11 November, 16.
24. W. Lowenstein quoted in N. Dexter (1978) 'A Depression Relived', *Melbourne Age*, 11 November, 16.
25. W. Green (190-?) 'Plan of Early Melbourne Showing Original Crown Allotments', http://handle.slv.vic.gov.au/10381/114752.
26. Anon (1861) 'Plan of Allotments of Land Situate in Waltham Terrace Richmond', http://handle.slv.vic.gov.au/10381/161872.
27. A. C. Allan (1888) Map, http://search.slv.vic.gov.au/MAIN:Everything:SLV_VOYAGER787513.
28. A. Roger-Gernersh and B. Carroll (1976) *Richmond and East Melbourne Sketchbook* (Adelaide: Rigby).
29. G. Davison (1980) 'Richmond', in G. Davison (ed.) *Melbourne on Foot: 15 Walks Through Historic Melbourne* (Adelaide: Rigby), p. 97.
30. Davison, 97.
31. D. S. Garden, 'Frencham, Henry (1816–1897)', Australian Dictionary of Biography, National Centre of Biography, Australian National University, http://adb.anu.edu.au/biography/frencham-henry-3577/text5537, accessed online 2 May 2019.
32. H. Frencham (1888) 'The Discoverer of the Bendigo Goldfield', *Melbourne Age*, 30 June, 4.

33. J. & T. O'Connor Architects and R. Coleman and H. Wright Architects (1985) *Richmond Conservation Study* (Richmond: City of Richmond, Australian Heritage Commission, Ministry for Planning and Environment), p. 3.
34. Heritage Council Victoria (1999) 'Pelaco Sign', https://vhd.heritagecouncil.vic.gov.au/places/4857#statement-significance.
35. NTAV Archive, Berry Street Area, B3223.
36. R. Howe (ed.) (1988) *New Houses for Old: Fifty Years of Public Housing in Victoria 1938–1988* (Melbourne: Ministry of Housing and Construction).
37. S. Downes (1981) 'A Man with High Ideals', *Melbourne Age*, 21 April, 11.
38. G. Davison (1991) 'A Brief History of the Australian Heritage Movement', in G. Davison and C. McConville (eds.) *A Heritage Handbook* (Sydney: Allen & Unwin), pp. 14–27.
39. B. Patterson (1973) '$500,000 Plan to Redevelop North Richmond', *Melbourne Age*, 5 April, 3.
40. NTAV Archive, 18 Berry Street Area, B3256.
41. Anon (1983) 'Advertisement', *Melbourne Age*, 22 June, 36; Anon (1989) 'Advertisement', *Melbourne Age*, 28 June, 78. 'D. Pownall' is *not* the British writer David Pownall (Pownell via A. Hewson, pers. comm. 22 May 2019).
42. R. Hillier (1967) *Let's Buy a Terrace House* (Sydney: Ure Smith); I. Evans, *Getting the Details Right: Restoring Australian Houses 1890s–1920s* (Yeronga: Flannel Flower Press).
43. R. Dredge (1991) 'Western Atmosphere at Alphington Sale', *Melbourne Age*, 14 September, 31.
44. Richmond Conservation Study; Victorian Heritage Database, H710 and HO226.
45. Anon (1984) 'How to Live in an Urban Conservation Area', *Melbourne Age*, 13 April, 35.
46. Victorian Heritage Database, H710 and HO226.
47. M. Boulton (2018) 'Statue Sensation: Melbourne to Honour Hutchence', *Melbourne Age*, 5 December, https://www.theage.com.au/entertainment/music/statue-sensation-melbourne-to-honour-hutchence-20181205-p50kb3.html.

'Making It': The Ears, INXS, and Music Scene Restructuring as Seen Through *Dogs in Space*

Sarah Taylor

'I was far more interested', Richard Lowenstein said in 1986, 'in doing, instead of your rags-to-riches pop star story, your rags-to-gutter story… by actually showing the ones that don't become famous'.[1]

At the time of its release in late 1986, *Dogs in Space* provided a compelling contrast between the heights of music industry success enjoyed by one of its stars, Michael Hutchence, and the vibrant but chaotic music movement it depicted.[2] By the time *Dogs In Space* had been re-released in 2009, alongside the documentary *We're Livin' on Dog Food*, the status of live music in Australian cities had shifted sufficiently that the scenes depicted in the film were not so much of bands experiencing entertainingly low levels of commercial success, but of a successful and exciting city scene.

What happened? In a word: restructuring. *Dogs In Space* provides multiple vantage points to a decades-long story of restructuring for live music in Australian cities. The concept of 'making it' provides an interesting

---

S. Taylor (✉)
RMIT University, Melbourne, VIC, Australia
e-mail: sarah.taylor@rmit.edu.au

subset of this restructuring. The fact that a film made in the 1980s about a band 'not making it' (The Ears), starring a musician who had 'made it' (Michael Hutchence), would go on become a cult classic in the 1990s and 2000s, to the extent that the bands who were 'not making it' would later be seen as both relatable and desirable, provides insights into broader contextual changes in these decades.

This chapter provides details and context for two real-life bands linked to *Dogs in Space*: The Ears and INXS. It maps their performances in Melbourne in the late 1970s and early 1980s, highlighting their different achievements and the contextual norms of their music scene participation. It then outlines the music industry restructuring that took place to shift many of these norms. The information in this chapter can help to contextualise the changing status of *Dogs in Space* and the music scene that it portrays. It can also be of general interest, since there is a reasonable argument to be put forward that whatever happens to other industries, happens to music first.[3]

Dogs in Context: Post-Punk, Punk, and New Wave

Dogs in Space was filmed, and released, in 1986. The dialogue, characters, music and locations were drawn from director Richard Lowenstein's observations of the 1978–1981 Melbourne music scene, a fact widely acknowledged at the time of release but apparently lost on some viewers in the film's ensuing decades as a cult classic and quotable party film.[4]

There is no literal mention of 'post-punk' anywhere in *Dogs in Space*, but it is a useful term for understanding the film. It is now used to refer to a music movement of the late 1970s and early 1980s. The Melbourne music scene depicted in *Dogs in Space*, along with its constituent bands, can now be quite comfortably grouped in the post-punk genre. Post-punk shared common values and lineage with punk but could be distinguished by three basic points. Firstly, the inclusion of new instruments and technology: in particular, keyboards, synthesisers, drum machines and assorted electronic gadgetry. Secondly, unapologetic romanticism and artiness, wherein it was acceptable to express artistic rather than political ambitions (cheerfully summed up by Phillip Brophy as 'artsiness, pretentiousness and being a wanker').[5] Thirdly, applying the do-it-yourself principle to broader musical styles other than to the chords and time signatures of rock and blues, thus losing the suffix punk-*rock*. The pre-punk David Bowie and Brian Eno were often admired by post-punk musicians.

All these post-punk elements can be seen in *Dogs in Space*: the entire soundtrack; the queue for David Bowie tickets; the ill-fated experimentation with electronic gadgets attempted by Tim (Nique Needles); the unapologetic artiness and oblique lyrics of the titular band; and the range of rackets made by different bands applying the do-it-yourself principle. A 1977 television interview with Melbourne band The Young Charlatans is also instructive: Ollie Olsen, later the musical director of *Dogs in Space*, describes his interest in Bartok, Wagner, and synthesisers.[6]

'New-wave' is another useful term to add context to *Dogs in Space*. The Young Charlatans interview mentioned above switches tellingly but subtly between references to 'punk' (from the interviewer) to 'new-wave' (from the musicians themselves). If one were to imagine a Venn diagram of new-wave and post-punk genres, one would see considerable overlap and a great number of late 1970s and early 1980s bands, but with Joy Division and Boys Next Door located at the more obviously post-punk end and Blondie, Devo, and Talking Heads at the more obviously new-wave end, edging into disco or synth-pop. New-wave was a suitable term for musical acts with post-punk characteristics but an ambition to become commercially successful. The origins of the genre name can be traced to a 1977 marketing campaign by Sire Records manager Seymour Stein, who felt that 'punk' would hinder sales for some of their newly signed acts, including Talking Heads.[7] The new-wave/post-punk distinction also demarked INXS from The Ears.

Dogs in Context: Links to the Australian Post-Punk Music Scene

The participants of *Dogs in Space* are busy with music, if not strictly in the music business. There are no music-biopic style scenes of musicians signing record deals, triumphing over personal adversity, thrilling at the sound of their recording on the radio, or happily scanning a surprisingly large and suitably impressed audience (*Purple Rain*, *La Bamba*, or even *Spinal Tap*-style). In fact, they do not obviously go anywhere with their music, except to gigs at the pub and parties with their friends. To 1986 audiences this might have been inexplicable, but to twenty-first-century audiences this could be termed a 'thriving music scene'. The depiction was, for the most part, an accurate one of the inner suburbs of Australian cities from approximately 1976 to 1982.

No doubt, other music scenes were thriving in other places, but if a music scene forms in a city and no one hears about it, does it make a sound? Several of the music scene participants went on, in subsequent years and decades, to achieve wider recognition.[8] In addition, it helped that there were people on the ground at the time with an interest in documenting the scene.[9] Community radio stations, established within a short-time frame in the mid-1970s, championed new local music acts.[10] Music journalist Clinton Walker compiled an influential collection, *Inner City Sound*, and continued to write about the merits of Australian independent music (see below).[11] A key impression was that the post-punk scene in Australia had been exciting in spite of, or because of, being geographically isolated.

While the film conveyed highly localised and not particularly glamorous happenings, the *Dogs in Space* cast included bona fide international rock star Michael Hutchence, lead singer of INXS, a band that was, at the time, kicking unusually high goals for Australian music in overseas markets. Hutchence's stardom contrasted with the characters in the film, for whom music was a central activity, but apparently undertaken in a mode of almost wilful anti-success. Commentary at the time seemed ambivalent as to whether the musical activities of 'the ones that don't become famous' were actually interesting enough to warrant a film.[12] Rather than a vibrant music scene, the 1980s reviewers saw 'musicians and drifters', 'chaos', a 'scroungy' house and 'a counterculture without a cause'.[13]

Dogs in Space featured a musician from a real-life band (INXS) performing in an almost-fictional band (Dogs in Space) based unabashedly on a real-life band (The Ears). INXS and The Ears began band-lives at similar times. In 1979, the Farriss Brothers changed their name to INXS and an assemblage of friends headed by Sam Sejavka played a debut show as The Ears at a Footscray party. The Ears performed at inner city venues in Melbourne for the next two years, typically once or twice a month.

The time span of The Ears maps closely to the timeline compressed into the film, beginning at the 1978 Bowie queue, where many of the band members first met, and ending shortly after the death of Sejavka's girlfriend in 1981. Along the way, The Ears garnered a following with local trendies, were written about in the local music press, and recorded and released two singles. Richard Lowenstein directed their 'Leap for Lunch' film clip in 1980, and, obviously, took a longer term interest in them.

Figure 1 maps the distribution of publicly listed live music performances in Melbourne by The Ears, from 1979 to 1981. The performances are grouped by venue, so that venues with more performances by The Ears have larger symbols and larger labels. Table 1 lists the venues by name and suburb, including their respective distances from the *Dogs in Space*/Berry Street house (an average of 4.7 km).

Here, The Ears can be seen performing primarily—overwhelmingly— in the inner suburbs of Melbourne, and at particular venues (namely the Seaview Hotel in St Kilda, the Champion Hotel in Fitzroy, and the Exford Hotel in the CBD) more than others. This geography was characteristic of their career, although elsewhere in this book the band's bass player Cathy McQuade recalls making occasional trips to perform further afield.

The Champion Hotel was a key venue for The Ears; it also features in *Dogs in Space*, and in their 'Leap for Lunch' film clip (mixed with footage of 18 Berry Street, Richmond in its original grungy condition). The Ears' association with The Champion may have contributed to later confusion about whether they (and, by extension, the semi-fictional *Dogs in Space* band) were a 'Little Band'.[14] A 1980 review notes:

> A now defunct venue 'The Champion' was like their garage and their friends, acquaintances, peers and so on were always there when they were just mucking around… But it seems that this band had a bit more to offer than the general run of the mill, off-beat, crazed band. So they grew, from that recognition of talent. Whereas so many others dropped by the wayside. In reality the band was pretty bad about a year or so ago… But now they're getting, they've got, so much better. They used to have the label of being the worst band in town and now they're getting some recognition…They

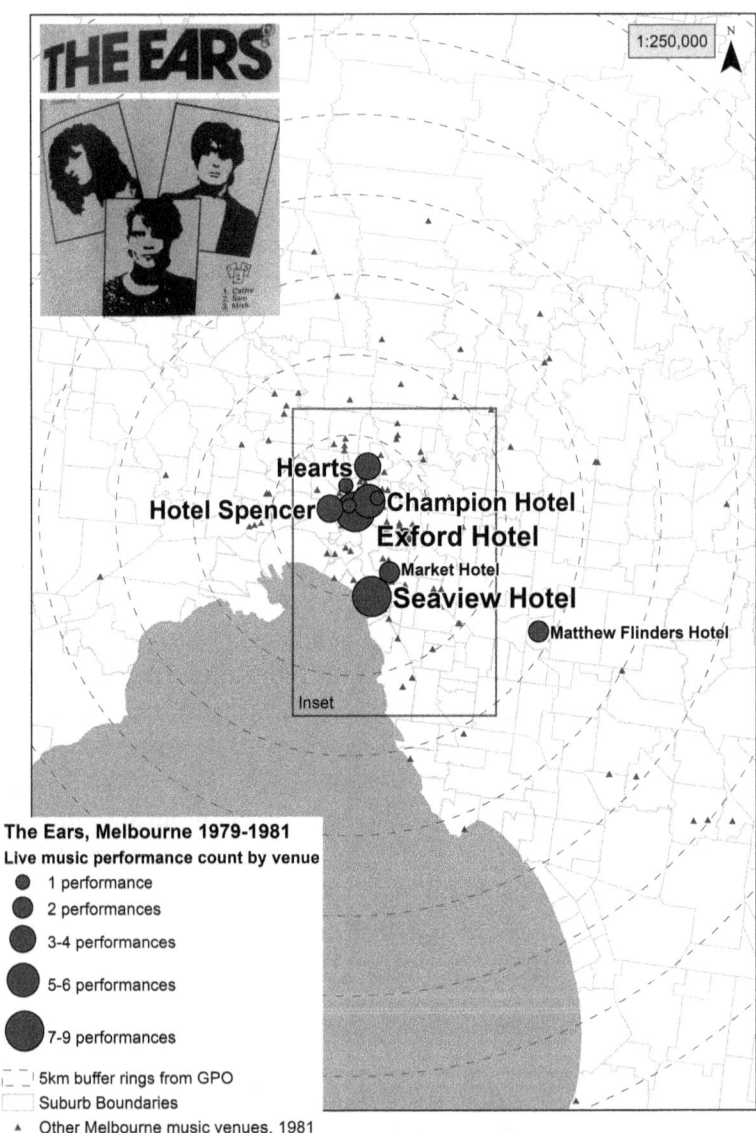

Fig. 1 Map of publicly listed live music performances by The Ears in Greater Melbourne, 1979–1981, grouped by venue. Details in Table 1

Table 1 Publicly listed live music performances by The Ears in Greater Melbourne, 1979–1981, grouped by venue

Venue name	Suburb	Count of Ears performances	Distance from 18 Berry Street, Richmond (km)
Exford Hotel	Melbourne CBD	9	3
Seaview Hotel	St Kilda	8	6
Champion Hotel	Fitzroy	6	3
Hearts	North Carlton	4	5
Hotel Spencer	Melbourne CBD	3	5
Market Hotel	South Yarra	2	4
Matthew Flinders Hotel	Chadstone	2	13
Central Club Hotel	Richmond	1	1
Jump Club	Collingwood	1	3
Melbourne University	Parkville	1	5
Oxford Hotel	Melbourne CBD	1	4
Martini's	Carlton	1	5
Total		39	
Average			4.7

Sources: *The Age*, *The Alternative Gig Guide*. Venues restricted to ABS definition of Greater Melbourne, 2011. Performances restricted to these publicly available sources. 'Seaview Hotel' also used to refer to venues located within the building (e.g. Paradise Lounge, Crystal Ballroom)

have enough confidence in themselves now to come out of their isolation, and they are as ambitious as the next person.[15]

Other reviews veered between admiration and loathing, and backhanders ('gifted idiots'[16]). Perhaps this was exacerbated by their arty, proto-hipster style, or by the fact that they were not active in the earliest years of the Melbourne post-punk scene (1977 and 1978), thus encouraging comparisons to predecessors like the Boys Next Door or Whirlywirld. Either way, The Ears managed to generate some startlingly negative press:

> The Ears are currently the dahlings (dahling) of Melbourne's 'arty punk' set… an imitation of the Boys Next Door, and a bad one at that.[17]
>
> Straining myself to think seriously about what they were offering, words such as banal, mundane and pretentious sprung to mind. Perhaps their only

saving grace was their filmclip... If this is all The Ears have to offer then perhaps they should take a hint from Van Gogh.[18]

The last Ears gig was in June 1981, at the opening of rock music nights at the Oxford Scholar Hotel, in the CBD. A music magazine in May of that year noted that 'The Ears are rumoured to be breaking up... the usual professional differences are cited as the reason...'.[19] The musical direction taken by the male members of The Ears, who regrouped later in the year as Beargarden (see below), is consistent with the 'professional differences' line. A review of their last gig suggested that the band could have expanded their scale of operations if they had only been more organised:

> ...the Ears confirmed rumours that they were splitting after 2½ years. I've never really understood the media's attitude to the Ears. Over the years, and most recently as well, they've been mercilessly hammered as a dismal punk band... Personally, I've often enjoyed them, and considered 'The Crater' from their single of 1980 as close to the best song for that year. My only criticism was their sloppy, unprofessional approach to gigging, which prevented their music from rising out of the new wave ruck.[20]

The Ears would never be accused, as INXS sometimes were, of being overly professional and, for better and for worse, they were neither cohesive nor strategic. In the present day, this gives the band the distinct sheen of not having tried *too hard*, a compliment rarely directed towards their contemporaries, INXS.

The funding and promotion of *Dogs in Space* was helped, in no small part, by the star power provided by Michael Hutchence, who exemplified the 1980s heights of 'making it' in the Australian music industry. While Hutchence later came to the attention of tabloids and met a tragic end in 1997, the band as a whole were remarkably uncontroversial and even industrious: travelling on some of the same roads as The Ears, but at different speeds. On an occasion when the band did encounter controversy it involved a certain amount of professionalism: their 1991 live album was alleged to have been polished up too much in the studio.[21]

INXS began in Sydney in the late 1970s with the nucleus of brothers Tim, Andrew, and Jon Farriss, later joined by Hutchence (who attended the same high school) then Kirk Pengilly and Garry 'Gary' Beers. This line-up remained remarkably unchanged for the ensuing decades. After a year in Perth, the band returned to Sydney in 1979 and began playing around the northern beaches, gaining many support spots for Midnight Oil, whose manager Gary Morris suggested their name change to INXS. By many accounts, INXS were confident and almost bizarrely professional from the start when approaching pub gigs large or small.[22]

In 1979, they hired Chris Murphy as their manager. Murphy was a 'colourful hard-arse'[23] and confident wheeler-and-dealer who had been working as a booking agent in Sydney throughout the 1960s and 1970s. In 1982, Murphy joined with INXS's touring manager Gary Grant to establish MMA (Murphy Media Academy). MMA was not a record company. Its role was to 'negotiate separate publishing, recording, video and merchandising deals',[24] operating within the established Australian music industry, but also in defiance of it, steering bands towards overseas contracts at the earliest opportunity. In 1982, INXS signed to WEA (a multinational) for Australian distribution, to Atco (a subsidiary of Atlantic Records) for American distribution, and to Mercury (yet another multinational subsidiary) for the UK.

Figure 2 maps the publicly listed live music performances in Melbourne by INXS during 1979 to 1981, the same years in which The Ears were active. Table 2 lists the venues and suburbs, and distances from the *Dogs in Space* Berry Street house. This can be compared to Table 1 (The Ears).

Between 1979 and 1981 INXS were beginning to crack the Australian charts but they were yet to break overseas. Some venue names appear in both Table 1 (The Ears) and Table 2 (INXS): the Seaview Hotel; Hearts in North Carlton; Martini's in Carlton, and the Exford Hotel in the CBD. INXS and The Ears found 'common ground'[25] in the inner-city music venues associated with the post-punk scene.

While they overlapped with The Ears, INXS also combined inner-city venues with suburban venues. They performed in Melbourne at an average of 9.1 km from the *Dogs in Space* house, compared to 4.7 km for The Ears, and with one-third of venues over 10 km away (compared to one twelfth for The Ears). They also played a higher number of performances overall: INXS played 84 publicly listed gigs in Melbourne between 1979 and 1981, while The Ears played 39 (and this is saying nothing of interstate tours, which INXS engaged in frequently). Two other venues frequented

184   S. Taylor

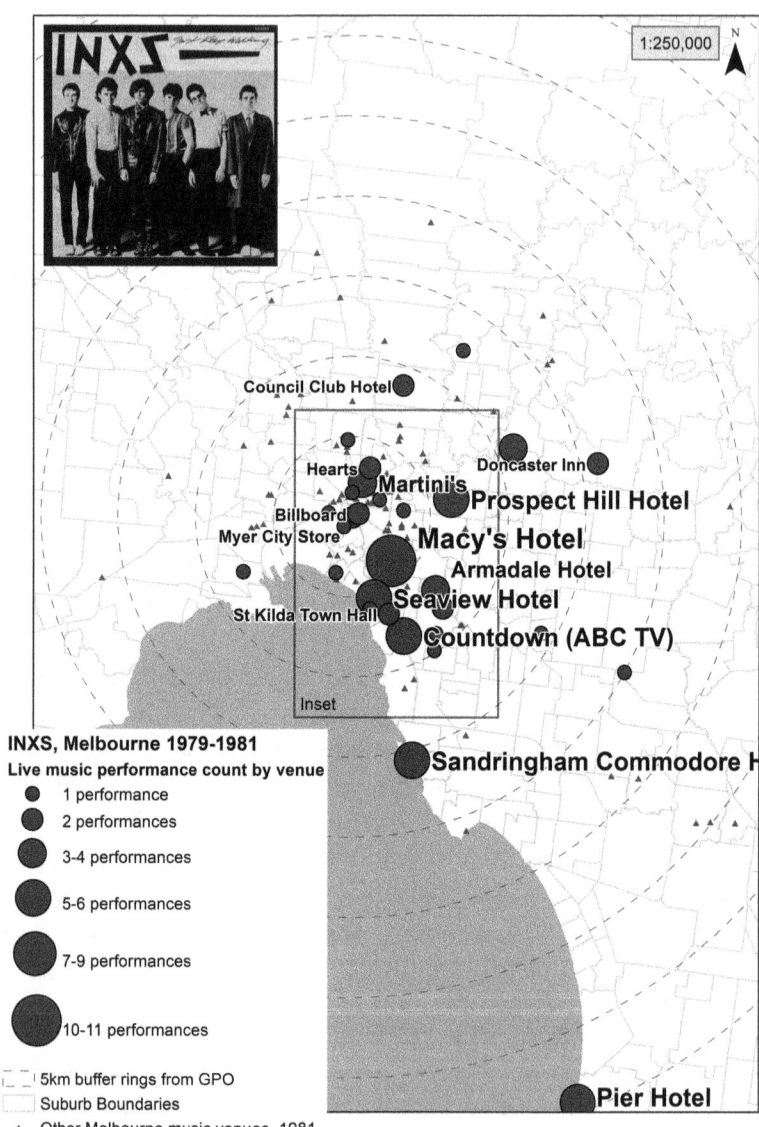

Fig. 2 Map of publicly listed live music performances by INXS in Greater Melbourne, 1979–1981, grouped by venue. Details in Table 2

Table 2 Publicly listed live music performances by INXS in Greater Melbourne, 1979–1981, grouped by venue

Venue Name	Suburb	Count of INXS performances	Distance from 18 Berry Street, Richmond (km)
Macy's Hotel	South Yarra	11	3
Seaview Hotel	St Kilda	7	6
ABC Studios (*Countdown*)	Elsternwick	6	8
Prospect Hill Hotel	Kew	6	4
Pier Hotel	Frankston	5	40
Sandringham Commodore Hotel	Sandringham	5	15
Armadale Hotel	Armadale	4	6
Martini's	Carlton	4	5
Ferntree Gully Hotel	Ferntree Gully	3	29
Sentimental Bloke Hotel	Bulleen	3	10
Billboard	Melbourne CBD	2	3
Bourke Street Mall	Melbourne CBD	2	3
Council Club Hotel	Preston	2	10
Doncaster Inn	Doncaster	2	14
Hearts	Carlton North	2	5
Railway Hotel	Malvern	2	7
St Kilda Town Hall	St Kilda	2	6
Bananas	St Kilda	1	7
Bombay Rock	Brunswick	1	8
Caulfield Arts Complex	Caulfield	1	9
Electric Ballroom	St Kilda	1	7
Eureka Hotel	Richmond	1	1
Festival Hall	West Melbourne	1	6

(continued)

Table 2 (continued)

Venue Name	Suburb	Count of INXS performances	Distance from 18 Berry Street, Richmond (km)
Grainstore Tavern	Melbourne CBD	1	4
Jump Club	Collingwood	1	3
Junction Hotel	Newport	1	12
La Trobe University	Bundoora	1	13
London Tavern	Caulfield South	1	10
Matthew Flinders Hotel	Chadstone	1	13
Melbourne College of Advanced Education	Carlton	1	5
The Venue	St Kilda	1	6
Village Green Hotel	Mulgrave	1	20
Windsor Hotel	Albert Park	1	6
	Total	84	
	Average		9.1

Sources: *The Age*, *The Alternative Gig Guide*, INXS 'gigography' at http://inxsonline.com/gigography/. Venues restricted to ABS definition of Greater Melbourne, 2011. Performances restricted to these publicly available sources. 'Seaview Hotel' also used to refer to venues located within the building (e.g. Paradise Lounge and Crystal Ballroom)

by INXS are important to note: many appearances at the ABC Ripponlea studios for *Countdown*, and at Macy's Hotel in South Yarra. Macy's was renovated in 1980 with 'ski lodge standard' upstairs accommodation, well-suited for touring bands like INXS.[26]

Rather than ups and downs, or a single meteoric rise followed by dramatic crash, the 1980s played out for INXS as a steady, gamified rise through available paths of opportunity. In 1982, their second album (*Shabooh Shoobah*) reached the Australian Top 10 and US Top 30; their fifth album, *Kick* (1987), went on to become their highest selling album: nine million copies and #1 in the USA. In 1985, they won seven *Countdown* awards and were part of the 'Rocking The Royals' gig for Princess Diana and Prince Charles in Melbourne. In 1986, they performed at Wembley Stadium with Queen. When *Dogs in Space* was released they were about to embark upon the 'Australian Made' arena tour with the 'cream of the crop' of Australian bands.[27]

A characteristic feature of INXS' career during the 1980s is that of expansion: each album sold incrementally more, and each tour extended further afield. This manifested spatially even in their early years of operation, with the mix of inner-city and suburban gigs. It also played out over the longer term and on a wider scale. One account suggests that later in the 1980s their management literally kept a map of the world on its office wall, with the effect akin to a 'war room'.[28] Now, an animated, year by year, world-scale map of all INXS gigs is provided on the official INXS website, with the subheading 'How INXS conquered the world'.

After The Ears

The Ears dovetailed quickly into two bands with more obvious mainstream ambitions and occasional successes. The (male) members of The Ears had by October 1981 reassembled under a new name, Beargarden. After leaving The Ears, Cathy McQuade formed funk-pop Deckchairs Overboard. With a record deal and a strong following in Sydney, the band presented an enticing alternative for McQuade, and she relocated to Sydney for several years. She also provided one of the 'singing voices' for the ABC TV series *Sweet and Sour*, a show which portrayed the ups and downs of a band striving, more earnestly than The Ears but less effectively than INXS, for music industry success in 1980s Sydney.[29]

The first Beargarden gig was in October 1981, and shortly afterwards they began to tour a slightly different circuit than The Ears, combining the inner-city circuit with big suburban pubs like the Ferntree Gully Hotel and the Prospect Hill Hotel. This signalled an intention to shed some of the edgier aspects of The Ears and operate at a wider scale. The resemblance to INXS was not coincidental: Beargarden came to the attention of Chris Murphy when both bands performed at the Seaview Hotel, and Beargarden subsequently signed to MMA and toured several times with INXS.

They became the first band to sign to Virgin Records Australia and even performed on *Countdown* in 1985, becoming (in the short term, at least) more widely known than 'notorious laughing stock' The Ears.[30] Beargarden was active from 1981 until 1987. As a less weird and slightly more ambitious version of The Ears, and a more weird and slightly less ambitious version of INXS, they achieved some successes but never reached anywhere near the commercial successes of INXS nor the legendary status of The Ears. This was summed up, not so generously, in a 2009 assessment of Sejavka as having 'shaken off the punk image and… reinvented himself as a 80s new-waver in a highly digestible form in the band, Beergarden [sic]'.[31]

For INXS, the decade after *Dogs in Space* was not great. The bands were not by any means destitute—far from it, they lived well-off lifestyles in different cities across the globe, and they continued to record and tour. But, just as in the 1980s they had sold successively more records at each release, the reverse was true in the 1990s. Characteristic of a band not given to erratic changes or outward displays of friction, this played out steadily rather than dramatically. In 1996, ten years after *Dogs in Space*, Hutchence was publicly dissed at an awards ceremony by the (then) new face of rock music, Noel Gallagher of Oasis, who announced that 'has-beens shouldn't give awards to gonna-be's'.[32]

Michael Hutchence died in 1997, but INXS did not officially cease operations until 2012. The surviving members made use of high-profile guest vocalists (Terence Trent D'Arby, Jimmy Barnes, and Jon Stevens) and continued touring and recording. In 2005, they ran a reality television programme to recruit a new singer, entitled *Rock Star: INXS*.[33]

Pick Me: Late Twentieth-Century Music Industry Restructuring

With hindsight, the 'apex of their fame'[34] for INXS can be placed squarely around the *Dogs in Space* years, 1986–1987. This was also a turning point for Australian musicians more generally: in successive years, both the music industry and Australian cities restructured significantly. Some key points are described below.

As a starting point, it is helpful to clarify what is meant by 'independent music'. The Ears and many (though not all) of their peers in the post-punk scene were independent musicians. Music is defined as 'independent' when it is created and distributed without funding from major labels. The term 'major label' is relative: major labels hold a large proportion of market share, 'more than 5% of the world market(s) for the sale of records or music videos…'.[35]

Through much of the late twentieth century, precisely defining a 'major label' was of trifling importance: in any given year, there were typically no more than six companies recognised as such, and though they engaged constantly in acquisitions and mergers, they were hard to avoid.[36] For several decades, major labels were a preoccupation for musicians: that is, much more than today.

The 'independent' term takes on a different nuance at different geographic scales. The Australian music industry has long displayed a hybrid of national and international power structures. In the late twentieth century, many of its most powerful gatekeepers could be defined as 'independent' on a global scale, but easily met the threshold for being 'major' at a national scale. The *Countdown* music television programme was not even a record label, but it certainly controlled more than 5% of record sales. The same was true of the Mushroom group, founded by Michael Gudinski in 1972.[37]

In the era in which both The Ears and INXS were active, one path to national success was relatively clear. With (for instance) a Mushroom Records recording contract, a live performance booking contract with the Premier-Harbour agency (also part of the Mushroom group), and exposure on *Countdown*, acts could potentially do very well nationally. But Mushroom was not the only option: subsidiary companies of the six global major labels were an important presence in Australia, establishing the ARIA group (Australian Recording Industry Association) in 1983. It was also possible to bypass the *local* majors by signing directly to a major label overseas. This path was taken by Little River Band, INXS, and Men at Work.[38]

The independent/major music industry power structure, and its subsequent disruption, can be partly understood through technology. In the present day, with cheap home-recording software and digital music platforms, it can be easily forgotten the actual process of recording and reproducing music was once very expensive. This was the case up to and including the post-punk era. Home-recording studios were extremely uncommon and professional studios were not cheap. Each song directly incurred more studio time and thus more up-front costs. Likewise, reproducing music on vinyl required time and money. Albums required an investment of several thousand dollars (not adjusted to inflation!), but sometimes horrifyingly even more than this.[39] Singles presented a cheaper option through the simple economics of using less time and less vinyl, but they were not actually cheap.

Thus, one option for musicians was to seek the assistance of a major label. This was typically undertaken as part of a record 'deal': music acts were picked up major labels, then signed to a contract that facilitated the recording, reproduction, and distribution of music. The arrangement could seem like winning the lottery, but in practice, it was also a mortgage: the labels fronted the cash, the acts paid it back over time. This debt relationship meant that some musicians were given the opportunity to have their music distributed at a scale that would otherwise be completely impossible. The trade-off was that record label executives were able to exert creative influence on who and what was recorded, reproduced, and distributed. For an introduction of the highs and lows that this relationship entailed, one can select at random from any rock and pop music biography of the twentieth century.[40]

For those rejected by, or rejecting, this system, the other options were to self-finance or to join with an independent label. In the post-punk era, this did not mean truly 'do it yourself' recording and reproduction of music: at some stage, a recording studio and a record press were required. The Ears self-funded their first single ('Leap For Lunch'), and for their second single worked with Missing Link, an independent record label. INXS signed up to major label deals in 1982. Though less common, it was also possible to travel in the other direction, from major label back to independent: The Boys Next Door released one album with Mushroom in 1979 but then defected to Missing Link. The 'deals' offered by independent labels were typically smaller in scale and budget but more open to artistic risk.

Throughout the 1980s, technological change impacted upon recording and reproduction processes. The technology for multitrack home recording to cassette tape (the Tascam four-track Portastudio) debuted in 1979 and became more widely available in 1982.[41] Throughout the 1980s and 1990s, the cost of professional studio time also declined. Economic geographer Andrew Leyshon argues convincingly that the introduction of recording console software in the late 1970s created downward price competition in the studio market.[42] This was mostly good news for bands, although record labels could increasingly count on bands to self-finance their early recordings.[43]

By the late 1980s, around the release of *Dogs in Space* and the apex of INXS's career trajectory, it was increasingly viable to engage in the tasks of recording, reproducing, and distributing music without major label assistance. At the same time, major labels were becoming more consolidated and powerful, so their success stories were more conspicuous. The 1990s was characterised by a crossover between the two worlds of independent and major label music production. Through this process, popular music became, at least superficially, less corporate and more open-minded than in the preceding decades. The top spots of recorded music charts were populated by a variety of acts that would, in all likelihood, have operated only in the independent scene in previous decades. In some cases, these literally were the same acts: R.E.M, Sonic Youth, and Nirvana all recorded with independent labels in the 1980s before either signing to or being absorbed into major labels.[44] The results were prodigiously successful and offered a sense of validation for those who had felt the merits of independent musicians had been too long overlooked.[45]

As Craig Mathieson (2000) describes in *The Sell-In*, from the early 1990s major labels courted Australian bands from the independent scene, 'plucking' them from obscurity and fast-tracking them to distribution streams. The process straddled geographic scales, described later as a 'glocalization' strategy.[46] Talent scouts ('A&R reps') worked for national subsidiaries of major labels; recordings were sold within domestic markets alongside those of global stars and promoted to global distribution channels when they seemed promising enough. Enforcement of copyright laws was crucial: exclusive ownership of copyright meant that if an act did become popular in a given region, there was only one way to purchase their recorded music.[47]

INXS's manager Chris Murphy was also involved in the plucking trend, founding the rooArt record label in 1988 and landing Australia's first 'alternative' #1 hit with Ratcat's 'That Ain't Bad' (1990). rooArt made use of major label distribution channels but sought out bands from the independent scene. The rapid plucking process applied to labels as well as bands: rooArt was purchased by BMG in 1996. Throughout the decade, many other independent record labels (including Mushroom Records) were acquired by major labels.[48] In spite of outward changes to the types of music acts on the charts, the global music industry reached a peak of agglomeration in the late 1990s. In 1997, five companies accounted for 90% of music sales in America, and 70–80% of music sales worldwide.[49]

One effect of music industry restructuring in the 1990s was to promote the idea that waiting to be picked was the best chance of success for musicians. The process was now rapid and suspenseful: bands recorded demos or entire albums at their own expense, sent them out into the ether, then waited for lift-off. A key case in point was silverchair, a group of teenagers from Newcastle who won the evocatively titled *Pick Me* demo competition run by SBS-TV and national youth radio network Triple J, then signed to a Sony subsidiary.[50] The waiting room dichotomy (picked or not picked) could be contrasted with the strongly hierarchical, longer term system that preceded it, and began to hollow out the steps on the ladder to 'making it'. It might also have begged the question, after reading this advice published in 1996, that if record companies were so fond of bands that did things themselves, what a recording contract actually did:

> So you're a young band, you know you're just as good as silverchair, but you don't have a deal. The A & R folk would love you if only they could hear you – how do the two parties get together? …With the price of making your own cds significantly lower, self-financed cds are a reality now for many bands. All the label representatives agree that if a band has previously made a good quality cd (or demo tape), it's a definite feather in their caps… "there's no point in sending out ten – send out two to three hundred, to all the radio stations all over the country."[51]

With the global music industry peaking in agglomeration in the late 1990s, it could be argued at this point that they were only nominally involved in recording: their true powers lay in reproducing and distributing music. Less generously, it could even be argued that they actually specialised in just stopping anyone else doing this. The prices of compact discs in Australia, buoyed by favourable copyright laws, were high enough to attract the attention of the Prices Surveillance Authority.[52] This situation did not last. From 1999 onwards, digital file sharing disrupted the market for music *reproduction and distribution*. Major labels reacted with 'fear and loathing'.[53] Record labels endured epic financial losses in the late 1990s and early 2000s and responded by quickly downsizing and merging, then, much more slowly, changing their business models to move away from physical album sales as a chief revenue stream.[54] This meant making use of the newer, legal digital platforms that proliferated after 2003, and branching into licensing streams for other commercial products like advertisements and the *Idol* television programmes. A particularly sought-after commodity in the twenty-first-century music industry is a single catchy enough to make a return on tiny digital download margins and to quickly propel tour sales, as described in *The Song Machine*.[55]

Writing at this stage of the twenty-first century, 'independent musician' is something of a tautology. The overwhelming majority of musicians operate without a major label recording contract, or any recording contract at all. To do it yourself as a musician (that is, record, reproduce, and distribute music) is now quite possible, with both positive and negative outcomes for musicians. Touring is an important revenue stream for established bands facing depleted revenue streams from sales of existing recordings. With this in mind, the *Rock Star: INXS* television programme and the decision of the surviving INXS members to continue touring seems more pragmatic than strange. For less established bands, the 1990s preoccupations with recording contracts have passed, but the paths to success are suspenseful and stressful in their own ways. Recording can be a very isolated endeavour that one is expected to do at home *before* performing live, alongside other individualised administrative and promotional tasks.[56] The 'buzz' of a music scene can be simply the buzz of many bands converging in one place, the 'it' that bands are doing themselves, comprises live music but also a great deal of the tasks previously undertaken (without any particular kindness, but undertaken nonetheless) by record labels.[57] In this climate, a socially cohesive music scene that is, if nothing else, low on stress begins to take on new significance.[58]

Changing Status of Live Music

Live music predated and now post-dates the twentieth-century music industry. The means of delivery remain essentially unchanged: audiences and performers show up at the same place and time. Where live music *has* changed is in its status and its geography.

Between the 1980s and the 2000s, descriptions of live music in Australian cities changed from that of being a booming but not particularly inclusive industry with close ties to alcohol sales and the recorded music industry, to something deserving of, and in need of, protection from external factors.[59] Reports of venue closures, particularly in Sydney, began in earnest in the late 1980s, and continued through the 1990s.[60] Accounts of live music in Melbourne also suggested the end of a boom time, but were less negative than those in Sydney.[61] While many of the early wave of independent crossover acts had been signed to Sydney record labels, throughout the 1990s Melbourne became a more attractive destination for musicians.[62]

Amidst the hubbub of recorded music changes in the 1990s, the status of live music was something of a sideshow. Attention from both musicians and the music industry remained focused on the national and global scale of operations, and the same could be true of interest for policy-makers. Marcus Breen defines the mid-1980s through to 1998 as a distinct 'policy moment' (marked, as it happens, at the beginning by the 'Rocking the Royals' concert in which INXS participated). During this time, a series of state and federal government initiatives attempted to fashion popular music as a stable employer and export commodity; the idea of the Australian music industry as a 'minnow somehow bestowed with the mighty jaws of a ravaging shark' was imagined and then rapidly downsized.[63]

Early in the 2000s, live music gained new status for policy-makers as a desirable feature of night-time economies and creative economies.[64] The 'creative city' rather than the 1990s concept of the 'creative nation' gained popularity as a potential strategy for cities grappling with deindustrialisation. While the creative cities framework was subject to critique, research into the factors affecting live music locations became increasingly sophisticated in this time frame, particularly from researchers with a background in urban planning.[65] A key finding in live music research was that on-paper support for live music counted little when policies inadvertently made live music a difficult choice for venue operators.

In the late 1990s, conflict over live music venues in Australian cities began to make headlines more regularly: from noise complaints, residential redevelopment, poker machines, and liquor licensing policy, music scene participants lobbied to protect live music venues from external stresses.[66] From the focus on inner-city music venues, it would be possible to reach the conclusion that aggregate live music venue decline was precipitous, or that it was a purely inner-city phenomenon brought on by gentrification. While the pressures were real, the conceptualisations of decline were only partly true. Decline in live music over time was evident, but this occurred geographically and individually, as restructuring rather than aggregate decline.

Table 3 shows a summary of live music data from Melbourne, collected from the same week in four respective years: 1981, 1991, 1996, and 2006.

Table 3 Publicly listed live music performances, same week of different years, Melbourne

	1981	1991	1996	2006
Number of live music performances listed	360	484	544	816
Number of live music venues listed	143	164	122	135
Number of bands/acts listed	231	394	438	645
Percentage of performances listed in top 5 venues	13%	16%	21%	22%
% of performances listed in CBD	9%	9%	13%	20%
% of performances listed in Fitzroy	4%	11%	15%	17%
% of performances listed in Richmond	3%	11%	9%	3%
% of performances listed in St Kilda	6%	11%	10%	13%

Sources: *The Age, Beat magazine*
Details in S. J. Taylor (2016) *Geographical Information Systems for Applied Social Research: The Case of the Live Music Industry in Sydney and Melbourne*, Doctor of Philosophy (PhD Geospatial Science), Mathematical and Geospatial Sciences, RMIT University

The data is drawn from a wider research project.[67] Here, we can glimpse some broad trends in Melbourne live music between the early 1980s and the mid-2000s. Firstly, the number of advertised live music performances increased over time: from 360 in 1981, through to 816 in 2006. The number of venues changed little: 143 in 1981 and 135 in 2006. The number of individual musical acts (referred to as 'bands' here for convenience) increased: 231 in 1981, through to 645 in 2006. These changes did not occur evenly. Over time, there were more bands, but they all performed less frequently, and with greater concentration into particular suburbs and venues.

Aside from the patchwork of live music concentrating into some suburbs more than others, a broader geographic change took place through the late 1980s and through the 1990s, wherein the suburban live music circuit quietly declined in importance. The idea of significant live music venues outside of the inner city, in suburbs like Ferntree Gully, Frankston, Sandringham, Doncaster, or Bulleen, can now seem a novelty. But all these suburbs can be seen in the list of live music performances by INXS, as they could for other well-known bands of the era.[68]

In the 1970s and 1980s, playing at large suburban venues was a stepping stone or brutal litmus test for artists on the road to national success. They reached large audiences and turned a reasonable profit (though not necessarily for the musicians) based on prodigious beer sales.[69] These venues were also allied with the recorded music industry. The suburban circuit benefited greatly from the national exposure of bands on *Countdown*. The venues were rarely booked directly by interactions between bands and publicans, but rather were facilitated by booking agencies with strong ties to the recorded music industry.[70]

For INXS, the booking agency connection was made through their manager, as Chris Murphy had worked as a booking agent for years. Whether through managers or booking agents vertically aligned with recording companies, bands received a geographic push when they signed up to contracts. There was a rationale to book bands at many venues, in both the inner city and in the suburban circuit: live shows were profitable, they helped to sell records, everyone (from the band through to bookers through to the record label) had a vested interest in selling records, and, in a happy coincidence, publicans also made a decent profit and had no obvious alternative uses for pub space (yet). When this set of push factors dissipated, the suburban circuit lost energy and quietly declined. In the 1990s in Melbourne, the introduction of poker machines and the increased enforcement of drink driving legislation helped to usher in new uses of suburban pub spaces.[71] But since musicians had rarely dealt with these venues directly, these threats were not so readily noticed as those presented years later by gentrification in the inner city.

In contrast to the costs and efforts of recording, the barriers to live music performance in the late 1970s and early 1980s were few. The only real difference lay in what kind of live music venue bands performed at, or how often. Less serious bands performed at inner-city venues outside of the booking agency system, less often, but still without a great deal of effort (after all, it was possible for The Ears to be impressively lacking in strategy, but still perform live at least once a month, sometimes more). More serious bands signed up to performing more frequently and in a wider geographic range: performing several times a week, in both the inner city and the suburban circuit, was not uncommon. For those who were less interested in pursuing major label success, live music was still accessible but at a smaller geographic scale. An 'independent' venue referred informally to venues (usually pubs) not answering to booking agencies. These tended to be located in the inner city, and they were closely aligned with the independent music scene, based as they were on face-to-face contacts and shared social contacts. The Ears did not work with a booking agency. Hence, unless they were playing a support spot for a band that was, they stuck to the inner city and to the venues they knew through social contacts.

This, as it happens, is a familiar situation in the present day, but the key difference is that it is difficult for musicians to actually *live* near these venues. In the late 1970s and early 1980s, renting a room in an inner-city share house accounted for about one-third of dole or student income: a more reasonable figure than over 100%, as in the present day.[72] The fact that it was once possible to live in the inner city and participate in the music scene on a low income, even only on government benefits, is a truly amazing proposition in the present day, discussed at length in the *Dog Food* documentary. In twenty-first-century Melbourne, recording music is cheap, but real estate is not. This has had a combined effect: the absence of a geographic push from booking agencies and record labels means that musicians more often operate in a small area; the increase in land values mean there is more pressure to pull audiences into these venues; and high rents mean that musicians and audiences live further from venues, and each other.

Dogs in Space/The Ears Reappraisal in the Late 2000s

The Ears overlapped with INXS in time and space, sharing several of the same inner-city Melbourne venues, and operating within the same industry. But they differed in terms of their operational model their geographic range. The key characteristics of The Ears' gigs in contrast to those of INXS are now defining features of the wider music industry: independent bands, performing less often, compressed into particular venues and into particular suburbs of the inner city. The suburbs in which The Ears performed are still recognisable to music scene participants in the present day: St Kilda, Fitzroy, and the CBD. Also familiar to contemporary audiences is their lack of obvious 'going somewhere': nobody expects to follow the same steady path to success as INXS, nor even to be 'picked up' like a 1990s independent band. Instead, what seems unusual and desirable about The Ears now are the casual proliferation of live music opportunities, the cheap rent and communal living, the proximity to live music venues, and devil-may-care attitude to success.

The status of the recording industry at the time of its release provides insights into the reception to *Dogs in Space*. The world depicted in the film presented a disjuncture with its major label star, and the structure of the music industry in the late 1980s. At the time, INXS were associated with commercial success and a kind of corny nationalism that celebrated certain bands who had 'made it', seemingly at the expense of those operating on the independent scene:

> You would have to have been living in a barrel not to have noticed the nationalistic tub-thumping about the qualities of 'Australian music' that has been going on in the past year - the failures of the jingoistic Australian Made tour notwithstanding. Sometimes I think no-one would bat an eyelid

if INXS, Jimmy Barnes and Pseudo Echo formed a supergroup to record Advance Australia Fair for their next assault on the lucrative American market, with a dub mix of Waltzing Matilda on the B-side...[73]

Ten years later, in 1997, INXS was cited as an example of what had been lost during a decade of music industry agglomeration, the lost possibility of 'making it' to something bigger by gradually increasing scale of operations:

> When we did have a healthy Australian industry was in the late 1970s, early 1980s, when the Cold Chisels, The Angels, INXS, Midnight Oil etc. were coming through the live scene and grabbing an audience. Radio and record companies had to sign them because of sheer weight of numbers. That's not happening now...The old adage of growing up in public doesn't happen anymore.[74]

In the 1970s and 1980s, trying one's luck as a musician in Australia typically took several years, in which the normal strategy was to perform live frequently (and in a lot of 'festering beer barns'[75]), build an audience, record when it could be afforded, tour to promote the recording, suck up to the right gatekeepers, and hope to proceed incrementally upwards (it was 'a long way to the top'). In the 1990s, the steps on the ladder began to hollow out, but the prospect of being 'picked' was sufficiently exciting (at the time) to override this. This was followed by rapid change in the status of recorded music in relation to live music.

In fact, the change was so great but is still so recent that engaging with material about the 1990s music industry induces, for this author, a certain cringe. The prevailing preoccupations with record labels and albums seem strange and stressful, especially with the knowledge that contracts were no longer financially necessary for recording. Above all, and in contrast to both The Ears and INXS, not many people in the 1990s seemed to be making money *or* having fun. Excellent examples can be found in rock music documentaries of the era: *The Fauves—15 Minutes to Rock* (in which affable Australian band The Fauves are berated over the phone by their record company) and *Dig!* (tracing the rivalry of two American bands during the 1990s, culminating in tears over a failed bid to score a record deal).[76] There is no such cringe in watching *Dogs in Space*.

Dogs in Space was not a commercial success on its release, but it has gone on to achieve cult status. Decades later, the Melbourne post-punk scene received renewed attention as a historical example of a thriving local music scene.[77] The film was remastered and re-released in 2009 as part of the Melbourne International Film Festival. In addition, Lowenstein directed a documentary, *We're Livin' on Dog Food*, which looked back to the making of *Dogs in Space*, and to the post-punk scene itself. 'Exciting' was a keyword throughout: it was an exciting time to be in a band, an exciting time to be in the city.

In comparison to the norms of the twenty-first-century Melbourne music scene, The Ears would just be 'a band', and not a particularly unsuccessful one, let alone a 'laughing stock'. They had gigs more than once a month, had a consistent (albeit niche) audience, worked with an independent record label, and were the subject of written reviews (some good, some bad, and with a certain amount of local notoriety). They also appeared, at the very least, to have had fun. They lived with other young people who were also engaged in creative endeavours, none of whom seemed to fret about precarious employment, high rent, time pressures, success pressures, or even food. As described by Nique Needles: 'there didn't seem to be any need to do anything, you got the dole…no one was really searching for anything except fun'.[78]

Meanwhile, INXS perfectly navigated the 1980s conditions for live music in Australian cities, working through available paths of opportunity year upon year, through to successively wider geographical scales. Their successes are still impressive, but also seem impossible to recreate, having traced a path that no longer exists. Successful in their own, less profitable way, The Ears might be seen to be expertly prepared for that great euphemism of twenty-first-century work skills: 'resilience'. By being out of fashion in the 1980s, and out of action for the entire 1990s, they ended up being perfectly dressed for the new century.

Notes

1. R. Lowenstein quoted in S. Coupe (1986) 'Generation of Sex, Drugs, Rock'n'roll', *Sydney Morning Herald* 14 December, 115.

2. J. Schembri (1986) 'Hutchence Sends a Message', *Melbourne Age*, 26 December, 8–9; S. Coupe (1986) 'Generation of Sex, Drugs, Rock'n'roll', *Sydney Morning Herald*, 14 December, 115.
3. J. Lanier (2010) *You Are Not a Gadget: A Manifesto* (London: Penguin); A. J. Scott (1999) 'The US Recorded Music Industry: On the Relations Between Organization, Location; and Creativity, in the Cultural Economy', *Environment and Planning A*, 31(11), 1965–1984.
4. K. Huffhines (1987) '"Dogs" Has a Bit of Bite About Aussie Decadence', *Detroit Free Press*, 22 November, 76; D. Nichols and S. Perillo (2016) 'Friday Essay: Dogs in Space, 30 years on—A Once Maligned Film Comes of Age', *The Conversation*, 15 April, https://theconversation.com/friday-essay-dogs-in-space-30-years-on-a-once-maligned-film-comes-of-age-56288, accessed 6 June 2019; B. Smith (1986) 'Dogged by Punk', *Juke*, 22 March, 4.
5. P. Brophy in R. Lowenstein (Director) (2009) *We're Livin' on Dog Food*. [Documentary film].
6. R. S. Howard and O. Olsen interviewed in ABC-TV (1977) *Music Around Us*, https://www.youtube.com/watch?v=KDIVaogpKls, accessed 6 June 2019.
7. T. Cateforis (2011) *Are We Not New Wave?: Modern Pop at the Turn of the 1980s* (Ann Arbor: The University of Michigan Press); V. Goldman (2019) *Revenge of the She-Punks* (Austin: University of Texas Press), 59; K. A. Gordon (2016) 'Fossils: Sire Records' Don't Call It Punk', *That Devil Music*, http://www.thatdevilmusic.com/2016/08/fossils-sire-records-dont-call-it-punk.html, accessed 6 June 2019.
8. I. McFarlane (1999) *The Encyclopedia of Australian Rock and Pop* (Sydney: Allen & Unwin); D. Nichols (2016) *Dig: Australian Rock and Pop Music 1960–85* (Portland, OR: Verse Chorus Press).
9. V. Riley (1992) 'Death Rockers of the World Unite! Melbourne 1978–80—Punk Rock or No Punk Rock?' in P. Hayward (ed.) *From Pop to Punk to Postmodernism: Popular Music and Australian Culture from the 1960s to the 1990s* (North Sydney: Allen & Unwin), 113–126.
10. D. Nichols (2016) *Dig: Australian Rock and Pop Music 1960–85* (Portland, OR: Verse Chorus Press), 272–273; MILESAGO (2004) 'Radio in Australia—An Overview', *MILESAGO*, www.milesago.com/Radio/radioinaustralia.htm, accessed 6 June 2019.
11. First published version of C. Walker (ed.) (1982) *Inner City Sound* (Glebe, NSW: Australia Wild & Woolley); see also 2005 revised updated version

and C. Walker (1996) *Stranded: The Secret History of Australian Independent Music, 1977–1991* (Sydney: Pan Macmillan).
12. R. S. Cauthorn (1988) '"Dogs in Space" Packs Small but Heartfelt Bite', *Arizona Daily Star*, 12 March, 29; Coupe (1986) 'Generation of Sex…'; Huffhines (1987) '"Dogs" Has a bit of Bite…'; L. Klady (1987) '"Dogs" Runs on Punk Power', *Los Angeles Times*, 9 October, 154.
13. Cauthorn, '"Dogs in Space" Packs Small but Heartfelt Bite'; S. Hunter (1987) '"Dogs in Space": Australian Hippie Meets Bad End', *Baltimore Sun*, 30 October, 98; Klady (1987) '"Dogs" Runs on Punk Power…'.
14. S. Wang (1980) 'Little Bands', *TAGG: The Alternative Gig Guide*, 17, 15–28 February, 46–47.
15. T. Lee (1980) 'Gig Review: The Ears', *TAGG: The Alternative Gig Guide (Melbourne)*, 24 October–6 November, 49–51.
16. 'TAGG Prospects: The Ears', *TAGG: The Alternative Gig Guide*, 16, 1–14 February, 18–19.
17. C. Walker (1980) 'The Ears…(Hearts, Melbourne)', *RAM*, 25 July, 31.
18. G. Gleeson (1981) 'Snakefinger! The Ears', *TAGG: The Alternative Gig Guide*, 47, 14–28 May, 15.
19. 'TAGG Magg' (1981) *TAGG: The Alternative Gig Guide (Australia)*, 1, 11–25 June, 9.
20. M. Lynch (1981) 'Models Again', *TAGG: The Alternative Gig Guide (Australia)*, 25 June–9 July, 16–17.
21. S. Carney (1992) '"Achtung Baby" Top for 1991', *Melbourne Age*, 2 January, 24.
22. J. Apter (2013) *Up From Down Under: How Australian Music Changed the World* (Scoresby: The Five Mile Press), 183–198; INXS and A. Bozza (2005) *INXS : Story to Story* (Sydney: Bantam Books); INXS, Y. Gamblin, and E. St John (1992) *INXS: The Official Inside Story of a Band on the Road* (Port Melbourne: Mandarin); D. San Miguel (2011) *The Ballroom: The Melbourne Punk and Post-Punk Scene: A Tell All Memoir* (Melbourne: Melbourne Books), 104–106; T. Sarno (1986) 'Can INXS Break the International Sound Barrier?' *Canberra Times*, 27 April, 42–47.
23. K. McCabe (2016) 'It was the Line-Up and the Party of a Lifetime, Australian Made Celebrates Its 30th anniversary', *news.com.au*, www.news.com.au/entertainment/it-was-the-lineup-and-the-party-of-a-lifetime-australian-made-celebrates-its-30th-anniversary/news-story/b865ee8bb2304476f164261baa3c44c1, accessed 6 June 2019.
24. W. Milsom, H. Thomas, and P. Hawkes (1986) *Pay to Play: The Australian Rock Music Industry* (Ringwood: Penguin), 4.

25. J. Lethlean (1980) 'Sydney Group Plays a Wide Range of Music', *Melbourne Age*, 11 December, 21.
26. K. Wakefield (1980) 'Her Majesty Rules to Rock', *Melbourne Age*, 29 August, 'Weekender' section, 5.
27. L. Barber (1987) 'Oz Rock: A Corporate Creation', *Sydney Morning Herald*, 29 August, 51; McCabe (2016) 'It was the Line-Up and the Party of a Lifetime...'.
28. Apter (2013) *Up from Down Under...*, 197.
29. R. Glover and T. Creswell (1984) 'Hey Hey It's The Takeaways', *Sydney Morning Herald*, 2 July, 36; I. McFarlane (1999) *The Encyclopedia of Australian Rock and Pop*, 129.
30. A. Ryan (1982) 'INXS, Beargarden', *Roadrunner*, May, 23.
31. P. Galvin (2009) 'We're Living on Dog Food. So What?' *SBS*, September 7, www.sbs.com.au/movies/article/2009/09/07/were-living-dog-food-so-what, accessed 9 June 2019.
32. 'Is Rock Band Oasis a Thing of the Past?' (1996) *Saskatoon Star-Phoenix*, 14 September, 44.
33. C. Adams and K. McCabe (2012) 'INXS's Demise After 35 Years Followed Years of Controversy', *Sunday Telegraph*, 18 November, https://www.dailytelegraph.com.au/news/opinion/inxss-demise-after-35-years-followed-years-of-controversy/news-story/e18ce388d7818f1bb056f3f7b57ee442, accessed 9 June 2019.
34. E. St John quoted in Adams and McCabe (2012) 'INXS's Demise ...'
35. J. Doorakkers (2018) 'Modern Day Music Industry: The Role of Money in Making Successful Albums', Bachelor Thesis in Economics, Universiteit van Amsterdam, 8, http://scriptiesonline.uba.uva.nl/document/668161, accessed 9 June 2019.
36. A. J. Scott (1999) 'The US Recorded Music Industry...'.
37. Milsom, Thomas and Hawkes (1986) *Pay to play...*; C. Walker, T. Hogan and P. Beilharz (2012) 'Rock 'n'Labels: Tracking the Australian Recording Industry in "The Vinyl Age" Part Two: 1970–1995, and After', *Thesis Eleven*, 110(1), 112–131.
38. Apter (2013) *Up from down under...*
39. B. J. Hracs (2012) 'A Creative Industry in Transition: The Rise of Digitally Driven Independent Music Production', *Growth and Change*, 43(3), 442–461; D. Nichols (2016) *Dig...*, 422; Milsom, Thomas and Hawkes (1986) *Pay to Play...*, 154. (Includes the note that Australian Crawl in 1985 owed $350,000 in studio time).

40. E. Forde (2015) 'Record Breaker: A Brief History of Prince's Contractual Controversies', *The Guardian*, August 11, https://www.theguardian.com/music/2015/aug/10/history-prince-contractual-controversy-warner-paisley-park, accessed 6 June 2019; K. Gordon (2015) *Girl in a Band* (London: Faber & Faber); M. Seymour (2008) *Thirteen Tonne Theory: Life Inside Hunters and Collectors* (Camberwell: Penguin); B. Springsteen (2016) *Born to Run* (London: Simon & Schuster); C. Walker (1996) *Stranded…*; S. Weller (2008) *Girls Like Us: Carole King, Joni Mitchell, Carly Simon: And The Journey of a Generation* (London: Ebury).
41. R. Alberts (2003) *Tascam: 30 Years of Recording Evolution* (Milwaukee, WI: Hal Leonard).
42. A. Leyshon (2009) 'The Software Slump?: Digital Music, the Democratisation of Technology, and the Decline of the Recording Studio Sector Within the Musical Economy', *Environment and Planning A*, 41(6), 1309–1331.
43. A. Howell (1989) 'Phantom of the Underground', *Sydney Morning Herald*, 21 September, 124; T. Winkler (1994) 'The CD Reality', *Melbourne Age*, 11 March, 16.
44. C. Schuftan (2012) *Entertain Us: The Rise and Fall of Alternative Rock in the Nineties* (Sydney: HarperCollins Australia).
45. C. Walker (1996) *Stranded…*
46. C. McLeay (2006) 'Government Regulation in the Australian Popular Music Industry: The Rhetoric of Cultural Protection, the Reality of Economic Production', *GeoJournal*, 65(1–2), 91–102; C. Mathieson (2000) *The Sell-In: How the Music Business Seduced Alternative Rock* (Sydney: Allen & Unwin).
47. McLeay (2006) 'Government Regulation…'; D. Rowe (2001) 'Globalisation, Regionalisation and Australianisation in Music: Lessons from the Parallel Importing Debate', in T. Bennett and D. Carter (eds.) *Culture in Australia: Policies, Publics and Programs* (Melbourne: Cambridge University Press), 46–65.
48. C. Mathieson (2000) *The Sell-In: How the Music Business Seduced Alternative Rock* (Sydney: Allen & Unwin); Walker, Hogan and Beilharz (2012) 'Rock 'n' Labels…'.
49. Hracs (2012) 'A Creative Industry in Transition…'; A. J. Scott (1999) 'The US Recorded Music Industry…'.
50. J. Apter (2003) *Tomorrow Never Knows: The Silverchair Story* (Port Melbourne: Coulomb Communications).

51. T. Bolster (1996) 'Young Talent Time: The Hunt for the Next Silverchair', *Beat*, 21 August, 16–17.
52. M. Breen (1993) *Rock Dogs: Politics and the Australian Music Industry* (Lanham, MD: University Press of America); M. Smith (1991) 'Musicians, Copyright and the PSA', *Drum Media*, 20 August, 21.
53. A. Leyshon (2001) 'Time—Space (and Digital) Compression: Software Formats, Musical Networks, and the Reorganisation of the Music Industry', *Environment and Planning A*, 33(1), 50.
54. M. Breen. (2004) 'The Music Industry, Technology and Utopia—An Exchange Between Marcus Breen and Eamonn Forde', *Popular Music* 23(1), 79–89; C. Mann (2000) 'The Heavenly Jukebox From Hell: Internet Piracy Isn't the Problem—The Music Industry is the Problem', *Atlantic Monthly*, September, 39–59.
55. J. Seabrook (2016) *The Song Machine: How to Make a Hit* (London: Vintage).
56. J. Heazlewood (2014) *Funemployed: The Life of an Artist in Australia, from Cradle to Centrelink* (Melbourne: Affirm Press); I. Rogers (2008) "You've Got to Go to Gigs to Get Gigs': Indie Musicians, Eclecticism and the Brisbane Scene', *Continuum*, 22(5), 639–649.
57. Hracs (2012) 'A Creative Industry in Transition…'
58. N. Danger (2018) 'Why I Quit the Music Industry to Join My Local Music Scene', *Music Think Tank*, September 13, http://www.musicthinktank.com/blog/why-i-quit-the-music-industry-to-join-my-local-music-scene.html, accessed 9 June 2019; B. J. Hracs, J. L. Grant, J. Haggett, and J. Morton (2011) 'A Tale of Two Scenes: Civic Capital and Retaining Musical Talent in Toronto and Halifax', *The Canadian Geographer/Le Géographe canadien*, 55(3), 365–382.
59. E. Carbines (2003) *Live Music Taskforce Report and Recommendations*, December 5 (Melbourne, Victoria: Department of Planning and Community Development); S. Homan (2008) 'A Portrait of the Politician as a Young Pub Rocker: Live Music Venue Reform in Australia', *Popular Music*, 27(2), 243–256.
60. C. Walker (2012) 'History is Made at Night: Live Music in Australia', *Platform Papers* (32), 2–60; J. Bilic (1989) 'It's Tough Times for Rock Bands', *Sydney Morning Herald*, 29 June, 104; S. Molitorisz (1999) 'Rock in a Hard Place', *Sydney Morning Herald*, 16 April, 4; D. Scatena (1991) 'The Great Rock 'N' Roll Dwindle,' *Juke*, 835, 27 April, 11.

61. D. Jellie (1995) 'The Prince Expires, but Pub Rock Wails on', *Melbourne Age*, 26 October, 3; L. Schwartz (1996) 'So You Want to Be a Rock Star?' *The Sunday Age*, 1 June, 3.
62. D. Adams (1994), 'Music in Melbourne, Sound Cheques in Sydney', *Melbourne Age*, Melbourne: Fairfax, May 12, 'Entertainment Guide' section, 3; P. Donovan (2000) 'For Those About to Rock, Melbourne Suits you', *The Sunday Age*, 11 June, 17; T. Duffy (1994) 'Melbourne Rises Up from Down Under: New Music Mecca Boasts Frente! & others', *Billboard*, 106(46), 1.
63. Breen (1993) *Rock Dogs...*, 3.
64. C. Beer (2011) 'Centres that Never Sleep? Planning for the Night-Time Economy Within the Commercial Centres of Australian Cities', *Australian Planner*, 48(3), 141–147; R. Florida (2002) *The Rise of the Creative Class and How It's Transforming Work, Leisure, Community and Everyday Life* (New York: Basic Books); S. Homan (2011). '"I Tote and I Vote": Australian Live Music and Cultural Policy', *Arts Marketing: An International Journal*, 1(2), 96–107; A. C. Pratt (2008). Creative Cities: The Cultural Industries and the Creative Class. Geografiska Annaler: Series B, *Human Geography*, 90(2), 107–117.
65. M. Burke and A. Schmidt (2012) 'How Should We Plan and Regulate Live Music in Australian Cities? Learnings from Brisbane', *Australian Planner*, 50(1), 68–78; C. Gibson and S. Homan (2004) 'Urban Redevelopment, Live Music and Public Space', *International Journal of Cultural Policy*, 10(1), 67–84; S. Homan (2000) 'Losing the Local: Sydney and the Oz Rock Tradition', *Popular Music*, 19(1), 31–49; S. Homan (2003). *The Mayor's a Square: Live Music and Law and Order in Sydney* (Sydney: Local Consumption Publications); B. Johnson and S. Homan (2003) *Vanishing Acts: An Inquiry into the State of Live Popular Music Opportunities in New South Wales* (Sydney: Australia Council and the NSW Ministry for the Arts); K. Shaw (2013) 'The Melbourne Indie Music Scene and the Inner City Blues', in L. S. Porter and K. Shaw (eds.) *Whose Urban Renaissance?: An international Comparison of Urban Regeneration Strategies* (New York: Routledge), 366–385; J. Wardle (2008) *A Comparison of State and Territory Legislation and Regulations for Live Entertainment Venues in Australia* (Sydney: Music Council of Australia).
66. G. Coslovich and P. Donovan (2003) 'Inner-City Blues', *Melbourne Age*, 11 June, 'A3' section, 4; S. Homan (2010) 'Governmental as Anything: Live Music and Law and Order in Melbourne', *Perfect Beat*, 11(2), 103–118; R. Lobato (2006) 'Gentrification, Cultural Policy and Live Music

in Melbourne', *Media International Australia, Incorporating Culture & Policy*, 120, August, 63–75; J. Roberts (2011) 'Life After Death', *Melbourne Age*, 18 August, 18, www.theage.com.au/entertainment/music/life-after-death-20110818-1izve.html, accessed 9 June 2019; K. Shaw (2005) 'The Place of Alternative Culture and the Politics of Its Protection in Berlin, Amsterdam and Melbourne', *Planning Theory & Practice*, 6(2), 149–169; VicMUSIC (2003) *Rock 'n' Roll Ain't Noise Pollution* (Fitzroy, Victoria: VicMUSIC), http://rollingthunder33.tripod.com/RocknRollAintNoisePollution.pdf, accessed 9 June 2019; C. Webb (2003) 'Noising off Over Live Music', *Melbourne Age*, 26 May, www.theage.com.au/articles/2003/05/23/1053585693534.html, accessed 6 June 2019.

67. S. J. Taylor (2016) *Geographical Information Systems for Applied Social Research: The Case of the Live Music Industry in Sydney and Melbourne*, Doctor of Philosophy (PhD Geospatial Science), Mathematical and Geospatial Sciences, RMIT University.

68. A. Duffield (2009), *The Countdown Generation: 1974–1987*, Honours Thesis, School of Music (Southbank), Faculty of the Victorian College of the Arts and Music, The University of Melbourne, 41–45; Seymour (2008) *Thirteen Tonne Theory*...

69. J. Fiske, R. I. V. Hodge, and R. Turner (1987) *Myths of Oz: Reading Australian Popular Culture* (Sydney: Allen & Unwin); S. Homan (2000) 'Losing the Local: Sydney and the Oz Rock Tradition', *Popular Music*, 19(1), 31–49; K. Legge (1981) 'Young Bands Get Payment Blues', *Melbourne Age*, 12 March, 10.

70. R. Guilliatt (1997) 'Between ROCK and a hard place', *Sydney Morning Herald*, Sydney: Fairfax, October 10, 14; Milsom, Thomas and Hawkes (1986) *Pay to Play*...; T. Robert (1988) 'A conversation with Frank Stivala', *Beat*, 108, September 7, 19.

71. S. Taylor (2018) 'A Place to Play: An Historical Geographical Perspective on Live Music and Poker Machines in Australian Pubs', *Historic Environment*, 30(2), 112–133.

72. S. O'Hanlon (2018) *City Life: The New Urban Australia* (Sydney, NSW: NewSouth), 195–217; K. Shaw (2005) 'Gentrification and the Inner City Blues', in C. Long, K. Shaw, and C. M. Merlo (eds.) *Suburban Fantasies: Melbourne Unmasked* (Melbourne: Australian Scholarly Publishing), 20–49.

73. Barber (1987) 'Oz Rock: A Corporate Creation'...

74. J. O'Rourke quoted in L. Schwartz (1997) 'Band Rights', *The Sunday Age* 16 November, 'Applause' section, 1.

75. S. Carney (1992) '"Achtung Baby" Top for 1991', *Melbourne Age*, 2 January, 24.
76. O. Timoner (Director) (2004) *Dig!* [Documentary film]; V. Stuart (Director) (1998) *The Fauves ... 15 minutes to rock.* [Documentary film].
77. P. Donovan and A. Murfett (2009) 'Post-Punk Revival', *Melbourne Age*, 3 July, 'Entertainment Guide' section, 3; S. O'Brien (Producer) (2010) *Do That Dance! Australian Post Punk, 1977–1983.* [TV documentary in two parts] Australian Broadcasting Corporation; San Miguel (2011) *The Ballroom...*
78. N. Needles quoted in R. Lowenstein (Director) (2009) *We're Livin' on Dog Food.* [Documentary film].

The Strange Life of 'Shivers' and Its Place in *Dogs in Space*

Lisa MacKinney

The history of popular music is littered with extraordinary achievements by adolescents. 'Shivers', dashed off in ten minutes by a teenaged Rowland S. Howard, unquestionably deserves a place in this canon. On the surface, it seems simple bordering on innocuous, but closer examination reveals a far more complex set of dynamics at work. As Rowland's brother Harry Howard observed while introducing a rare performance of 'Shivers' in conjunction with Edwina Preston,

> Rowland wrote fantastic songs, and I've never really learnt any of his songs before, but I was really amazed at how incredibly simple they are. Yet with the same chords…he creates such an incredibly different, evocative song.[1]

This chapter looks closely at the origins and construction of 'Shivers' in order to arrive at a more informed understanding of just how this deceptively simple song worked so well at speaking to so many. As British writer and critic Jack Sargeant said of 'Shivers',

L. MacKinney (✉)
Melbourne, VIC, Australia

Everyone I know in Australia seems to know that song - they remember it from school discos and so on. It seems to have had a huge cultural impact.[2]

Sargeant made that observation in 2003, but even when Richard Lowenstein was gearing up to make *Dogs in Space* in 1985, 'Shivers' had already run away from home and joined the circus, accumulating a reputation and standing that consistently irritated and frustrated its author. 'It's bizarre', Howard mused, 'that you can write something and once it goes out to the public domain you no longer have any control over how it's perceived'.[3] Its status as a kind of home-grown underground cult ballad was central to its inclusion in *Dogs in Space* and further cemented by the role it played in the film. 'Shivers' has survived an array of cover versions, from a rendition by Sam Sejavka at a Triple R community radio benefit in 1986, directly inspired by the film, to an incongruous working-over from mainstream rock band the Screaming Jets that was released as a single in 1993 and sold enough copies to reach #19 on the ARIA singles chart.[4] 'Nick Cave fans were appalled', Rachel Gibson told readers of *The Age* two years later.[5] The ability of 'Shivers' to operate in a bewildering variety of contexts is a direct result of the complex realities it is able to convey in pop song form, and as a result, it occupies a very particular place in the visual and sonic landscape of *Dogs in Space*.

Thanks to a short-lived Melbourne fanzine called *Alive 'n' Pumping*, a party that took place at 'Janet's and Lucy's place in Camberwell' on Saturday 23 July 1977 exists in the historical record.[6] Janet Austin was a music enthusiast whose friend Rowland Howard had mentioned to her that Bruce Milne wanted writers for a new punk fanzine that he and Clinton Walker were putting together. Austin contacted Milne, quickly became involved, and the first issue of *Pulp* came out in August 1977.[7] As a consequence of Austin's immersion in this musical community, the guests at her Camberwell party included, according to the *Alive 'n' Pumping* chronicler,

> everyone they knew who liked all the new rock'n roll (sic) bands as well as a few of Melbournes (sic) own bands, as yet unknown by the masses, but not for long. Of course I'm talking about the Reals, Boys Next Door, Obsessions and the Babeez (who wanted to come but couldn't).[8]

The Obsessions was Rowland Howard's second band, formed with school friends Simon McLean and Graham Pitt, both of whom he had played with after joining Tootho and the Ring of Confidence (TATROC) in 1975. Howard described the Obsessions as:

> a high school band and it didn't really ever become more than that. It was like me and my best friend and it was like a lot of bands that formed that way. It was almost like an in-joke and we wrote songs that were amusing to us. The idea of actually making a record was just so far from our minds that there was no attempt to do anything other than exactly what we wanted to do.[9]

The Obsessions' existence was brief (likely less than a year) and while it appears that at least some band members attended Janet Austin's party, there is no evidence that they performed there, or elsewhere. McLean, the band's singer, recalled that:

> I may well have been at the party and some of those bands may have played there, that was the way of things then, but I'm pretty sure that we didn't play there. We rehearsed a lot, spent a fair bit of time looking for a drummer, had some fun making a lot of racket…and that was it, so no, we didn't do any gigs.[10]

The Reals, whose line-up included Garry Gray, Chris Walsh, and Ollie Olsen, did perform, if the attendee writing for *Alive 'n' Pumping* can be relied upon: he reported that 'Janet saw the Reals and thought they were quite good, even if they were only playing in Chris' bedroom'.[11] It is also unclear whether the Boys Next Door played—at this point they had only a few, if any, shows to their credit. These three bands were scheduled to play a 'new wave rock show' at Ethel Hall, Swinburne Technical College in Hawthorn on Friday 19 August 1977 with the Reals headlining, but the Obsessions pulled out at the last minute (apparently after being unable to secure a suitable drummer) and were replaced by the Babeez. The Boys Next Door, as newcomers and doing mainly covers, were on the bottom of the bill.[12]

Nevertheless, the Obsessions received attention in locally produced zines to which the group members also contributed pieces of writing.

The first issue of *Pulp* includes, alongside Janet Austin's lengthy Radio Birdman interview/feature, coverage of a Birdman show by McLean and fascinatingly, a live review of The Reals by Howard, whose observations as a teenager were already astute, especially about his soon-to-be collaborator, Olsen.[13] Howard also designed the *Pulp* dripping ink-style logo.[14] It was around this time, while The Obsessions were operational (as much as they ever would be) and within a small community of like-minded, precociously creative young people fighting Australia's stifling dreariness and galvanised by the punk sounds trickling in from the USA and UK, that Howard wrote what remains his best-known piece of music, 'Shivers'.[15] According to Howard, he was sixteen and it took him ten minutes.[16]

The Obsessions folded when Howard departed to form the Young Charlatans with Ollie Olsen, Jeff Wegener and Janine Hall; the Reals also ceased as a consequence.[17] The Young Charlatans only lasted a little over six months and played a total of thirteen gigs, as both Howard and Olsen have testified.[18] Among the handful of surviving recordings made by the group is the earliest extant version of 'Shivers', likely dating from around mid-1978. None of this (essentially demo) material was released at the time, but in 1981 'Shivers' was issued, in a very low-key way, as a track on the fourth issue of *Fast Forward* cassette magazine. The accompanying text relates that the track 'comes from their only recording session, on a 4 track at their rehearsal studios (Rowland singing), about a week before internal friction sent them on their separate ways'.[19] The following year *Fast Forward* featured another version of 'Shivers', this time a live version by Big Bang Combo (referred to in the accompanying booklet as 'Big Bang Band'). The group is described as 'specially formed for the [Virgin Press Benefit] event, with various members of HUNTERS AND COLLECTORS and BANG as the basis. The BIG BAND played energetic renditions of a number of old rhythm 'n' blues standards'.[20] This context is noteworthy, and regardless of how one feels about this version, it is clear that 'Shivers' translated quite easily into a country-blues arrangement.[21]

Although both these recordings are significant artefacts, it is unlikely that they would have been released at all were it not for the interest generated by the legendary 'underground anthem' status of the version of 'Shivers' recorded when Rowland Howard joined the Boys Next Door in 1978. It became the last song on their debut album *Door, Door*, released as a single in May 1979. Famously, it was not Howard, but his new bandmate Nick Cave, who sang the song on record. Cave's performance, along with a substantially altered arrangement, transformed 'Shivers' to such an extent that twenty years later, Howard would lament, 'it's just so long ago, it doesn't even seem like anything to do with me – I feel like I'm sort of playing a cover version when I play it'.[22]

In terms of construction, 'Shivers' is a remarkably simple song, and what follows refers primarily to Howard's performance(s), although much is applicable to the later Cave/Boys Next Door version. It contains a total of four chords: E (tonic), A (sub-dominant), B (dominant) and C# minor (relative minor) which is used only once as the song's final chord.[23] Essentially, it's a three-chord song, and these three E-A-B chords form the classic I-IV-V blues progression that is the basis of countless rock, pop, blues and folk songs. This is one of the reasons that 'Shivers' sounds instantly familiar, because beyond all its cult/underground cachet, it is constructed from the same building blocks as, among many others, 'Louie Louie', 'Wild Thing' and 'Get Off of My Cloud'. However, where these songs use the sub-dominant (IV) as a stepping stone (hence the sub-) to get from the tonic (I) to the dominant (V), 'Shivers' uses the *dominant* (V) as a passing chord or stepping stone between the tonic (I) and the sub-dominant (IV), rendering the dominant (V) peripheral and, in fact, not dominant at all. This inverts the standard rock power dynamic in favour of a two-chord tonic/sub-dominant (E/A) progression that simply rocks gently back and forth, like a boat swaying left to right in a sea breeze but not moving from its mooring. Harmonically, this is the entirety of what happens in 'Shivers'— the chorus uses the same pattern but with variation in rhythmic emphasis and melody. Significantly, the use of the 'weaker' A/IV/sub-dominant in conjunction with the tonic means that the harmonic resolution suggested by the passing B/V/dominant never occurs; the song could conceivably go on and on forever.

This lack of resolution in conjunction with the metronomic movement back and forth between the E and A chords establishes a harmonic stasis that is maintained throughout. This simultaneously creates a sense of tension and of languid torpor that functions as a marvellously effective method for conveying musically the themes and concerns with which 'Shivers' is preoccupied. At the outset, this is juxtaposed with what would surely be a finalist in any competition for most attention-grabbing opening line of a song, 'I've been contemplating suicide...' This extraordinary jolt of clashing sensibilities grabs the listener, plunging them headlong into the song, before they can get their bearings. While in this destabilised state, the listener is then informed by the song's narrator

> But it really doesn't suit my style,
> So I think I'll just act bored instead
> And contain the blood I would've shed.

By this point, it's apparent that the narrator is in no serious danger of taking their life and that the opening line is a melodramatic conceit. Nevertheless, the listener is already hooked, still reeling but lulled by the singer's world-weary delivery, the song's gently rocking harmonic movement and tick-tock rhythm, all of which soon culminate in the song's distinctive 'Spy-yi-yi-yi-yi-yi-yi-yi-yine' refrain. Thus, two central concerns of the song are established—teenage melodrama and the young Howard's bored exasperation with it:

> When I was still at Swinburne Community School I wrote this song 'Shivers' which was intended as an ironic comment on the way I felt people I knew were making hysterical things out of what were essentially high school crushes.[24]

He noted in an earlier interview that

> It started off being a very cynical song about their behaviour and the way that they talked and acted about being in love which I found to be incredibly insincere and blown out of all proportion, although I'm hardly one to speak because I had a little glass heart pinned to my sleeve most of the time...[25]

Here, Howard (perhaps unintentionally) put his finger on one reason for the song's success when it was released as a single after undergoing a transformation during its recording with the Boys Next Door. Discussing 'Shivers' in a lengthy 1994 interview, Howard observed,

I wrote that when I was still in the Obsessions and it's turned out to be the most productive five minutes of my life! Also when I wrote it, I sat down to write a 'hit single' and it's fairly ironic that one of the few songs in my life that I've ever written that wasn't out of a desire to express something and it's the song that's moved the most people. I don't know what that proves but it proves something in an extremely cynical way.[26]

What it might prove is that in seeking to expose the (perceived) insincere histrionics of his friends' behaviour and love lives, Howard actually conveyed a core truth about the nature of teenage love and the perils of navigating new adult emotions. In this insecure, constantly shifting emotional landscape, the wearing of masks, acting 'bored instead', and 'keeping a poker face' are essential protections against the exposure of one's true, insecure, 'ill-at-ease', highly emotional self to misunderstanding and ridicule. The other extreme, 'contemplating suicide', ostensibly to demonstrate extreme depths of devotion ("If you leave me, I'll kill myself!") can be seen as another mask—if sincerity needs to be manufactured, it is automatically rendered absent. On the other hand, veering between extremes of feeling unable to live and utterly detached boredom is fairly textbook teenage emotional terrain and is no less genuine for being experienced by people who are young. 'Shivers' operates on these dual levels, exposing tensions between the desire to be genuine and sincere, and the impossibility of actually doing this.

In the chorus of 'Shivers', all this receives expression in elegantly clear poetic language:

> My baby's so vain
> She is almost a mirror
> And the sound of her name sends
> A permanent shiver down my
> Spine

Like Narcissus, the song's romantic object threatens to be consumed by her own reflection, disappearing into her mirror and being absorbed by her mask. The narrator is reduced to a bystander, lamenting the inability of both himself and his 'baby' to transcend the falseness of their facades. Set atop a simple but achingly beautiful melody, the tentatively anthemic chorus aspires to resolution and fulfilment, but has to be content with a resigned acceptance that these tensions will remain unresolved. 'Permanent shivers down my spine' is a perfectly natural, instinctive and, importantly, subconscious bodily response to the realisation of being trapped, suspended in this web of falsity. If the listener is in any doubt about this, the sudden appearance after several repetitions of the 'spi-yi-yine' refrain of a hitherto unheard C# minor chord brings the song to an abrupt end with an emphatic musical question mark. Although it may not have been his intention, Howard nevertheless communicated this with an unselfconscious authenticity that resonated with people because they recognised it, as he did, in their own behaviour and impulses. It is a mark of the song's sophistication that these multiple layers of meaning are present, and as much as Howard may have objected, Cave's elevation of a variant layer in his reading of 'Shivers' is perfectly legitimate.

Howard made it clear in numerous interviews that he remained frustrated that 'Shivers' had never been recorded to his satisfaction. As part of this process, he felt he had lost control of the song and that it had been misunderstood by the majority of its audience:

> Nick's performance of it is so hammy and overblown that it certainly wasn't the listener's fault that they interpreted it that way, but it was not the song I wrote.[27]

Cave's 'hammy' performance cannot be held solely responsible for the recorded fate of 'Shivers' though—it also received a significant rearrangement in the studio.[28] The distinctive rhythm of the strummed distorted guitar was removed and replaced with a sparse, chord-based piano phrase that made the back-and-forth two-chord pattern described earlier even more pronounced. What little guitar remained was reduced to repeated, ornamental note-based repetitive phrases, and the drums were muted and splashy with reverb. The key was changed to A, presumably to accommodate Cave's considerably deeper and richer voice, and the tempo slowed from pop song to ballad pace. In short, 'Shivers' underwent an MOR/soft-rock makeover and became an 'adult' song in the process.[29] Given the punk context of the milieu in which it was recorded and the transformation (into the Birthday Party) that the Boys Next Door would soon undergo, 'Shivers' remains a fascinating anomaly. As Ollie Olsen later observed,

> 'Shivers' went on to then get recorded by the Boys Next Door and Nick Cave sang it and stuff and it became this kind of miserable anthem for a certain generation and became quite a big part of the Australian punk rock scene which is kind of weird because it's a ballad![30]

Despite Howard's eternal dissatisfaction with 'Shivers' and Cave's eventual admission he was never able to do the song justice and that he wished Howard had sung it, the Boys Next Door version is remarkable for several reasons.[31] The 'soft-rock' arrangements and Cave's deep-voiced, boots-and-all inhabiting of the song not only transformed it into an adult record, but in the process took all that teen posturing, awkwardness, melodrama and insecurity with it into adulthood.[32] It legitimated the intensity and reality of those feelings and, it seems, made an awful lot of people feel heard, acknowledged and understood. It did all this while remaining completely accessible, partly because (as noted earlier), it was grounded in such familiar pop/rock structures and possessed a marvellous earworm chorus. 'Shivers' had already established itself as a live favourite by the time *Door, Door* was released in mid-1979, as is evident from this discussion with a young Michel Faber at University of Melbourne student magazine *Farrago*:

> *Nick*: 'Shivers' generally is never boring. It always goes over really well when we play it. People always shout out for it.
> *Farrago*: Everywhere you play?
> *Rowland*: It would probably go over best in outer suburbs, it usually goes over much better than most of our other songs.
> *Nick*: It's only because it has all this sort of mock emotion, you know: clenching the heart and stuff like that –
> *Phil*: Hand motions, you know.
> *Nick*: – which people for some reason seem to like.
> *Rowland*: And also we're not making a tremendous amount of noise which they object to most of the time because they can't talk, so that when we allow them to talk to their friends *[laughter]*, they clap us for it.[33]

Although typical of Howard's wry humour, this flippant remark may have been intended to deflect discussion away from 'Shivers' and 'mock emotion', a topic with which he would develop a long-term discomfort. In any case, the band's core audience, which had developed without the aid of a single or LP, seemed not to share any of the misgivings about 'Shivers' that would soon be evident in responses from their record label Mushroom and the wider media landscape (*Countdown*, in particular).[34] As Cave later observed, speaking about Howard's authorship of the song,

> It was something that was so total and so loved by everybody and it talked to everybody and all that stuff that a great song should be able to do…it's just so accomplished.[35]

Even Howard's mother was a fan. When asked by an interviewer in the 1980s (for reasons that remain unclear) how his mother felt about all his musical activity, Howard responded, 'She wishes that I'd write more songs like Shivers…'[36]

Dogs in Space

'Shivers' arrived in *Dogs in Space* with this rich repository of cultural resonances intact, landing, unlike a piece of Skylab, on a plot of ground that had been carefully cleared for it. The songs used in the film and on its soundtrack included well-known tracks by Iggy Pop, Gang of 4, Brian Eno and New Zealand's Marching Girls (who had relocated to Melbourne in 1979), but all the Australian 'of the scene' songs used in *Dogs in Space* were previously unrecorded, relics of the 'little bands' milieu excavated and recorded properly for the first time. As the film's musical director Ollie Olsen related in a 1987 feature in *RAM*,

> "Basically he [Lowenstein] just wanted a degree of authenticity…the bands that were around at the time, and I knew them all, so it wasn't hard to get together."

Ollie organised the reformation of bands like the Primitive Calculators and his own band Whirlywirld, and took them into Richmond Recorders to record a track or two each. They were songs of the era, maybe up to ten years old but most never before having been recorded, so there was present all the requisite enthusiasm…

"It's just great to hear all this stuff recorded properly," said Ollie. "Like, being a big fan of the Primitive Calculators, I just always wanted to hear them sound good on record, and now this is it."[37]

The great exception to this was 'Shivers', which instantly accorded it a special significance in the context of the *Dogs in Space*, so much so that it appears in two versions: the 'hit' by the Boys Next Door, and a rendition by 'Marie Hoy and Friends', recorded and performed especially for the film. Both appear on the soundtrack album released in 1986.[38] Although an exact contemporary of the 'little bands' material, 'Shivers' had not emerged from this scene and by the time of the making of *Dogs in Space* was a nearly decade-old underground anthem instantly recognisable to the film audience's rock cognoscenti. Its first appearance is in the form of the Boys Next Door film clip made in 1979 by Paul Goldman to accompany the song and is ostensibly projected, with the song audible, on the wall of the Crystal Ballroom, where performances by several of the 'little bands' are taking place.[39] It functions as the backdrop to Tim's (Nique Needles) imminent ejection from (the band) Dogs in Space, as Sam (Michael Hutchence) and Lisa (Glenys Osborne) plot his expulsion at the bar while he remains alone at the recently vacated table, suspicion darkly etched on his face. Significantly, the audio of 'Shivers' remains present as the action cuts to a sequence of Anna (Saskia Post) and her friends getting ready to attend the gig, laughing, singing, drinking laced tea, carefree, and chaotically getting dressed.

Presaged by its appearance approximately ten minutes earlier, 'Shivers' returns to the film in its second incarnation, performed live on stage by a group billed as Marie Hoy and Friends. They are the gig's headliners, the last in a series of bands with semi-rotating membership that has performed over the course of the night. These include Too Fat to Fit Through the Door and Thrush and the Cunts, two 'little bands' with whom Hoy played in the 1970s; the (resurrected) Primitive Calculators also appear, and of course, Dogs in Space, based on Sam Sejavka's band the Ears. Marie Hoy and Friends also includes Ollie Olsen, with whom Hoy had already collaborated in Orchestra of Skin and Bone; they would later form NO with Michael Sheridan and Kevin McMahon. Hoy had known both Olsen and Rowland Howard for many years and according to Hoy, it was at Howard's insistence that if 'Shivers' was to be used in the film, it could only be with Hoy singing it.[40]

This performance of 'Shivers' by Marie Hoy and Friends falls somewhere in the middle of Howard's sarcastic detachment and Cave's hyperemotionalism. While the instrumentation retains key elements of the Boys Next Door version—piano, synthesiser, a sparse, atmospheric arrangement—it is notable that the rhythm guitar is restored to audibility, and with it the distinctive under-beat that was all but lost in the Boys Next Door recording. Since Olsen had played guitar on the earliest surviving account of 'Shivers', it is likely that he was at least partially responsible for the decision to restamp it with Howard's input.[41] Hoy's delivery is beautifully in keeping with the spirit of the song, the rich warmth of her voice cloaked in detachment but interrupted with subtle vocal catches that evoke a hurt teenager trying to be tough. Poised and controlled, she is aloof with a slight supercilious sneer that suggests contempt but never erupts into full-blown scorn. Shot exquisitely with stunning red lighting, Hoy is mysterious and enigmatic—a punk Juliette Greco anti-chanteuse.

It is clear that this is a *moment* in the film, recognised and treated as such by the band room audience, who stand quietly, watching and listening with an attention that borders on reverence. This is in stark contrast to the chaotic musical performances that have preceded it, during which audience members jump/dance/pogo into each other; some are off shooting heroin in the toilets, picking fights or buying/spilling/downing drinks at the bar; almost everyone is yelling. At this point, it is also worth noting that from the outset, the film's sound world is a constant cacophonous riot: multiple conversations happening at once, screeching tyres, car motors, indistinguishable dialogue, bands rehearsing, TV and radio, phones ringing.[42] As Clinton Walker observed at the time,

To look at, it's as messy and busy as hell – and that's echoed in the soundtrack, which (excluding music) consists of a miasma of cross-cut dialogue and sound-effects – positively Altmanesque, it is – but it flows beautifully, with an infectious energy and unstoppable momentum.[43]

This 'unstoppable momentum' screeches to a halt during Hoy's performance of 'Shivers', a rare moment of stillness that commands attention. While Hoy is still mid-song, the action shifts outside onto the street where, among other chaotic happenings, Dogs in Space are packing their gear into a car. Luchio's (Tony Helou) country bumpkin girlfriend Leanne (Sharon Jessop), drunk, out of place and out of patience with the hipsters, staggers out of the Ballroom shouting, 'Fakes and phonies, that's all they fucking-well are!' While she smashes a glass on the footpath for emphasis, 'Shivers', a song that exposes the irreconcilability of falsity with genuine feeling, continues to be audible in the background. Sam then approaches Tim to inform him that he and the rest of the band have decided to get a new keyboard player. Only partially succeeding at keeping a poker face, Tim responds, 'Doesn't matter, I was gonna leave anyway', lingering briefly before turning on his heel and walking back upstairs. The camera follows him into the band room where Hoy is still singing and he stands still, watching her, as the betrayal and his new post-band reality sinks in. With 'Shivers' still playing, the action cuts back to the house where Anna and Sam are in bed, post-gig, and Sam shoots her up with heroin for the first time. Anna vomits and the song ends on that questioning, uncertain relative minor chord while the camera cuts back to Hoy on stage, resting her chin on the microphone and peering ominously out the tops of her eyes at the audience.[44]

'Shivers' marks a turning point in the film, an apex of the action where, as Andrew de Groot put it,

> the two dramas are played out with Nique Needles' character [Tim] and his life suddenly becoming disappointing and friendships collapsing, and then it quite gently moves to an even bigger thing that's unfolding with Anna, and everyone's life is suddenly changing.[45]

'Shivers' is an augur, a portent marking the point at which both the band and house begin to fracture, heralding the eventual, inevitable demise that culminates in Anna's accidental death from an overdose. Ultimately, this subcultural plane of existence, created by a group of middle-class kids slumming it to escape the safety and boredom of their suburban origins, will be shortly rendered unsustainable. *Dogs in Sp*ace is an anthropological excursion into this landscape of masks and acting, another planet where everyone is high and 'normal' people who enter the house might well be on the moon, a point loosely underscored by the spacecraft and Skylab references that permeate the film. 'Shivers' is part of the glue that binds all this together; a seemingly simple song replete with layers of meaning, a conduit for complex realities while remaining elusive enough to function as a cipher.

Notes

1. H. Howard and E. Preston (2011) performing 'Shivers', October, https://www.youtube.com/watch?v=TEFBjmz5qu4, accessed 6 June 2019.
2. J. Sargeant (2003) 'Dead Letter Tales: The Rowland S. Howard Interview', *BB Gun Magazine*, 6 reprinted at https://rowland-s-howard.com/articles/2003-bb-gun-mag.php, accessed 5 June 2019.
3. R. S. Howard quoted in P. Donovan (1998) 'Song of Rowland', *The Age* (Melbourne), 17 July, p. 45.
4. For a brief overview with audio and video links, see D. Laing (2019) 'Celebrating 40 Years of Shivers by the Boys Next Door', https://www.ilikeyouroldstuff.com/news/celebrating-40-years-of-shivers-by-the-boys-next-door, accessed 9 June 2019.
5. R. Gibson (1994) 'Last of the Cavemen?' *The Age* (Melbourne), 29 July, p. 48.
6. Unknown author (1977) Alive 'n' Pumping, reproduced at http://www.fromthearchives.com/bnd/BND23_Jul_77.jpg, accessed 25 May 2019. I would like to acknowledge the DIY archiving achievement of Hans from www.fromthearchives.org whose site makes available many other historical documents that would otherwise have been lost.
7. Interview with J. Austin (2017) for *Self-Made: Zines and Artist Books*, exhibition at State Library of Victoria curated by M. Syrette,

https://www.slv.vic.gov.au/self-made-audio-extras/stops/7/, accessed 25 May 2019; see also interview with B. Milne, https://www.slv.vic.gov.au/self-made-audio-extras/stops/2/, accessed 25 May 2019. For *Pulp*, see C. Walker, http://www.clintonwalker.com.au/fanzines-1970s.html, and for full first issue https://www.flipsnack.com/B89E97BA9F7/pulp-fanzine-1977.html, both accessed 25 May 2019.
8. Unknown author (1977) Alive 'n' Pumping, reproduced at http://www.fromthearchives.com/bnd/BND23_Jul_77.jpg, accessed 25 May 2019.
9. I. McFarlane (1994) Prehistoric Sounds 1:2, 24 November reproduced at https://rowland-s-howard.com/articles/1994-prehistoric-sounds.php, accessed 26 May 2019.
10. Precise dating of the Obsessions' existence is difficult but seems likely to have covered a lengthy chunk of 1977, possibly commencing in late 1976. I thank Simon McLean for his generous input and for allowing me to cite our personal email correspondence of 27 May 2019.
11. Unknown author (1977) *Alive 'n' Pumping* reproduced at http://www.fromthearchives.com/bnd/BND23_Jul_77.jpg, accessed 26 May 2019.
12. See The Obsessions—Chronology which includes two hand-drawn flyers for the show, http://www.fromthearchives.org/rsh/chronology2.html, accessed 25 May 2019, and https://www.discogs.com/Boys-Next-Door-Live-Swinburne-College-Melbourne-Aug-77/release/4608232, accessed 27 May 2019. The Eastern Suburbs Technical College was founded in 1908 by the Honourable George Swinburne and now operates as Swinburne University of Technology in Hawthorn. Ethel Hall was part of the Ethel Swinburne Centre, built in 1959–1961 and dedicated to George's wife Ethel. It also housed the student cafeteria. See https://commons.swinburne.edu.au/items/ead65256-bbbd-4e67-ad84-a18fb264fdab/1/ for footage of the building's construction; the last three minutes contains footage of Ethel Hall. The Ethel Swinburne Centre was demolished in 2008, https://commons.swinburne.edu.au/items/8afe4a07-831c-461e-90ba-3596257d9cc1/1/, both accessed 25 May 2019.
13. *Pulp* 1 (1977), August, pp. 1, 3, 4, 7, 10, 12, https://www.flipsnack.com/B89E97BA9F7/pulp-fanzine-1977.html, accessed 25 May 2019.
14. http://www.clintonwalker.com.au/fanzines-1970s.html, accessed 25 May 2019.
15. See http://www.fromthearchives.org/rsh/chronology2.html, accessed 25 May 2019; C. Walker (2009) 'Planting Seeds', in T. Dalziell and K. Welberry (eds.) *Cultural Seeds: Essays on the Work of Nick Cave* (London: Taylor

& Francis), pp. 31, 37; see also 'Juvenalia' and 'Art School' DVD Special Features, L. Milburn and R. Lowenstein (2012) *Autoluminescent: Rowland S. Howard*, Ghost Pictures/Umbrella Entertainment.

16. C. Ubu (2003) Rowland S. Howard interview, *Overeasy*, October, reproduced at http://rowland-s-howard.com/articles/2003-overeasy-mag.php, accessed 25 May 2019. On several occasions Howard has declared that he wrote 'Shivers' when he was sixteen, but he has also consistently stated that he wrote it while in the Obsessions, which Simon McLean's recollections also support. Howard's date of birth was 24 October 1959; if the Obsessions were operational mainly during 1977, this would make Howard seventeen. As noted earlier, it is difficult (and unnecessary) to make definitive pronouncements regarding minutiae of timing, so I will leave the last word to Howard.

17. Pitt attempted to recruit new personnel and keep the Obsessions going, but to no avail, http://www.fromthearchives.org/rsh/chronology2.html, accessed 26 May 2019; see also http://www.fromthearchives.org/rsh/chronology3.html, accessed 26 May 2019 and C. Walker, 'Planting Seeds', p. 37.

18. Interviews with O. Olsen and R. Howard in R. Lowenstein (2009) *We're Living on Dog Food* (Melbourne: Ghost Pictures). See http://www.fromthearchives.org/rsh/chronology3.html, accessed 30 May 2019 for a Young Charlatans chronology that includes a selection of gig posters.

19. 'The Young Charlatans', *Fast Forward* 004, http://spill-label.org/FastForward/ff04/ff04-05.mp3, accessed 30 May 2019; 'Shivers' audio, http://spill-label.org/FastForward/ff04/ff04.php, accessed 30 May 2019.

20. R. Barden, 'Virgin Press Benefit', *Fast Forward* 013, p. 9, http://spill-label.org/FastForward/ff13/ff13-zine05-large.jpg, accessed 30 May 2019.

21. For audio of Big Bang Combo's performance of 'Shivers', http://spill-label.org/FastForward/ff13/ff13-08.mp3, accessed 30 May, 2019.

22. Interview with C. Walker for Howard's performance on ABC TV's *Studio 22*, 1999; see (with performance of Shivers) https://www.youtube.com/watch?v=L7ChSy6FhxQ, accessed 30 May 2019. These events are well-documented: see C. Walker (1982) *Inner City Sound* (Glebe: Wild & Woolley); C. Walker (1996) *Stranded: The Secret History of Australian Independent Music 1977–1991* (Sydney: Macmillan); David Nichols (2016) *Dig: Australian Rock and Pop Music* (Portland, OR, and Melbourne: Verse Chorus); R. Lowenstein (2009) *We're Living on Dog Food* (Melbourne: Ghost Pictures); and L. Milburn and R. Lowenstein (2012) *Autoluminescent: Rowland S. Howard*, Ghost Pictures/Umbrella Entertainment.

23. It is not clear what key Howard composed 'Shivers' in (the quality of the extant Young Charlatans version resists definitive pronouncements) but given that Howard played it in E on *Studio 22* in 1999 and that this version is substantially similar (if a little slower), I use this version, in E, for reference: see https://www.youtube.com/watch?v=L7ChSy6FhxQ, accessed 31 May 2019. The Boys Next Door recorded the song with the I-IV-V progression in A, so with A-D-E as the tonic, sub-dominant and dominant, respectively.
24. Interview with R. Howard in R. Lowenstein (2009) *We're Living on Dog Food* (Melbourne: Ghost Pictures).
25. Archival interview footage in Milburn and Lowenstein (2012) *Autoluminescent: Rowland S. Howard*.
26. I. McFarlane (1994) *Prehistoric Sounds* 1:2, 24 November, reproduced at https://rowland-s-howard.com/articles/1994-prehistoric-sounds.php, accessed 26 May 2019.
27. Interview with R. Howard in R. Lowenstein (2009) *We're Living on Dog Food* (Melbourne: Ghost Pictures).
28. The complicated genesis of *Door, Door* has been recounted elsewhere; for an overview see Walker, *Stranded*, pp. 40–45
29. MOR: Middle of the Road.
30. Interview with O. Olsen and R. Lowenstein (2009) *We're Living on Dog Food* (Melbourne: Ghost Pictures).
31. N. Cave interview in Milburn and Lowenstein (2012) *Autoluminescent: Rowland S. Howard*; see also interview with *Door, Door* producer Tony Cohen, who asserts that he argued for Howard to sing his own material but was refused by Cave.
32. I thank my dear friend and fellow historian Dr Corinne Manning for this observation.
33. M. Faber (1979) 'Conversations with Boys Next Door', Farrago 57:12, 29 June, pp. 20–21; Nick Cave, Rowland Howard and Phill Calvert were present for the interview. See also M. Faber (2011) 'A Boy Next Door', in M. Snow (ed.) *Nick Cave: Sinner Saint—The True Confessions, Thirty Years of Essential Interviews* (London: Plexus), pp. 15–27. Michel Faber is an acclaimed novelist and author of *The Crimson Petal and the White* (2002).
34. I. McFarlane (1994) *Prehistoric Sounds* 1:2, 24 November, reproduced at https://rowland-s-howard.com/articles/1994-prehistoric-sounds.php, accessed 26 May 2019; see also Faber, 'A Boy Next Door'.

35. Nick Cave interview in Milburn and Lowenstein (2012) *Autoluminescent: Rowland S. Howard*.
36. Archival interview footage in Milburn and Lowenstein (2012) *Autoluminescent: Rowland S. Howard*.
37. C. Walker and P. Stafford (1987) '1979—An Inner Space Odyssey', *RAM*, 14 January, pp. 30–31.
38. R. Lowenstein (2009) *Dogs in Space: 2 Disc Collector's Edition*, Ghost Pictures/Umbrella Entertainment.
39. Although this sequence was filmed at the Crystal Ballroom, in the film's narrative the gig was in fact taking place at the Champion Hotel in Fitzroy, a locus for 'little band' activity.
40. Interview with Marie Hoy conducted by David Nichols, 17 December 2015.
41. This is even more evident in Howard's later Studio 22 performance, https://www.youtube.com/watch?v=L7ChSy6FhxQ, accessed 5 June 2019.
42. Richard Lowenstein (2009) *Dogs in Space: 2 Disc Collector's Edition*, Ghost Pictures/Umbrella Entertainment. On the audio commentary by Richard Lowenstein and Ollie Olsen that appears as an extra feature on this release, Lowenstein notes that *Dogs in Space* was one for the first films to feature dialogue in surround sound. This was usually frowned upon as it rendered dialogue indistinguishable, but in the case of this film, it added to the sonic chaos that mirrored the film's action.
43. C. Walker and P. Stafford (1987) '1979—An Inner Space Odyssey', *RAM*, 14 January, p. 30.
44. R. Lowenstein (2009) *Dogs in Space: 2 Disc Collector's Edition*, Ghost Pictures/Umbrella Entertainment. There is lengthy discussion in the audio commentaries (Richard Lowenstein with both Ollie Olsen and Andrew de Groot) included as extra features on this release about the complexities of filming and timing this sequence.
45. R. Lowenstein (2009) *Dogs in Space: 2 Disc Collector's Edition*, Ghost Pictures/Umbrella Entertainment, audio commentary with Richard Lowenstein and Andrew de Groot.

'The Fucked Room': Situating the *Dogs in Space* Soundtrack and 'Rooms for the Memory' in the Diffusion of the *Dogs in Space* Story

David Nichols

This chapter examines the lineage and legacy of one key aspect of the *Dogs in Space* story: the film's soundtrack, compiled and in many instances composed and produced by Ollie Olsen. Examination of the soundtrack and its component parts—notably but not exclusively the material recorded specially for the film—helps us understand not only the power of the film but also its context(s) as a 1986 production ostensibly portraying events set less than a decade earlier. While this chapter concentrates heavily on the song 'Rooms for the Memory'—an Australian chart hit in early 1987 and one of Michael Hutchence's many important contributions to the film—it also examines the album as a whole, in its numerous permutations. Just as the testimonials from key players which appear throughout this book illustrate the context of the film's key characters' personal development, so too does examination of the soundtrack songs position *Dogs in Space* as a music film, a document (after a fashion) of a cultural phenomenon, and as presaging future projects and creations since its creation.

D. Nichols (✉)
University of Melbourne, Parkville, VIC, Australia
e-mail: nicholsd@unimelb.edu.au

'The fucked room' is, according to Ollie Olsen and Richard Lowenstein's commentary from the 2009 DVD reissue of *Dogs in Space*, the room in 18 Berry Street 'where everyone put their shit'. It is also the room in which the band Dogs in Space rehearse in the film, shattering peace in the house (and possibly the street). To give this chapter such a title is not to suggest that the soundtrack album is 'fucked' or a repository of 'shit'. It is nonetheless to suggest that, just as much of the film itself was a luxurious exploration of multifaceted storytelling (or antinarrative), the album was also a place for associated odds and ends: a storehouse or a treasure trove. Importantly many consumers, as will be seen, saw it as a revelatory, life-changing, trove of riches.

Commenting on Anthony Neild's article about *Dogs in Space* on *The Quietus* online magazine, one Lara Hrycaj, of Detroit, Michigan says:

> I became obsessed with this movie via the soundtrack. I bought the soundtrack on a cassette at a record store in the mall and listened to it over and over. Yes, I bought the soundtrack initially because of the Michael Hutchence/INXS connection but it opened me up to musical world I never knew existed and still love today… While I wore out the cassette I am very happy to have the soundtrack on vinyl (I have two copies, just in case). I would LOVE to see this film on FILM! Oh, *Dogs in Space* – rooms for the memories.[1]

Suitably for a film many see as non-linear, *Dogs in Space* has a multitude of endings. Strongest in most viewers' recollection of the film's conclusion—neon limousine aside—is, no doubt, the sight of Michael Hutchence performing 'Rooms for the Memory' in a 'nifty double breasted suit', according to Craig McGregor's review of the film on its release. Hutchence performs on a stage with only two other musicians while some minor, poignant aspects of the narrative are resolved in what McGregor describes as a 'closing funeral tableau'.[2] These include Anna's elaborately attired friends leaving her freshly prepared grave and Deanna Bond as 'the girl' rescuing a scarf, as a memento of Anna, from the front room of 18 Berry St. We also see the final eviction of the house's occupants—not for their debauchery, squalor, the damage they had done to the property or the fact that a young woman had died in the house, but because they had not been paying their rent. The hitherto utterly ineffectual local policemen are shown to be finally performing *a* duty, in the service of the house's unseen landlord. It is clear that even here, the policemen had not directly evicted the tenants, that job having been undertaken by hired thugs, but instead appeared the following day to commiserate. As well as the 'Rooms for the Memory' ending there is, of course, an extra conclusion to *Dogs in Space*—a long credit montage of the actors, in scenes from the film, a reminder of what and who we have just seen. This is set to a 1980 version of Whirlywirld's 'Win/Lose', rather than the newer recording included on the film's soundtrack album.

It is the song 'Rooms for the Memory', credited to Michael Hutchence and released as a single, which is the most affecting and important song to the film, the two versions of Rowland S. Howard's 'Shivers' (discussed in its own chapter within this book) notwithstanding. Walker writes in his sleevenote to the album:

> Rooms for Memory, another classic old Whirlywirld song Ollie Olsen recorded for the film with Michael Hutchence on vocals, is like a rejoinder to everything that's preceded it. A deeply affecting song about the haunting persistence of memory – which, in one way, Dogs In Space itself is all about – it brings to mind that old saying about history, that by ignoring it we are doomed to repeat it, in all its tragedy.

This chapter seeks to locate 'Rooms for the Memory' on the film's soundtrack album and within the charts, and other appearances it made, at the time it was released and at the peak of its consumer popularity. Within the understanding that a Michael Hutchence solo single—at the moment when Hutchence himself was nearing the height of his popularity—was an issue within INXS' presentation as a coherent, unified group, what did 'Rooms for the Memory' mean to fans, to music consumers, and to critics? How was it promoted and sold, and what does such promotion tell us about the expectations of the film's producers and marketers?

Michael Hutchence, Film Soundtracks and 'Rooms for the Memory'

INXS joined with Cold Chisel's Jimmy Barnes to remake the Easybeats' song 'Good Times' for a single released in December 1986—the month *Dogs in Space* was most heavily publicised. Originally recorded to promote the Australian Made tour, which featured both bands (the film of the tour was directed by Richard Lowenstein), the song would also become part of another film soundtrack, for Joel Schumacher's *The Lost Boys*; it opened the album. While this was plainly *not* in any sense a Hutchence solo record—it was credited to 'INXS and Jimmy Barnes'—its inclusion of Barnes as second vocalist, and the video which accompanied release of the song as a single, highlights Hutchence as vocalist, personality and celebrity at the same time as it consolidates his place as just one member of a six-part group. It does so by dint of 'explaining' and 'introducing' Barnes—famous in Australia, but barely known elsewhere—to an international audience as INXS' collaborator. The single was recorded, its cover proclaims, 'over 3 days of madness & mayhem', and this is what the video strives to promote, though the 'madness' is closer to the madcap Monkees than the debauched Stones. The video portrays good clean fun: minimal or merely implied alcohol or cigarettes and of course no recreational drugs are shown. The traditional nature of the song and video ('No one rocks like the Aussies', one commenter suggests on YouTube)[3] and its down-to-earth, throwaway humour is a strong contrast to the material found in *Dogs in Space* (exceptions that prove the rule like the Marching Girls' 'True Love' notwithstanding). If, as some commentators suggest, there was anxiety in the INXS camp over the potential damage done to Hutchence's image by playing Sam in *Dogs in Space*, upbeat material like 'Good Times' and its video would have at very least presented an alternative ideal.

Michael Hutchence had laid groundwork as a nominal solo artist in film soundtrack work many years prior to the recording of 'Rooms for the Memory' as his first 'solo single'. The precedent for 'Good Times' as a key element of the soundtrack to *The Lost Boys* is a lesser-known album from five years before. Don Walker's music for Scott Hicks' 1982 film *Freedom* forms, in essence, a Cold Chisel album from which their main (but not sole) vocalist Jimmy Barnes is notably absent. Almost half of the album is instrumental, and the remainder features vocals by Walker, Kayellen Bee, Liz Watters, Jason Currie and Jenny Hunter-Brown. Hunter-Brown is now known as Jen Jewel Brown and is co-author with Tina Hutchence of a 2018 memoir of Tina's brother Michael. She is credited on this release both as performer 'Quito Ray' and under her own name as one of three 'co-ordinators'.[4] Two tracks also feature lead vocals by Michael Hutchence; one of these, 'Speed Kills', was issued as a single credited, with crafted awkwardness, to 'Vocals: Michael Hutchence and Don Walker'. The other Hutchence track, a 'slow, slightly Spanish-sounding piece' called 'Forest Theme' features Hutchence speaking, rather than singing.[5] It is not only because it is a spoken word track that this bears some resemblance to Hutchence's 'The Green Dragon' on the *Dogs in Space* soundtrack.

Hutchence does not appear in *Freedom*. Yet his association with the production was marked by a promotional video which, in an unconventional move, combines the first two songs from the soundtrack album—Walker's 'Port Adelaide' and 'Speed Kills'—in edited versions; Hutchence mimes his part good-humouredly, and alone, on a mountain of rusty car bodies (on the album, 'Speed Kills' appears between 'Port Adelaide' and 'Port Adelaide II'). The relevance of this foray to *Dogs in Space* and to 'Rooms for the Memory' is that it served as a dry run for INXS and Hutchence's management in experiments exploring the way they might manage the band's lead singer's fame above and beyond the group itself. It is evidence of his willingness to work outside the band format and his comfort level when it came to being depicted in unglamorous, 'gritty' settings. This song was included as the final track on the 2002 compilation album of early INXS material, *Stay Young: the Deluxe Years*, credited to 'Michael Hutchence and Cold Chisel'—a counterpoint to the 'INXS and Jimmy Barnes' credit used on 'Good Times'. Richard Clapton has claimed that the experience of working with Walker was a strong influence on Hutchence's approach to his work. He adds that for INXS' second album, which Clapton produced, Hutchence would record vocals 'almost like a gig, one song after the next'.[6] This might suggest an approach closer to the pursuit of 'feel' rather than technical perfection which might have served Hutchence in his later work outside the band. As mentioned, there are only two Hutchence tracks on the *Freedom* album, so while Walker may have been an influence, Hutchence was unlikely to be replicating a process.

'Rooms for the Memory': Four Versions of the Song

'Rooms for the Memory' began life as a song by Whirlywirld. On the commentary track to the DVD of the film from 2009, Olsen dates the song to 'probably around 1978':

> I remember writing the song when I was waiting in a waiting room at a hospital when my girlfriend of the time had been checked for cancer… the lyric is pretty obvious, a memorial plaque on the wall, there literally was, in the waiting room.

The group went through two incarnations and released a single and a 12" EP, nine tracks: enough material to be combined on an album (indeed, *The Complete Studio Works* was released in 1986) but the band did not release its version of 'Rooms for the Memory'. One article from 1987 suggests Whirlywirld did not even play the song live (thus Walker's suggestion that the song is a 'classic' simply indicates that he thinks it's very good) although guitarist Dean Richards claims otherwise.

There are at least three versions of Michael Hutchence's 'Rooms for the Memory'. The song was released on 7" and 12"; the 12" seems identical to the version featured on the soundtrack album. These are, however, different mixes (if not different recordings) to the version included at the end of the film, in which the Andrew Duffield's emulator is much lower, Hutchence's vocal is less treated and chorus vocals appear towards the song's end.

The single, as released, was mixed (the back cover claims 'produced') by Nick Launay, who had also produced all but one song on the 1984 INXS album *The Swing*. In Tina Hutchence and Jen Jewel Brown's biography of Michael Hutchence, Bruce Butler—whose connections to the *Dogs in Space* stories are multiple—recalls being present when Hutchence received Launay's cassette of final mixes of the single. 'It really was a turning point', Butler says; 'the band heard what Michael could do without INXS'.[7] The group were supporting English band The The in Strasbourg that night, Butler recalls, and while he is adamant that 'Rooms for the Memory' was '100% Ollie', he is clear that the moment in Strasbourg 'started Michael on a very different way of thinking'. Of course, his fellow INXS members had heard Hutchence do *something* as a solo artist some years before, but clearly this was at a different level; not least because he was now an internationally renowned performer.

Butler was, of course, an insider to the *Dogs in Space* and 'Bowie Queue' scene; he, like many, might well have seen the film and 'Rooms for the Memory' as recognition of talent that had originally been passed over by the mainstream. Clinton Walker, in his sleevenotes to the *Dogs in Space* soundtrack album, suggests:

> Like their American equivalent Suicide, Whirlywirld never made a real commercial mark for themselves – simply they were ahead of their time.

The assumption amongst so many of the commentators on the Olsen-Lowenstein-Hutchence collaboration was to resort to a literal reading of the notion that Whirlywirld (for instance; by implication, of course, other groups and artists were similarly caught up in this idea) was 'ahead of its/their time'. Interviewed by Paul Fleckney for the book *Techno Shuffle*, Olsen provides some clues to the ways in which Whirlywirld might arguably have been musically 'other' in the 1970s; like the Primitive Calculators (see Stuart Grant's chapter in this book) he 'loved disco even in the punk era' and embraced elements of this music in the late 1970s when few others were experimenting in this realm.[8] The 1985/1986 'Rooms for the Memory' was, in essence, a Whirlywirld recording by dint of its instrumental personnel—Dean Richards on guitar, Andrew Duffield on emulator, and Olsen as songwriter, producer, drum programmer and auteur; all had been members. Bass player Tim Millikan, who Olsen had recruited to play on most of the songs he recorded for the album, was not involved in the original group (he was in fact only 20 years old at time of recording).

Of course, Hutchence, who had minimal if any connection to Olsen or Whirlywirld prior to this, sang 'Rooms for the Memory'. Richards had recorded Whirlywirld playing the song on his four-track recorder and believes it was either this version, or a live recording, which Hutchence heard. He recalls that Hutchence adhered closely to Olsen's vocal melody from original versions, although both men used the opportunity to improvise extensively on the new recording.

The idea of a group or artist being 'ahead of its/his/her time' is flattering to the object of the assessment but, of course, problematic in other ways. Walker did, after all, call Whirlywirld 'Australia's Suicide', that is, a version of the infamous New York synthesiser and vocal duo which had made a splash in certain circles in the mid-1970s (Hugo Race's character Pierre's evocation of 'Frankie Teardrop' early in *Dogs in Space* is a Suicide reference; Olsen himself even extrapolates, in a sung introduction to the 'live' version of 'Win/Lose', of a 'Frankie' in his one key appearance in the film; there are further veiled references to this group—see below). Yet, there are other ways in which defenders of the notion might underpin its veracity. Dean Richards was (and remains) a highly respected guitarist and composer, who wrote with the popular Stephen Cummings and who also penned Jules Taylor's second, unreleased, single; Andrew Duffield had, as a member of Models, played on a number of charting singles and indeed had co-written 'Barbados', a top 40 hits for the band the year before. John Murphy, who had been a constant in Whirlywirld and could surely lay some claim to 'Rooms for the Memory's' creation, appeared on the b-side of the single as part of the ersatz Ears 'Dogs in Space' band. Murphy had played in The Associates and featured on that Scottish band's 1982 album *Sulk*, a top ten hit in the UK. The former members of Whirlywirld had, in effect, become connected with the mainstream and their commercial and artistic potential, by the mid-1980s, was realised. Clinton Walker writes:

> The results are successful because not only, as Olsen pointed out, 'There's been this eight year gap where everybody got better at what they did, but also, as nobody had ever had the opportunity to record any of this material before, it was a fresh challenge they were eager to tackle.'

'Rooms for the Memory' in the Film

Like much of *Dogs in Space*, the film's conclusion and the inclusion of the song is ripe for interpretation. It is possible that many viewers are in sympathy with Stuart Coupe, who felt that to end the film with Hutchence miming to (what would prove to be) a hit song was at best a non-sequitur, but at worst crass commercialism. Coupe wrote:

> After almost two hours you've begun to forget that Hutchence is a semi-famous rock 'n' roll star, only to be reminded of this in *Dogs in Space*'s only unnecessary three minutes – the last three, nothing more than a promotional video clip for Hutchence.
>
> The video clip features Hutchence performing 'Rooms for the Memory' which is, surprise, surprise, to be made available as a single to coincide with the Australian release of the film.[9]

There is, indeed, ample reason to view the film this way. It is highly unlikely that there would have been a *Dogs in Space* without Hutchence's involvement; more importantly, his musical contributions in the rest of the film are the largely unlistenable songs by the band Dogs in Space (these songs, though they are based on songs by the Ears, are incidentally much worse than even the earliest relics of the Ears' recorded legacy: they are deliberately rendered as terrible in the film, but fare slightly better on record). That he, Lowenstein and Olsen close the film with a song that INXS fans might actually recognise as a produced and realised pop-rock song might well be seen as a cop-out. (One writer suggested in 2018 that 'we're never under any illusions that [the band Dogs in Space are] destined for greatness.')[10] Where Coupe is arguably mistaken is in seeing *Dogs in Space* as promotion for Hutchence's career, rather than as piece of work which relies on his fame for its existence: the months he spent on *Dogs in Space* could clearly have been much more financially beneficially used continuing to tour with INXS. Of course, Hutchence's 'credibility' did, ultimately, increase in certain quarters by dint of his participation in *Dogs in Space*, but this was hardly a foregone conclusion in 1986–1987 (and credibility is not commerciality).

It is easy to imagine, and this is clearly an impression deliberately contrived by the filmmakers, that the performance of 'Rooms for the Memory' in the film is mimed by Hutchence at Anna's graveside. When the music begins, he is kneeling at Anna's grave and jolts backwards, his head upturned, as if about to begin performing a song. The song continues on the soundtrack as we are shown, firstly, the mourners leaving the graveside; the (semi-comic) eviction by the police; the Girl and the empty rooms of the house and finally, two minutes into the rendition of the song, Hutchence onstage.

It is, firstly, notable that Hutchence is dressed, and made up, to look most unlike 'Michael Hutchence of INXS' and indeed it is credit to the film-makers' skill that he more properly looks like Sam Sejavka as he portrayed himself in Beargarden in 1984–1985. Parallels in the careers of Hutchence and Sejavka are explored in Sarah Taylor's chapter in this book. Sejavka had lobbied for a song he had written to be the closing track for the film, and it jostled for favour for some time with 'Rooms for the Memory'. It is important to note that in 1984–1985 Sejavka had risen to become a pop star, appearing on Countdown and similar programmes, and that the two videos that band produced portrayed Sejavka as an elegant dandy; the Hutchence at the end of the film reflects this figure more than his own pop star style. Secondly, as per the 'Speed Kills' video, there are two depersonalised male musicians around him; if there is any inference intended to be derived from this fact, it is that no one should mistake this song for an INXS creation (the band's management did ask whether INXS could appear in the film; Lowenstein suggested, wryly, they appear at the end, presumably at this juncture—the possibility was not pursued). INXS had a distinct persona—as Richard Lowenstein was, of course, very well aware and indeed Lowenstein made a significant contribution to the creation of that persona. The band's videos not only featured all six members but presented it as a group of many vibrant and equal personalities.

There are clearly grounds for an interpretation that Sam—jolted into reality at Anna's graveside—comes to appreciate either that her faith in, and support for, him is the reason he must make something of himself to make her emotional investment worthwhile; or at very least that her death brings about an epiphany that the bacchanal of the 'boy's house' in Richmond could not last forever, that there is a time when one must grow up. Lowenstein does not depict Sam and the cleaned-up, sanitised Dogs in Space performing on *Countdown* or at national stadiums (as Beargarden did, in support of Culture Club during that band's 1984 Australian tour). In that regard, the final scene might either be Sam's vision or fantasy for what he might achieve in a post-Anna, post-Berry St world; or it might as easily be Sam's ideal for becoming, if not a good person, at very least a good artist. Whatever else we can take from the final scene, it is clearly intended that the Dogs in Space songs as performed in the film—'Golf Course' in particular, with its opening lines borrowed from the Beatles' 'Help' and its meandering nursery rhyme elements—constitute a foolish racket, but that 'Rooms for the Memory' is a synth-pop epic with an emotional core commensurate to its grandiosity.

Rooms for the Memory: The Video Clip

The five-minute video clip for 'Rooms for the Memory' is substantially different from the presentation of the song in *Dogs in Space*, although both end with the camera pulling away from Hutchence on a stage. The video features hand-coloured black-and-white stills from the film—focusing very strongly on Saskia Post as Anna and Deanna Bond as The Girl—interposed with a stark black-and-white footage of Hutchence in what appears to be a single-take multiple-camera performance. Lowenstein and his team had pioneered the use of coloured black-and-white images in INXS' video for 'What You Need' in 1985; beyond the very minimal illusion of movement provided by the rapid presentation of a few comparable images in this video, 'Rooms for the Memory' visuals are far starker, yet must surely have been an allusion for many viewers to Lowenstein et al.'s work for INXS.

For the first three minutes of this video, Hutchence is only shown from the top of his head to his shoulders—miming the song into a microphone. For the last minute-and-a-half into the clip, the camera pans back to reveal Hutchence alone on a stage, dressed simply in white shirt and black pants. The stage is spotlit from above; in certain respects, one might imagine the Hutchence footage is at least in part inspired by Stanley Dorfman's clip for David Bowie's '"Heroes"', the notable absence being, of course, the spotlight in '"Heroes"' shines behind Bowie in that production, and between his legs: but the Hutchence clip, the singer's own innate attractions aside, is not attempt to be sexy, alluring or even fun. Paul Goldman's understated video for 'Shivers', from the previous decade, shows Nick Cave performing less kinetically—but every bit as theatrically—with the almost motionless Boys Next Door in a similar understated 'onstage' scenario.

In the case of 'Rooms for the Memory', a more distinct performance from that of 'Good Times' cannot be imagined; Hutchence does not smile or, indeed, do anything more than stand and perform until, at the very end of his vocal, he falls to his knees. As mentioned above, he begins his performance in the film version *on* his knees, though it is difficult to interpret this coherently, in part because of the way this scene is edited.

1987 Hits Out as a Context for Consuming 'Rooms for the Memory'

The top 40 hits album is an artefact no longer in currency: consumers today can choose to listen to songs they already know they like, online, with new tracks recommended to them only by dint of 'similarity'. In the twentieth century, new music exposure was arguably provided in a more linear—perhaps a better word would be 'temporal'—fashion, through radio or television programmers as mediators, or often, through tangible programmed works on LP or cassette which necessitated listening to a range of songs to hear the ones preferred. The blank cassette, of course, provided a short circuit to this process through which one might choose to programme one's own range of tracks from radio, vinyl or another cassette source.

Top 40 albums maintained, however, a significant input particularly into younger music consumers' evolving tastes and the development of their experiential palettes. As the compiler of a website in tribute to such albums opines, they 'would usually have some new songs that you already knew (and hence would make you want to buy the record) and… some songs that you hadn't heard before'.[11] Such albums were apparently compiled in expectation of what might make the charts by the time the album in question was released, but there was and remains little science to this; many of the songs on such compilations were actually not hits, yet songs included received extraordinarily high sales as a component to the 'package'. Presumably deals were done in which compilers were permitted new tracks from major artists, for instance, as long as songs by up-and-comers in which the label also had a stake were included. The top 40 albums must surely be a package of predictions, aspirations and songs by artists with a proven track record.

For the consumer, one can imagine—there seems to have been little research undertaken on the consumer or producer process for what is admittedly a fringe concern—that top 40 albums provided a host of services. Primarily, of course, they were a cheaper way to access a larger range of current songs than would be possible from purchasing individual singles, and a chance to 'buy in' to the current pop world. Almost certainly, as one was compelled to listen to the putative 'gristle' between the choice cuts on such albums (who had the patience to pick up and reposition the stylus on an LP, or to fast forward a prerecorded cassette?) one might develop new favourite songs or artists. Might they also have been a way to own and enjoy songs and genres, be they disco or hard rock, which parents or friends disapproved of? Notably in 1977 and 1978 The Saints—the seminal Australian punk band which failed to gain any significant purchase on the nation's charts in its initial incarnation—had songs placed on three major top 40 album releases which were surely amongst the biggest selling pop records of 1977 (*Devastator*, *Explosive Hits '77* and the World Record Club's *Austrock '77*). I remember, at the age of 12, a friend's strong interest in the Supernaut song 'I Like it Both Ways', a power-pop song concerning 'Johnny', a young bisexual man ('It's about poofs', I was told). Purchased as part of a package (*Ripper '76*) one need not fear being tainted by owning, much less having consciously bought, a paean to sexuality outside the norm.

Into this métier, we find 'Rooms for the Memory' placed on *1987 Hits Out*, an album released by RCA in April. Perception is, of course, unique to each individual and it is virtually impossible to understand how strange or 'weird' the song might have seemed to consumers at the time. This is particularly so in the late 20-teens, when the pop music of the 1980s is de rigueur for commercial radio. *1987 Hits Out* begins with Dead or Alive's 'Something in My House', a dance track which lyrically explores themes similar to 'Rooms for the Memory'—the emotional emptiness and sadness that can derive from an empty house. A long way away emotionally and geographically, 'Rooms for the Memory' is third from last on side 2, and programmed (for surely these albums were programmed, not randomized) between two other up-tempo, nominally 'electronic' tracks which would be regarded by many as residing in the category of 'dance': Wa Wa Nee's 'Sugar Free' and Cameo's 'Word Up'. Other songs on the compilation—giving a temporal place for 'Rooms for the Memory' in pop history—include New Order's 'Bizarre Love Triangle' and Europe's 'The Final Countdown'.

The bombastic 'Final Countdown' was, incidentally, used as the theme for the literal final episode of the original *Countdown*, the Sunday night television show which plays such a vital role in *Dogs in Space* itself. The program's last episode was broadcast on 19 July 1987,[12] by which time the programme was regarded by many as a tawdry anachronism. INXS reportedly attended—albeit briefly—the show's farewell party at the Sydney club Jamison Street.[13] The decision to terminate *Countdown*—arguably a short-sighted one, but one which also allowed Australians to reassess the program and its meaning to the lives of any Australian sentient between 1974 and 1987—marked a shift in the different perceptions of 'pop' and 'rock' at the very time *Dogs in Space* entered cinemas.

The *Dogs in Space* Soundtrack: Five Iterations

While 'serious' music fans might readily disparage hits compilations as limiting the artist's wider vision, the fact is that the *Dogs in Space* soundtrack is also, in its way, a hits compilation. Four official versions exist of the album, divisible into two varieties of 'uncensored' (black cover) and 'censored' (white cover). The version most commonly seen is a vinyl LP with a black cover, marketed with stickers covering the name of Thrush and the Cunts. Others are in CD and vinyl versions, with a white cover notable for blanking out this band's name and featuring the song 'Diseases' with only a portion of the vocal and the Primitive Calculators' 'Pumping Ugly Muscle' in an instrumental version. Six of the album's fourteen tracks are 'vintage' selections from the 1970s, and five of those—by Gang of 4, Brian Eno, Marching Girls and Iggy Pop, who contributes a song each from his *New Values* (1979) and *Soldier* (1980) albums—are non-Australian.[14] Seven of the remaining eight are recordings which recreate Australian songs (largely, hitherto unrecorded) from the late 1970s, and one is a spoken word piece by Hutchence ('The Green Dragon'—a particularly ambiguous moment in a film riddled with ambiguity, which Lowenstein reveals on the DVD commentary to have been the work of one Sarah Newsome).

In 2009 Connecticut-based owner-operator of the blog *Psychotic Leisure Music*, Kevin Sartori, assembled an 'expanded' Dogs in Space soundtrack album. Sartori utilised not only the Japanese compact disc version of the original release (so, a digital version) but also music sourced from the film itself which was not available on the original. He discusses the two CD versions in existence: one which he claims was issued in Germany (which he says 'mixed in dialogue from the movie and the tracks segue into each other')[15] and the Japanese iteration which ('presents the songs individually' without segues or dialogue). The Japanese version also, however, includes the instrumental versions mentioned above *and* a longer ('more complete') 'Green Dragon'.

Sartori added five songs found on the soundtrack that were not included on any release. These were 'Frankie Teardrop' by Stamphyl Revega; 'Skullbrains' by Too Fat to Fit Through the Door; 'Window to the World' by Whirlywirld and two songs by The Birthday Party: 'Mr. Clarinet' and 'Happy Birthday'. The first two of these tracks were unreleased, and Sartori surmises that Stamphyl Revega is an Ollie Olsen pseudonym (the blending of Suicide's Martin Rev and Alan Vega into one word may be a clue, although to what?!). Sartori added two short pieces of music for which Olsen claims credit on the film's DVD commentary. Sartori titled these for the moments in the film they accompany: 'Anna Betrayed' and 'Sam & Anna Reunited'. Two songs in the film are absent from Sartori's version. Chuck Río's 'Tequila' was, he says, too fragmented in the film to be adequately 'ripped' in a listenable version, and a third version of 'Win/Lose' is also missing from the album. This song was released as a second single from the soundtrack (credited to Ollie Olsen) after 'Rooms for the Memory', with a remixed version on the b-side, though it did not chart. Another piece of music he omits is a 3RRR jingle, written by Martin Armiger and Stephen Cummings and sung by Jane Clifton, which is heard early in the film.

On the DVD commentary from 2009, Lowenstein and Olsen posit the imminent arrival of an expanded, two-CD soundtrack album, which would include 'Tequila' and Olsen's score music, and presumably other material, though this is not specified. Sartori reported the same year, however, that Lowenstein had been unable to obtain the required licences to reissue the album in this or indeed its original form. The director therefore sanctioned Sartori's extended version: 'As a 50% owner of the DIS Soundtrack copyright', he wrote, 'you have my blessing! If anyone tries to scare you into taking it down, please put them onto me'.[16]

The Soundtrack to...?

> I'm not angry, I just wish you'd brought those Max Q lyrics to the band! They're really good! – Andrew Farriss to Michael Hutchence, *Never Tear Us Apart* (2016).[17]

In 1989, Tim Farriss began work on a film variously described as 'an arty documentary' and an exploration of environmentally sensitive big game fishing, which he called *Fish in Space*. Other members of the group were to contribute soundtrack music; it is unclear whether the film was released.[18] Its title may have been a good-humoured joke, but it was surely a joke seeking to prick the grandiosity, if not pomposity, of INXS' singer's 'grungy' film. This is not the place to explore the five INXS instrumentalists' ambivalence (or antipathy) to Michael Hutchence's ambitions to work outside the band. Yet there is a strong indication, in both the sanctioned INXS miniseries quoted above, in *Mystify* and in many other quarters, that Hutchence was seen—perhaps saw himself—as capable of 'deeper' work outside the realm of the million-selling pop group.

As is clear elsewhere (for instance, in Laura Carroll's and Simona Castricum's chapters) in this book, the soundtrack to *Dogs in Space*, quite apart from its validity as an artefact in and of itself, took on a special status as a cultural signifier for those who identified with the film and the world it represented. The extreme fluctuations in quality of material involved notwithstanding, the album remains a remarkable piece of work and more than an adjunct to, or memento of, a stirring cinema experience. Much of this is surely down to the compelling qualities of 'Rooms for the Memory' as a song, and Hutchence's role in its creation.

There is a coda to the 'Rooms for the Memory' story which should inform any reading of Hutchence's life—the subsequent decade—following *Dogs in Space*. In late 1989, the product of Hutchence and Olsen's renewed partnership, an album by studio band Max Q, was released. Hutchence funded the album himself, and 'forgot to tell' the rest of INXS that he was working on it.[19] Olsen took the lion's share of the songwriting duties for the album, indeed, just as Hutchence's *Dogs in Space* songs were reworkings of songs by The Ears or Whirlywirld, two of the key tracks on *Max Q* were remakes of material from the self-titled Orchestra of Skin and Bone album from 1986; another track, 'Ghost of the Year', was a reworking of a song from the Young Charlatans days. As was the case with *Dogs in Space*, Olsen took the opportunity to recruit his friends, in this case six men from the Melbourne 'underground' scene—many of whom had participated in the *Dogs in Space* soundtrack—to be the group which Hutchence was at pains to point out 'doesn't exist beyond this album'.[20] Critics were bamboozled or enticed by the new record: 'the primitive Third World goes beat-to-beat with the modern high-tech world', the Hackensack *Record's* music reviewer Barbara Jaeger rhapsodized in a review which only gave the record three stars but nonetheless described it as 'exciting' and 'enthralling'.[21]

Olsen's subsequent work has been sporadic and multifaceted and has remained an innovator until recently when, following the demise of his group with Lisa MacKinney and Mathew Watson, Taipan Tiger Girls, he announced on Facebook in 2019, 'Hi all, I've decided to retire from music. Thanks for your support'.[22]

The only true Hutchence solo album—self-titled and posthumously released in 1999—was produced by Andy Gill of the Gang of 4, whose 'Love Like Anthrax' was featured in *Dogs in Space*. Gill and Hutchence co-wrote 9 of the album's 13 tracks. Bruce Butler, an insider friend to Hutchence and Olsen, states that, amongst other plans, Hutchence hoped in 1997 to leave INXS and to record again with Olsen. Plainly this is an unknowable scenario, not least because Hutchence was (as the 2019 film *Mystify* shows) depressed, unfulfilled and locked in grotesque legal battles at the time.

The attraction Hutchence himself had towards experimental and 'underground' music—a far cry from INXS even in its earliest 'new wave' days—is apparent from his solo work, as far back as the *Freedom* album and as recently as his one genuine 'solo' album. The *Dogs in Space* soundtrack—like the film itself—was an opportunity Hutchence took to lend his name to a showcase of experimental work; in no other conceivable way would (for instance) Thrush and the Cunts, or for that matter the Primitive Calculators, have been heard around the world.

Laura Hrycaj's comment above—which has resonances with other testimonials in this book and elsewhere—suggests that the *Dogs in Space* soundtrack and its hit single has had a lasting impact. The album is a jumpy, 'fucked', mishmash of ideas and sounds, the unlistenable rubbing shoulders with the quixotic and the sophisticated. Both album and single took on lives of their own and introduced thousands, if not tens of thousands, to a new aesthetic from which many have yet to recover.

Notes

1. Comment on A. Neild, 'Films for Music: Dogs in Space Revisited', The Quietus, 9 July 2013, https://thequietus.com/articles/12709-films-for-music-dogs-in-space-revisited, accessed 9 June 2019.
2. C. McGregor (1986) 'Now on Film: A Generation Lost in Space', *Sydney Morning Herald*, 6 December, p. 52.
3. 'WickedNightAlbel' comment on https://www.youtube.com/watch?v=sqdNcAjj9p4, accessed 28 October 2018.
4. T. Hutchence with J. J. Brown (2018) *Michael: My Brother, Lost Boy of INXS* (Crows Nest: Allen and Unwin), p. 72. Brown says that in her use of a pseudonym she was 'just being a shape shifter', pers. comm., 20 October 2018.
5. Hutchence with Brown, *Michael: My Brother…*, p. 72.
6. R. Clapton quoted in Creswell, 'Shine Like It Does', p. 43.
7. Hutchence with Brown, *Michael: My Brother…*, p. 112.
8. P. Fleckney (2018) *Techno Shuffle: Rave Culture and the Melbourne Underground* (Melbourne: Melbourne Books), pp. 48–50.
9. S. Coupe (1986) 'Generation of Sex, Drugs and Rock 'n' Roll', *Sydney Sun-Herald*, 14 December, p. 118.

10. Anon, 'Rooms for the Memory: 'Dogs in Space' and the Getting of wisdom', SBS Movies, https://www.sbs.com.au/movies/article/2018/11/19/rooms-memory-dogs-space-and-getting-wisdom, accessed 17 April 2019.
11. http://oz-compilation-albums.com, accessed 28 October 2018.
12. P. Speelman (1987) 'The End of an Um, Er… era', *Melbourne Age*, 20 July, p. 14; R. Oliver (1987) '9 in by a Ratings Whisker', *Melbourne Age*, 30 July, p. 9.
13. M. McConnell (1987) 'Molly's Barefaced Farewell Ends Without a Whimper', *Sydney Morning Herald*, 23 July, p. 24
14. The Marching Girls' 'True Love' was, however, recorded in Melbourne and the group had relocated there by that time. The track was produced by Daffy, also known as David Williams, who also engineered the Ears' 'Leap for Lunch'.
15. The online record collecting database does not list a German release, but does feature a white LP issued in 'Europe' and an LP and cassette issued in the Netherlands. https://www.discogs.com/Various-Dogs-In-Space-Original-Motion-Picture-Soundtrack/master/38340, accessed 17 April 2019.
16. http://p-l-m.blogspot.com/2009/01/dogs-in-space-expanded-1986.html, accessed 17 April 2019.
17. Never Tear Us Apart: The Untold Story of INXS, directed by Daina Reed, 2014.
18. As a testament to the vagaries of memory (or at least one person's memory), this author has a strong recollection of *Fish in Space* being released—but can find no evidence of its existence. It was periodically discussed by Farriss in interviews, including B. Thomas 'INXS—"Two Year" Break from Tours', *Sydney Morning Herald*, 23 April 1989, p. 5; D. Lockwood, 'Taking the Cure', *Sydney Morning Herald*, 7 March 1998, p. 219. Of course for the purposes of this discussion its name is the primary concern.
19. Hutchence quoted in D. Hunt (1989) 'INXS' Hutchence Rejects Rock Star Image', *Los Angeles Times*, 30 September, p. 53.
20. Hutchence quoted in D. Hunt (1989) 'INXS' Hutchence Rejects Rock Star Image', *Los Angeles Times*, 30 September, p. 53.
21. B. Jaeger (1990) 'INXS' Lead Sings a New Tune', *Hackensack Record*, 9 November, p. 112.
22. O. Olsen (2019) Facebook announcement 11 January.

Say Clitoris: Queers in Space

Simona Castricum

While I keep getting older, endless streams of teenage kids emerge into young adulthood through the familiar conduits of sex, drugs, fashion and music. It's a beautiful thing, and while that apparent trend remains, each evolves significantly in context, substance and preference. Each put their own take on gender and sexuality. The party, the club or the gig are exciting events of new possibilities where a special kind of magic occurs. Through Generation X to Millennial eras; at day raves, kick-ons, and housewarmings; from horse, to meth, on pingas, nangs and ketamine, one event never dies of burn-out; the Victorian terrace share house party. It has a different set of rules for unexpected outcomes. Deep within the chaos and void can be a room with a view, a liminal space within which to find ourselves. That is something inherent about queerness.

S. Castricum (✉)
University of Melbourne, Melbourne, VIC, Australia
e-mail: castricums@student.unimelb.edu.au

Two iconic party scenes in Richard Lowenstein's 1986 movie *Dogs in Space* remain the most definitive cinematic record of the inner-city Melbourne party. The Berry Street household is cast as the frenetic heartbeat of a wild post-punk musical community; of the seemingly unlimited housemates. Sam and Anna—alternatively Michael Hutchence and Saskia Post—live out a romantic synth-punk tragedy within the depraved, anarchistic belly of Melbourne's underground musical community of 1978 on a strict diet of Countdown, cough mixture, David Bowie, dog food, Iggy Pop and heroin.

The lives, looks and lifestyles depicted in *Dogs in Space* seemed so real, so cool, so desirable. Even though the film is set in 1978, it was so easy to feel immersed in something unique to a Melburnian experience that transcends cultural generations. As the share house and extended circle reassemble their living room in the middle of Berry Street for kick-ons, I could not help but feel deeply connected to a lineage through my own young-adult aspirations and experiences of parties in these homes. As they watched TV in the glow of the red neon Pelaco sign, hovering above from the top of the street, I watched them on my VHS from my art-deco club lounge and lamp ensemble in a Geelong living room.

In the mid-1990s studying architecture, I'd just moved out of home and was emerging into my adulthood. My girlfriend at the time was a big fan of the movie, and I'd just found my first group of queer friends who I started hanging out with. Everyone loved this movie. I dubbed a copy of the soundtrack on cassette which introduced me to so many bands; Primitive Calculators, Whirlywirld, Thrush and the Cunts. At parties in Ocean Grove or Belmont, someone would always yell out 'Ballarat!!'. Thankfully the 7-Eleven stores were more conveniently located by then. But Melbourne was still an hour away; still a long way to the shop if you wanted a sausage roll—so to speak.

By 1994 St Kilda had just begun to gentrify out of reach, the Seaview Hotel's Crystal Ballroom and The Venue had long closed their doors the late 1980s. Melbourne's musical underground instantly fascinated me. I remember watching Kim Salmon and The Surrealists play at St Kilda Bowls Club and loving it. Half way through the set I became self-conscious of my yuppie Country Road outfit, turtle-shell round glasses and slick blonde hair. These days that outfit would do very nicely at a Community Radio

Live-To-Air, but in 1996 that get-up just had to go. I left the gig in shame, jumped in my 1975 mustard Volkswagen Superbeetle and drove back to Geelong. As soon I got home, I ripped my clothes off, threw them on the back veranda and set them on fire. I sprayed my glasses frames black and I started wearing my ex-girlfriends' black jeans. I've literally never looked at a blue denim, beige collarless shirt and rust woollen vest combination with any respect ever since. A week later I dyed my hair purple with a Napro colour from Pakington Street Safeway during pre-drinks with my friend Melissa; as if to emulate the narrative of the unnamed schoolgirl-runaway who Anna befriends in the Berry Street house.

I first saw *Dogs in Space* as I turned twenty years old, ten years after it was released. I knew of the film upon its release through Michael Hutchence's debut solo single 'Rooms for The Memory', produced by Ollie Olsen it's still one of my all-time favourite songs. As an eleven-year-old an R-rated independent film—albeit apparently about heroin—wasn't that easy to see, so it had mystery to me. ABC TVs Countdown, then both a television show and magazine, sold the movie to teenagers through the image of Hutchence and his magnetic sexuality. Given my adoration for him and INXS, it remained a curiosity that I still peel back layers to reveal its secrets to this day. This journey is so often a place of geographical, historical and cultural reference. The lines of Hutchence's role in *Dogs in Space* are blurred between the character of an eccentric intoxicated electro-punk; The Ears frontman Sam Sejavka, or as himself the frontman of INXS. An interview between Hutchence and Melbourne scene influencer Troy Davies—who stars in the film both as a frightening misogynistic, homophobic skinhead in the opening scene and a violent unhinged country bogan—reveals something of the double life Hutchence plays between INXS and *Dogs in Space*; 'Do you almost wish they (INXS) were in the film sometimes?' asks Davies. Hutchence replies succinctly; 'No'. Davies finishes in observation; 'not at all — it's completely separate'.

Hutchence was seen to emerge from a shyness in this role and to add something queer to his existing sex-symbol status. He toys with a decadent aspect of his sexuality, even Sam claims to Anna; 'he wanted to go to bed with me, but I'm straight. He said what do you mean?' In Lowenstein's 2015 documentary on the life of Davies *ECCO HOMO*, film producer Michele Bennett remarks; 'Michael was quite shy and liked what Troy brought out of him. If Troy was around it just gave you license to be bolder. I think that was something Michael really valued'. Troy Davies was something of a gatekeeper to Lowenstein's casting of *Dogs in Space*. In her memoir *Butterfly on a Pin* (2018), Alannah Hill recounts Davies as 'a powerbroker, the grey eminence hovering over the *Dogs in Space* shoot… Richard's glittering court jester'.[1]

Perhaps it's Troy Davies' mysterious fingerprints and make-up dusted all over *Dogs in Space* that give its queer depth; but it's certainly one of confrontation and discomfort. In the opening scene, Skinhead Davies shouts; 'Are you from the planet poofta or from the planet stupiter?' as he lays a platform boot into Sam who is sleeping out for Bowie tickets by the old Western Stand of the Melbourne Cricket Ground. What seems like a frightening pretext to the familiar refrain of 1980s 'poofta bashing' is acted out by Davies; himself one of Melbourne's most creative queers and gender nonconformists. While it might hint to an internalised homophobia and transphobia, it stands to reason Davies would know how to play that kind of villain well, given his own experience at the hands of it. Film-maker Greg Perano recounts of Davies—aka Vanessa; 'there was this innate intelligence that could put people in their places the way no one else could, she had that baring about her of someone who was a performer; dealing with people on the street; you had to learn how to manipulate those people to keep them happy and not bring out the abuse and the violence'.

It's this very marginalised and oppressed view of homosexuality and gender variance that *Dogs in Space* has in common with genre films of its canon; specifically, Haydn Keenan's 1983 movie *Going Down*. Keenan casts Sydney's queer, drag and transgender underbelly of Sydney as an exotic perverted sideshow through gay character Greg, also drag queen Trixie. The moment 'poofta bashing' is suggested as a pre-party activity is chilling in its casual suggestion, particularly in the context of Sydney's gay hate murders on the North Head's gay beat in 1988. It's symptomatic of queer themes in late twentieth-century Australian cinema; that three-quarters of the way into the movie an exotic queer tragedy is exploited to spice up the heterosexual hedonist standpoint. While that is completely boring for queer and trans people to sit through, for a while it was all we had to see ourselves reflected in. It wasn't until films like Ana Kokkinos' *Head On* (1998), Emma-Kate Croghan's *Love and Other Catastrophes*

(1996) and Stephan Elliott's *The Adventures of Priscilla, Queen of the Desert* (1994) came along, where lived experiences of gay, lesbian, and gender nonconforming people became the genuine subjects of Australian feature film.

To this end, *Dogs in Space* became a how-to guide for destroying my straight edge cis-het presenting teenage self. It was so exciting. There was something so real and tangible about it that felt like a yesterday I viewed at a distance, vicariously through MTV, *Smash Hits* and my older sister and brothers. The inner north-east of Melbourne had not yet gentrified so greatly from Lowenstein's world; it was still so recognisable. In the years prior to seeing it, I'd worked as a student in a landscape architecture studio off Lennox Street and Bridge Road, driving my Superbug around the bluestone laneways and shortcuts around Richmond Hill. I felt somewhat located and reflected in the story's urban geography and culture. I became deeply inspired by it; I photographed the house. I took the laneway leading to Bridge Road as my shortcut to my Dad's house on River Street. I eventually moved from Geelong to an apartment in Church Street. It felt like the right place to connect with to the experimental life I needed to express. I looked to all the movie's characters for inspiration, their creative hedonistic aspirations became something to interpret and find myself. In the pre-internet era, finding queer people, creating a vernacular language to express yourself and coming to some understanding of your identity was accessed through searching deep into alternative cinema, magazines and music in real time. It was all we had, it was enough. That process of discovery was beautiful in its uncertainty as it was frightening and lonely. It didn't have the immediacy or archive we have today through search engines. It was in those moments of patience and frustration we came into our own invention.

I was obsessed with Anna's character and style; I think I only smoked Peter Stuyvesant because she did—that and its catchphrase; 'the international passport to smoking pleasure'. My dad smoked them, he used to have a carton in the glove box of his red Porsche 944. That and the Concorde on the packet seemed like a good reason to smoke them. I miss 1980s cigarette packaging. I was a bit of a sucker for the looks and the lifestyle. Anna became symbolic of a classy indie Melbourne underground aesthetic. Her bleached white hair and retro-1960s dresses and sequinned jumpers reminded me of my girlfriend who introduced me to this film; rebellious, open to risk, yet still one degree connected to her suburban Polish migrant roots. The scene of Anna crying with her mother in her childhood home after busting Sam kissing 'the girl', her face illuminated in stark blue light from the lounge room television was so familiar to me. That room could have been that of my girlfriend's babcia and dziadziuś' house in North Geelong, three-piece lounge suite included.

As Sam and Anna became references, house parties excited me as opportunities to live out those characters. I used to rate every party I went to against a *Dogs in Space* share house fling. I'd literally go up to somebody the moment when the night went sideways and be like; 'yep - it's a *Dogs in Space* kinda night'. Hopefully somebody might have the slightest idea what I'm talking about and concur by suggesting a trip up to the shops for an Egg Flip Big M, or yell back at me; 'Did someone say Ballarat?'.

A party's quality and virtues were assessed against specific criteria that defined these scenes.

1. Peak attendance—nobody can move freely through hallways or doorways for at least three hours at capacity, the lounge room, stairs, balcony and backyard are heaving with hundreds of trashed people.
2. Bedroom activity—every bedroom is the anchor of a party's disparate social cliques, their doors shut, behind are lines of drugs and hair bleaching, people rooting, or some poor student housemate cramming for an exam and trying to resist their crushes coming in for a kiss and mouthful of cough syrup. At a friend's fortieth birthday party in a Fitzroy warehouse, someone ripped LCD Soundsystem off the CD player and dropped Brian Eno's 'Saint Elmo's Fire'; at which point we had to break it to him that it wasn't that kind of party. The concept of putting on a vinyl record to have sex in the age of streaming playlists seems like a terrible inconvenience. Perhaps that's why people only said rooting was a fifteen-minute task; you had to get one off before you changed sides.
3. Kitchen vibe—the most important space at a house party, crammed with people leaning on the kitchen bench. Shouting across the dining table in deep political conversation in fierce agreement bordering on violent confrontation brings out the depth of a scene amongst

the boring anecdotes from stoner housemates about chainsaws or vaudevillian actors. The kitchen is my favourite place to party. It acts as the critical threshold between inside and out, and it always felt rebellious to use a place of food preparation and cleanliness to get very messy in, a lino kitchen floor is the ultimate ashtray. I did use the benchtop of a Drummond Street terrace house as a dancefloor once at a dead Rockstar party (in case you're wondering; no, I didn't dress up at Ian Curtis, but others might have). It was so packed the only place I could find my feet was in the sink playing air guitar to David Bowie's 'Blue Jean' on a pinger. I decided to get out of the sink in case I went through the bench, I didn't want to be 'that guy', but I fear by that stage I already was.

4. Drug use—selling it, buying it, stealing it, but most importantly everybody doing it, whatever it is, for the first time, the next time or the very last time. For a place to go sideways, it's got to have good drugs and everyone's kicking in around the same 45-minute window, that's when the magic happens. It's at that moment when time stands still. Only then can an entire Melbourne terrace house open into a completely new dimension of reality and channel the spirit of each party before it through all who enjoy it. I threw the worst house party during a Boxing Day flood in a morbid Charles Street terrace in Fitzroy. We were pretty much all on acid as the water came through the laneway wall. Everything just felt really humid. Acid is a very sweaty drug. Memorable moments include 1990s Melbourne drag icon Feral Beral coming, so it can't have been that bad. All I remember is her asking me if I was wearing any underwear, to which I replied; 'Yes, several pairs in fact'. I think she clocked my body shaping hip pads, I'd found a friend.

5. Police and emergency services attendance—they came, they blew a siren, knocked on the door, told you to turn the music down and with that they left into the night as someone yelled out 'fuck off', kicking in the balcony balustrade. While I never had the cops turn up, the fire brigade was close to coming to my twenty-first birthday in these fabulous art-deco apartments on La Trobe Terrace in Geelong. We kinda took over the whole block, the neighbours even came. I had a smoke machine, black lights and strobe going most of the night;

bringing the rave. I thought it was a nice touch. A passing motorist stopped and ran out of his car to check if the house was on fire. He came running up the back stairs through the kitchen yelling at everyone to get out. A friend stopped him from calling the fire brigade; 'Yeah-nah mate, it's just a smoke machine'. Thanks Sally.

6. Rooftop Access—people had to get on the roof by any means possible, particularly at sunrise. This is where most unique connections are formed looking across the silhouettes of rooftops, backyards and garages of your immediate neighbourhood. It brings a serenity and perspective that forms the closest of personal bonds—before separation anxiety kicks in. Good way to piss the neighbours off, looking into their backyards, making out and gurning your face off like a gaggle of drug-fucked gargoyles.

7. The impromptu excursion—there's always one designated driver who's up for facilitating a road trip, usually a renegade group of adventurers looking to add something spontaneous to the evening, photo-bombing your mate in his pyjamas who lives with his parents because he didn't make it, a trip to the country to steal a sheep. Nothing—not even shortages of Egg Flip Big M at the local Sevs—will prevent more supplies of booze, or the arrival of a drug dealer even if your car rolled at a Victoria Street tram track. Many a close relationship can begin through suggesting a little trip to the nearest convenience store for a Chupa-Chop or a Chomp; a cute fifty-cent consumable to have with a pack of tobacco, papers and filters. A great way to flirt.

8. An angry neighbour—you need at least one, an angry bastard with a broom in their terry-towelling dressing gown who knows exactly how loud the music's at and what time it is; usually 4 o'clock in the morning. The weekend of the Black Saturday heatwave of 2009, my neighbours were partying so hard in their garage one oppressive 46-degree night until sunrise. As they finished singing 'Wonderwall' to acoustic guitar and moved into 'American Pie'—I lost my shit, I became that angry neighbour. I ran out my apartment fully naked and ran up their rear laneway to their open garage door screaming at them in my most psychotic death metal singer-cum-scorned Collingwood Cheer Squad feral. They were so frightened; the door closed immediately. The Oasis/Don Mclean megamix was over. It wasn't so

much the singing or partying, it was just those two songs—I mean they really are just the worst you could think of; I just couldn't believe somebody could do that, not in North Fitzroy at least. It was a sign the neighbourhood around Edinburgh Gardens had well and truly gentrified by then. It was time to move. Ten years later, I ended up at a party at that very same house. This time Oasis, acoustic guitars and 'American Pie' had been replaced with a serious house rave. It was thrown by a guy who later that year would fall out the toilet window of Hugs and Kisses nightclub onto the crowded laneway below. He walked away from it, only to end up in hospital with a fractured pelvis. I guess I was at the right party that night.

9. Kick-ons—The moment you realise you don't have to go home, but you can no longer stay there. Drug-induced separation anxiety can bring about the strangest of behaviours but setting the television on fire and arguing whose it is to burn is a good way to get people to go to bed. There is always that moment where the drugs and booze move into the next weird phase. I usually completely misinterpret the most innocent comment and bury myself in a hole of shame over it. At this point, I put on sunglasses and stop talking, only to ghost after I think about it for two hours. The walk home is the silver lining; it's like having another line of ketamine when you've run out of drugs.

10. The music—there must be a live set by at least one cool emerging underground electronic band, anything else is bullshit. Between sets is a random selection mainstream pop that pisses all the hipsters and bogans off equally as they bond together into one passionate hate-sponge of raw emotion. Got to be attended by representatives of all four degrees of separation to make it truly relevant; that also meant Indy labels execs, community radio hosts, DJs knocking off for kick-ons, or the video makers and photographers spruiking for underpaid work. Nothing is funnier than taking over the music at 5 a.m. with queer top-forty bangers to really piss of the techno-bros in the K-hole on the couch. I call it the obnoxious four-song challenge; Destiny's Child, Kylie, Madonna and Spice Girls has gotta be in it.

And the last one;

11. The Monday myth—when the dust settles and suicide Tuesday turns into Westgate Wednesday, spinning a good yarn can take the edge

off. I've heard so many myths about Melbourne house parties as I've gone through a few generations of queer, creative and student communities. The best one is that AFL football legend 'Lethal' Leigh Matthews bounced out Nick Cave from Paul Hester's 21st Birthday in St Kilda. Now, I don't even know if that's true—but why let the truth get in the way of a great story? How we fictionalise these events as vernacular storytelling is gold, it sets the personalities within the homes, the suburbs and seasons in folklore. I wonder if the Berry Street house parties that we saw in *Dogs in Space* were as exaggerated? If the get-up of the people in Mark Zenner's short music film *Big Risk* is any indication of the punk scene fashion of Melbourne in 1978, wardrobe was close. Definite hard butch-dyke looks. 1970s bogans and Melbourne Sharpies look so camp in hindsight.

The one-liners Richard Lowenstein peppers throughout the movie are so typical of the scenes that make a cooked party. Still, it amazes me how everything remains the same. Barry—played by Gary Foley—might agree that nothing has changed; 'You look at any society in the world today and on the bottom rung of the ladder you'll find women and blacks - do you understand that you stupid cunt?!' An empty bottle of Southern Comfort to one's throat has never looked so politically weaponised. Indigenous sovereignty hasn't come very far 40 years later. At least fundraisers for First Nations causes and acknowledgement of country at live gigs are increasing in 2019.

'Are you a Maoist or a Trot?' asks Barbra from the Socialist Youth Alliance of Berry Street resident snag-cum-chick magnet Grant. The morning after the second party, he complains to Luchio; 'Just typical of a bunch of spoilt middle-class brats – pathetic. Have you seen some the girls they have in here – they can't be more than 14!' as a lamb walks past a syringe stick in the kitchen wall. Through these random incoherent scenes, *Dogs in Space* exposes the contradictions of sexuality, gender, race, class, privilege, drug use and social capital that play out through random narratives. It tells us something uniquely Melburnian about share house communities. But that's the genius of *Dogs in Space*; the treasure is deep within Lowenstein's script. You need to watch the film at least twenty times. In the 1990s on a

Say Clitoris: Queers in Space   257

VHS player with a remote control in hand I'd rewind back to catch everything that was said; isolating each of the four simultaneous conversations happening. It was this chaotic style that made the film such an obsession, watching it repeatedly to understand the film in its entirety; the narratives, the characters, the personalities, the comedy, the quotes—so thorough was its layering of narrative. The party, pre-drinks and kick-ons scenes revealed the gold. It would be the first film I had seen queer characters, a look into how Melbourne queers navigated, endured, survived music scenes that were predominantly heterosexual and cisnormative.

As Anna holds court from her bed to a group of friends in bed, she turns to one of her goth girlfriends; played by Melbourne fashion designer Alannah Hill, and yells across the room; 'Hey Pierre, say clitoris!'. Pierre; played by former Bad Seed Hugo Race, sporting a slick-back haircut, black and white striped T-Shirt and blazer combo looks back curiously suspicious, and replies rather campishly; 'What?'. Anna continues; 'say clitoris; oh, go on — it's easy; cli-tor-is'. After a longer pause and embarrassment, Pierre gets up walks out of the room, only to be ridiculed by Anna and her girlfriends; 'oh he's all upset - such a little coward'. To me, Pierre looks like one of the few queers at the party. In those days, forcing gay men to talk about vaginas or lesbians to talk about dicks was shit-talking. Anna's question is homophobic in her bullying of Pierre—bitchily egged on by Hill's character—to stir him to deal with the reality of female sexuality and anatomy from a heterosexual standpoint in front of an audience as if to suggest he's never been near one in his life. It spoke to me about the disdain queers endured in social groups in the 1980s, that queer sexuality or gender identity was so often out on the spot. Pierre's reaction is baited by Anna to embarrass him about his sexuality for theatre. To me, the inaudible conversation between Anna and her friend that is the pretext to this moment; '*C'mon, he must be gay. Let's find out. I know I'll put him on the sport and see how he reacts to a clitoris*'.

Rough-as-guts straight country girl bogan Leanne—who mistakenly lands in the middle of art-wank hipsterville is definitely not a fan of lesbians. She is responsible for some of the most scathing and brutal one-liners of the movie. 'The one thing I hate more than fucken blokes, it's fucken dykes!'; this one slapped directly into the face of party guest Lisa, kitted out in a wonderful light pink jumpsuit. She gave me perhaps my strongest introduction to 'fuck the patriarchy' rhetoric as she slams some random bro against a wall; 'It's assholes like you who perpetuate the state of male oppression. How many other societies do you know of where the main form of male abuse is the word for female genitals. Women are the slaves of slaves, and the outcasts of outcasts bonded into marital prostitution and your male dominated society'. Barry follows up; 'Are we getting through to you shit head?' She continues to Jenny, Tone's girlfriend; 'I can't believe you're living in this place. These men are praying on the naivety and inexperience of young girls. It's pure sexual exploitation'. At which point she leans forward and runs her fingers through Jen's fringe; 'you know; you've got beautiful hair. Are you involved with anybody at the moment?'. The next morning, they lie arm in arm together in a makeshift bed on the balcony. Jen breaks up with Tone and leaves with Lisa for Sydney.

Cowgirl is one of my favourite characters. 'Get out of my bloody way fuckwit—assholes—get out of my house ya fuckwits get out! Fuck off!!' she screams, storming though the middle of a house party as a couple of guests raid her kitchen cupboards. Meanwhile, Ollie Olsen and Whirly-World play '*Win/Loose*' live in someone's bedroom; still the best electronic handclap/gated snare drum combo in Australian music. In a later scene at the Seaview Ballroom, Cowgirl cuts an epic melancholic moment of solitude, alone at a table to The Birthday Party's 'Shivers', as she tips the remaining dregs of her flat beer over a pyramid of empty beer pots. When I feel that angry, shit and alone, I want to look as effortlessly cool as Cowgirl; dumping my red quiff into a fingerless gloved hand, smoking out the end of a cigarette, blowing smoke rings that read; '*take it all why don't ya, take all my fucking food!*'.

I don't know who the bleached-blonde punk in the silver-studded leather jacket and thick-rimmed glasses is at the Primitive Calculators gig, but I wanted to be him for a hot minute. He looked like one of the drummers in Big Pig, and probably was. Anyone who was anyone was in Dogs in Space. It was like the legend of the Sex Pistols 1976 gig at Lesser Free Trade Hall in Manchester. Everyone ten years older than me said they were an extra in the movie. If that was true, there would have to have been a scene at a VFL footy game to hold the numbers, in the way

David Williamson's *The Club* (1980) did. There was no way of proving otherwise.

'*I don't wanna live my life like everybody else*' sing The Babeez in Zenner's *Big Risk* juxtaposed against cuts of people exiting the cinema after watching Randal Kleiser's 1978 box office smash *Grease*, with Olivia Newton-John and John Travolta in big letters above the footpath. The people of *Big Risk*, indeed, *Dogs in Space, Going Down* and it's other contemporary Bert Deling's *Pure Shit* (1976) are the antithesis of Grease lightning. 'Boredom is counter revolutionary' reads a poster in the Berry Street household. While Deling's cooked heroin epic lacks the depth beyond the pursuit of the next hit of smack, Anna had something else in her life beyond horse fresh out of Thailand customs. That's the tragedy of her overdose, indeed of *Dogs in Space*. She leaves behind a rich community of love, friendship and creativity. I'm glad ecstasy came along when it did in the late 1980s, it was a safer bet than smack. By the time the Melbourne rave scene was at its peak, it had changed the way the kids of Generation X partied and used drugs; at least until the dealers flooded the market with crystal meth disguised as speed in their pre-millennium tension. By the time HIV/AIDS had taken a generation of queers, intravenous drug use stopped being the weapon of choice in musical communities. That pressure was never there through the 1990s as it was in the 1980s, yet it still lurked between Bourke and Smith Street. I can't imagine bedroom opium dens facilitating the kinds of household kick-ons we have these days. People are too interested in enjoying the personal connection after the lines that an individual pursuit a needle would bring. It might explain why ketamine is a Melbourne favourite though, for the love of downers. Just take my advice; don't eat it off a key, it's the wrong way.

When I came out as transgender (for the third and last time) in 2012, I literally went from being married with a three-year-old son and a Brunswick mortgage to separated and homeless over Christmas. I had no idea that what lay ahead for the next five years would be a second chance at adolescence. What was fascinating was how those same *Dogs in Space* points of reference remained transferable to emerging once again into a musical community. Even Primitive Calculators were about to release a new album at this stage. This time the universe connected me to a couple of share houses in Melbourne's inner north; Fame Street and Barkly Street.

Those parties fulfilled every criterion with distinction and created their own legends. I still see a great relevance in *Dogs in Space* to Melbourne's queer and gender nonconforming music scene; from the Tote, to Hugs and Kisses. There are such amazing characters and personalities that have amazing stories; a soundtrack created weekly by HABITS, Female Wizard, KT Spit, Geryon, June Jones, Kandere, Trans Pixies, Spike Fuck, Callan and Race Rage to name but a few. This time around, these queer and trans lived experiences are visible and proud, all of which would make a great feature film one day. As disparate and disconnected a community as it is, it still manages to come together in very similar ways to the Berry Street house. One thing is sure; how we archive queer and gender nonconforming narratives in film has a rich reference point.

Note

1. Hill, A. *Butterfly on a Pin* (Richmond: Hardie Grant), p. 162.

Fun House: DIY House Venues and the Melbourne Underground

Carolyn Hawkins

Independent subcultures are, by definition, built on a rejection of the mainstream.[1] DIY ('Do-It-Yourself') live music venues provide a compelling example of the creative underground's use of unconventional strategies and self-sufficiency as the guiding principles in side-stepping the limitations of regulated spaces and the mainstream music industry.[2] The alternative approach of these spaces is rarely in accord with official protocols surrounding where and how live music is consumed.[3] They skirt and defy legal boundaries, often finding refuge in 'grey areas' of planning and licensing regulations, or operating in ways that allow them to remain overlooked or undetected. Their tendency to bypass permits, avoid liquor licenses, and produce noise at late hours often causes headaches for councils, neighbours, and landlords.[4] Conversely, their autonomous organisational structure and covert existence allow unique opportunities for performers, organisers, and punters, by fostering experimentation, self-expression, collaboration, and community building.[5] This chapter

---

C. Hawkins (✉)
Melbourne, VIC, Australia

investigates the distinct character and value of informal venues, focusing specifically on spaces operating in Melbourne—a place considered, at least by its state government, to be the 'leading music city in Australia'.[6] These themes will be explored with reference to three recent case studies of venues operating out of inner Melbourne share houses, an exploration of the relationship between alcohol and live music in Australia, and Richard Lowenstein's 1986 film *Dogs in Space*.

Information relating to the case studies was gathered through both primary and secondary sources, including face-to-face interviews and email correspondence with key organisers of Catfood Press in East Brunswick, The Bank in Preston, and a third anonymous venue, still in operation at time of writing, referred to under the pseudonym 'Secret Location' in order to protect those involved.

Catfood Press was a venue located in a shopfront dwelling on Lygon Street in East Brunswick. According to Steph Hughes, who lived and organised shows at Catfood Press from 2006 until 2008, the space began as a squat, until the landlord eventually struck up a rental deal with one of the squatters. Named after the 'amount of cat food...left around the place', it originally began with the intention of starting a screen-printing studio however the t-shirts never quite took off but the gigs 'kinda went gangbusters'.[7] Jack Petty, a tenant at Catfood Press from 2010 until 2014, emphasises the importance of Catfood Press as 'providing an all ages space'.[8] The space still functions as a creative share house space, although regular live shows ceased in 2014.

The Bank, situated on Plenty Road in a 'not-quite-gentrified pocket of Preston', was a share house and creative space incorporating artist studios, a recording and rehearsal space, and a live music venue set up by Liam Barton in 2011.[9] Housed within a former State Savings Bank of Victoria building,[10] events held at The Bank ranged from quieter afternoon shows to all night raging parties with live music. It ran until 2016.

The venue I have called 'Secret Location' is currently operating out of a house in Melbourne's northern suburbs, hosting weekly shows.

The selected case studies are a part of a much wider phenomenon of Australian DIY venues, which has recently included house venues such Lacklustre HQ and Crossroads in Canberra,[11] warehouse venues such as Dirty Shirlows, Maggotville and the Red Rattler in Sydney,[12] Animal House in Adelaide,[13] and 208 Punk House in Perth.[14] Historically, DIY house venues have also included spaces such as Victim Manor in Perth,[15] Club 76/No. 4 Petrie Terrace in Brisbane,[16] and various house shows occurring as part of the Little Bands scene in Melbourne in the late 1970s, as immortalised in the film *Dogs in Space*.[17] A fictionalised account of the Melbourne punk/post-punk community at the time, the film is set against the backdrop of a share house located at 18 Berry St., Richmond. Having shared this house in real life while at film school, director Richard Lowenstein witnessed first-hand the bourgeoning experimental post-punk Little Bands music scene.[18] This was an artistic community defined by anti-commercialism, DIY ethos, unconventional instrumentation (e.g. synthesizers, drum machines), rampant drug use, and opposition to a mainstream 'totally subservient to Anglo/American imperialism'.[19] *Dogs in Space* is a vivid portrayal of the integral connection between the domestic realm, community, and creative production, which resonates just as strongly today as it did when it was first released. At times, certain qualities of *Dogs in Space* can feel exaggerated: an inevitable outcome considering that Lowenstein condenses an enormously multifaceted community into the space of a single household and a running time of less than two hours. Nonetheless, the film provides a clear depiction of how a creative subculture operates within the urban landscape and provides a rich source of comparison to how Melbourne's independent music community operates today.

Live Music, Alcohol, and the Origins of the DIY House Venue in Australia

When investigating the distinction between regulated and unregulated music performance spaces in Melbourne, the role of liquor licensing is particularly significant. Tracing the origins of the licensed live music venue and the subsequently changing relationship between live music and alcohol provides historical context for the demand for live music venues to exist outside of these frameworks. These combined factors illuminate possible sources of motivation behind house shows in the late 1970s inner-city

Melbourne within the punk scene. Although much has changed since this time, the legacy of independence from the music industry and separation from mainstream culture within an Australian context lives on in present-day DIY house venues.[20]

In order to chart the history of regulation surrounding live performance spaces and alcohol consumption in Victoria, it is necessary to step back to a time when these two things were less closely connected. In the 1960s, most live music performances were alcohol-free, as the liquor licensing laws at the time did not permit alcohol to be served after 6 p.m.[21] Live music events were held at churches, community halls, universities, civic centres, and unlicensed 'clubs' such as Berties, Q Club, Reefer Cabaret, and Much More Ballroom.[22] The phasing out of 6 p.m. closing times in 1966 opened up empty time and space in pubs which had previously been filled with hundreds of beer-guzzling men, and live music presented itself as a profitable new way of filling these unused spaces and boosting alcohol sales. With the further extension of pub business hours to 1am in 1968, and the lowering of the legal drinking age from 21 to 18 the following year, the potential profitability of pubs as music venues was becoming apparent and the economics of the music industry began to shift. The establishment of much larger licensed 'beer barns' (e.g. the Village Green in Mulgrave, the Pier Hotel in Frankston, and the Croxton Park Hotel in Thornbury) developed into a thriving 'pub circuit' awash with 'inebriated crowds and extreme volumes' of amplified music.[23] There was a sentiment felt by some that live shows had shifted from an environment based around social and creative connection, to one where bands were booked based on how much cash their audiences spent at the bar.[24] In addition to this, the entertainment at many of these venues was controlled by larger agencies such as Premier Artists and Mushroom Music, which routinely booked shows for bands within their stable.[25] Musicologist Bruce Milne reflects that 'in general, it meant that the bands that catered (or pandered) to a drinking crowd got the work'.[26] Namely highly masculine, loud guitar music made for suburban, heavy-drinking, male-dominated audiences.

By 1976, there was a surge of Melbourne bands playing fast-paced, stripped-back, confrontational, and nihilistic guitar-driven music.[27] These bands, soon to be labelled 'punk', were beginning to find an audience, however, there were few venues available for these bands to play.[28] The first punk gig, Punk Gunk, held on New Year's Eve in 1977, was forced to change venues at the last minute from a St Kilda church hall to a sidewalk in Faraday St, Carlton after church authorities heard the word 'punk'.[29] Gavin Quinn of Babeez, one of three bands billed to play, explains how the community took matters into their own hands: 'the footpath is a stage, a street is an auditorium, we just have to put the speakers on the stage and play'.[30] In her 2011 memoir, Dolores San Miguel (booker of the Crystal Ballroom) recalls 'many young musicians unleashed their raw energy and adrenaline performing at inner suburban parties' and live music 'pour[ing] out of the windows of inner-city squats and share houses every weekend'.[31] Gigs began to be organised independent of the agency-controlled venues and were often self-promoted by bands. In the introduction to *Inner City Sound*, Clinton Walker declares that punk bands have no interest in engaging in 'massively loud mindless boogie and gallons of beer', feeling that their music 'hadn't been acknowledged by its homeland' or 'been allowed to...dominate the charts'.[32] These bands would have to find alternate outlets for their music, separate to mainstream tastes, and share houses were one of few readily available spaces that could be adapted to this purpose.

By the late 1970s, there were numerous punk shows taking place in smaller inner-city pubs, although house shows remained popular. Gradually punk morphed into the more socially accepted 'new wave', the suburban 'beer barns' largely disappeared in the 1990s with the introduction of pokies,[33] and in the twenty-first century, there is a smorgasbord of venues welcoming a range of musical genres. Yet, DIY house venues still exist in Melbourne. It is evident that these settings have distinct qualities unable to be replicated in formal music venues, and that the originating principles of self-sufficiency and a rejection of regulated space are still an important factor for underground creative communities.

Unexpected and Unsupervised Encounters with Space

Henri Lefebvre emphasises the importance of structured and unstructured interactions with space in urban society. These interactions are closely linked with the fundamental social needs for 'certainty and adventure...

work and play… the predictable and unpredictable', which he suggests as being two oppositional yet complementary sides of the anthropological coin.[34] The highly regulated nature of licensed late-night music venues, whether it be in the physical spaces themselves or the legislation that surrounds them, allows for a fairly narrow spectrum of encounters between audience, performers, and space. The desire to work around and outside of these structures is a response to their rigidity, resulting in the existence of informal spaces for live music performance.

The Victoria Police website advocates Crime Prevention Through Environmental Design (CPTED), the theory that 'the design of a physical environment can produce behavioural effects that will reduce both the incidence and fear of crime' through three basic strategies: access control, surveillance, and territorial reinforcement.[35] Likewise, the Design Guidelines for Licensed Venues document from the Victorian Commission for Gambling and Liquor suggest that a deliberate management of 'furniture, lighting, climate, and sound' can 'provide powerful behavioural cues to patrons'.[36] These combined factors contribute to the regulation of space in licensed live music venues.

Surveillance of patrons is paramount in formal music venues and is heavily regulated by design guidelines. Clear lines of sight are maintained by constructing open plan spaces, keeping circulation areas free of clutter, working to prevent areas of concealment, and installing sufficient lighting, security guards and CCTV cameras.[37] These measures allow venues monitor patron behaviour and ensure they remain within the realm of permitted experiences.

Territorial reinforcement is the clear delineation between public and private space, and ensuring all areas are designed and managed for their purpose to create a 'sense of ownership'.[38] In his work on 'third places', Ray Oldenburg argues that newer venues are 'more wedded to the purpose for which they were built',[39] and often include separate areas specifically designed for paying entry fees, watching live music, performing live music, purchasing alcohol, consuming alcohol, smoking, dancing and other activities.

Access control involves the physical design or alteration of a space directly aimed at 'decreasing criminal activity'.[40] Architectural features may be modified (e.g. walls knocked down) to maximise surveillance, as well as allowing a flow of people through rooms and avoiding 'bottlenecks' at entry and exit points. Of course, these measures play an undeniable role in ensuring the well-being of venue patrons, however, one cannot help but feel that the combined effect of these interventions results in a set of heavily mediated and often sanitised interactions between physical space and those circulating within it.

The concept of house-as-venue or venue-as-house provides the possibility for new and unexpected encounters with space: houses appear less house-like, and venues appear less venue-like. To borrow from sociology, this fluid house/venue dichotomy presents ideas of *bricolage* as discussed by Dick Hebdige in his 1979 book *Subculture: The Meaning of Style*. Hebdige, quoting a text by the surrealist Max Ernst from 1948, describes:

> the subcultural bricoleur, like the author of a surrealist collage, typically juxtaposes two apparently incompatible realities (i.e. 'flag': 'jacket'; 'hole': 'teeshirt'; 'comb': 'weapon') on an apparently unsuitable scale…and…it is there that the explosive junction occurs.[41]

The conflation of the house and music venue is one such juxtaposition, causing a similar 'assault on the syntax of everyday life'[42] and what we expect to occur in these realms. However, this logic doesn't just apply to shows taking place in domestic environments. Before organising shows at The Bank, Liam put on gigs at Thornbury Bowls Club and 'an old piano store in Reservoir', simply because 'it's just nice to go to a new place and see a gig'.[43] The mundane is thus transformed into a slightly surreal experience. This disconnect jolts us out of the familiar and ultimately facilitates a more exciting and creatively charged environment to consume and perform live music within.

As renters rather than homeowners, the occupants of houses operating as DIY venues are often limited in how much they can modify the space to align with live music venue guidelines. Organisers must capitalise on the existing topography of the building, rather than structurally altering the space to influence what activities take place within its walls. Steph 'instantly wanted to do shows' after discovering the possibilities afforded by the shopfront space at Catfood Press: an open room (aka band room) big enough to house an audience but small enough to feel intimate, direct access to street, and a staircase winding up into a loft which provided prime viewing access for those keen to keep clear of the mosh. Steph describes the venue as being 'a smaller space but... the layout worked well for crammed but visible shows'.[44]

DIY house venues, with their often semi-concealed, pokey and chaotic rooms, are unlikely to conform to design recommendations for licensed music venues.[45] Unsupervised and often disorderly, these spaces can afford a wider gamut of potential experience and encourage the 'adventurous', 'playful' and 'unpredictable' encounters which, according to Lefebvre, are integral to our social well-being. DIY house venues reveal haphazard accumulations of signs and signifiers that do not relate to a single function, but instead suggest 'places of simultaneity'.[46] When Liam gives the cameraman a tour of The Bank in the 2018 film *Now Sound*, the first things he points out are the incongruous scenes of 'record player...dishes...piles of music equipment that doesn't have a proper home'.[47] A 'lived-in' quality permeates every corner of the space, constantly being rearranged and added to. The house is a dynamic vessel of cluttered material leftovers, where the realms of domestic/creative, private/public, ordinary/transcendent coalesce and new meanings can be formed.

The physical environment of share houses is more effective in expressing aspects of personal or collective identity, rather than explicitly communicating a defined purpose or function of a space. The interior of Secret Location is adorned with an ever-changing display of artworks made by friends and staff. Organisers describe Secret Location as 'a reflection of us, an extension of ourselves', providing a more intimate, inviting and personalised environment.[48] Similarly, The Bank's walls were 'covered from floor to ceiling with paintings, instruments and musical equipment'.[49] In *Dogs in Space*, the ephemera of share house life almost reaches the point of caricature. Described by Lowenstein as a 'spider web, womb-like place',[50] the mise-en-scène is a densely chaotic and detailed visual feast. The house, located in a run-down area, is already in a state of disrepair and therefore acts as a blank canvas onto which its inhabitants can freely project their values and tastes: music posters and political flags cover the walls, tin cans hang in the shower, and empty beer bottles populate most surfaces. The room where Dogs in Space (the band) rehearse seems to be at the heart of this chaos, which Lowenstein explains as being based on 'The Fucked

Room' of the real-life Berry St share house, 'where everyone put their shit'.[51] It is not surprising that this room is also the household's epicentre of creativity and expression, facilitating not only rehearsals but also house gigs with a party atmosphere. In these spaces, the physical environment becomes another means of self-expression for the creative community, fostering a greater sense of belonging, and creating a more meaningful and stimulating environment in which to perform and watch live music.

The chaos and confusion of The Fucked Room facilitates another important quality of house shows—the lack of hierarchy between band and audience. This is consistent with the do-it-yourself philosophy of the Little Bands scene, which embraces the ethos that anyone can start a band regardless of technical ability, gender, or commercial viability. There are two key party scenes in *Dogs in Space*: the first at a share house where Whirlywirld are playing, the second at Berry St where Dogs in Space (the band) are playing. In both these scenes, the bands are playing to living room crowds who stand on the same physical level as the band, resulting in very little distinction between the partying audience and the musicians performing. According to Yasmine Sharaf, a regular at Secret Location as both an audience member and musician, this flattening out of physical space contributes to a 'spirit of camaraderie and community'.[52] The audience, in both a literal and figurative sense, can become the band thus making the 'symbolic crossing from the dance floor to the stage'.[53] In *Dogs in Space*, the intimacy between band and audience is somewhat lacking in the gig scenes shot at live music venues. The Primitive Calculators' performance provides the soundtrack to an argument between Anna and Sam, and similarly Marie Hoy's rendition of 'Shivers' marks the end of the night as too-drunk Leanne makes a scene, Tim gets kicked out of Dogs in Space (the band), and Anna injects heroin, apparently for the first time, before vomiting out the window. Although none of these events are related to the formal venue spaces themselves, the darker mood of these scenes provides a stark contrast to the lively atmosphere of the house gigs, suggesting that the latter allows a certain freedom not available in the formality of public spaces.

In both Lowenstein's account of share house living in *Dogs in Space* and contemporary DIY house venues in Melbourne, the domestic environment allows its inhabitants to create their own private universe according to the aesthetic of the scene. The self-directed transformation and personalisation of physical space by its inhabitants presents a collage of symbols that speak to both the inhabitants and the community that walk through its doors, and thus feels symbolic of the morphing collective identity by the Melbourne underground.[54] Interestingly, the feelings of intimacy, autonomy, and collective identity fostered by this environment contradict those of dislocation and subjugation often felt by tenants in rented share houses at the hands of landlords, real estate agents, and property developers. The subversion of private domestic space in this way can therefore be an empowering experience for those that feel disenfranchised by mainstream capitalist society.

External Pressures and Makeshift Solutions

For many organisers of these venues, there is no intention of operating legally: they simply wish to prolong the venue's existence by remaining undetected by regulatory bodies and law enforcement. For others, there may be a desire to establish a more legitimate operation but perceive an unrealistic number of bureaucratic hoops to jump through, or conforming with the legal requirements is simply outside of their financial means. Additionally, the transience of renting means that the lifespan of a venue could have wrapped up by the time tenants have managed to navigate the red tape required to apply for the appropriate licences and permits. In short, there are many reasons why organisers do not conform to the regulations set by planning authorities, liquor licensing and law enforcement.

One heavily regulated aspect of live music venues is alcohol consumption. For venues such as The Bank and Catfood Press, liquor licences were not necessary as alcohol is not being sold (audiences can 'B.Y.O'), and the consumption of alcohol would thus be considered part of the standard use of residential premises. However, if gigs were to run every week then concerns may be raised as to whether the site was transforming beyond its normal domestic use. Secret Location, on the other hand, has a dedicated bar where alcohol is sold and there is no BYO. The venue would be unlikely to get a late-night (general) liquor licence: there are residential properties nearby,[55] it is dilapidated and therefore unlikely to meet building standards, and would probably fail design recommendations for licensed venues.[56] So instead, Secret Location has been organising limited liquor licences for each event. These licences provide a cheap and relatively straightforward solution. 'It's like sixty bucks for three… it takes ten minutes and for the first forty we got them straight away', explain organisers.[57] However, temporary limited licences are technically granted for 'one-off events or a series of one-off events', so the serving of alcohol 1–2 nights per week at Secret Location is bending the rules.[58] Recently, the Victorian Commission for Gambling and Liquor Regulation started rejecting these applications, so organisers began applying under other names—which worked for a while. Organisers also discussed the possibility of applying for a permit to run it as a gallery space, which would include limited licences for every 'exhibition opening', allowing them to 'exist in that grey area…for a while'.[59] Again, costliness and red tape proved to be hurdles too big to overcome. In my most recent correspondence with organisers, they had attempted to apply for a permanent liquor licence but needed a council planning permit first. 'The response was not good', organisers explained, 'we think the property might have had a red mark against it. A senior council person responded asking for a heap more info, making us jump through numerous hoops that…made it not possible, as well as very expensive. That was a real bummer and very stressful, we thought it might end soon after that'.[60] However, the venue continues, albeit illegally instead of inhabiting the 'grey area' afforded by the limited licences, and organisers have not heard anything more from planning and liquor licensing.

Noise complaints can be difficult to evade and are intensified with the growing gentrification and densification of the inner city.[61] Live music venues are required to 'protect noise sensitive residential use within 50 metres of the venue',[62] which was met by Secret Location's soundproofing of the band room to minimise sound projecting out the front of the building. However, organisers have found the most effective response to noise complaints is befriending the neighbours, who now complain directly to them rather than to the council or liquor licensing. Organisers must also be mindful of what kinds of shows can occur in the space and take into consideration what the soundproofing can handle, stating 'we've had to not do raves…the bass is so hectic and relentless'.[63] Both Steph and Jack spoke of Catfood Press's various encounters with 'the neighbour / council / real estate holy trinity', as well as numerous visits from Victorian Police responding to noise complaints.[64] In the end, these pressures resulted in effectively preventing Catfood Press from hosting live shows. Jack describes a mounting intensity from a number of regulatory bodies:

> Vicpol started to come semi-regularly and ask our neighbours for all sorts of information about us. Sometimes undercover police would come to our events, I kicked one out once for trying to find and buy drugs. On top of that there were constant visits and letters from organisations like the liquor licensing board, the local council and APRA… Surprise inspections started occurring for the first time in almost a decade and you could just kind of tell that regularly hosting events was no longer sustainable… A disadvantage of spaces that are both domestic and public is that they fulfil a variety of different needs to different people. At first we tried to just reduce the frequency of shows but eventually it became apparent that the risk of several people losing their home was too much.[65]

At The Bank, local musician and tenant Romy Vager explains 'we thought we were being clever I think, and it turned out the council was quite aware of things'.[66] After an intimidating meeting with the local council and 'a big fine', Liam let the heat die off and ran afternoon shows, however, pressure from neighbours, the landlord, and local council ultimately resulted in The Bank's closure in 2016.[67] These pressures always put a question mark over the lifespan of DIY venues, as spaces can be terminated at any given moment. However, the constant threat of closure, combined with the thrill of participating in something subversive, adds to the unique atmosphere of DIY venues. Yasmine remarks that 'events always run the risk of being shut down by police, but that too can add to the element of excitement… There is always a sense of immediacy, possibility. It is a little bit like the parents have gone away for the weekend'.[68]

The rapid rate of gentrification in twenty-first-century Melbourne and the subsequent decreasing availability of affordable and appropriate space present another difficulty for DIY house venues. Melbourne's inner northern suburbs, historically an industrial and working-class area, are today considered 'fertile musical ground…with rampant cross pollination in venues, studios and share houses'.[69] It is ironic that the colonisation of the post-industrial environment by predominantly middle-class students and bohemians in the 1970s also marks the beginnings of gentrification in the inner city of Melbourne.[70] *Dogs in Space* vividly portrays the inner city well before rents skyrocketed and multi-storey apartments were the norm—the urban environment is depicted as a cheaply available and unsupervised playground for groups and individuals engaging in alternative lifestyle choices. By the second decade of the twenty-first century, the underground has become the mainstream, and a predominantly low-income creative class is facing displacement at the hands of gentrification.[71] These factors combined make it increasingly difficult for not just DIY house venues, but indeed live music venues in general, to exist. It is these challenges which spark the innovation, problem solving and makeshift solutions developed by creative subcultures, who by definition are inclined to 'think outside the box'. Liam describes 'a resilience…some weird survival mentality' and that moving further out may be the key: 'there are heaps of disused shopping strips… all the way out in Reservoir and Thomastown and stuff. It seems crazy far away but maybe it won't in a couple of years'.[72] But at what point do these places become inaccessible and will the scene become so geographically fragmented that the underground community loses connection and strength? The Internet connects people virtually, but as this chapter argues, physical spaces play an important and irreplaceable role in the consolidation of underground scenes.

Fostering a Creative Community

One of the most unique and treasured aspects of DIY venues is their ability to nurture a tight-knit community, and their typically secretive nature is a key contributing factor in facilitating this. Since these spaces are often operating illegally or semi-legally in unauthorised or unconventional locations, it is necessary to maintain a low profile to avoid detection by local councils, licensing authorities, neighbours, and police. As a result, they are rarely signed or made obviously visible from street level. Described by Oldenburg as the 'protective colouration' of third places, the inconspicuous appearance of house venues deters 'a high volume of strangers or transient customers'.[73] Therefore, those that do visit these venues are either already part of the community or a 'friend of a friend', and have made a conscious effort to seek out this environment, rather than simply wandering into it by chance on a night out. Details about shows are not openly advertised to the public, and so it is often necessary to interact with other community members in order to find out the address, who is playing, and sometimes specific procedures on how to enter the venue. Secret Location exemplifies this discreet approach: the name and address cannot be posted in promotional material for shows due to both items 'being flagged early on' by planning authorities, and an Instagram account used to post about upcoming events is set to private.[74] The fact that audience numbers depend on word of mouth is not a problem, with organisers stating 'it can only fit 150 people in. Functionally it doesn't need more'.[75]

More than just the desire to be subversive, there is also the thrill that comes with being privy to a world that is not visible to the general public.[76] Steph describes the thrill of 'feeling you're stumbling across a bit of a secret or special thing', which 'helped to nurture a really great crew of regulars'.[77] This sentiment is reflected by Yasmine, a frequent attendee at Secret Location both as a musician and an audience member, who describes a 'feeling of belonging to a secret club'.[78] Organisers at Secret Location admit that they 'struggle a bit with the fact that there is this exclusivity', but acknowledge that it is a necessary step in remaining undetected by planning and licensing authorities.[79] It is also important in managing their own security and that of others:

> We feel like we know the pop/punk underground scene a bit more. There's not going to be too many surprises, or weird maniacs showing up... the secrecy of the venue does help with the self-policing nature of a space like this too, not just anyone knows where it is and generally people look after each other and are respectful of the venue.[80]

DIY house venues are often founded on a not-for-profit basis by tenants who have strong networks and connections within the creative scene, instilling these spaces with a greater sense of affinity between organisers and audience members than typically found at licensed venues.[81] For example, both Liam and Steph are visual artists and play in numerous local bands. The result is a mutual respect and understanding within the community that just one instance of bad behaviour could destroy the venue. Organisers of Secret Location know this well, explaining that 'most of the events here we know more than half the people... Everyone's happy to keep this little secret'.[82] The intimate community at DIY house venues creates the relaxed atmosphere found at places like Secret Location, The Bank, and Catfood Press. Yasmine describes Secret Location as being:

> so much more welcoming than a formal venue. It is also a lot of fun, you never know how long it will stay open, and if you play your cards right you may be able to hang out playing dice until 5am. It has a much smaller capacity than most formal venues which creates an intimate atmosphere amongst the audience. People seem more willing to talk and mingle at Secret Location than at a larger traditional venue... As a performer, you really do feel looked after. It is not uncommon for organisers to make you a midnight snack or a cup of tea... There is a real family spirit.[83]

The Bank had a similar community focus. Al Solly, resident of The Bank, organised a series of afternoon gigs called 'Hootenanny' shows at the venue once the council had had enough of the night shows. He explains that:

> It was really necessary to have something at The Bank, a place that people could walk to instead of having to pay for a taxi or public transport. There are a lot of people in the area living off Centrelink or a student allowance. The idea for the Hootenannys all happened from there – putting on good music and bringing people together.[84]

Third places such as The Bank thrive 'where walking takes people to more destinations than does the automobile', and casual and informal interactions invite human connection, imparting an 'attachment to the area and the sense of place' for locals.[85] In contrast to the necessary concealment of Secret Location, Solly's statements speak to a desire to not only foster a social set within the walls of venues such as The Bank, but to share the value of the space with the local community.

At Catfood Press, there was particular focus on facilitating all-ages shows, something which organisers felt was severely lacking in the Melbourne music scene. In 2004, Victorian liquor licensing placed a four-month ban on underage gigs after a bouncer was attacked at the Metro nightclub in Melbourne's CBD at an all-ages event. When the ban was lifted, a number of amendments were made to the Liquor Control Act including the requirement that venues submit an application 45 days prior to the event, a restriction to under 18s only (rather than the previously 'all-ages' gigs), a 10 p.m. finishing time, at least two security guards at the entrance plus one for every 100 patrons, and a no 'pass-outs' rule.[86] Unsurprisingly, licensed venues, particularly smaller pubs, were reluctant to host these shows. Jack describes all-ages shows as something that organisers 'were passionate about, because we had that access [growing up] and it really shaped us'.[87] In this way, places like Catfood Press are an example of how DIY venues provide an inclusive and welcoming community for those that are excluded from the intensely surveilled and restrictive environment of formal music venues.

The importance of DIY spaces as a community hub is significant for groups or individuals rendered 'outsiders' by mainstream capitalist values of economic productivity.[88] Returning to *Dogs in Space*, the share house is presented as hive of social activity where the creative community can thrive. The Berry St kitchen serves as a confluence of diverse social factions, and a space where their various political and creative ideologies can circulate. Many of the activities that take place at Berry St are outside of mainstream social norms, and Berry St very much embodies the personal freedoms afforded by share house living in the changing social and cultural landscape of the time.[89] The film still provides an accurate depiction of share house life, a reason why it still strongly resounds with audiences over 35 years later.

The supportive communities that are formed around DIY spaces make them important sites for collaboration, learning, and experimentation. The do-it-yourself mentality means that all aspects of venues' operation are managed at a grassroots level, resulting in opportunities for growth and learning in a wide range of areas for those involved. As Yasmine explains, 'DIY venues often hinge on collaboration, rather than hierarchical systems [that are] in place at formal venues'.[90] Community members are encouraged to build, share and develop new strategies around events management, promotion, graphic design, networking, financial organization, and administration within an arts context. For example, since running The Bank, Liam has gone on to start his own record label and has plans to run a 'more legit venue' in the future.[91] The 'hands-on' approach of DIY venues is empowering for organisers, musicians, and audiences alike, and thus acts as a catalyst for cultural consumers to become cultural producers, thereby enriching the wider creative landscape.[92]

The outlay and operation costs of DIY house venues are low: rent is covered by existing tenants, promotion for events is run through social media, sound systems can generally be sourced at little or no cost through community networks, and the cost of liquor licensing, permits, security, and building requirements are bypassed.[93] Being inexpensive to run, and with any money made going straight back into the local community, DIY house venues also grant organisers the curatorial freedom to program more experimental performances.[94] The experience of musicians performing, rehearsing, or songwriting at The Bank expresses similar sentiments about the openness to experimentation in these spaces. Resident and local musician Reuben Bloxham explains there were not 'the pressures of a traditional gig space' and therefore felt 'more open to experimentation than they usually would', and Liam describes performances at The Bank that 'would go for like two or three hours and were just total chaos and noise'.[95] Similarly, Secret Location has provided 'a safe space for experimentation in my music' for Yasmine during her performances.[96] This need for experimentation is important to the creative process and is part of what Lefebvre describes as the basic human need to 'accumulate energies and…waste them in play'.[97] In her work on creative 'knowledge workers' in cities, Kate Shaw describes the importance of 'engag[ing] in the kind of experimentation that requires…products that sometimes fail' in creative production.[98] The Little Bands scene provides another example of creative production through experimentation. The concept of band members constantly collaborating, creating, breaking apart, reshuffling, and regrouping into new configurations to begin the process all over again embodies the transient and ephemeral nature of experimentation afforded by informal environments, and suggests a creative process driven by trialling, failure, and discovery, rather than a final end product.

Conclusion

It is clear that the autonomy afforded by DIY house venues can provide a rich source of social connection, creative expression, cultural production, and learning for organisers, performers and punters alike that feeds back into the wider creative scene. The subversive nature of DIY house venues forces them to lead a precarious existence by carefully circumventing regulatory boundaries, however, the transient nature of these venues adds to their charm. The attraction of such spaces is evidently acknowledged by more 'legitimate' operations: websites like House Concerts Australia[99] and Parlour Gigs[100] (who provide platforms for registered hosts to put on gigs in their home) offer somewhat sanitised versions of the DIY house venue experience. Boasting 'well-paying performances', 'engaged audiences' and the promise that hosting a house show is 'easy' and 'fun',[101] one can't help but feel that these websites seem to miss the point: that the thrill of house shows comes from engaging in an act of rebellion, the challenge and rewards of discovering a like-minded community, and organising events autonomously.

The existence of DIY house venues could be largely attributed to the failure of dominant cultural, commercial and political structures to satisfy the human desire to engage in unexpected, unstructured, and unsupervised encounters with space. This fundamental creative need has only 'somewhat parsimoniously taken into account by planners'[102] and is demonstrated clearly in the highly systematised environment of 'legitimate' music venues. Building upon the DIY ethos pioneered by the punk movement, house venues provide an impressive example of the ways in which independent communities employ radical approaches to develop their own methods of cultural production and consumption and continue to provide a dynamic and viable space for creative expression that is not aligned with the mainstream.

Notes

1. K. Shaw (2013) 'Independent Creative Subcultures and Why They Matter', *International Journal of Cultural Policy*, XIX(III), 333–352.
2. S. Albini (2014) Keynote Address: Steve Albini, Face the Music Conference, Melbourne, 15 November 2014, https://www.youtube.com/watch?time_continue=5&v=Lz_CPzuwSk4, accessed 17 May 2019.
3. S. Homan (2010) 'Governmental as Anything: Live Music and Law and Order in Melbourne', *Perfect Beat*, XI(II), 103–118; S. Taylor (2016) 'Geographical Information Systems for Applied Social Research: The Case of the Live Music Industry in Sydney and Melbourne', PhD diss., Mathematical and Geospatial Sciences, RMIT University.
4. Department of Environment, Land, Water and Planning (2016) 'Planning Practice Note 81: Live Music and Entertainment Noise', State Government of Victoria, https://www.planning.vic.gov.au/resource-library/planning-practice-notes, accessed 11 November 2018; Victoria Commission for Gambling and Liquor Regulation (2017) 'Design Guidelines for Licensed Venues', State Government of Victoria, https://www.vcglr.vic.gov.au/resources/design-guidelines, accessed 24 October 2018.
5. H. Pereira (2017) 'The Bank', *Swampland*, III, 62–71.
6. Department of Environment, Land, Water and Planning (2016) 'Planning Practice Note 81: Live Music and Entertainment Noise', State Government of Victoria, https://www.planning.vic.gov.au/resource-library/planning-practice-notes, accessed 11 November 2018, p. 1.
7. S. Hughes (2018) pers. comm., 29 October.
8. J. Petty (2019) pers. comm., 20 May.
9. H. Pereira (2017) 'The Bank', *Swampland*, III, 62–71 (63).
10. Heritage Council Victoria (2011) 'State Savings Bank of Victoria (Former)', Victorian Heritage Database, http://vhd.heritagecouncil.vic.gov.au/places/27132/download-report, accessed 15 October 2018.
11. I. Hellyer (2016) 'Why Canberra Is the Best City in Australia: A Chat with the Capital's Busiest Musician', Noisey Australia, https://noisey.vice.com/en_au/article/ryz4mj/canberra-is-the-best-city-in-australia-a-chat-with-the-capitals-busiest-musician, accessed 25 October 2018.
12. A. Critchley (2010) 'Sydney's Unlicensed Venues', *Cyclic Defrost*, https://www.cyclicdefrost.com/2010/09/sydney%E2%80%99s-unlicensed-venues-by-alyssa-critchley/, accessed 25 October 2018.

13. L. Godwin (2018) 'Keep Animal House Open', GoFundMe, https://au.gofundme.com/keep-animal-house-open, accessed 18 May 2019.
14. R. En (2017) 'The Bank', *Swampland*, II, 60–65.
15. A. Trainer (2016) 'Perth Punk and the Construction of Urbanity in a Suburban City', *Popular Music*, XXXV(I), 100–117.
16. C. Walker (1996) *Stranded: The Secret History of Australian Independent Music 1977–1991* (Sydney: Pan Macmillan).
17. R. Lowenstein (2009) 'We're Livin' on Dog Food'.
18. R. Lowenstein and A. De Groot (2009) 'Dogs in Space: Audio Commentary with Richard Lowenstein and Andrew De Groot', DVD special feature.
19. C. Walker (2005) *Inner City Sound*, 2nd edn (Portland, OR: Verse Chorus Press), p. 7.
20. P. Fleckney (2018) *Techno Shuffle: Rave culture and the Melbourne Underground* (Melbourne: Melbourne Books).
21. S. Taylor (2016) 'Geographical Information Systems…'.
22. D. Kimbell (2018) 'Australasian Popular Music of the 1960s and 1970s: An Overview', MILESAGO: Australasian Music and Popular Culture 1964–1975, http://www.milesago.com/MainFrame.htm, accessed 1 November 2018; D. Nichols (2016) *Dig: Australian Rock and Pop Music, 1960–85* (Portland, OR: Verse Chorus Press).
23. P. Oldham (2013) 'Suck More Piss: How the Confluence of Key Melbourne-Based Audiences, Musicians, and Iconic Spaces Informed the Oz Rock Identity', *Perfect Beat*, XIV(II), 120–139 (129).
24. M. Engleheart (2010) *Blood, Sweat and Beers: Oz Rock from the Aztecs to Rose Tattoo* (Sydney: HarperCollins).
25. S. Taylor (2015) 'Lost Venues, Long Nights: An Introduction to Historical maps of Live Music in Sydney and Melbourne', *Cordite Poetry Review*, http://cordite.org.au/essays/lost-venues-long-nights, accessed 1 November 2018.
26. B. Milne (2018) pers. comm., 28 October 2018.
27. M. Von Wayward (2019), 'Punk and Post-punk', Punk Journey, http://www.punkjourney.com/punk-and-postpunk.php, accessed 18 May 2019.
28. D. San Miguel (2011) *The Ballroom: The Melbourne Punk and Post-punk Scene* (Melbourne, VIC: Melbourne Books).
29. R. Stapleton (1978) 'Takin' It to the Streets (or Punkin' It up in Carlton)', *Juke Magazine*, CXL, 4.

30. The Australian Music Vault (2017) 'Punk Gunk: The Birth of Punk', mini documentary (Gatherer Media).
31. D. San Miguel (2011) *The Ballroom: The Melbourne Punk and Post-punk Scene* (Melbourne, VIC: Melbourne Books), p. 39.
32. C. Walker (2005) *Inner City Sound*, 2nd edn (Portland, OR: Verse Chorus Press), p. 7.
33. S. Taylor (2016) 'Geographical Information Systems …'.
34. H. Lefebvre (1996) *Writings on Cities*, translated by E. Kofman and E. Lebas (Oxford: Blackwell), p. 147.
35. Victoria Police (2019), 'Crime Prevention Through Environmental Design', https://www.police.vic.gov.au/business-and-commercial#crime-prevention-through-environmental-design, accessed 12 May 2019.
36. Victoria Commission for Gambling and Liquor Regulation (2017) 'Design Guidelines for Licensed Venues', State Government of Victoria, https://www.vcglr.vic.gov.au/resources/design-guidelines, accessed 24 October 2018 p. 41.
37. Victoria Commission for Gambling and Liquor Regulation (2017) 'Design Guidelines…'
38. Victoria Police (2019), 'Crime Prevention…'
39. R. Oldenburg (1999) *The Great Good Place: Cafes, Coffee Shops, Bookstores, Bars, Hair Salons, and Other Hangouts at the Heart of a Community*, 3rd edn (New York: Avalon), p. 36.
40. Victoria Police (2019), 'Crime Prevention Through Environmental Design', https://www.police.vic.gov.au/business-and-commercial#crime-prevention-through-environmental-design, accessed 12 May 2019.
41. D. Hebdige (1979) *Subculture: The Meaning of Style* (London, UK: Routledge), p. 106.
42. Hebdige, p. 107.
43. L. Barton (2018) pers. comm., 3 October 2018.
44. S. Hughes (2018) pers. comm., 29 October 2018.
45. Victoria Commission for Gambling and Liquor Regulation (2017) 'Design Guidelines…'.
46. Lefebvre, p. 148.
47. T. Willis (2018) 'Now Sound: Melbourne's Listening', documentary (KEWL).
48. Anonymous (2018) pers. comm., 5 November 2018.
49. H. Pereira (2017) 'The Bank', *Swampland*, III, 62–71 (63).

50. R. Lowenstein and A. De Groot (2009) 'Dogs in Space: Audio Commentary with Richard Lowenstein and Andrew De Groot', DVD special feature (Ghost Pictures Pty Ltd).
51. R. Lowenstein and O. Olsen (2009) 'Dogs in Space: Audio Commentary with Richard Lowenstein and Ollie Olsen', DVD special feature (Ghost Pictures Pty Ltd).
52. Y. Sharaf (2019) pers. comm., 15 May 2019.
53. Hebdige, p. 110.
54. Hebdige.
55. Live Music Roundtable (2012), 'Best Practice Guidelines for Live Music Venues', Music Victoria, http://www.musicvictoria.com.au/assets/2016/reports/Best-practice-guidelines-for-live-music-venues.pdf, accessed 2 November 2018.
56. Victoria Commission for Gambling and Liquor Regulation (2017) 'Design Guidelines…'.
57. Anonymous (2018) pers. comm., 5 November 2018.
58. Victorian Commission of Gambling and Liquor Regulation (2018), 'Liquor Licensing Fact Sheet: Temporary limited license', State Government of Victoria, https://www.vcglr.vic.gov.au/sites/default/files/uploadLiquor_licensing_fact_sheet_-_Temporary_limited_licence.pdf, accessed 24 October 2018, p. 1.
59. Anonymous (2018) pers. comm., 5 November 2018.
60. Anonymous (2018) pers. comm., 5 November 2018.
61. K. Shaw "Knowledge Workers' and the contradictions of the Creative City', Paper presented at the Melbourne 2010 Knowledge Cities World Summit, 16–19 November 2010, https://katesshaw.files.wordpress.com/2013/06/e28098knowledge-workers_-and-the-contradictions-of-the-creative-city.pdf, accessed 25 October 2018.
62. Department of Environment, Land, Water and Planning (2016) 'Planning Practice Note 81: Live Music and Entertainment Noise', State Government of Victoria, https://www.planning.vic.gov.au/resource-library/planning-practice-notes, accessed 11 November 2018.
63. Anonymous (2018) pers. comm., 5 November 2018.
64. S. Hughes (2018) pers. comm., 29 October 2018.
65. J. Petty (2019) pers. comm., 20 May 2019.
66. T. Willis (2018) 'Now Sound: Melbourne's Listening', documentary (KEWL).
67. H. Pereira (2017) 'The Bank', *Swampland*, III, 62–71.
68. Y. Sharaf (2019) pers. comm., 15 May 2019.

69. T. Willis (2018) 'Now Sound: Melbourne's Listening', documentary (KEWL).
70. R. Howe, D. Nichols, and G. Davison (2014) *Trendyville: The Battle for Australia's Inner Cities* (Clayton: Monash University Publishing); J. McCalman (1984) *Struggletown: Public and Private Life in Richmond 1900–1965* (Carlton: Melbourne University Press).
71. Shaw, K. (2008) 'Gentrification: What It Is, why It Is, and What Can Be Done About It', *Geography Compass*, II(V), 1697–1728; Throsby and K. Petetskaya (2017) 'Making Art Work: An Economic Study of Professional Artists in Australia', The Australia Council, https://australiacouncil.gov.au/research/making-art-work/, accessed 19 May 2019.
72. L. Barton (2018) pers. comm., 3 October 2018.
73. R. Oldenburg (1999) *The Great Good Place: Cafes, Coffee Shops, Bookstores, Bars, Hair Salons, and Other Hangouts at the Heart of a Community* (New York: Avalon), p. 36.
74. Anonymous (2018) pers. comm., 5 November 2018.
75. Anonymous (2018) pers. comm., 5 November 2018.
76. P. Fleckney (2018) *Techno Shuffle: Rave culture and the Melbourne Underground* (Melbourne: Melbourne Books).
77. S. Hughes (2018) pers. comm., 29 October 2018.
78. Y. Sharaf (2019) pers. comm., 15 May 2019.
79. Anonymous (2018) pers. comm., 5 November 2018.
80. Anonymous (2018) pers. comm., 5 November 2018.
81. D. Stuart (2017) 'Mulgara and the DIY Music Scene in Canberra', *The Riot Act*, https://the-riotact.com/mulgara-and-the-diy-music-scene-in-canberra/197371, accessed 28 October 2018.
82. Anonymous (2018) pers. comm., 5 November 2018.
83. Anonymous (2018) pers. comm., 5 November 2018.
84. H. Pereira (2017) 'The Bank', *Swampland*, III, 62–71 (65).
85. Oldenburg, p. 210.
86. Arts Victoria (2011), 'Economic, Social and Cultural Contribution of Venue-Based Live Music in Victoria', Deloitte Access Economics, https://musicvictoria.com.au/assets/Documents/DAE_Live_music_report_2011.pdf, accessed 21 May 2019; J. Topsfield and P. Donovan (2005), 'Under-Age Gigs Return', Melbourne *Age*, 19 March, https://www.theage.com.au/national/under-age-gigs-return-20050319-gdztfg.html, accessed 21 May 2019.
87. J. Petty (2019) pers. comm., 20 May 2019.

88. K. Shaw (2013) 'Independent Creative Subcultures and Why They Matter', *International Journal of Cultural Policy*, XIX(III), 333–352; Stanford Encyclopaedia of Philosophy (2018) 'Social Norms', Centre for the Study of Language and Information, Stanford University, https://plato.stanford.edu/entries/social-norms/, accessed 28 October 2018.
89. M. McKew (2017) 'Share Houses and Women's Liberation: A Forgotten History', *The Conversation*, https://theconversation.com/share-houses-and-womens-liberation-a-forgotten-history-84069, accessed 2 October 2018; R. Howe, D. Nichols, and G. Davison (2014) *Trendyville: The Battle for Australia's Inner Cities* (Clayton: Monash University Publishing).
90. Y. Sharaf (2019) pers. comm., 15 May 2019.
91. H. Pereira (2017) 'The Bank', *Swampland*, III, 62–71.
92. K. Shaw (2013) 'Independent Creative Subcultures and Why They Matter', *International Journal of Cultural Policy*, XIX(III), 333–352.
93. D. Stuart (2017) 'Mulgara and the DIY Music Scene in Canberra', *The Riot Act*, https://the-riotact.com/mulgara-and-the-diy-music-scene-in-canberra/197371, accessed 28 October 2018.
94. K. Shaw (2004) 'FG4LM and Anarchism, Lefebvre and the Situationist International, and the Politics of Place in Alternative Culture', Paper presented at Deakin University Cultural Heritage Centre for Asia and the Pacific seminar series, September 2004, https://katesshaw.files.wordpress.com/2013/06/fg4lm-and-anarchism.pdf, accessed 25 October 2018.
95. H. Pereira (2017) 'The Bank', *Swampland*, III, 62–71 (63).
96. Y. Sharaf (2019) pers. comm., 15 May 2019.
97. Lefebvre, p. 147.
98. K. Shaw (2010) "Knowledge Workers' and the Contradictions of the Creative City', Paper presented at the Melbourne 2010 Knowledge Cities World Summit, 16–19 November 2010, https://katesshaw.files.wordpress.com/2013/06/e28098knowledge-workers_-and-the-contradictions-of-the-creative-city.pdf, accessed 25 October 2018, p. 2.
99. House Concerts Australia (2019), 'Welcome to Our House!', https://houseconcertsaustralia.com/, accessed 12 May 2019.
100. Parlour Gigs (2019), 'Parlour Gigs', https://parlourgigs.com/, accessed 12 May 2019.
101. House Concerts Australia (2019), 'Welcome to Our House!', https://houseconcertsaustralia.com/, accessed 12 May 2019.
102. Lefebvre, p. 147.

Finding 'Places to Be Bad' in Social Media: The Case of TikTok

Sorcha Avalon Mackenzie and David Nichols

Dogs in Space is concerned with a group of non-conformist musicians, activists and general 'outsiders' who live in inner-city Melbourne in the late 1970s. The film shows the way in which it is possible for such people to make a place for themselves either inhabiting pre-existing spaces—the pubs and houses of the down-at-heel inner city—while recycling or referring to elements of everyday materialism and social tropes (typified best of all by the pop culture trash mound of 18 Berry St itself). Here they express themselves performatively in both senses of that term—as artist(e)s or simply 'acting out' as members of cliques or subcultures.

If that was all that these characters did, that would be enough in itself. However, it is clear by looking at the subsequent careers of many (of course, by no means all) of the key players in the Melbourne 'postpunk'

S. A. Mackenzie
Melbourne, VIC, Australia

D. Nichols (✉)
University of Melbourne, Parkville, VIC, Australia
e-mail: nicholsd@unimelb.edu.au

music scene in the 1970s that the scene was a crucible for development of artistic perspectives and performance or other creative skills. It is also clear that the 'subversive' use/appropriation of space and culture was key to these cultural developments: to rework and react was to generate new ideas.

The closed universe of the characters in *Dogs in Space* is in many respects a given. Their global reference points, and any expectation of making an international impact, are unspoken and undeveloped. Yet they are part of a culture and an economy that requires them to consistently reflect on the world around them as broadcast or otherwise supplied to them in tropes, ideals, consumer choices, rhetoric and even *news* from the outside world. They are, in essence, constantly responding to the culture in their conversation and actions, and also for the musicians in the house, in public performances that could be classified as reaction.

In this chapter, we ask not whether a *Dogs in Space*-style world could exist in the present day (assuming that in its superficial detail it could not, but that in the broader sense part of the continued appeal of the film is the universality of youth subcultures) but whether there are any arguably comparable fora for 'anti-social' or subversive expression in any media with as much impact as pop music had in the 1970s. Shane Homan wrote presciently in 2003 of the irrelevance of local music to twenty-first-century youth and the need to recognize 'the ways in which youth cultures are constituted beyond national borders' requiring, amongst other things, 'the use of cultural technologies' and the 'adaptation of global popular culture'.[1] Is it possible to insert oneself into the cracks in mainstream, to—as much as this is in itself a cliché—upset dominant paradigms in the way that the punks of the late 1970s were definitively offensive, sparking a moral panic?

Examining one social media phenomenon in its first two years of existence, we look into the way it is maintained and adapted to advantage its users. This multipronged study of the TikTok phenomenon begins with a contextualization of the form and historic precedents for similar, globally appealing, examples which have for at least a century generated exploitable content from amateur talent through contest and competition. It does this at least in part to dispel the idea that concepts such as TikTok are so entirely novel as to be impossible to examine within conventional understandings of social behaviour and cultural production. We then discuss TikTok specifically as a social media brand; its internal tropes, issues and ideals. Thirdly—and in the knowledge that a significant proportion of academic analysis of social media trends, values and expectations are conducted via observation rather than participation—one of the two present authors discusses her own experience as a TikTok creator. Finally, we present our own analysis of TikTok, outlining where we see it now and what, if anything, it portends. Within all of this we seek to establish whether TikTokkers have agency to 'subvert' the generic tropes of the platform, or whether it is subversion-proofed either by dint of its design or the very nature of twenty-first-century social media. We see this through a lens perhaps best typified by 'PsBattleMod' in an online comment from early 2019 which could as easily have been directed to the 'punk' scene of the late 1970s: '*What is it with that app and bringing out the oddest people in this society, what is that gives them the confidence to do this shit*'.[2]

TikTok videos are not memes, but they exist within a meme-friendly space of social media. Seffert-Brockmann et al. assign to memes 'three types of communication logic: wasteful play online, social media political expression, and cultural evolution'.[3] In this way, they assert, memes are 'acts of subversive speech'.[4] We would suggest that TikTok can fill a similar role in many regards, with the caveat that the delivery and exposure of TikTok videos, regulated by an algorithm and somewhat haphazardly polices and censors certain content.

The app encourages comedy in videos, though ironic videos that might be perceived as mocking other users are discouraged and suppressed. The TikTok creator program gives selected TikTok users information about upcoming 'challenges' and trends within the app, as well as the opportunity to become featured if users comply and create videos with certain predetermined narratives under particular hashtags. In December 2018, videos tagged 'Christmas Look' were featured, with users showing off Christmas outfits, makeup looks or looks involving their pets.

We feel the need to countenance the truth that there is a sinister seam amongst TikTok users (as indeed there is to most elements in the social media universe—and indeed the universe). While TikTok's operators do not engage overtly with the issue, one online commentator's assessment— 'I don't think it's unreasonable to say that most of TikTok's user base is comprised of people under 14 and over 45'[5] stands for many who believe that there is a significant audience of paedophiles using the app either for passive titillation or even to contact children. While we cannot deny the likelihood of this, neither are we interested in exploring it in this chapter; we certainly do not see such activity as falling under our definition of 'subversion' or being 'bad'. This is true as much as we acknowledge it is undeniably an example of use of the platform outside sanctioned or conventional approaches, although as with all online content providers, TikTok's owners must surely have been aware of the likelihood of this.

TikTok removes videos deemed inappropriate quickly. One only needs to use the app for a short amount of time to see posts from regular users captioned 'reuploaded, because TikTok removed'. Many users post the number of violation notices they have received in their bio. However, while this may be a badge of pride for some, it is often unclear *why* videos are removed. Those in the creators program need only message the partner manager if they are experiencing trouble with their posts to easily have the post investigated and, most likely, brought back online. TikTok users without this connection have to contact TikTok through the app, which many have complained is highly ineffective.

TikTok: The Platform, Its Precedents and Its Participants

TikTok manifested in September 2017 from the Chinese app Douyin. Its owners, ByteDance, purchased another, similar, app—musical.ly—and merged the two in August 2018. After this time musical.ly users found that, if they refreshed or updated the app, it was recreated as TikTok. The following month, ByteDance claimed 150 million daily active users worldwide for their product.[6] The app has been downloaded, it is reputed, over a billion times.

The app's appeal appears to be, in large part, its brevity and light good humour, as well as the opportunity to follow featured contributors who, in search of 'likes', regularly add new videos. Content is user-generated albeit suggested and/or provided cues, music, 'challenges' and arguably other, subtler guidance, usually in the form of moderator intolerance for certain elements. Prohibitions include the use of weaponry, real or implied (with a few, surprising, exceptions such as mimicking gunfire); activities perceived as bullying—which might take the form of satire, in the form of 'irony'—and, unsurprisingly, sexualized content (of course, this may be in the eye of the beholder).

In the second decade of the twenty-first century, much writing about, and analysis of, social and digital media continues—despite or because of its almost near-ubiquity in modern life—to regard it as signifying a disturbing trend, or rather, a simultaneous channelling of disturbing trends, leading almost inexorably to social deterioration or mass exploitation and/or control, by business, governments, or both. In many instances, such descriptions are reminiscent of, for instance, mid-twentieth century alarmism over the pernicious influence of television; ongoing unease over particular forms of music or cinema, or what has been called 'pulp' and/or romance fiction. Railing against cultural novelty is, of course, much older than these examples.

Our interest here, however, is not in the history of warnings of the deleterious impact of various media and nor is it to pass judgment on the realities of such warnings. Rather, we are concerned with examples of the 'D.I.Y.' character and rebellious spirit of TikTok's content. Like many of the most popular social media platforms, TikTok is primarily populated by original user content; in many instances, new content 'riffs' on earlier work, and is in most cases soundtracked by audio provided as suggestions by TikTok itself.

Dave Centeno has explored the internet's 'stakeholder ecology' and 'democracy-enabled co-creations' in detail.[7] It is unclear from pronouncements by TikTok's participants how frequently they see involvement in the platform as a career step, although it is plain that many are honing performance skills and, given that it is possible to achieve a million likes through a modicum of short videos, celebrity of some sort is a reality. A minority of users do suggest via their profiles that they are, for instance, (aspirant?) fashion models, and in this regard they are arguably using TikTok as advertising for further exposure.

There are some superficial similarities between the world of late 1970s subcultures and TikTok—particularly the 'riffing' on and parodying of conventional ideas, myths and values. It would not be drawing too long a bow to connect a phenomenon such as the Little Bands—deliberately, self-consciously amateurish, created to challenge the idea of professionalism—with some TikTok activity. However, where we see the roots of TikTok forming in the modern era is in the talent contest. This user-generated (to use modern parlance) competition came to prominence in the late nineteenth century, at least in its currently familiar form. The beauty contest, another style of 'free' competition, appears to have gained popularity slightly later, and the two forms naturally crossed over both in audience appeal and in content or were in some instances combined.

Participants in nineteenth or early twentieth-century talent contests were usually expected to be amateurs (it would have been deemed unfair for professional performers to participate) and might typically work up a short, single act such as a novel interpretation of a popular song, poem or comedy monologue. Audiences and judges would be looking, it is clear, for an act both familiar and original; something which would allow audiences to 'hit the ground running' in comprehension and appreciation by use of familiar songs, texts or at very least, tropes (for instance, the use of blackface comedy). Notably, the format of a series of sketches, songs and stories was typical for vaudeville: a talent contest audience, it is to be assumed, adjusted their expectations in terms of performer skill but was, similarly to an audience in a professional show, kept engaged by dint of the fact that however redundant or disappointing one act might be, another would follow shortly.

Harrisburg, Philadelphia's Orpheum Theatre announced a talent contest in 1908 at which, it was announced, 'embryonic stars who crave honors in the footlights' glare will be invited to use the Orpheum stage as a stepping stone to greater things'.[8] At the Strong City, Kansas Auditorium in April 1912 Marion Plummer performed a Piano Solo, Marguerite Ryan a recitation, Hurbert Carter something referred to as a '(colored) dance' and Fred Apel an acrobatic act; Apel won the night.[9]

No doubt many 'indie' musicians of the late 1970s and today would be offended to be compared to the above, but there are genuine similarities which should be acknowledged. Not the least of these is the status of local legend conferred on individuals who act the part of a professional performer—exist, in a manner of speaking, creatively in the genre—yet could not feasibly exist on payment for performance. Scenes in *Dogs in*

Space surrounding the band's performance at the Seaview/Crystal Ballroom—not least the 'fans' fawning over Sam—are a case in point.

TikTok users—and indeed social media users generally—would readily recognize some of these features as germane to the 'challenges' and presentations they participate in, to be a functioning and practical member of TikTok. While it is true that participants in competitions described above were in many instances competing for not insubstantial amounts of money, for many the same impulse must surely have been in play as that experienced by social network participants today: the search for 'likes', as described by Jill Walsh in her study of adolescent Facebook users.[10] Such tropes have reached the present day through more recent iterations; the television talent show and YouTube are good examples, though TikTok's best known obvious precedent is Vine, which was operated by Twitter and sustained between 2013 and 2017. A Tiktokkers' reward is something arguably more valuable than cash; it is popularity and approbation, or social capital, within the TikTok community. TikTokkers will frequently make a self-referential video expression their pleasure at reaching '100k' or similar.

Tropes, Ideals, Processes and Issues

As has been the case in popular and 'fringe' culture for over a century, social media relies on borrowing from (if not outright appropriation of) tropes, references and ideas from broader or older cultures. Creative users of TikTok in 2018 mimed to, or even 'retooled', ideas within the TikTok world. Many videos on TikTok were originally based on comedic miming to songs or dialogue, and the viewer's expectations are raised when a familiar snatch of song, or image, begins each video. Popularity and value of videos is then gauged by the talent—usually, comedic—of the performer as well as, it is to be assumed, their physical attractiveness ('No-one can be prettier than you', @chris_23k tells @angrylittlebitch).

Examples proliferate. In late 2018, many TikTok contributors created videos acting out the opening lines of Dolly Parton's song '9 to 5'. Usually, the videos are cut together with a different scene for each line, beginning with the TikTokker 'tumbling out of bed' in slapstick fashion. Curiously—perhaps suggesting no more than a difficulty in tangibly realizing metaphor in the everyday—many found it problematic in particular to act pouring 'a cup of ambition', with dishwashing liquid, mysterious purple-black liquid, or the mere act of pouring illustrating this phrase (i.e. pouring a cup of *something*). The videos almost always strive to desexualize any potentially salacious element of 'tumbling out of bed' and the line which usually ends the video, referring to showering, which participants tend to enact in a bathroom but fully clothed. One noteworthy aspect of these videos, which may be no more than a non-sequitur, is the enacting of 'yawning, stretching' in which the 'stretching' is usually interpreted as the warm-up preceding exercise.

Because TikTok videos are not dated, and presented to the user in a continuous reel, it is not possible to track the development of such interpretations and influences. Seiffert-Brockmann et al., writing not about user-generated videos but about memes, nevertheless proffer relevant observations: that the 'public discursive relevance' of such works 'is that they are part of a decentralized game' centred on play, 'the waste of energy just for the sake of it'.[11] Everyone is joining in on an activity, and producing their own interpretation, in some instances merely the creation of their own version distinguishable from others primarily because *they* are doing it. The greatest difference between memes and TikToks is that TikTok itself often prescribes themes as 'challenges', though of course for the creators along the chain, the source is arguably irrelevant.

While it is not necessarily important, it is also unclear how familiar the TikTokkers and their consumers are with the entirety of songs used. In some instances, it is plain that the source of humour is in certain respects simply the length of a song's intro, which thereby allows the performer to construct a convoluted lead-up to a simple joke 'beginning'—at which point the song begins, but the video ends. Other soundtrack songs appear disconnected lyrically or conceptually from the scenes they are brought into illustrate, such as the intro to a 2015 track by French DJ and producer Breakbot which is frequently put forward to illustrate a paradigm in which users 'google search' phrases such as 'who do I look like'. Breakbot (feat. Irfane)'s 'Baby I'm Yours' has no lyrical or conceptual connection to such activities.

It is more likely that the future of TikTok lies with creators such as Bricknermon, a notable TikTok user who has gained widespread attention in the app and beyond. A video featuring him sitting on the toilet staring into the camera, as his mother fed him yoghurt, went viral. Bricknermon's TikTok character is of a socially awkward, overly indulged, un-self aware, technologically naïve kid. Many of his videos feature his mother and brother, and reference his Polish heritage. Thousands of contributors have used hashtags such as '#bricknermonsquad', '#bricknermonisdaddy', '#bricknermom' and '#shoutoutbricknermon.'

Can TikTok Be Subverted? Sorcha Mackenzie's Experience with TikTok

I first downloaded TikTok in October 2018. I only understood the application to be a karaoke app. I'd seen videos on Instagram reposted from the application Music.ly and downloaded it with the intention of ironically singing over the popular 2018 hit 'In My Feelings' by Drake. The app was initially difficult to understand, but I spent the day making horribly jerky, absurd videos with my friends; lip syncing on top of many of the songs that popped up in the app's Top 20 Trending list. In the proceeding weeks, I'd occasionally open up the app and scroll through what seemed to be endless music and acting videos.

The more I engaged with the app and liked certain content TikTok's algorithm sent more comedic and ironic videos into my feed. After two of my best friends downloaded the app, we began posting more regular videos. After using the app quite briefly and posting an ironic video dueting a featured video my friend found overnight they'd received over 100k views. I was inspired to continue creating my own content for the app as there seemed to be a great community of people posting ironic videos.

I began to see TikTok as a platform, like Vine, which had a great potential for comedic videos. As an artist who relies heavily on Instagram for promotion and selling work, I also saw the value in using TikTok to promote my art: my TikTok account could be directly linked to my Instagram and I saw it as an opportunity to gain more Instagram followers.

I'd gain a bit of traction on the app due to some absurd and ironic videos I'd posted referencing memes and tropes within the app. As someone with a background in music, art and videography I found it easy to download videos with popular sounds, extract audio and then use simple music editing software to change or 'remix' the audio in humorous ways. I then would record videos and using a mix of the video editing software on my computer (Final Cut Pro) I would make more complex videos with original sounds that I could then upload back into the app. Editing videos through external and sophisticated editing software means I can create content without the restraints imposed by the program to be user friendly; a path to creating more complex, impressive content.

The first video that I created which received a lot of attention referenced the well-known 'overwatch meme' on the app. The audio from the original video was extracted from the song 'No Mercy' by The Living Tombstone. The theatrical song was created as a comment on players of Overwatch who act as 'bad sports' by blaming others for not choosing to be supporting characters, such as healers, while subsequently and ironically being the most useless person on the team. The bridge of the song involves a dialogue between two players and is as follows:

P.1 Maybe I'll be Tracer
P.2 I'm already Tracer
P.1 What about Widowmaker?
P.2 I'm already Widowmaker
P.1 I'll be Bastion
P.2 Nerf Bastion
P.1 You're right, so, Winston
P.2 I wanna be Winston
P.1 I guess I'll be Genji
P.2 I'm already Genji
P.1 Then I'll be McCree
P.2 I already chose McCree

The original viral video began through a popular TikTokker who posted a video lip syncing to this audio while holding controllers. The sound then became viral.

Upon seeing the large number of ironic videos made using and referencing the sound, I began thinking of ways to incorporate the sound in my own videos. During a conversation with a friend on the phone remaking on the audio, a friend remarked that the actual dialogue isn't logical in a chronological sense; if the dialogue were logical it would read:

P.1   Maybe I'll be Tracer
P.2   I'm already Tracer
P.1   What about Widowmaker?
P.2   Thats fine, I'm already Tracer

I exported the original audio and removed the female vocals from it and created a soundfile. I then recorded a video of myself speaking over the audio awkwardly in that fashion as if I was confused by 'Player 2's' dialogue.

The video was soon popular, reaching 600,000 views by the end of 2018. I gained a large following quite quickly and continue to amass followers and likes on videos daily. It was featured in a few YouTube compilations which also resulted in more followers both on Instagram and TikTok.

Immediately after this video was posted, I received a large amount of likes on nearly anything following it; these slowly decreased to a more 'normal' amount. Maintaining engagement and popularity on TikTok truly has a lot to do with maintaining momentum and being able to keep creating content and posting regularly. While I do enjoy creating content I can find it stressful as it is time consuming, and as a perfectionist with an obsessive personality it can truly take up my whole day.

Recently I was approached by TikTok Australia official to be an official Australian 'Creator' for the app. This means being included in a group chat to be told first the upcoming 'challenges' and 'trends' that TikTok will be promoting. It's a useful tool for those who post regularly and a supportive group to discuss ideas, show videos and talk to. It is, however, a reminder that many of the trends on TikTok are not organic, but rather contrived by the app developers.

Recently I was informed by a few friends that one can easily be shadow banned from the app by posting too much ironic or 'meme' related content. Unconfirmed rumours swirled that posting hashtags under 'meme' 'ironic' or 'gamer' would have your content blocked from, or minimized in, the feed. I had a few videos tagged 'ironic' that gained no views once posted despite my audience and I suspected these had been blocked from the 'for you' page. The hashtag 'gamer' itself has been blocked from TikTok. Other 'ironic' TikTok users had suspected the block had been created as there was a high amount of bullying under the 'gamer' hashtag. A popular trope within the app had developed telling women to 'stay in the kitchen' or 'make me a sandwich' which 'gamer girls' were often referred to as property. These jokes were often made self-deprecatingly by female users.

Ironic videos on TikTok could be seen as a form of bullying, regardless. They are essentially making fun of the application, the videos of others who make 'genuine' or 'sincere' videos by trivializing them. On the app it has become a popular trope to duet famous TikTok members who make 'funny faces' by filming oneself deadpan and staring into the camera. It also became a popular trope to make fun of these users while sarcastically laughing when the user in the original video made jokes.

I am a TikTok user who mainly makes ironic videos which are centred around twisting and merging tropes together and trivializing them. I think many of the ironic and 'subversive' videos created on TikTok are a great critique on the app and can be very clever and humorous. However, I completely disagree with, and refuse to engage with, videos that rely on ironic or dark humour to thinly veil racism, homophobia, transphobia and ableism. Many of the videos under the ironic and gamer tag do engage in this kind of bigotry and bullying and it becomes clear why some people, including the application itself, want to distance themselves from it.

However, I think TikTok's attempts to ban this kind of content lies more in the realm of it being concerning to have children bullied through their application and the possible negative consequences of this. It is a form of self-preservation.

Conclusion: The Future of/Is TikTok

It is clear that TikTok is an engaging, connective and innovative platform for expression: a soothing endless stream of 15-second videos, entirely 'mindless' yet entirely mindful to engage with. It also invites contributions;

users have the option to upload or create videos through a fairly user-friendly video editing system. The possibilities are endless, unless those possibilities involve something the app, its algorithm or any one of a host of users deem inappropriate.

In the 1970s and 1980s, those wishing to interact with popular culture, art or music, or to be 'countercultural' (the difference, in hindsight, seems far more meagre than it did forty years ago) were impeded. This took place in ways which, if they did not entirely thwart all activity, made it very clear about who could and could not participate. Examples abound in this book, but one can stand in for many: the response of the powers that were at the British Rough Trade label to the EP of Melbourne's Little Bands, which was considered too weird to be saleable. Of course, there was a back story to the Little Bands which perhaps enhanced their appeal; but present generations are comparatively immured to designations such as 'too weird', by dint of their exposure to (albeit often decontextualized) examples of strange, extraordinary and fascinating cultural product from anywhere, at all times.

Thus, what is perhaps most exciting about TikTok is its value as a platform to experiment and engage. A 12-second video by a TikTokker called femaledoglasagna (all signs point to a real-world identity as Canadian teenager Sarah Fung) is a case in point. The narrative—such as it is—is simple: taking a sip of coffee, Sarah spits it out as too cold; there follows nine jump cuts of walking a suburban footpath (with two amusing asides, including the kicking of a newly delivered parcel off her doorstep with 'ew, whatever'), the tossing of the coffee cup into a microwave, then the ascent to the first floor of her suburban home to play a sound effect on her computer: 'bruh'. The entire production is surreal and comic, with reference points far beyond the skeletally meagre storyline; whether it is anything more than funny-peculiar is perhaps in the eye of the beholder.

In 1978, anyone wishing to inhabit a counterculture would be limited by geography and social mores. Now, it is TikTokkers like femaledoglasagna (23,900 followers in June 2019) or others such as the much more popular Bricknermon (159,300 followers in June 2019) who are breaking new ground in social media. The freedom within the platform is, undeniably, fragile and also, undoubtedly, controlled by unseen hands in ways users can only incidentally understand. However, the creativity and cleverness of many users should also not be underestimated; whatever its pernicious possibility, the beauty of TikTok is in both its accessibility and in its capacity to convey the most simple, bizarre and indeed subversive messages, worldwide. While it would be disingenuous to describe TikTok as 'punk', it would also be naïve to ignore its potential as a place to be 'bad', 'subversive' and 'ironic'.

Notes

1. S. Homan (2003) 'From Bankstown to the Globe, and Home: Popular Music in Sydney', in Melissa Butcher and Mandy Thomas (eds.) *Ingenious: Emerging Youth Cultures in Urban Australia* (North Melbourne: Pluto Press), p. 188.
2. PsBattleMod, 'What the Fuck Is up with Tiktok Making so Much Shit', Reddit, https://www.reddit.com/r/teenagers/comments/9s5iea/what_the_fuck_is_up_with_tiktok_making_so_much/, accessed 25 April 2019.
3. J. Seiffert-Brockmann, T. Diehl, and L. Dobusch (2018) 'Memes as Games: The Evolution of a Digital Discourse Online', *New Media & Society* 20(8), 2862–2879 (2862).
4. Seiffert-Brockmann et al., p. 2868.
5. https://www.youtube.com/watch?v=rFNDa48eYbE&feature=youtu.be, accessed 25 April 2019.
6. Q. Chen (2018) 'The Biggest Trend in Chinese Social Media Is Dying, and Another Has Already Taken Its Place', CNBC, https://www.cnbc.com/2018/09/19/short-video-apps-like-douyin-tiktok-are-dominating-chinese-screens.html, accessed 18 December 2018.
7. D. Centeno (2018) 'Social Media Stakeholder Co-creation of Celebrities as Human Brands' in B. Rishi and S. Bandyopadhyay (eds.) *Contemporary Issues in Social Media Marketing* (Oxon: Routledge), pp. 60–74.
8. Anon (1908) 'Two Men and a Bottle', *Harrisburg Daily Independent*, 19 March, 4.
9. Anon (1912) 'At the Auditorium Last Week', Strong City *News-Courant*, 18 April, 1.
10. J. Walsh, 'Adolescents and Their Social Media Narratives', p. 47.
11. Seiffert-Brockmann et al., p. 2868.

Coda: 'What It Feels Like When a Subculture Appears'—Richard Lowenstein Interview, 2009

Trevor Block

In August 2009, a restored *Dogs in Space* and Richard Lowenstein's documentary *We're Livin' on Dog Food* were shown on consecutive days one weekend at the Melbourne International Film Festival. Both were released as one DVD set at the end of the month. In between those two events, the Ears reformed to play at the Corner Hotel, Richmond, at a night called 'Sails of Oblivion', which also included appearances by Hugo Race and Ollie Olsen. Trevor Block interviewed Lowenstein for *Mess + Noise*. The feature, part of the magazine's 'Icons' series, appeared only in the online version of the magazine.

TB: *You must be pleased to be getting the reissue out.*
RL: Yes, I am, I'm pleased that I'm finally able to do it, legally and all that stuff. It's cost me—me, personally, I mean—a hell of a lot of money to do. It's not like you can just go to a DVD company and have them say 'Yeah, we'll do it, we'll spend fifty grand on restoring this and putting it out'. So I'm glad that I've done it myself, I felt it was worth it. Most places would have done it on the cheap, you know, not put in HD, they just would

---

T. Block (✉)
Melbourne, VIC, Australia

have done it as economically as possible. But I felt that, considering for the past twenty years it hasn't been available on anything but bad VHS tapes, it should be done right. Though having said that, we actually used a copy of the VHS version as a colour guide and so on for the work we did. At the time I thought the VHS looked pretty good but then you put it up in a large format, and look closely, and it's like 'Oh, Jesus'.

It was great to be able to put the original negative up and scan it in at high definition. I probably wouldn't say that about all my films. Like, say, *Strikebound*, which is now about thirty years old, I don't think I would have spent so much time and energy on that. But when I saw *Dogs*, in high definition, I did feel that it has a kind of timeless quality, and it really was worth making the effort to fix it up.

There's some additional footage, but that's been put into the *Dog Food* documentary, not into the film. There was a 16 mm crew on set while we were filming, and just by luck, pure coincidence, we found their footage twenty years later. There is one scene missing from the film, that I wish I could find a copy of, but there hasn't been anything added. Actually, if I did find that missing scene, I'm not sure I would have put it back in. It was a subplot about Gary Foley's character, having an affair with the blonde rockclimbing girl. They're in the film as it is now, but there was a subplot where she was cheating on him, and he comes home one day and terrorizes her with a knife. The punks are all just sitting there, rigid, as she runs through the house bleeding and screaming, and he staggers into the room holding this bloody knife up. To give Gary credit, he did all that, he did it well. It was a good scene, but it seemed to be too long in the initial release and too confrontational.

I watched a crappy VHS bootleg of the film on the weekend, to prepare for this talk, and to me it didn't feel like a nostalgia trip at all. And, you know, I bought Bowie tickets, and saw the Ears play.

It's a fantasy, really, a mid-80s fantasy. Which has kind of become clearer in making the documentary, which has a section in it about the real Bowie queue at the MCG, with all the photographs I could find of it, and another section about the Crystal Ballroom, with all the original footage we could find. I wasn't in the Bowie queue, but I was very much at the Ballroom. It's now very obvious that when we made the film, we were recreating that earlier era, through the rose-coloured glasses of both the cinema and the mid-80s. As Ollie Olsen says in the documentary, people are dressed a lot better in *Dogs in Space* than they actually did at the time. We were heading in that direction, but when you see the original footage from the late 70s, it was a real mixed bag back then. As opposed to the post-punk thing of, you know, looking pretty. In the early days, it was predominantly a very suburban crowd, and it was a much more suburban look.

I remember standard Ballroom wear for a lot of people being sneakers, jeans, a band tshirt and an op-shop suit coat with a few badges on the lapels.

Yes, you can see in the old footage that for some people it was sort of like 'I'm waving the flag for the punk movement, but I'm not going to do anything too extravagant'. And then you had people like Sam who was trying to be a bit more out there, and outrageous. There were a few people who would bleach or dye their hair, and give themselves strange haircuts, but, especially in the early days, they were very few and far between. And if you saw someone walking down the street, who looked a bit odd, the chances were that you knew them. And there were a lot of people who went to the Ballroom just for a look at this new place, maybe hoping for a fun night out, you know, the reason anyone goes to a club. It was pretty obvious at the time we made the film that, even though we weren't thinking consciously about it, we were exaggerating the look and feel of things a bit, both to suit the time we were in by then, and also for the needs of cinema. I mean, poor old Primitive Calculators were asked to wear berets onstage for their appearance, for some reason. Although to their credit they absolutely refused, so at least they look the same in the film as they did back in the day.

I think that the very fact the film and its soundtrack existed, that they were out there to be found, kept alive the music and the memory of a lot of the bands featured.

Well, I would never have thought that, until I sat down at this very table with the Primitive Calculators to talk to them for the documentary. At the time, in the late 70s, I kind of idolized them, and that carried through until we made the film. I always thought they and the other bands were going to go down in the record books, in the annals of music history. And so they came in to talk, and initially, Stuart was very abrasive—as he can be, but that's just him. He was all 'We weren't one of the Little Bands, we were a real band'. Which is true, when people talk about the Little Bands scene they often mention the Primitive Calculators, but they were a bit apart from that, as well as being one of the great punk bands of the era. But, once he calmed down, he was—well, they all were—incredibly effusive about having been in the movie, even though a film like *Dogs* wasn't in their mindset at any point in time. It was too mainstream for them. But, that one day of shooting that they came and did, which I think was only half a day actually, has made them some kind of icons in the subculture hall of fame. And they said, you know, that twenty years later they have people emailing them, or approaching them in the street, saying things like 'You people changed our lives'. And when they ask 'Well, how did you hear us, hear our two little independent releases?', the answer is always 'I saw you and heard you in that movie, *Dogs in Space*, and then I went and chased up everything else I could find, the soundtrack, bootlegs, whatever'. So at the time, they were a bit hesitant about appearing, but I think now they realize it worked out well for them. I haven't seen them since they reformed, though I have watched them playing at All Tomorrow's Parties on YouTube. They told me they didn't really like doing that, it was a bit too big and 'industry' for them. They've always preferred playing in little places, hidden in back streets. Although that ATP show, more people probably saw them play at that one gig than ever saw them when they were around back then.

They were one of your favorites first time round, obviously.

Oh, yeah. But having said that, I probably didn't see them all that often, because they didn't play live much. They rehearsed a lot though, like Whirlywirld. Whirlywirld only played something like thirteen shows, but they became legends too. At the time we thought all the bands were just going to keep on playing, even if they did only play now and again. But of course a lot of them disappeared, and it was all over before it really began.

Aside from having to listen to the music while doing the restoration work on the film, do you still listen to it much?

Oh, yes. I've always been keen on Whirlywirld. And you know, I wasn't averse to *Door, Door*, either. A lot of people knocked it at the time, but it was when they became the Birthday Party that they lost me. But Whirlywirld were always the ones for me. I mean, their music is in the movie itself, and over the end credits. And the great thing about Ollie, and one of the reasons I asked him to do so much in the movie, is that his songs have always had a feel to them, a kind of mood that fitted in with what we were doing. You'd die to make a video for some of his songs, he uses so many great images, and the rhythms he uses are amazing as well.

I only recently got the Primitive Calculators' CD, they gave me a copy when they came in. And, you know, you certainly couldn't just listen to the Ears all the time. They were in the film partly because they were so ridiculous in many ways. And they didn't ever see themselves as something serious, they were just having fun.

And as well as interviewing him for the documentary, Ollie was one of the people you got in to do a commentary track on the reissue DVD.

Yes, there's one track that's me and Ollie, one of me and Andrew De Groot, the cameraman, and one of Chuck Meo and Tim McLaughlan, who give a bit of insight from the Ears' perspective as well. Funnily enough, one of the reasons that the documentary happened is that people who had heard about the reissue were ringing me up and saying they wanted to be on the narration. But technically there's a problem, you can't have more than three commentary tracks. So the documentary idea came about. Sam was one of the first people we got in to interview for it, and him talking, him and Mick Lewis, really got me thinking that there are were actually a lot of other peoples' stories out there. And those original stories, that the film was based on, were far more interesting than the film itself. So we thought, well, let's get Rowland in, and let's get Ollie in, and let them tell their oral histories, their stories of the time.

What do you think that people who are newcomers to the film, to those stories, will take from the film and the documentary?

Well, to be honest I'm much more interested in the documentary at the moment. But I think that what comes through in *Dogs in Space* is that it's about a band that wasn't necessarily all that great, and that's the point of putting them in it. You know, I wasn't making a movie about the Models, or the Boys Next Door or anything. And what also comes across is the spirit of the times, the enthusiasm and the excitement. There was a feeling that we were onto something new, that really could get us out of the grey huddled masses of the rest of society in 1979. I think that feeling comes through in both of them, actually. Hopefully, people will come away from them with a taste of what it feels like when a subculture appears, or ideas go through a renaissance. Like when music and culture gave us the beats, who were one of the first distinct subcultures of the twentieth century, and who were initially underground and out of the mainstream. And then you had the hippies, who very quickly became part of the mainstream. But I'm sure both of them started as small eclectic groups, with the same spirit. And they must have been very exciting, with new music, new art and new ideas. That's what I think both films have captured, that feeling of excitement that you get when you are on the cutting edge.

I don't think you can underestimate how conservative Australian society was back at that time. And also, there was a bit of a technological revolution going on, with the introduction of cheap synthesizers. Of course, synthesizers had been around for a while, but they were these huge clunky things, and they were hugely expensive—only people like ELO and Yes could afford them. But for the first time, you could buy a Korg for less than a thousand dollars and pretty much anyone could play one. I think those Korgs did a lot to change Australian pub music. They transformed it, made this strange new wave or post-punk possible.

So you had this anti-conservative feeling, and this new technology, and a lot of the members of this very small subculture jumped onto both, and got very excited. And that's what I'm hoping to show.

Back then it felt like a lot of the world was asleep, or just didn't notice, and so no one minded when a few kids took over the back room of a little pub to play music. As opposed to now, where things are regulated, and entertainment is a very big business.

I sometimes get the feeling—and I may be talking as an outsider, because I'm no longer in any kind of music scene, unlike someone like say Bruce Milne, who is still very heavily involved—I get the feeling that because there are less and less boundaries on behaviour, people just keep pushing further, looking for the limits. Things like the tattoos, and the extreme piercings, it like, how far do you have to go, or can you go, to be an outsider, to be seen as a rebel? Dyeing your hair just doesn't do it anymore. I'm not against it, I think it's fine, but it is like there's some kind of vacuum out there, and that people have run out of ways to rebel, because rebellion has become mainstream. In a way, perhaps you could theorize that a new form of conservatism is the only way to be different. Not necessarily politically, but visually.

I agree with Philip Brophy, when in his interview for the documentary, he says that he always finds some excitement in music, and it's when you start to think that there is nothing new any more, that there is nothing exciting any more, it's a sign that you've really lost it. But then again, music has always been interested in regurgitating it's own past every so often. But I have no idea what the current state of young peoples' musical culture is like these days.

All I can say is that the times I lived through were great times, take what you want from it, and let's treat it seriously as a part of our musical history. This stuff never got on Countdown, as you know, and there's only been one book written about it, Clinton Walker's *Inner City Sound* and while Nick Cave recently got inducted to the ARIA Hall of Fame, I was in complete agreement with him when he said all his bandmates should have been inducted, too. And why weren't they? Why isn't someone like Ollie Olsen in there? Because they didn't sign up to the big labels, they didn't play the game, the way that someone like Ross Wilson did. And so they're not recognized, and Ollie has to work in a record store and has had to fight to get the royalties he's owed.

I wonder if I can chuck a few phrases at you?

(*laughs*) Sure, what sort of thing did you have in mind?

'*Oi, dogface!*'

Oh, dear (*laughs*) 'Show us your snatch!' I can't claim to have written that one, my friend Troy did, the guy who actually does the line in the film.

'*Are you from the planet Poofter?*'

'Or the planet Stupider?' I can't take credit for that one either, that was something that Chuck Meo used to say. Chuck and Tim, for all their failings as musicians, are really funny guys. Only he could have come up with that line.

'*I wrote a song about you*'. '*Oh yeah, what?*'

'It's called 'Brick Woman''. Is this a test? That was actually a real song, which Sam wrote about a friend of someone else in the band. I think it was a fairly accurate comment on her physique, from memory, but I probably shouldn't say any more. The reason I remember all these is not from them being in the film, but from the time when I first heard them being said. That's why I put them in the film, because they were common lines or sayings from around then.

'*How do you know when you had a good time at a party?*'

'When you throw your knickers at the wall, and they stick there'. That really happened, that. I remember the real girl who said this, it was outside the Champion Hotel one night, I think after a Little Bands night. I couldn't stop laughing at it.

Bibliography

Books

Alberts, R. (2003) *Tascam: 30 Years of Recording Evolution* (Milwaukee: Hal Leonard).
Allen, T. (1995) *Roar, and Quieter Moments from a Group of Melbourne Artists 1980–1993* (Roseville: Craftsman House).
Apter, J. (2003) *Tomorrow Never Knows: The Silverchair Story* (Port Melbourne: Coulomb Communications).
Apter, J. (2013) *Up from Down Under: How Australian Music Changed the World* (Scoresby: Five Mile Press).
Arns, I., and Horn, G. (eds.) (2007) *History Will Repeat Itself: Strategies of Re-enactment in Contemporary (Media) Art and Performance* (Frankfurt: Revolver Books).
Barnes, J. (2017) *Working Class Man* (Sydney: HarperCollins).
Blackburn, S. (ed.) (2015) *Breaking Out: Memories of Melbourne in the 1970s* (Willoughby, NSW: Hale and Iremonger).
Bloom, H. (1975) *A Map of Misreading* (Oxford: Oxford University Press).
Bolin, A. (2018) *Dead Girls: Essays on Surviving an American Obsession* (New York: HarperCollins).
Bongiorno, F. (2015) *The Eighties: The Decade That Transformed Australia* (Collingwood: Black Inc.).

Breen, M. (1993) *Rock Dogs: Politics and the Australian Music Industry* (Lanham: University Press of America).
Carbines, E. (2003) *Live Music Taskforce Report and Recommendations* (Melbourne: Department of Planning and Community Development).
Cateforis, T. (2011) *Are We Not New Wave? Modern Pop at the Turn of the 1980s* (Ann Arbor: The University of Michigan Press).
City of Richmond (1988) *Copping It Sweet: Shared Memories of Richmond* (Richmond: City of Richmond).
Clifton, J. (2011) *The Address Book: A Memoir About My Homes* (Camberwell: Penguin).
Creswell, T. (2017) *Shine Like It Does* (Richmond: Echo).
Davison, G. (ed.) (1980) *Melbourne on Foot: 15 Walks Through Historic Melbourne* (Adelaide: Rigby).
Dick, P. K. (1979) *Do Androids Dream of Electric Sheep?* (New York: Ballantine).
Engleheart, M. (2010) *Blood, Sweat and Beers: Oz Rock from the Aztecs to Rose Tattoo* (Sydney, NSW: HarperCollins).
Evans, I. (1989) *Getting the Details Right: Restoring Australian Houses 1890s–1920s* (Yeronga: Flannel Flower Press).
Fiske, J., Hodge, R. I. V., and Turner, R. (1987) *Myths of Oz: Reading Australian Popular Culture* (Sydney: Allen & Unwin).
Fleckney, P. (2018) *Techno Shuffle: Rave Culture and the Melbourne Underground* (Melbourne, VIC: Melbourne Books).
Florida, R. (2002) *The Rise of the Creative Class and How It's Transforming Work, Leisure, Community and Everyday Life* (New York: Basic Books).
Garner, H. (1980) *Honour and Other People's Children* (Melbourne: McPhee Gribble).
Goldman, V. (2019) *Revenge of the she-Punks* (Austin: University of Texas Press).
Gordon, K. (2015) *Girl in a Band* (London: Faber & Faber).
Haese, R. (2011) *Permanent Revolution: Mike Brown and the Australian Avant-Garde 1953–1997* (Carlton: Miegunyah).
Haese, R., Brown, M., and Nodrum, C. (1995) *Power to the People: The Art of Mike Brown* (Melbourne: National Gallery of Victoria).
Heazlewood, J. (2014) *Funemployed: The Life of an Artist in Australia, from Cradle to Centrelink* (Melbourne: Affirm Press).
Hebdige, D. (1979) *Subculture: The Meaning of Style* (London, UK: Routledge).
Hill, A. *Butterfly on a Pin* (Richmond: Hardie Grant).
Hillier, R. (1967) *Let's Buy a Terrace House* (Sydney: Ure Smith).
Homan, S. (2003) *The Mayor's a Square: Live Music and Law and Order in Sydney* (Sydney: Local Consumption Publications).

Howe, R. (1988) *New Houses for Old: Fifty Years of Public Housing in Victoria 1938–1988* (Melbourne: Ministry of Housing and Construction).
Howe, R., Nichols, D., and Davison, G. (2014) *Trendyville: The Battle for Australia's Inner Cities* (Clayton: Monash University Publishing).
Hutchence, T., and Glassop, P. (2000) *Just a Man: The Real Michael Hutchence* (London: Sidgwick and Jackson).
Hyde, M. *All Along the Watchtower* (Carlton North: The Vulgar Press).
INXS, and Bozza, A. (2005) *INXS: Story to Story: The Official Autobiography* (New York: Atria).
INXS, Gamblin, Y., and St John, E. (1992) *INXS: The Official Inside Story of a Band on the Road* (Port Melbourne: Mandarin).
Jameson, F. (1991) *Postmodernism, or the Cultural Logic of Late Capitalism* (Durham: Duke University Press).
Johnson, B., and Homan, S. (2003) *Vanishing Acts: An Inquiry into the State of Live Popular Music Opportunities in New South Wales* (Sydney: Australia Council and the NSW Ministry for the Arts).
Koch, C. J. (1986) *The Doubleman* (London: Triad Grafton).
Lanier, J. (2010) *You Are Not a Gadget: A Manifesto* (London: Penguin).
Lec, S. (1962) *Unkempt Thoughts* (New York: St Martin's Press).
Lees, L., Slater, T., and Wyly, E. K. (2007) *The Gentrification Reader* (London: Routledge).
Lefebvre, H. (1996) *Writings on Cities*, translated by E. Kofman and E. Lebas (Oxford, UK: Blackwell).
Mathieson, C. (2000) *The Sell-In: How the Music Business Seduced Alternative Rock* (Sydney: Allen & Unwin).
McCalman, J. (1984) *Struggletown: Public and Private Life in Richmond 1900–1965* (Carlton: Melbourne University Press).
McFarlane, I. (1999) *The Encyclopedia of Australian Rock and Pop* (Sydney: Allen & Unwin).
Milsom, W., Thomas, H., and Hawkes, P. (1986) *Pay to Play: The Australian Rock Music Industry* (Ringwood: Penguin).
Morrissey (2013) *Autobiography* (London: Penguin).
Nichols, D. (2016) *Dig: Australian Rock and Pop Music, 1960–1985* (Portland: Verse Chorus).
Nietzsche, F. W. (1957) *The Use and Abuse of History* (New York: Liberal Arts Press).
O'Connor, J., O'Connor, T., Coleman, R., and Wright, H. (1985) *Richmond Conservation Study* (Richmond: Corporation of the City of Richmond).
O'Hanlon, S. (2018) *City Life: The New Urban Australia* (Sydney: NewSouth).

Oldenburg, R. (1999) *The Great Good Place: Cafes, Coffee Shops, Bookstores, Bars, Hair Salons, and Other Hangouts at the Heart of a Community* (New York, NY: Avalon Publishing Group).
Overton, N. (1986) *The Neon Eclipse* (Ringwood: Penguin).
Perec, G. (1997) *Species of Spaces and Other Pieces* (London: Penguin).
San Miguel, D. (2011) *The Ballroom: The Melbourne Punk and Post-punk Scene—A Tell All Memoir* (Melbourne: Melbourne Books).
Schuftan, C. (2012) *Entertain Us: The Rise and Fall of Alternative Rock in the Nineties* (Sydney, Australia: HarperCollins).
Seabrook, J. (2016) *The Song Machine: How to Make a Hit* (London: Vintage).
Seymour, M. (2008) *Thirteen Tonne Theory: Life Inside Hunters and Collectors* (Camberwell: Penguin).
Smith, N. (1996) *The New Urban Frontier: Gentrification and the Revanchist City* (London: Routledge).
Springsteen, B. (2016) *Born to Run* (London: Simon & Schuster).
Stratton, J. (2007) *Australian Rock: Essays on Popular Music* (Perth: Curtin University Press).
Tevis, W. (1976) *The Man Who Fell to Earth* (London: Pan Macmillan).
Walker, C. (ed.) (1982) *Inner City Sound* (Glebe, Australia: Wild & Woolley).
Walker, C. (1996). *Stranded: The Secret History of Australian Independent Music, 1977–1991* (Sydney: Pan Macmillan).
Wardle, J. (2008) *A Comparison of State and Territory Legislation and Regulations for Live Entertainment Venues in Australia* (Sydney: Music Council of Australia).
Weller, S. (2008) *Girls Like Us: Carole King, Joni Mitchell, Carly Simon—And the Journey of a Generation* (London: Ebury Press).
Wittgenstein, L. (1966) *Lectures and Conversations on Aesthetics, Psychology and Religious Belief* (Oxford: Blackwell).

Book Chapters
Brown, J. J. (2014) 'Ghost of the Year: Was Michael Hutchence Happy?', in C. Ryan (ed.) *The Best Music Writing Under the Australian Sun* (Melbourne: Hardie Grant), pp. 279–296.
Centeno, D. (2018) 'Social Media Stakeholder Co-creation of Celebrities as Human Brands', in B. Rishi and S. Bandyopadhyay (eds.) *Contemporary Issues in Social Media Marketing* (Abingdon, Oxon: Routledge), pp. 60–74.
Davison, G. (1991) 'A Brief History of the Australian Heritage Movement', in G. Davison and C. McConville (eds.) *A Heritage Handbook* (Sydney: Allen & Unwin), pp. 14–27

Faber, M. (2011) 'A Boy Next Door', in M. Snow (ed.) *Nick Cave: Sinner Saint— The True Confessions, Thirty Years of Essential Interviews* (London: Plexus), pp. 15–27.

Garden, D. S. 'Frencham, Henry (1816–1897)', *Australian Dictionary of Biography*, National Centre of Biography, Australian National University.

Homan, S. (2003) 'From Bankstown to the Globe, and Home: Popular Music in Sydney', in Melissa Butcher and Mandy Thomas (eds.) *Ingenious: Emerging Youth Cultures in Urban Australia* (North Melbourne: Pluto Press).

Riley, V. (1992) 'Death Rockers of the World Unite! Melbourne 1978–80— Punk Rock or No Punk Rock?', in P. Hayward (ed.) *From Pop to Punk to Postmodernism: Popular Music and Australian Culture from the 1960s to the 1990s* (North Sydney: Allen & Unwin), pp. 113–126.

Roger-Gernersh, A., and Carroll, B. (1976) *Richmond and East Melbourne Sketchbook* (Adelaide: Rigby).

Rowe, D. (2001) 'Globalisation, Regionalisation and Australianisation in Music: Lessons from the Parallel Importing Debate', in T. Bennett and D. Carter (eds.) *Culture in Australia: Policies, Publics and Programs* (Melbourne: Cambridge University Press), pp. 46–65.

Shaw, K. (2005) 'Gentrification and the Inner City Blues', in C. Long, K. Shaw, and C. M. Merlo (eds.) *Suburban Fantasies: Melbourne Unmasked* (Melbourne: Australian Scholarly Publishing), pp. 20–49.

Shaw, K. (2013) 'The Melbourne Indie Music Scene and the Inner City Blues', in L. S. Porter and K. Shaw (eds.) *Whose Urban Renaissance? An International Comparison of Urban Regeneration Strategies* (New York: Routledge), pp. 366–385.

Films and Related Media

Albini, S. (2014) Keynote Address: Steve Albini, Face the Music conference, Melbourne, 15 November, https://www.youtube.com/watch?time_continue=5&v=Lz_CPzuwSk4, accessed 17 May 2019.

D. O'Brien, S. (Producer) (2010) Do That Dance! Australian Post Punk, 1977–1983 [TV documentary in two parts], Australian Broadcasting Corporation.

Howard, H., and Preston, E. (2011) Performing 'Shivers', October, https://www.youtube.com/watch?v=TEFBjmz5qu4 accessed 6 June 2019.

Lowenstein, R. (director) (1986) Dogs in Space.

Lowenstein, R. (director) (2009) We're Livin' on Dog Food.

Lowenstein, R. (director) (2019) Mystify.

Milburn, L., and Lowenstein (directors) (2012) R. Autoluminescent; Rowland. S Howard.

Reed, D. (director) (2014) *Never Tear Us Apart: The Untold Story of INXS*.
Stuart, V. (director) (1998) *The Fauves … 15 Minutes to Rock*.
The Australian Music Vault (2017) 'Punk Gunk: The Birth of Punk', mini documentary (Gatherer Media).
Timoner, O. (director) (2004) *Dig!*

Journal and Magazine Articles
Anon (1980) 'TAGG Prospects: The Ears', *TAGG—The Alternative Gig Guide*, 16, 1–14 February, 18–19.
Anon (1987) 'Dogs in Space', *The New Yorker*, 26 October, 22.
Bail, K. (1987) "Putting the Bite into Dogs in Space", *Cinema Papers*, 61, January, 7.
Beer, C. (2011) 'Centres That Never Sleep? Planning for the Night-Time Economy Within the Commercial Centres of Australian Cities', *Australian Planner*, 48(3), 141–147.
Bolster, T. (1996) 'Young Talent Time: The Hunt for the Next Silverchair', *Beat*, 21 August, 16–17.
Breen, M. (2004) 'The Music Industry, Technology and Utopia—An Exchange Between Marcus Breen and Eamonn Forde', *Popular Music*, 23(1), 79–89.
Burke, M., and Schmidt, A. (2012) 'How Should We Plan and Regulate Live Music in Australian cities? Learnings from Brisbane', *Australian Planner*, 50(1), 68–78.
Davison, G. (2009) 'Carlton and the Campus: The University and the Gentrification of Inner Melbourne 1958–75', *Urban Policy and Research*, 273, 253–264.
Duffy, T. (1994) 'Melbourne Rises Up from Down Under: New Music Mecca Boasts Frente! & Others', *Billboard*, 106(46), 1.
Edwards, P., Jones, J., and Edwards, J. (1986) 'The Social Demography of Shared Housing', *Journal of Population Research*, 3, 130–143.
En, R. (2017) 'The Bank', *Swampland*, II, 60–65.
Faber, M. (1979) 'Conversations with Boys Next Door', *Farrago*, 57(12), 29 June, 20–21.
Gibson, C., and Homan, S. (2004) 'Urban Redevelopment, Live Music and Public Space', *International Journal of Cultural Policy*, 10(1), 67–84.
Gleeson, G. (1981) 'Snakefinger! The Ears', *TAGG: The Alternative Gig Guide*, 47, 14–28 May, 15.
Griffin, A. (2016) 'A Brief History and a Short Future of the Imaginary Sharehouse', *Voiceworks*, 104, 19–25.

Harkins-Cross, R. (2013) 'Punks in Share Houses, Dogs in Space', *Lifted Brow* (17), April.
Homan, S. (2000) 'Losing the Local: Sydney and the Oz Rock Tradition', *Popular Music*, 19(1), 31–49.
Homan, S. (2008) 'A Portrait of the Politician as a Young Pub Rocker: Live Music Venue Reform in Australia', *Popular Music*, 27(2), 243–256.
Homan, S. (2010) 'Governmental as Anything: Live Music and Law and Order in Melbourne', *Perfect Beat*, 11(2), 103–118.
Homan, S. (2011) '"I Tote and I Vote": Australian Live Music and Cultural Policy', *Arts Marketing: An International Journal*, 1(2), 96–107.
Hracs, B. J. (2012) 'A Creative Industry in Transition: The Rise of Digitally Driven Independent Music Production', *Growth and Change*, 43(3), 442–461.
Hracs, B. J., Grant, J. L., Haggett, J., and Morton, J. (2011) 'A Tale of Two Scenes: Civic Capital and Retaining Musical Talent in Toronto and Halifax', *The Canadian Geographer/Le Géographe canadien*, 55(3), 365–382.
Hussey, S. (2009) 'Punk Moments: A Conversation with Richard Lowenstein', *Metro Magazine: Media and Education Magazine*, 162, 157–159.
Kitson, M. (2004) 'Saskia and Hutch: Doggy style', *MetroDate*, 1 June.
Lee, T. (1980) 'Gig Review: The Ears', *TAGG: The Alternative Gig Guide* (Melbourne), 24 October–6 November, 49–51.
Leyshon, A. (2001) 'Time—Space (And Digital) Compression: Software Formats, Musical Networks, and the Reorganisation of the Music Industry', *Environment and Planning A*, 33(1), 50.
Leyshon, A. (2009) 'The Software Slump? Digital Music, the Democratisation of Technology, and the Decline of the Recording Studio Sector Within the Musical Economy', *Environment and Planning A*, 41(6), 1309–1331.
Lobato, R. (2006) 'Gentrification, Cultural Policy and Live Music in Melbourne', *Media International Australia, Incorporating Culture & Policy*, 120, August, 63–75.
Lynch, M. (1981) 'Models Again', *TAGG: The Alternative Gig Guide* (Australia), 25 June–9 July, 16–17.
Maher, C. (1985) 'Building Activity and Socio-Economic Change in Inner Melbourne 1961–1981', *Urban Policy and Research*, 3(1), 3–12.
Mann, C. (2000) 'The Heavenly Jukebox from Hell: Internet Piracy Isn't the Problem—The Music Industry Is the Problem', *Atlantic Monthly*, September, 39–59.
McLeay, C. (2006) 'Government Regulation in the Australian Popular Music Industry: The Rhetoric of Cultural Protection, the Reality of Economic Production', *GeoJournal*, 65(1–2), 91–102.

McNamara. S., and Connell, J. (2007) 'Homeward Bound? Searching for Home in Inner Sydney's Share Houses', *Australian Geographer*, 38(1), 71–91.
Oldham, P. (2013) 'Suck More Piss: How the Confluence of Key Melbourne-Based Audiences, Musicians, and Iconic Spaces Informed the Oz Rock Identity', *Perfect Beat*, XIV(II), 120–139.
Penman, I. (2017) 'Wham Bang, Teatime', *London Review of Books*, 39(1), 5 January, 21–26, 10.
Pereira, H. (2017) 'The Bank', *Swampland*, III, 62–71.
Pratt, A. C. (2008). 'Creative Cities: The Cultural Industries and the Creative Class', *Geografiska Annaler: Series B, Human Geography*, 90(2), 107–117.
Rogers, I. (2008) '"You've Got to Go to Gigs to Get Gigs": Indie Musicians, Eclecticism and the Brisbane Scene', *Continuum*, 22(5), 639–649.
Rowe, G. (1984) 'Richard Lowenstein: On the Rock Clip Road to Feature Films', *Metro Magazine: Media & Education Magazine*, 64, 20–23.
Ryan, A. (1982) 'INXS, Beargarden', *Roadrunner*, May, 23.
Scatena, D. (1991) 'The Great Rock 'n' Roll Dwindle', *Juke*, 835, 27 April, 11.
Scott, A. J. (1999) 'The US Recorded Music Industry: On the Relations Between Organization, Location; and Creativity, in the Cultural Economy', *Environment and Planning A*, 31(11), 1965–1984.
Seiffert-Brockmann, J., Diehl, T., and Dobusch, L. (2018) 'Memes as Games: The Evolution of a Digital Discourse Online', *New Media & Society* 20(8), 2862–2879, 2862.
Shaw, K. (2005) 'The Place of Alternative Culture and the Politics of Its Protection in Berlin, Amsterdam and Melbourne', *Planning Theory & Practice*, 6(2), 149–169.
Shaw, K. (2008) 'Gentrification: What It Is, Why It is, and What Can Be Done About It', *Geography Compass*, II(V), 1697–1728.
Shaw, K. (2013) 'Independent Creative Subcultures and Why They Matter', *International Journal of Cultural Policy*, XIX(III), 333–352.
Smith, B. (1986) 'Dogged by Punk', *Juke*, 22 March, 4.
Smith, M. (1991) 'Musicians, Copyright and the PSA', *Drum Media*, 20 August, 21.
Speed, L. (2019) 'Win or Lose: Subculture and Social Difference in Dogs in Space', *Metro*, 162, September 2009, 160–165.
St. John, E. (1986) 'Dogs in Space and Other True Stories', *Stiletto*, 36, December, 33.
Stanton, G. (2017) "Dog Days: The Making of Dogs in Space", *FilmInk*, 22 November, 2017.

Stapleton, R. (1978) 'Takin' It to the Streets (or Punkin' It Up in Carlton)', *Juke*, 4.
Taylor, S. (2018) 'A Place to Play: An Historical Geographical Perspective on Live Music and Poker Machines in Australian Pubs', *Historic Environment*, 30(2), 112–133.
Trainer, A. (2016) 'Perth Punk and the Construction of Urbanity in a Suburban City', *Popular Music*, XXXV(I), 100–117.
Vider, S. (2015) 'The Ultimate Extension of Gay Community: Communal Living and Gay Liberation in the 1970s', *Gender & History* 27(3), 865–881.
Walker, C. (1980) 'The Ears…(Hearts, Melbourne)', *RAM*, 25 July, 31.
Walker, C. (2012) 'History Is Made at Night: Live Music in Australia', *Platform Papers*, 32, 2–60.
Walker, L. (2012) 'Share Houses', *Meanjin* 71(4), 60–67.
Walker, C., and Stafford, P. (1987) '1979—An Inner Space Odyssey', *RAM*, 14 January, 30–31.
Walker, C., Hogan, T., and Beilharz, P. (2012) 'Rock 'n' Labels: Tracking the Australian Recording Industry in "The Vinyl Age" Part Two—1970–1995, and after', *Thesis Eleven*, 110(1), 112–131.
Wang, S. (1980) 'Little Bands', *TAGG: The Alternative Gig Guide*, 17, 15–28 February, 46–47.
Wright, F. (2017) 'Perhaps This One Will Be My Last Share House', *Sydney Review of Books*, https://sydneyreviewofbooks.com/perhaps-this-one-will-be-my-last-sharehouse/.
Young, G. (2004) '"So Slide Over Here": The Aesthetics of Masculinity in Late Twentieth-Century Australian Pop Music', *Popular Music*, 23(2), May, 173–193.

Newspaper Articles (Print)
Adams, D. (1994) 'Music in Melbourne, Sound Cheques in Sydney', *Melbourne Age*, 12 May, 'Entertainment Guide' section, 3.
Anon (1908) 'Two Men and a Bottle', *Harrisburg Daily Independent*, 19 March, 4.
Anon (1912) 'At the Auditorium Last Week', *Strong City News-Courant*, 18 April, 1.
Anon (1967) '14-Hour Day "Underwork"', *Melbourne Age*, 12 April, 1.
Anon (1970) 'Labor Would Stop House Wrecker', *Melbourne Age*, 16 May, 3.
Anon (1970) 'National Service', *Melbourne Age*, 21 March, 11.
Anon (1984) 'How to Live in an Urban Conservation Area', *Melbourne Age*, 13 April, 35.

Anon (1996) 'Is Rock Band Oasis a Thing of the Past?', *Saskatoon Star-Phoenix*, 14 September, 44.
Barber, L. (1987) 'Oz Rock: A Corporate Creation', *Sydney Morning Herald*, 29 August, 51.
Basile, V. (1970) 'The Force Triumphs: Stronghold Falls in Siege of Mahony Street', *Melbourne Age*, 15 May, 3.
Bilic, J. (1989) 'It's Tough Times for Rock Bands', *Sydney Morning Herald*, 29 June, 104.
Carney, S. (1992), '"Achtung Baby" Top for 1991', *Melbourne Age*, 2 January, 24.
Cauthorn, R. S. (1988) '"Dogs in Space" Packs Small but Heartfelt Bite', *Arizona Daily Star*, 12 March, 29.
Coslovich, G., and Donovan, P. (2003) 'Inner-City Blues', *Melbourne Age*, 11 June, 'A3' section, 4.
Coupe, S. (1986) 'Generation of Sex, Drugs, Rock 'n' Roll', *Sydney Sun Herald*, 14 December, 115.
Dexter, N. (1978) 'A Depression Relived', *Melbourne Age*, 11 November, 16.
Donovan, P. (2000) 'For Those About to Rock, Melbourne Suits You', *The Sunday Age*, 11 June, 17.
Donovan, P., and Murfett, A. (2009) 'Post-punk Revival', *Melbourne Age*, 3 July, 'Entertainment Guide' section, 3.
Downes, S. (1981) 'A Man with High Ideals', *Melbourne Age*, 21 April, 11.
Dredge, R. (1991) 'Western Atmosphere at Alphington Sale', *Melbourne Age*, 14 September, 31.
Frencham, H. (1888) 'The Discoverer of the Bendigo Goldfield', *Melbourne Age*, 30 June, 4.
Gibson, R. (1994) 'Last of the Cavemen?' *Melbourne Age*, 29 July, 48.
Glover, R., and Creswell, T. (1984) 'Hey Hey It's the Takeaways', *Sydney Morning Herald*, 2 July, 36.
Guilliatt, R. (1997) 'Between Rock and a Hard Place', *Sydney Morning Herald*, 10 October, 14.
Holding, C. (1964) 'Labor's Policy on Education', *Melbourne Age*, 16 June, 2.
Howard, R. S. quoted in Donovan, P. (1998) 'Song of Rowland', *Melbourne Age*, 17 July, 45.
Howell, A. (1989) 'Phantom of the Underground', *Sydney Morning Herald*, 21 September, 124.
Huffhines, K. (1987) '"Dogs" Has a Bit of Bite About Aussie Decadence', *Detroit Free Press*, November 22, 76.
Hunt, D. (1989) 'INXS' Hutchence Rejects Rock Star Image', *Los Angeles Times*, 30 September, 53.

Hunter, S. (1987) '"Dogs in Space": Australian hippie meets bad end', *Baltimore Sun*, 30 October, 98.
Jaeger, B. (1990) 'INXS' Lead Sings a New Tune', Hackensack *Record*, 9 November, p. 112.
Jellie, D. (1995) 'The Prince Expires, but Pub Rock Wails on', *Melbourne Age*, 26 October, 3.
Klady, L. (1987) '"Dogs" Runs on Punk Power', *Los Angeles Times*, 9 October, 154.
Legge, K. (1981) 'Young Bands Get Payment Blues', *Melbourne Age*, 12 March, 10.
Lethlean, J. (1980) 'Sydney Group Plays a Wide Range of Music', *Melbourne Age*, 11 December, 21.
Lockwood, D. (1998) 'Taking the Cure', *Sydney Morning Herald*, 7 March, 219.
Loughnan, C. A. (1924) 'Richmond Slum Areas', *Melbourne Age*, 12 August, 12.
McConnell, M. (1987) 'Molly's Barefaced Farewell Ends Without a Whimper', *Sydney Morning Herald*, 23 July, 24.
McGregor, C. (1986) 'Now on Film: A Generation Lost in Space', *Sydney Morning Herald*, 6 December, 52.
Molitorisz, S. (1999) 'Rock in a Hard Place', *Sydney Morning Herald*, 16 April, 4
O'Rourke, J. quoted in L. Schwartz (1997) 'Band Rights', *Sunday Age*, 16 November, 'Applause' section, 1.
Oliver, R. (1987) '9 in by a Ratings Whisker', *Melbourne Age*, 30 July, 9.
Patterson, B. (1973) '$500,000 Plan to Redevelop North Richmond', *Melbourne Age*, 5 April, 3
Rickey, C. (1988) 'Dogs in Space Takes a Look at Punk Rockers in Australia', *Philadelphia Inquirer*, 19 January, 5.
Sarno, T. (1986) 'Can INXS Break the International Sound Barrier?', *Canberra Times*, 27 April, 42–47.
Schembri, J. (1986) 'Hutchence Sends a Message', *Melbourne Age*, 26 December, 30–31.
Schwartz, L. (1996) 'So You Want to Be a Rock Star?', *The Sunday Age*, 1 June, 3.
Speelman, P. (1987) 'The End of an Um er... Era', *Melbourne Age*, 20 July, 14.
Thomas, B. (1989) 'INXS—"Two Year" Break from Tours', *Sydney Morning Herald*, 23 April, 5.
Wakefield, K. (1980) 'Her Majesty Rules to Rock', *Melbourne Age*, 29 August, 'Weekender' section, 5.
Warneke, R. (1973) 'Children with Their Own Police Dossiers', *Melbourne Age*, 28 December, 2.

Winkler, T. (1994) 'The CD Reality', *Melbourne Age*, 11 March, 16.

Unpublished Sources

Andrews, P. (1973) 'Blessed Are the POOR—Part 1', transcript of *By The Way*, ABC Radio broadcast 12 November, in possession of D. Nichols.

Doorakkers, J. (2018) 'Modern Day Music Industry: The Role of Money in Making Successful Albums', Bachelor Thesis in Economics, Universiteit van Amsterdam.

Duffield, A. (2009) 'The Countdown Generation: 1974–87', (Honours Thesis) School of Music (Southbank), Faculty of the Victorian College of the Arts and Music, The University of Melbourne.

Gilmour, G. (1974) 'Richmond Stereotype—A Demographic Analysis', University of Melbourne Thesis held in Architecture, Building and Planning Library.

King, D. (1974) 'Richmond Survey', University of Melbourne Essay held in Architecture, Building and Planning Library.

Mutton, A. *Then and Now*, memoir in possession of D. Nichols.

Taylor, S. J. (2016) 'Geographical Information Systems for Applied Social Research: The Case of the Live Music Industry in Sydney and Melbourne', Doctor of Philosophy (PhD Geospatial Science), Mathematical and Geospatial Sciences, RMIT University.

Websites and Online Sources (Including Newspaper Items Accessed Online)

Adams, C., and McCabe, K. (2012) 'INXS's Demise After 35 Years Followed Years of Controversy', *Sunday Telegraph*, 18 November, https://www.dailytelegraph.com.au/news/opinion/inxss-demise-after-35-years-followed-years-of-controversy/news-story/e18ce388d7818f1bb056f3f7b57ee442.

Anon (1960) 'Ethel Swinburne Centre', https://commons.swinburne.edu.au/items/ead65256-bbbd-4e67-ad84-a18fb264fdab/1/.

Anon (1977) 'Alive 'n' Pumping', reproduced at http://www.fromthearchives.com/bnd/BND23_Jul_77.jpg, accessed 25 May 2019.

Anon (2017) Interview with B. Milne, https://www.slv.vic.gov.au/self-made-audio-extras/stops/2/.

Anon (2017) Interview with J. Austin for *Self-Made: Zines and Artist Books*, exhibition at State Library of Victoria curated by M. Syrette, https://www.slv.vic.gov.au/self-made-audio-extras/stops/7/.

Anon, 'Rooms for the Memory: 'Dogs in Space' and the Getting of Wisdom' SBS Movies, https://www.sbs.com.au/movies/article/2018/11/19/rooms-memory-dogs-space-and-getting-wisdom.

Bibliography

Arts Victoria (2011) 'Economic, Social and Cultural Contribution of Venue-Based Live Music in Victoria', Deloitte Access Economics, https://musicvictoria.com.au/assets/Documents/DAE_Live_music_report_2011.pdf, accessed 21 May 2019.

Barden, R. (1982) 'Virgin Press Benefit', *Fast Forward* 13, 9, http://spill-label.org/FastForward/ff13/ff13-zine05-large.jpg.

Buckmaster, L. (2015) 'He Died with a Felafel in His Hand Rewatched—A Tour of Sharehouse Excess', *The Guardian*, 1 May, https://www.theguardian.com/film/2015/may/01/he-died-with-a-felafel-in-his-hand-rewatched-a-tour-of-sharehouse-excess.

Butler, B., and Jones-Dean, A. R. (2019) 'Dogs in Space: The Melbourne Ticket Queue', Bowiedownunder.com, http://www.bowiedownunder.com/lowheroes/14.html.

Chen, Q. (2018) 'The Biggest Trend in Chinese Social Media Is Dying, and Another Has Already Taken Its Place', CNBC, https://www.cnbc.com/2018/09/19/short-video-apps-like-douyin-tiktok-are-dominating-chinese-screens.html.

Critchley, A. (2010) 'Sydney's Unlicensed Venues', *Cyclic Defrost*, https://www.cyclicdefrost.com/2010/09/sydney%E2%80%99s-unlicensed-venues-by-alyssa-critchley/, accessed 25 October 2018.

Danger, N. (2018) 'Why I Quit the Music Industry to Join My Local Music Scene', Music think tank, 13 September, http://www.musicthinktank.com/blog/why-i-quit-the-music-industry-to-join-my-local-music-scene.html, accessed 9 June 2019.

Department of Environment, Land, Water and Planning (2016) 'Planning Practice Note 81: Live Music and Entertainment Noise', State Government of Victoria, https://www.planning.vic.gov.au/resource-library/planning-practice-notes.

Discogs.

Fitzsimons, S. (2012) 'Dogs in Space Share House Up for Sale for $1 Million', *The Music*, 2 October. http://themusic.com.au/news/all/2012/10/02/dogs-in-space-house-up-for-sale/.

Forde, E. (2015) 'Record Breaker: A Brief History of Prince's Contractual Controversies', *The Guardian*, 11 August, https://www.theguardian.com/music/2015/aug/10/history-prince-contractual-controversy-warner-paisley-park, accessed 6 June 2019.

Fuller, G. (2019) 'Mystify: Michael Hutchence', *Screen Daily*, 27 April, https://www.screendaily.com/reviews/mystify-michael-hutchence-tribeca-review/5138837.article.

Godwin, L. (2018) 'Keep Animal House Open', GoFundMe, https://au.gofundme.com/keep-animal-house-open.

Gordon, K. A. (2016) 'Fossils: Sire Records' Don't Call It Punk', *That Devil Music*, http://www.thatdevilmusic.com/2016/08/fossils-sire-records-dont-call-it-punk.html, accessed 6 June 2019.

Hellyer, I. (2016) 'Why Canberra Is the Best City in Australia: A Chat with the Capital's Busiest Musician', *Noisey Australia*, https://noisey.vice.com/en_au/article/ryz4mj/canberra-is-the-best-city-in-australia-a-chat-with-the-capitals-busiest-musician, accessed 25 October 2018.

Heritage Council Victoria (2011) 'State Savings Bank of Victoria (Former)', *Victorian Heritage Database*, http://vhd.heritagecouncil.vic.gov.au/places/27132/download-report, accessed 15 October 2018.

House Concerts Australia (2019) 'Welcome to Our House!', https://houseconcertsaustralia.com/, accessed 12 May 2019.

Kimbell, D. (2018) 'Australasian Popular Music of the 1960s and 1970s: An Overview', *MILESAGO: Australasian Music and Popular Culture 1964–1975*, http://www.milesago.com/MainFrame.htm.

Laing, D. 'Celebrating 40 Years of Shivers by the Boys Next Door', https://www.ilikeyouroldstuff.com/news/celebrating-40-years-of-shivers-by-the-boys-next-door.

Live Music Roundtable (2012) 'Best Practice Guidelines for Live Music Venues', Music Victoria, http://www.musicvictoria.com.au/assets/2016/reports/Best-practice-guidelines-for-live-music-venues.pdf, accessed 2 November 2018.

McCabe, K. (2016) 'It Was the Line-Up and the Party of a Lifetime. Australian Made Celebrates Its 30th Anniversary', news.com.au, www.news.com.au/entertainment/it-was-the-lineup-and-the-party-of-a-lifetime-australian-made-celebrates-its-30th-anniversary/news-story/b865ee8bb2304476f164261baa3c44c1.

McFarlane, I. (1994) 'Prehistoric Sounds', 1(2), 24 November, reproduced at https://rowland-s-howard.com/articles/1994-prehistoric-sounds.php.

McKew, M. (2017) 'Share Houses and Women's Liberation: A Forgotten History', *The Conversation*, https://theconversation.com/share-houses-and-womens-liberation-a-forgotten-history-84069.

Michael Hutchence, https://michaelhutchence.org.

MILESAGO (2004). 'Radio in Australia—An Overview', MILESAGO. www.milesago.com/Radio/radioinaustralia.htm.

Neild, A. 'Films for Music: Dogs in Space Revisited', *The Quietus*, 9 July 2013, https://thequietus.com/articles/12709-films-for-music-dogs-in-space-revisited.

Nichols, D., and Perillo, S. (2016) 'Friday Essay: Dogs in Space, 30 Years on—A Once Maligned Film Comes of Age', *The Conversation*, 15 April.

Parlour Gigs (2019) 'Parlour Gigs', https://parlourgigs.com/.

PsBattleMod 'What the Fuck Is Up with Tiktok Making so Much Shit', Reddit, https://www.reddit.com/r/teenagers/comments/9s5iea/what_the_fuck_is_up_with_tiktok_making_so_much/.

Pulp fanzine, https://www.flipsnack.com/B89E97BA9F7/pulp-fanzine-1977.html.

Rajgor, H. (2018) 'TikTok: One Person's Cringe Is Another One's Cool', qrius.com, https://www.arre.co.in/pop-culture/tiktok-musically-india-social-media-content-video-app/.

Sargeant, J. (2003) 'Dead Letter Tales: The Rowland S. Howard Interview', *BB Gun Magazine*, 6, reprinted at https://rowland-s-howard.com/articles/2003-bb-gun-mag.php.

Schaller, M. (2017) 'From the Danube to the Yarra River', https://www.sbs.com.au/yourlanguage/german/en/explainer/danube-yarra-river.

Sejavka, S. (2015) 'David Bowie and Me: Sam Sejavka on the Moment His Melbourne Changed Forever', Melbourne *Age*, 3 July, https://www.smh.com.au/entertainment/david-bowie-and-me-sam-sejavka-on-the-moment-his-melbourne-changed-forever-20150627-ghz1hc.html.

Sejavka, S. *Sails of Oblivion* (blog), https://sailsofoblivion.blogspot.com.

Shaw, K. '"Knowledge Workers" and the Contradictions of the Creative City', Paper presented at the Melbourne 2010 Knowledge Cities World Summit, 16–19 November 2010, https://katesshaw.files.wordpress.com/2013/06/e28098knowledge-workers_-and-the-contradictions-of-the-creative-city.pdf, accessed 25 October 2018.

Stanford Encyclopaedia of Philosophy (2018) 'Social Norms', *Centre for the Study of Language and Information*, Stanford University, https://plato.stanford.edu/entries/social-norms/, accessed 28 October 2018.

Stuart, D. (2017) 'Mulgara and the DIY Music Scene in Canberra', *The Riot Act*, https://the-riotact.com/mulgara-and-the-diy-music-scene-in-canberra/197371, accessed 28 October 2018.

Taylor, S. (2015) 'Lost Venues, Long Nights: An Introduction to Historical maps of Live Music in Sydney and Melbourne', *Cordite Poetry Review*, http://cordite.org.au/essays/lost-venues-long-nights, accessed 1 November 2018.

Throsby, D., and Petetskaya, K. (2017) 'Making Art Work: An Economic Study of Professional Artists in Australia', The Australia Council, https://australiacouncil.gov.au/research/making-art-work/, accessed 19 May 2019.

Topsfield, J., and Donovan, P. (2005), 'Under-Age Gigs Return', *The Age*, 19 March, https://www.theage.com.au/national/under-age-gigs-return-20050319-gdztfg.html, accessed 21 May 2019.

Ubu, C. (2003) 'Rowland S. Howard Interview', *Overeasy*, October, reproduced at http://rowland-s-howard.com/articles/2003-overeasy-mag.php, accessed 25 May 2019.

VicMUSIC. (2003) *Rock 'n' Roll Ain't Noise Pollution* (Fitzroy, Victoria: VicMUSIC), http://rollingthunder33.tripod.com/RocknRollAintNoisePollution.pdf.

Victoria Commission for Gambling and Liquor Regulation (2017) 'Design Guidelines for Licensed Venues', State Government of Victoria, https://www.vcglr.vic.gov.au/resources/design-guidelines.

Victoria Police (2019) 'Crime Prevention Through Environmental Design', https://www.police.vic.gov.au/business-and-commercial#crime-prevention-through-environmental-design.

Von Wayward, M. (2019) 'Punk and Post-punk', Punk Journey, http://www.punkjourney.com/punk-and-postpunk.php, accessed 18 May 2019.

Walker, C. (2019) http://www.clintonwalker.com.au/fanzines-1970s.html.

Webb, C. (2003) 'Noising off Over Live Music', Melbourne *Age*, 26 May, www.theage.com.au/articles/2003/05/23/1053585693534.html.

Willis, T (2018) 'Now Sound: Melbourne's Listening', documentary (KEWL). www.sbs.com.au/movies/article/2009/09/07/were-living-dog-food-so-what.

Index

A

AAV (recording studio) 31
ABC Studios 185
Abeyratne, Sherine 30
AC/DC (group) 38, 112
'According to my Heart' (song) 55
Acland St, St Kilda 65
'Across the Universe' (song) 79
4AD (record label) 70
The Adventures of Priscilla, Queen of the Desert (film) 251
'After the News' (song) 55
Alive 'n' Pumping (fanzine) 210, 211, 222, 223
All Tomorrow's Parties 302
Alphaville (film) 75
'American Pie' (song) 254
Amphlett, Chrissy (Christina) 110
"Anarchy in the UK" (song) 41
Andrews, Philip 159, 160, 171

Angels, The (group) 82
Animal House (Adelaide) 263
'Anna' (character) 4, 20, 131, 141, 159, 251
'Anna Betrayed' (music piece) 241
Antoniades, Tony 28
Apel, Fred 290
Armadale 9–11, 185
Armadale Hotel 185
Armiger, Martin 241
Arns, Inke 125
Associates, The (group) 234
As Time Goes By (film) 78
Atco (record label) 183
Austin, Janet 210–212, 222
Australian Ballet Company 51
Australian Made (tour) 113, 187, 198, 202, 230
Australian Performing Group 148

© The Editor(s) (if applicable) and The Author(s) 2020
D. Nichols and S. Perillo (eds.), *Urban Australia and Post-Punk*,
https://doi.org/10.1007/978-981-32-9702-9

Index

Australian Recording Industry Association (ARIA) 107, 189, 210, 305
Austrock '77 (album) 239
Avondale Heights 65

B

Babeez 29
Babeez, The (group) 210, 211, 259
'Baby I'm Yours' (song) 292
'Baby's on Fire' (song) 29
Bad Seeds, The 56
Ballarat 248, 252
Bananas 18, 29, 54, 114, 185
The Bank (venue) 262, 267, 268, 270, 272, 275, 277
'Barbados' (song) 234
'Barbra' (character) 256
Barker, Nick 76
Barnes, Jimmy 110, 121, 188, 199, 230, 231
'Barry' (character) 131, 137, 256
Bartok, Bela 177
Barton, Jim 31
Barton, Liam 262, 281, 283
Bauhaus (group) 70
Bayswater 152
Beach Boys, The (group) 41
Beargarden (group) 70, 75, 79, 83, 87, 182, 187, 188, 236
Beatles, The (group) 237
Bee, Kayellen 231
Beers, Garry 'Gary' 111, 121, 182
Beggars Banquet (record label) 70
Belmont 248
Belvoir Street Theatre 77
Bennett, Michele 56, 113, 249
Berchtesgaden 13

Berry St, Richmond 6, 164, 170 *See also* 18 Berry St
18 Berry St 157, 158, 160, 163, 165–170, 173, 179, 181, 185, 186, 228, 263, 285
Berties (venue) 264
Bertolucci, Bernardo 84
Big Bang Combo (group) 212, 224
Big Pig (group) 258
Big Risk (film) 256, 259
Billboard (venue) 185
The Birthday Party (film) 28
Birthday Party, The (group) 70, 113, 217, 241, 252, 302
'Bizarre Love Triangle' (song) 240
Bliss (film) 77
Blondie (group) 52, 111, 177
'Blue Jean' (song) 253
BMG (record label) 192
Bombay Rock 185
Bond, Deanna 228, 237
Bongiorno, Frank 112, 121, 136, 139
2001 (book) 15
Borderline personality disorder 53
Bose speakers 55
Bosler, Danae 170
Bourke Street Mall 185
Bowen St., Richmond 157, 160
Bowie, David 4, 6, 10, 15, 16, 18, 24, 41, 87, 125, 126, 137, 177, 179, 237, 248, 250, 253, 300
Boys Next Door, The (group) 18, 19, 29, 53, 54, 62, 69, 75, 177, 181, 190, 210–212, 214, 217, 219, 220, 222, 225, 238, 303
Breakbot (feat. Irfane) 292
Breen, Marcus 194, 205, 206
Bricknermon 293, 297
'Brick Woman' (song) 25, 85, 305

Bridge Road, Richmond 4, 58, 159, 164, 166, 251
Briscomb, Adam 86
Brophy, Philip 177, 201, 305
Brosnan, Tim 28
Brother McCarthy 16
Brown, Jen Jewel 122, 231, 232, 244
Brown, Mike 135
Buckmaster, Luke 146, 154
Bukowski, Charles 79
Bulleen (Vic) 185, 196
Bum Steers, The (group) 44
'Burn for You' (song) 112, 114, 115
Burnie 12
Burroughs, William 10, 15, 16
Butler, Bruce 6, 18, 25, 87, 89, 93, 138, 232, 233, 243
Butterfly on a Pin (book) 118, 250, 260
Butters, Marshall 74
Buzzcocks (group) 52, 54
ByteDance 288

C

Cairns, Jim 160
Caledonian Lane 52
Camberwell Market 70
Cameo (group) 240
Camilleri, Joe 28, 165
Campbell, Ken 84
Camus, Albert 76
Cannes 56, 57, 114, 115
Captain Beefheart 54
Carey, Peter 77
Carlton 2, 27–29, 144, 147, 148, 150, 152, 159, 181, 185, 186, 265
Carroll, Brian 164, 172

Carroll, Laura 6, 242
Carrum 73
Carson (group) 38
Carter, Hurbert 290
Carter, Steve 31
Casinader, Robin 64
Castricum, Simona 7, 242
Catfood Press 262, 267, 270, 272, 275, 276
Caulfield 53, 185, 186
Caulfield Arts Complex 185
Cave, Nick 56, 69, 75, 116, 126, 213
CBS (record label) 31
Centeno, Dave 289, 298
Chadstone 36, 181, 186
Chain (group) 38
Champion Hotel 6, 11, 26, 42, 61, 74, 179, 181, 226, 306
Champion Ruby (tobacco) 82
Chapter (record label) 5–7, 47, 48, 87, 107, 141, 144, 158, 176, 209, 227–229, 233, 236, 242, 261, 273, 286
Charles Street, Fitzroy 253
Chase (record label) 47, 124
Cheks, The (group) 31
Chelsea 57
Chuck (character) 131
Church of Scientology 10
Church Street, Richmond 164, 251
Chynoweth, Adrian 76
Clapton, Richard 231, 244
Clarke, Arthur C. 15
Clash, The (group) 114
Clayton TAB 54
Clayton Technical College 36
Clifforth, John 5, 84
Clifton, Jane 52, 148, 150, 241
Climax records (store) 68–70

Club 76 (Brisbane) 263
Clyde St, St Kilda 62
Cobain, Kurt 108
Cocteau Twins (group) 70
Cohen, Leonard 15
Cohen, Tony 45, 225
Cold Chisel 33, 55, 110–112, 121, 199, 230, 231
Cole, Peter 70
Coles, Martii 164
Collingwood 181, 186, 254
Coloured Balls 27, 38
Compact, Boyd *See* Brosnan, Tim
Conroy, Nick 32
Conway, Deborah 32
Cook, John 75
Cookson St., Camberwell 82
Corner Hotel 70, 299
Costello, Elvis 111
Council Club Hotel 185
Countdown (TV series) 5, 26, 33, 74, 105–107, 117, 170, 186, 188, 189, 196, 218, 236, 240
Countdown 55, 305
Coupe, Stuart 117, 122, 200, 234, 235, 244
'The Crater' (song) 19, 25, 182
Crauford-Wall sisters 18
Creswell, Toby 203
Critter Canyon 32
Croghan, Emma-Kate 250
Crossroads (Canberra) 262
Croxton Park Hotel, Thornbury 264
Cruise, Tom 128
Crystal Ballroom 26, 42, 45, 46, 54, 56, 181, 186, 219, 226, 248, 265, 291, 300
Cuckoos, The 27
Culture Club (group) 236

Cummings, Stephen 234, 241
Cure, The (group) 43
Currie, Jason 231
Curse, The (group) 75, 76, 79
Curtis, Ian 253
'Cut my Toad' (song) 25

D

Daddy Cool (group) 52
Daffy (David Williams) (recording engineer) 19, 43
Dandenong 36
D'Arby, Terence Trent 188
Darlinghurst 56
Davies, Peter 'Troy' 5, 30, 114, 116, 249, 250
Davies, Robert 'Bomba' 64
Davison, Graeme 154, 164, 283, 284
Dead Can Dance 75
Dead or Alive (group) 239
Deckchairs overboard 5, 6, 31–33, 84, 187
De Clario, Emma 118, 119
De Groot, Andrew 158, 221, 226, 280, 282, 303
Delaney, Cornelius 6
Del Conti, Mariella 65
Deling, Bert 259
Della, Harry 111
Deluxe, Buzz *See* Leeson, Steve
Destiny's Child (group) 255
Devastator (album) 239
Devo 177
Dig! (flim) 199
Din (group) 79
Dire Straits 114
Dirty Pool 33
Dirty Shirlows (Sydney) 263

Discurio (record store) 51
'Diseases' (song) 71, 240
Ditty Dimwits (band) 32
Divinyls 113
'Dogs in Space' (song) 8, 23–25, 121, 122, 153, 170, 234, 280, 282
Domestic violence 37
Doncaster Inn 185
Door, Door (album) 212, 217, 225, 302
Dorfman, Stanley 237
Douyin 288
Down and Out in Paris and London 10
Dragon (group) 70
'Dream Kitchen' (song) 54
Drummon St, Carlton 253
Duffield, Andrew 54, 207, 232–234
Dum Dum Fix (group) 64
Dylan, Bob 51

E

Eagles, The (group) 52
Earls, Mick 44
Ears, The 5–7, 10, 14, 19–21, 23–26, 31, 42–44, 54, 63, 75, 77, 79, 81, 82, 84, 87, 92, 96, 141, 159, 163, 176–183, 187–190, 197–200, 202, 220, 235, 243, 249, 299, 303
East Brunswick 262
East Doncaster 73
East Melbourne 157, 159
Easybeats, The (group) 230
Eccohomo (group) 30
Edinburgh Gardens 51, 255
The Eighties: The Decade that Transformed Australia 112

7-Eleven 248
Elliott, Stephan 251
ELO (group) 304
EMI (record label) 33
English, Evan 70
Eno, Brian 24, 29, 177, 218, 240, 252
Eric Gradman's Man & Machine 54
Erin Street, Richmond 161
Ernst, Max 267
Esplanade, The (St Kilda) 18, 29
Ethel Hall, Swinburne Technical College 211, 223
Eucalyptus St, Richmond 159, 165
Eureka Hotel 185
Europe (group) 69, 127, 240, 245
Evictions (film) 163
Exford Hotel 79, 179, 181, 183
Explosive Hits '77 (album) 239
Eyres, Anthea 161
Eyres, David 161

F

Faber, Michel 217, 225
Fabinyi, Martin 32
Fabulous Marquises, The 61
Farnell, Ross 83
Farrago (magazine) 148, 217
Farriss Brothers, The 109, 178
Farriss, Andrew 242
Farriss, Jon 106, 113, 182
Farriss, Tim 106, 242
The Fauves – 15 minutes to Rock 199
Female Wizard 260
Ferntree Gully Hotel 185, 187
Ferrets, The 18
Festival Hall 185
Fidock, Stephan 54

1900 (film) 84
'The Final Countdown' (song) 240
Fish in Space (film) 242, 245
Fitzroy 4, 28, 42, 61, 75, 130–132, 144, 147–149, 152, 159, 179, 181, 195, 252, 253
Fitzroy Street, St Kilda 4, 16, 152, 159, 198
Five Great Gift Ideas (EP) 55
Fleckney, Paul 233, 244, 280, 283
Flett, Uschi 52
Foley, Gary 131, 256, 300
Footscray 179
'Forest Theme' (song) 231
Fortran 56
France 56, 57, 115, 120
'Frankie Teardrop' (song) 65, 234, 241
Freedom (film) 57, 146, 230, 231, 244, 276, 277
Frencham, Henry 165, 170
Fung, Sarah 297

G

Gallagher, Noel 188
Gang of 4 (group) 218, 240, 243
Garner, Helen 131, 136, 146
Geelong 248, 249, 251–253
Geldof, Bob 57
Genesis (group) 64, 108, 225
Georgetown 12
Georgiopoulos, Antonia 162
Gerrard, Lisa 74
Geryon 260
'Get Off of My Cloud' (song) 213
'Ghost of the Year' (song) 122, 243
Gibson, Rachel 210, 222
Gilbert, Andrew 32

Gill, Andy 243
Gilmour, G. 160, 161, 172
Glassop, Patricia 116, 121, 122
Glebe 55, 107
Go-Betweens, The 113
Going Down (film) 250, 259
Goldman, Paul 14, 19, 44, 70, 219, 237
'Golf Course' (song) 237
'Good Times' (song) 230, 231, 238
Gow, Michael 77
Grainstore Tavern 186
Graney, Dave 126
Grant (character) 131
Grant, Denise 68, 69
Grant, Gary 183
Grant, Stuart 62, 301
Gray, Garry 62, 211
Grease (film) 259
Greeks 36, 162
'The Green Dragon' 231, 241
Greswell 12
Griffin, Alex 146, 155
Gudinski, Michael 31, 189

H

Hacienda, The 33
Hall, Janine 212
Hanna, Arne 42, 44
'Happy Birthday' (song) 241
Harding, Anne 63
Harding, Christine 20, 63, 159
Harding, Tony 20
Hardware Lane 25
Harkins-Cross, Rebecca 144
Harry, Debbie 52
Hawthorn 19, 25, 160, 211, 223
Hay, Colin 33

Head On (film) 158, 250
Hearts (venue) 38, 42, 65, 181, 183, 185
Hebdige, Dick 267, 281
He Died With a Felafel in his Hand (film) 8, 146, 154
Hefner, Des 75
Heidelberg Town Hall 27
Helou, Tony 80, 221
Hendrix, Jimi 28
'"Heroes"' (song) 237
heroin 10
Hester, Paul 31, 33, 84, 256
Hicks, Scott 230
Hill, Alannah 2, 118, 250, 257
Hillcoat, John 70
Hill, Steve 47
1987 Hits Out (album) 238, 239
Hoddle Street 160
Hodgson, James 164
Holding, Clyde 160, 162, 166
Holmesglen 152
Homan, Shane 205–207, 279, 286, 298
Hong Kong 106, 110
Hooper, Craig 55
Hotel Spencer 181
House Concerts Australia 278, 284
House, Lynda 70
Housing Commission of Victoria 166
Howard, Harry 18, 209, 222
Howard, Rowland 2, 52, 126, 209–212, 220, 222, 224, 225, 229, 303
Hoy, Marie 18, 45, 54, 128, 219–221, 226, 269
Hoyts Cinemas 117
Hrycaj, Lara 228, 244
Hughes, John 117

Hughes, Steph 262, 279, 281–283
Hunter-Brown, Jenny *See* Brown, Jen Jewel
Hunter, Ian 62
Hunters and Collectors 112, 204, 212
Hussey, Sally 122, 152, 153, 156
Hutchence, Michael 6, 55, 57, 58, 78, 84, 107–109, 111, 114, 117, 119, 120, 124, 126, 169, 170, 175, 176, 178, 182, 188, 219, 227–232, 242, 248, 249
Hutchence, Tina 231, 232
Hyde, Michael 150

I

I Can't Remember (band) 25, 32
Icehouse 31, 33
Ida May Mack (group) 38
'I Like it Both Ways' (song) 239
India 37
Inner City Sound 178, 224, 265, 305
Instagram 293, 295
INXS 6, 7, 32, 55, 56, 59, 79, 83, 105–118, 120–122, 176–178, 182–194, 196, 198–200, 202, 228–233, 235–237, 240, 242, 243, 245, 249
Italians 36

J

Jab 29
Jaeger, Barbara 243, 245
Jaffers, Jeff 59
Jagger, Mick 108
Jamison Street (club) 240
Japan (group) 83

'Jen' (character) 131, 132, 137, 142, 143
Jessop, Sharon 221
Johnson, Stephen 28, 133
Jones, June 154, 260
Journey to the Centre of the Earth (album) 86
Joy Division (group) 77, 177
Juke (magazine) 64, 280
Jump Club, The 21, 54, 181, 186
Junction hotel 186

K

Kandere 260
Keenan, Haydn 250
Kelly, Brenda 70
Kennedy, Jo 77
Kick (album) 32, 106, 113, 114, 186
The Kid (play) 77
King Crimson (group) 64
Kings Cross 10
Kingston Hotel 29, 159
Kings Way 71
Kleiser, Randal 259
Kokkinos, Ana 250
Korg synthesiser 54, 304
Krautrock 41
Krupa, Gene 52

L

La Bamba (film) 178
Lacklustre HQ (Canberra) 262
Lafayette, Nicky *See* Smith, Nick
La Femme (group) 73, 82
La Grande Bouffe (film) 75
Lane, Anita 69
Latrobe Street 73

La Trobe University 186
Latvia 12
Launay, Nick 232
LCD Soundsystem (group) 252
'Leanne' (character) 106, 130, 131, 221, 257, 269
'Leap for Lunch' (song) 19, 179, 190, 245
Leapfrogs, The (group) 42
Leeson, Steve 28
Lefebvre, Henri 265, 268, 277, 281, 284
Lennon, John 79
Lennox Street, Richmond 251
Lewis, Michael (Mick) 10, 19, 24, 25, 63, 64, 77, 82, 85, 92, 159, 303
Lewis, Miles 167
'Lisa' (character) 62, 74–76, 257, 258
Listen Like Thieves 59, 113, 118
Little bands 6, 42, 43, 46, 48, 62, 68, 69, 71, 75, 78, 109, 163, 179, 218, 219, 226, 263, 269, 277, 290, 297, 301, 306
Little Bourke Street 52
'Little Mark' 92
Little River Band 189
Live Aid 57, 112
Living Daylights (magazine) 146
Living Tombstone (group) 294
London Tavern 186
Loriso, Giovanni 167
Los Angeles 110, 202
The Lost Boys (film) 230
Loughnan, C.A. 160, 171
'Louie Louie' (song) 213
Love and Other Catastrophes (film) 4, 250
Lovece, Frank 68

Lowenstein, Richard 1, 5, 7, 11, 26, 39, 43, 44, 48, 56, 57, 72, 77, 107, 108, 112–114, 121, 141, 153, 156, 168, 170, 175, 176, 179, 200, 201, 208, 210, 224–226, 228, 230, 236, 248, 256, 262, 263, 280, 299
Lowenstein, Wendy 163
Lowe, Shane 27
LSD 10
'Luchio' 84, 131
Lygon Street 149, 262

M

MacKinney, Lisa 7, 243
Macy's (Hotel) 186
Madigan, Mary 'Doody' 52
Mad Max (film) 76, 117, 125
Madonna 72, 255
Maggotville (Sydney) 263
Malvern 19, 23, 159, 185
Manchester 33, 258
Mannix, Brian 105
Manzil Room 32
Marching Girls, The (group) 75, 218, 230, 240, 245
Mario's (café) 70
Market Hotel 181
Martini's 29, 45, 54, 181, 183, 185
Mason, Dave 54
Mathieson, Craig 191, 204
Matthew Flinders Hotel 181, 186
Matthews, Leigh 256
Max Q (group) 58, 59, 113, 120, 242, 243
MC5 (group) 41
McCalman, Janet 159, 171
McCutcheon, Andrew 166

McGregor, Craig 117, 228
McIntyre, Vonda 15
McLaughlan, Tim 10, 19, 20, 24, 25, 79, 81, 159, 303, 305
Mclean, Don 254
McLean, Simon 211, 223, 224
McMahon, Kevin 220
McQuade, Cathy 5, 6, 24, 25, 31, 159, 179, 187
Melbourne College of Advanced Education 186
Melbourne Grammar 64
Melbourne on Foot 164
Melbourne State College 25
Meldrum, Ian 'Molly' 170
Men at Work 31, 33, 189
Mental as Anything 113
Mentals *See* Mental as Anything
Meo, Chuck 19, 303, 305
Mercury (record label) 183
Microfilm (group) 6, 74–76
Middlesex Poly 56, 57
Midnight Oil 55, 183, 199
Milburn, Lynn-Maree 56, 57, 64, 114, 225, 226
Millikan, Tim 233
Millionaires, The (group) 27, 28
Milne, Bruce 210, 264, 280, 304
Milton Street, Elwood 159
Minogue, Danielle (Dannii) 107
Minogue, Kylie 107, 119
Mitchell, Joni 24, 204
Mitre Tavern 29
Models (group) 18, 26, 113, 193, 234, 289, 303
Monash University 8, 37, 144, 150
Monkees, The (group) 230
Monkey Grip (book) 146
Monkey Grip (film) 146

Moodists, The (group) 75
'Moonage Daydream' (song) 27
Morales, John 33, 84
Mornington Peninsula 73
Moroder, Giorgio 54
Morrison, Jim 108
Morrissey 126
Moths, The (group) 41, 47
'Motorcycle Baby' (song) 30, 31
Mount Beauty 53
Mr Bum and Ruby (group) 44
'Mr Clarinet' (song) 241
Much More Ballroom (venue) 264
Mulgrave 36, 186, 264
Multiple Sclerosis 53
Munich 157
Munzibai, Sergio 33
Murphy, Chris 111, 114, 183, 187, 192, 196
Murphy, John 2, 42, 80, 234
Murphy Media Academy (MMA) 183, 187
Mushroom (record label) 31, 44, 133, 189, 190, 192, 218, 264
Musical.ly 288
Mutton, Annemarie 157, 160, 161, 171, 172
Mutton, Frank 157, 161
'My Hair' (song) 31
Mystify (film) 8, 108, 119–121, 242, 243

N

Nagorcka, Ron 25
Narcissus 215
Needles, Nique 6, 74, 177, 200, 208, 219, 221 *See also* Delaney, Cornelius

Neild, Anthony 228
Nepal 37
Newcastle 32, 138, 192
'New Dress' (song) 31
Newham, Polly 55
New Order (group) 240
NEWS (group) 80, 107, 170, 191
Newsome, Sarah 241
Newton-John, Olivia 259
New wave 29, 83, 111, 177, 182, 211, 243, 265, 304
New York 33, 41, 84, 234
New Zealand 68, 110, 218
Nice 21, 56, 71, 83, 254, 267
Nichols, Phil 44, 46
Nick Cave and the Bad Seeds 113
Nimrod Theatre 77
Nirvana 191
'No Mercy' (song) 294
North Carlton 181, 183
Northcote 52, 79
North Fitzroy 42, 51, 255
Northland 36
North Melbourne Association 161
North Queensland 38, 114
North Springvale 36

O

Oasis (group) 188, 203, 254, 255
Obsessions, The (group) 3, 210–212, 215, 223, 224
Ocean Grove 248
Oldenburg, Ray 266, 273, 281, 283
Olsen, Ollie 19, 31, 42, 45, 52, 58, 62, 68, 69, 71, 78, 113, 116, 118, 120, 128, 165, 177, 211, 212, 217, 218, 220, 224–229,

232–235, 241, 243, 245, 249, 258, 282, 299, 301, 305
'The One Thing' (song) 113, 257
Orchestra of Skin and Bone (group) 220, 243
'Original Sin' (song) 111
Orpheum Theatre (Harrisburg) 290
Orwell, George 10
Osborne, Glenys 219
Overwatch 294
Oxford Hotel 181

P

Pace, Aldo 84
Pack rape 37
Pakistan 37
Parkdale 150
Parkville 181
Parlour Gigs 278, 284
Parton, Dolly 291
Pelaco 128, 165, 166, 171, 248
Pelaco Brothers (group) 159, 165
Pengilly, Kirk 106, 109, 182
Perano, Greg 28, 250
Perry, Brendan 75
Petrie Terrace, Brisbane 263
Pettingill, Kath 16
Petty, Jack 262, 279, 282, 283
Pew, Tracey 65
Pew, Tracy 54
Piano Piano (group) 61
Pick Me 192
Pier Hotel, Frankston 185, 264
Pini, Karen 113
Pipe Music (record store) 24
Pitt, Graham 211
Pitts, Gordon 74
Plant, Robert 108

Plays with Marionettes (group) 61, 64
Plenty Road, Preston 262
Plummer, Marion 290
Polaris Inn 65
Pop, Iggy 4, 30, 77, 124, 218, 240, 248
'Port Adelaide' (song) 231
'Port Adelaide II' (song) 231
Portland, Vic 32
Post-punk 2, 176–178, 181, 183, 189, 190, 200, 248, 263, 301
Post, Saskia 63, 80, 108, 118, 159, 219, 237, 248
Potts Point 32
Pownall, D. 168
Pownall, V. 168
Prahran 144, 150
Prahran Technical College 144
Pram Factory 148
Premier-Harbour Agency 189
Preston, Edwina 209
Prices Surveillance Authority 193
Priest, Christopher 15
Priestley, Ray 144
Primitive calculators 19, 42–44, 46–48, 62, 219, 220, 233, 240, 244, 248, 258, 259, 269, 301–303
Prince 32, 47
Prince Charles 112, 187
Princess Diana 112, 187
Prospect Hill Hotel 185, 187
Psychedelic Furs (group) 77
Psychotic Leisure Music (album) 241
Pulp 210, 212
Punk Gunk 265
Purbrick, Simon 85
Pure Shit (film) 259

Purple Rain (film) 178

Q
Q Club 27, 264
Quasimodo's Dream (album) 55
Queen (band) 187
Queensland 37, 68, 114
Quinn, Gavin 265
'Quito Ray' *See* Brown, Jen Jewel

R
Race, Hugo 64, 234, 257, 299
Race Rage 260
Radio Birdman (group) 18, 212
Railway Hotel 185
Ramones (group) 40, 41, 77
Ratcat 192
Razorback (film) 76
Razor (club) 72
RCA (record label) 239
Reals, The (group) 62, 210–212
Red Rattler (Sydney) 263
Reed, Lou 4, 24, 56
Reefer Cabaret (venue) 264
Reels, The 54–56
Regular (record label) 31, 84
R.E.M 191
Reservoir, Vic 267, 273
Residents, The (group) 26
Rev, Martin 241
Richards, Dean 232–234
Richards, Keith 74
Richards, Laurie 62
Rich Kids 70, 72
Richmond 4, 6, 10, 11, 53, 54, 124, 128, 141, 157–166, 168–170, 173, 179, 181, 185, 186, 195, 236, 251, 263, 299
Richmond Association 161, 162, 166, 167
Richmond Recorders (recording studio) 45, 80, 219
Richmond Town Hall 160
Rich Kids 70, 72
Rieschbeth, Nick 53
Río, Chuck 241
Ripper '76 (album) 239
The Rise and Fall of Marvellous Melbourne 164
RMIT 80, 195, 279
"Rocket USA" (song) 40
'Rock Rock Daddy' (song) 72
Rock Star: INXS 188, 193
Rodgers, Nile 111
Roger-Genersh, Arno 164
Rogers, Terry 74
Roland CR78 drum machine 42
Roland System 100 syntheziser 42
Rolling Stones, The (group) 230
Ronnie and the Rhythm Boys 68
rooArt (record label) 192
'Rooms for the Memory' (song) 227–243, 249
Rooty Hill RSL 79
Rough Trade (group) 69, 297
Rowe, Glenys 70, 122, 169
Rowell, John 76
Rowville 62
Roxy Music 28, 41
Rozelle 79
Rude, Ron 61, 74
Rundgren, Todd 28, 55
Rundle Street 40
Russell Street 73

Russell Street Police Station *See* Russell Street
Ryan, Marguerite 290

S

'Sagging Insects' (song) 25
'Saint Elmo's Fire' (song) 252
Saints, The 113, 114, 239
Salmon, Kim and the Surrealists (group) 248
'Sam & Anna Reunited' (music piece) 241
Sandown Park 36
Sandringham Commodore Hotel 185
San Miguel, Dolores 265
Sargeant, Jack 209, 210, 222
Sartori, Kevin 241, 242
Sartre, Jean-Paul 76
'Scarecrow' (song) 20, 83
Scavengers, The (group) 75
Schembri, Jim 116, 117, 122, 201
Schumacher, Joel 230
Scott, Bon 112
Scott, Graeme 76
Seaview Ballroom 73, 75, 77, 258
Seaview Hotel 179, 181, 183, 185–187, 248
Seditionaries (store) 52
Seiffert-Brockmann, Jens 292, 298
Sejavka, Sam 5, 9, 24, 79, 81, 87, 93, 97, 99, 109, 116, 126, 128, 141, 151, 152, 158, 159, 163, 178, 179, 188, 210, 220, 236, 301
The Sell-In 191
Sentimental Bloke Hotel 185
Serious Young Insects 26
Sex Pistols (group) 15, 52, 258

Sex (store) 52
Seymour, Mark 82, 204
Seymour, Nick 54
Shabooh Shoobah 113, 186
Sharaf, Yasmine 269, 282–284
Shaw, Kate 277
Shaw, Robert 28
Sherbet (group) 75
Sheridan, Michael 220
'Shivers' (song) 7, 135, 209, 210, 212–222, 224, 225, 229, 237, 258, 269
Silverchair 192, 205
Simon of the Desert (film) 75
Sire Records 177
Skipping Girl Vinegar 165
'Skullbrains' (song) 241
Skyhooks 28, 46, 47, 75, 112
Skylab 218, 222
Smash Hits (magazine) 251
Smith, Lee 42
Smith, Nick 27, 171
Smith, Patti 4, 24
The Smiths (group) 107
Snowy Mountain Project 53
Solly, Al 275
Solomon, Shepherd 33
The Song Machine 193
Sonic Youth 191
Sony (record label) 192
Southern Cross Hotel 63
Southland 36
South Yarra 18, 181, 185, 186
South Yarra Station 17
'Space Oddity' (song) 15
'Speed Kills' (song) 231, 236
Speed, Lesley 118, 122, 143, 154
Spice Girls 255
Spielberg, Stephen 58

Spike Fuck 260
Spinal Tap (film) 178
Spit, KT 260
Spotswood (film) 158
Spring Street, Melbourne 51
Springvale North State School 36
Stein, Seymour 177
Stephenson St, Richmond 16
Stevens, Jon 188
St John Vianney's Primary School 36
St Kevin's College 9, 15
St Kilda 9, 15, 41, 47, 62, 73, 75, 179, 181, 185, 186, 195, 248, 256, 265
St Kilda Bowls Club 248
St Kilda Town Hall 185
St Martin's Theatre 65
Stooges, The (group) 41
Storey Hall (RMIT) 80
Stuyvesant, Peter 251
Starkie, Bob 54
Starstruck (film) 77
State Savings Bank 262
Status Quo (group) 81, 147
'Stay Young' (song) 55
Stiletto (group) 52
Stratton, Jon 111, 121
Strikebound (film) 56, 78, 114, 163, 300
Strong City (Kansas) Auditorium 290
Struggletown (book) 159, 169
Subculture: the Meaning of Style 267
'Sugar Free' (song) 240
Suicide (group) 31, 40–42, 120, 214, 233, 234, 241, 255
Sulk (album) 234
Sunbury 38
Supernaut (group) 239
Sussex, Lucy 10

Sutcliffe, Pierre (group) 61
Sweaty Weather (play) 65
Sweet and Sour (tv series) 6, 187
Swinburne College 26
Swinburne Community School 214

T

Taipan Tiger Girls (group) 243
Talking Heads (group) 29, 31, 32, 43, 111, 177
'Talking to a Stranger' (song) 56, 113
Tangerine Dream (band) 24
Taylor, Noah 3, 58
'Tequila' (song) 241
'That Ain't Bad' (song) 192
'That's the Way' (song) 84
Thomastown 273
Thompson, Hunter S. 79
Thornbury Bowls Club 267
Thorpie (Billy Thorpe) 38
Thrush and the Cunts (group) 6, 68, 69, 71, 219, 240, 244, 248
Tibbits, George 160
Tiger Lounge 18, 29, 42, 54, 159
Till, Gus 64, 83
Tintin 58
Tip Top bread 14
Too Fat to Fit Through the Door (group) 69, 219, 241
Toorak Anglers Hall 29
Tootho and the Ring of Confidence (TATROC) (group) 211
Top Tone (guitar) 19
Trade Union Club (Sydney) 33
Trans Pixies 260
Trash (store) 52–54
Travolta, John 259
Triffids, The 113, 114

Triple J (radio station) 192
Triple R (3RRR-FM) (radio station) 210
True Wheels (group) 28
Turner, George 10

U

Uncanny X-Men (group) 105
Underneath the Colours (album) 55
Universal Theatre, Fitzroy 70
University of Melbourne 81, 144, 148, 160, 217
Uren, Tom 166
Use No Hooks (group) 44

V

Vager, Romy 272
Valmorbida, Elise 10
Vega, Alan 241
Velvet Underground, The 56
Velvet Underground, The (group) 41
The Venue (St Kilda) 186, 248
Victim Manor (Perth) 263
Victoria Police 266, 281
Victorian Heritage Register 166
Victoria Street, Richmond 160, 165
Village Green, Mulgrave (venue) 186, 264
Vine 291, 293
Vonnegut, Kurt 56
Vynhil, Henry 28

W

Waffen SS 12
Wagner, Richard 177
Waits, Tom 44

Walker, Clinton 178, 201, 202, 204, 210, 220, 233, 234, 265, 305
Walker, Don 230, 231
Walsh, Chris 62, 211
Walsh, Jill 291, 298
Walsh, Peter 21, 84
Waltham Street, Richmond 160, 165, 166
Wasp synthesiser 42
Waters, Erica 93
Watson, Matthew 243
Watters, Liz 231
Wattletree Road, Malvern 23–25, 159
Watts-Russell, Ivo 70
Wa Wa Nee (group) 240
WEA (record label) 33, 183
Weevils in the Flour 162
Wegener, Jeff 212
Wembley Stadium 187
Werder, Felix 54
We're Livin' on Dog Food (film) 118, 175, 299
West Heidelberg 27
Westwood, Vivienne 52
'What You Need' (song) 118, 237
Whirlywirld (group) 19, 42, 54, 181, 219, 229, 232–234, 241, 243, 248, 269, 302
White Ox (tobacco) 82
Whitlam, Gough 37, 41, 166
'Wild Thing' (song) 213
Wilson, Ross 305
Windsor Hotel 186
'Win/Lose' (song) 229, 234, 241
Withnail and I (film) 85
Women's liberation 36
'Wonderwall' (song) 254
'Word Up' (song) 240

Wreckery, The (group) 61

X
X-Ray Spex (group) 52, 54
XTC (group) 43

Y
Yarra River 159
Yates, Paula 57, 120
Yes (group) 61, 64, 228, 253, 299, 301–304

Young Charlatans, The 177, 212, 225, 243
The Young Doctors (tv series) 113
Young, Greg 112, 121, 122
YouTube 291

Z
Zenner, Mark 256, 259
Ziggy Stardust and the Spiders from Mars (album) 27

GPSR Compliance
The European Union's (EU) General Product Safety Regulation (GPSR) is a set of rules that requires consumer products to be safe and our obligations to ensure this.

If you have any concerns about our products, you can contact us on

ProductSafety@springernature.com

In case Publisher is established outside the EU, the EU authorized representative is:

Springer Nature Customer Service Center GmbH
Europaplatz 3
69115 Heidelberg, Germany

www.ingramcontent.com/pod-product-compliance
Lightning Source LLC
LaVergne TN
LVHW010335260326
834688LV00036B/720